The Great Wines of America

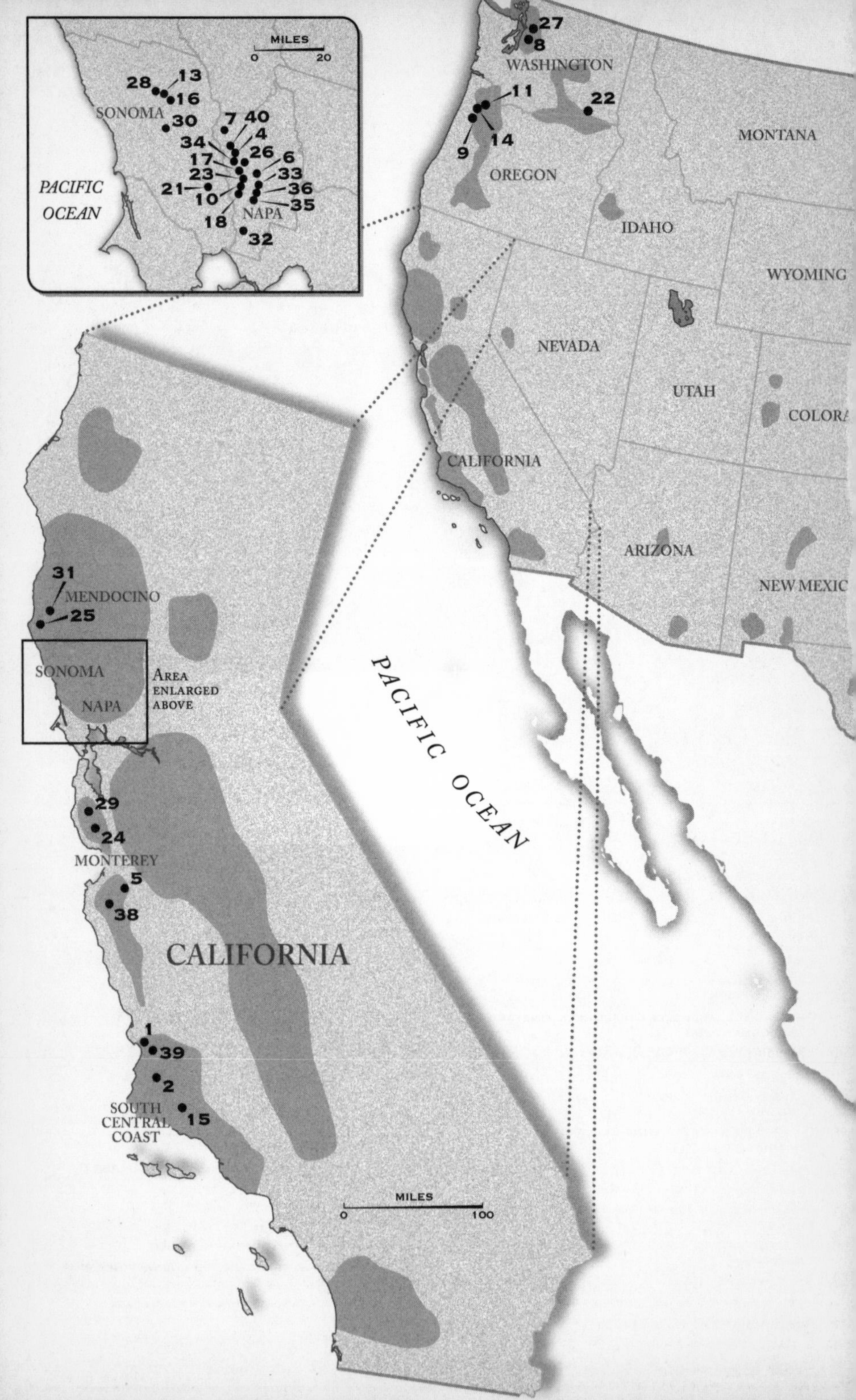

MILES
0
20
28
13
16
SONOMA
30
7
40
4
34
26
6
17
33
23
36
21
10
35
NAPA
18
32
PACIFIC
OCEAN
27
8
WASHINGTON
11
22
14
9
MONTANA
OREGON
IDAHO
WYOMING
NEVADA
UTAH
COLORA
CALIFORNIA
ARIZONA
NEW MEXIC
31
MENDOCINO
25
SONOMA
NAPA
AREA
ENLARGED
ABOVE
PACIFIC OCEAN
29
24
MONTEREY
5
38
CALIFORNIA
1
39
2
SOUTH
CENTRAL
COAST
15
MILES
0
100

Great Wines of America

ALSO BY PAUL LUKACS

American Vintage:
The Rise of American Wine

THE

Great Wines *of* America

The Top Forty
Vintners, Vineyards, and Vintages

PAUL LUKACS

W. W. NORTON & COMPANY
New York · London

To Marguerite

peas in pods

Printed in the United States of America
First published as a Norton paperback 2006

Manufacturing by RR Donnelley, Harrisonburg, VA
Book design by Barbara Bachman
Cartography by Justin Morrill
Production manager: Andrew Marasia

LIBRARY OF CONGRESS CATALOGING-IN-PUBLICATION DATA

Lukacs, Paul (Paul B.)
The great wines of America : the top forty vintners, vineyards, and vintages / Paul Lukacs— 1st ed.
p. cm.
Includes index.
ISBN 0-393-05138-2
1. Wine and wine making—United States I. Title.

TP557.L875 2005
641.2'2'0973—dc22
2005004945

ISBN-13: 978-0-393-32941-4 pbk.
ISBN-10: 0-393-32941-0 pbk.

W. W. Norton & Company, Inc.
500 Fifth Avenue, New York, N.Y. 10110
www.wwnorton.com

W. W. Norton & Company Ltd.
Castle House, 75/76 Wells Street, London W1T 3QT

1 2 3 4 5 6 7 8 9 0

CONTENTS

ACKNOWLEDGMENTS

...

If I'd a knowed what a trouble it was to make a book I wouldn't a tackled it." So writes Huck Finn in the last chapter of his *Adventures*, and I must admit I sometimes felt that way during the course of work on this book. Four years ago, when I proposed the idea of *The Great Wines of America* to my agent, Georges Borchardt, and then to my editor, Maria Guarnaschelli, I thought it would be an easy book to write. After all, I told myself, it'll just be a set of separate stories, none too long, all interesting, so simple to get down on paper. Boy was I wrong. First came the challenge of selecting the wines—easy for about twenty-five of them, complicated, even agonizing with the others. Then came the actual writing, and the difficulty of making each chapter or profile seem sufficiently distinct and different from the others. The idea all along was to paint a picture of high-quality American wine through a set of detailed but miniature portraits. I'll leave it to others to decide how well I succeeded, but I certainly learned how difficult painting with a small brush can be.

Over the course of working on the book, a number of people helped in various ways. Without them, my difficulties would have been far greater. I based the choice of the forty wines I profile primarily on my own palate and judgment, but I also solicited advice from people whose palates and judgments I respect. I am grateful for the sage guidance offered by Jim Laube, Archie McClaren, Michael Rubin, Pierre-Antoine Rovani, Lisa Shara Hall, and especially my good friend and colleague, Michael Franz, who as always listened patiently and counseled wisely.

I visited all of the producers whose wines are featured in the book, and to a person the vintners proved unfailingly generous. A cliché of the wine business has it that people who work with wine are especially good-hearted. At least with these forty, it proved true.

As to the book itself: Many thanks to Georges Borchardt for believing in and advocating this project. Thanks too to Rose Levy Beranbaum for first putting me in touch with Maria Guarnaschelli at W. W. Norton. And to Maria (and her former assistant, Erik Johnson, and his successor, Aaron Lammer) many, many thanks for your support, enthusiasm, and encouragement. Closer to home, I'm grateful to Mary Zajac, who helped me check facts and figures, secure permissions, and get labels and pictures. Finally, the photographs that didn't come from vintners all were taken by the woman to whom this book is dedicated. She traveled with me to most of the wineries, tasted the wines with me, asked the important questions I forgot, and in a myriad of ways kept me on track. I wouldn't have finished the book without her. More important, I know that without her love and companionship, my whole life, not just my writing, would be in mighty big "trouble."

INTRODUCTION

...

Only a generation ago, a book about great American wine would have been regarded as a joke. That's because there simply weren't great wines in the United States—wines, that is, with a sufficiently consistent record of excellence to be ranked with the world's best. Today, all that has changed. At the start of the twenty-first century, the finest American wines hold their own with the finest made anywhere. More to the point, they, or at least some of them, have become world leaders, with qualities emulated by vintners all across the globe. But which wines? And who are the people responsible for them? This book answers those questions by profiling forty different wines—not wineries, but individual wines, a veritable hit parade of vintners, vineyards, and vintages. Each profile is discrete. But considered as a whole, the individual portraits fill a larger canvas; they provide a panoramic picture of contemporary American wine at its highest level.

There certainly was wine in America a generation ago, just not great wine. That situation, however, was about to change. In 1973, when the journalist and publicist Leon Adams published his *Wines of America*, he already could talk about a "wine revolution" in the country. Adams used that phrase to refer to two separate but related phenomena—a developing appreciation for wine in a culture that previously had little use for it; and an improving level of quality in the nation's vineyards and wineries. Both trends have continued over the past three decades. American per capita wine consumption has more than doubled (to roughly 2.7 gallons annually per adult, an admittedly still low number compared to, say, the roughly 15 gallons in France or Italy). And technical advances in viticulture and enology have led to better and better wines, especially in regions east of the Rockies where grape growing can prove difficult. But the most important factor in this revolution, surely, was the raised ambition of vintners across the country. Before the 1960s, few American winemakers dared even dream of crafting wines that might compete with the great European growths or *crus.* But beginning in that decade, and then gaining momentum in the 1970s, 1980s, and 1990s, more and more winemakers started pursuing just that goal—to make wines qualitatively equivalent to the world's very best.

To understand how daring that goal was, one has only to remember the tragic farce of National Prohibition. Wine, like all alcohol, was contraband in America for fourteen long, dark years, and Prohibition's insidious legacy lingered longer still. (That legacy can be felt even now, particularly in the tangled thicket of laws that govern the distribution and sale of wine in the United States.) There had been more than a thousand commercial wineries in the country in 1919. At Repeal, in December 1933, slightly more than 150 opened for business. Many pre-Prohibition vineyards had been replanted to other crops. Those that remained tended to be overgrown and in disrepair. Most wineries contained dilapidated, often rusted equipment, and vintners with firsthand knowledge of how to make wine were few and far between. Not many people in the midst of the Depression had money to invest, so improvement inevitably came slowly. Even more problematic, the market for wine in America was small and impoverished. The word "wino," a derogatory euphemism for a poor drunk, had entered the lexicon around 1910, but the post-Prohibition era was when wine became widely figured in the popular imagination as something hidden in a brown paper bag. Not all wine. Not Champagne in a French restaurant, for instance, or Chianti in an Italian one. But American wine, cheap and often fortified, labeled with bastardized generic names like "Sauterne" or marketing monikers like "Thunderbird," was what winos drank.

The rise of American wine, a phenomenon culminating with the emergence of legitimately great American wine, is thus all the more remarkable once one considers how far American wine had fallen in the first half of the twentieth century. Many things came together to make progress possible—economic prosperity following World War II; technological improvements in winemaking (particularly involving temperature control); isolated, inspirational evidence of higher quality; a gradual cultural shift in perception away from wine as booze and toward wine as a mealtime beverage. It's a fascinating story, one that I tell in my earlier book, *American Vintage: The Rise of American Wine*. But that chapter in the nation's vinous history has ended. American wine is no longer notable simply because it's on dinner tables rather than skid row. What's important now is that top examples are qualitatively equivalent to top wines anywhere—those from Europe, fine wine's historic homeland, but also those from other New World wine countries such as Australia, Argentina, Chile, New Zealand, and South Africa. Different wines may differ stylistically, but the finest American ones evidence the attributes that distinguish any great wine—an evocative bouquet, depth and length of flavor, complexity, and balance.

Because wine at one level is just something to drink, the very concept of greatness may seem out of place when discussing it. Yet at its highest level, wine long has been regarded as something more, a (minor) art created by man and nature together. For most of American history, few vintners on these shores aspired to craft what might be considered artistic wines. In much of the country, nature conspired against them, as a harsh climate coupled with vineyard disease rendered growing classic wine grapes (all of which are of the European *Vitis vinifera* species) difficult if not impossible. Vinifera vines did fare well in California, and Golden State winemakers did make some highly regarded wines in the nineteenth century. But Prohibition's dagger had struck especially deep there, and hardly any California vintners thought of wine as anything remotely artistic until Leon Adams's American wine revolution began in the 1960s.

Now that the revolution has run its course, now that American wine has risen to unprecedented heights, it makes sense to step back and survey the scene. What are the country's great wines, and what makes them so? Where do they come from, and whose visions have inspired them?

People have evaluated and classified wine for a long time. They have identified, celebrated, and even venerated great wines for hundreds of years. Indeed, in many European wine-growing countries, qualitative distinctions between wines coming from particular vineyards or estates have become so established that they literally carry the force of law. In the United States, however, great wine is something new. There are no official lists or classifications, no established hierarchies or traditional points of reference. Instead, there are simply the wines themselves. Many wines from America win medals in international competitions, earn critical plaudits, and fetch prices comparable to their European counterparts. They clearly are judged great. What might not be so clear, though, is the rationale underlying such judgments.

One traditional criterion of greatness is price. When officials in Bordeaux decided to classify the region's best red wines some 150 years ago, they separated them in tiers on the basis of price. The wines that consistently sold for the most money became what we know as the first growths. In today's America, however, price is an unreliable barometer. For one, certain types of wines tend to fetch higher prices than others. For another, prices for some wines have more to do with scarcity (whether real or perceived) than inherent quality. This book, then, does not simply catalog the country's most expensive wines. It honors achievement not luxury, no matter whether the achievement results in a $150 Cabernet or a $15 Riesling.

Another criterion of greatness might be place, as certain locales are known to grow better grapes resulting in better wines than others. This is the Burgundy model. In that famed northern French region, the traditional home of Chardonnay and Pinot Noir, particular vineyards are distinguished as *crus*. They may have multiple owners who use different techniques when making different wines, but the site itself is what renders one wine a *grand cru*, another a *premier cru*, and still another a commune or village wine. (Chambertin-Clos de Bèze as opposed to Gevrey-Chambertin Cherbaudes as opposed to Gevrey-Chambertin, for example, even though vines for these all grow within a quarter mile of each other.) In this system, only certain grape varieties are permitted to be grown in certain places, history having determined the almost magical affinity of grape and place.

The difficulty in America is that, without centuries of experience on which to draw, no one can be sure which site deserves which classification or distinction. With wine, as with so much else in today's fast-paced world, history seems to be moving quickly; and certain grapes already have become associated with certain places—Cabernet Sauvignon with the Napa Valley, for example, and even more to the point, with a subregion of Napa like the Stags Leap District. Yet within such places, other grapes sometimes yield superlative wines. The federal government approves the establishment of American Viticultural Areas (AVAs), the geographical indicators found on domestic wine labels, but the regulators say nothing about what grapes should be grown within an AVA's boundaries, or about what the wine should taste like. Perhaps someday America's finest wines will find definition through an association of place. At this stage, though, AVAs provide geographical, not qualitative, reference.

A third, more contemporary criterion of greatness might be critical acclaim, specifically numbers or points. A wine rated 95 points surely is superior to one rated 85. Might not it fairly be considered great? Perhaps, but the illusion of objectivity with such scores is just that—an illusion. It matters a great deal who is assigning the points—not only in terms of the critic's personal preferences but also in terms of context. Moreover, greatness in wine surely is a function not of a single instant but rather of a sustained record of merit. And numerical scores by their very nature do not take into account the past.

In selecting the wines to be profiled in this book, I paid attention to price, place, and points, but I did not base my decisions on them. Nor did I attempt simply to list what I thought of as *the* top forty American wines today, a catalog that ultimately would reflect little more than my own personal bias. Instead, I tried to choose wines with inherent high quality in the glass as well as some significance that transcends the glass. That significance might be historical or regional (or both), but I wanted the story of each wine to be more than an extended tasting note. That is, every wine in the book is representative, tasting of itself and of more than itself—a grape variety perhaps, or a place, style, or winemaking vision.

As Henry James once wrote, "The effort really to see and really to represent is no idle business." In this case, the issue involved tasting rather than seeing, but the selection was certainly far from idle. Other tasters might pick other wines, but I'm confident that this set of forty reflects not only distinction but also diversity—the diversity of varietals, regions, and styles that defines contemporary American wine at its best.

The one firm criterion in my selection process was that any wine needed to have at least a ten-year track record of superiority in order to be considered for inclusion. In Bordeaux or Burgundy, ten years means virtually nothing. In America's vineyards, it means a great deal, and so seemed a sufficient span in which to assess quality over time. (I made one small exception. Au Bon Climat's "Nuits Blanches au Bouge" Chardonnay has been produced only since 2000; the winery, though, has made excellent Chardonnay for twenty-five years, and this particular cuvée marks an evolution in, not a departure from, that record.) No wine profiled in this book is thus a proverbial flash in the pan. Each has demonstrated sustained excellence—a fair definition of greatness with this minor art.

A generation ago, when America's wine revolution was just beginning, the best domestic wines were stylistic clones of prestigious foreign, primarily French, ones. Chardonnays echoed white Burgundy, Cabernets red Bordeaux. Some of that imitation still goes on. Today's finest American wines, however, have identities all their own. They may resemble the time-honored, European classics, but they also evidence individualistic, sometimes idiosyncratic personalities. Put another way, they taste distinctive as well as delicious. This book celebrates them.

The Great Wines of America

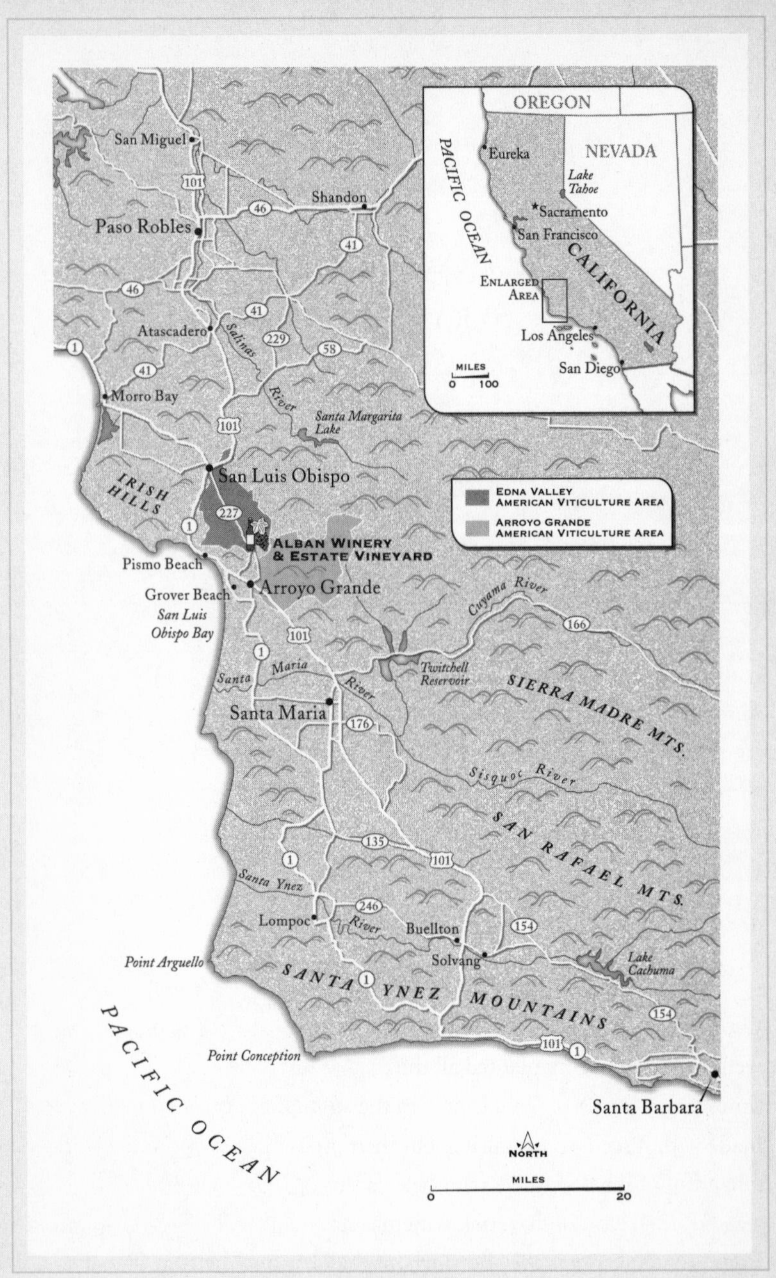

THE SAN LUIS OBISPO AVAs

CHAPTER 1

Alban Vineyards Syrah, "Reva"

Edna Valley, California

...

John Alban

Syrah, all the rage these days, was virtually unknown in the United States a generation ago. In 1970, fewer than five acres were planted to this grape throughout the entire country. Fifteen years later, that number had grown to over 100—a significant increase to be sure, but a mere pittance compared to the roughly 25,000 then devoted to Cabernet Sauvignon. Today, there are over 18,000 vineyard acres of Syrah in America, most in California and Washington, but some in Oregon, Texas, and other states as well, with more being planted all the time. This *parvenu* varietal is now in the spotlight because so many wines made with it seem so promising, but their promise stems from the work of a handful of rebel vintners who believed in it back when it was well off-stage. Because these maverick winemakers usually took their inspiration from French Rhône Valley bottlings, a small band of them, at first all Californian, became known as the "Rhône Rangers." Randall Grahm, with his wittily labeled and cleverly marketed wines from Bonny Doon Vineyard, was initially the most recognizable member of this informal group. But the ultimately more influential figure has turned out to be John Alban of Alban Vineyards. For over fifteen years, Alban has worked arduously to produce world-class American wines from the various grapes native to the Rhône Valley, first researching clones and selections, then propagating vines, and finally making the Syrahs and other varietals that have come to set the standard for a whole new category of American wine. Today, Rhône-styled wines rank among the most exciting being produced in the country. Syrah in particular, so long underappreciated, has emerged as a serious challenger to Cabernet, Chardonnay, and Merlot, the three security-blanket varietals most wine drinkers know. Vintners and consumers alike have embraced it, and the outlook seems extremely bright, with compelling new wines emerging every year, and literally thousands of young vines beginning to bear fruit.

John Alban trod plenty of uncharted ground in his quest to produce top-quality American wines from Rhône Valley grapes. He was not the first person to plant these varieties in the United States, but he distinguished himself from his fellow pioneers because of his single-minded devotion to them. Most of the early Rhône Rangers thought of Syrah and other Rhône grapes as sidelights. Even if they shared Alban's passion, they hedged their bets, usually planting less commercially risky grape varieties as well. Alban, however, never wanted to make anything but Rhône-styled wines of the highest order. Beginning with his first vintage in 1991, the unswerving quality of his production, coupled with its consistent style, paved the way for a host of ambitious producers, many of whom today willingly acknowledge Alban Vineyards as a reference point. His wines made with such Rhône grapes as Grenache, Rousanne, and Viognier rank among the country's finest, but his "Reva" Syrah is even more significant—if only because Syrah is the one Rhône varietal that to date has become widely accepted by consumers. Other American renditions may occasionally be its equal, but none shares its record of sustained merit.

Syrah has a somewhat obscure history in America. It was planted in California before the advent of Prohibition in 1919, often as part of a field blend, the old-fashioned custom of planting different grapes together in one vineyard, and often alongside Petite Sirah, a related but quite different variety known in France as Durif. Most of those nineteenth-century vines either died or were grafted over to other varieties after Prohibition, and Syrah only reemerged when Joseph Phelps devoted a block of his Napa Valley vineyard to it in 1974. Back then, few people knew much about this grape. Its linguistic resemblance to Petite proved confusing, and the variety was widely regarded as something pedestrian, good only for humble, jug wines.

This negative perception came in part because wines from the northern Rhône, Syrah's Old World homeland, had not yet been (re)discovered. The prominent American critic Robert Parker helped bring about their renaissance. Beginning in the early 1980s, he loudly and somewhat idiosyncratically championed wines from the northern Rhône appellations of Cornas, Côte-Rôtie, and Hermitage as the qualitative equivalent of classified-growth Bordeaux and *grand cru* Burgundy. Over the years, as Parker's influence grew, his praise helped fuel international demand, which in turn enabled Rhône producers to reinvest in their vineyards and wineries, thus elevating overall quality, leading to greater demand and then to even better wines—a rapidly moving upward spiral. At much the same time, Australian producers were turning their attention to the export market, first in Britain and then in the United States. And their most distinctive wines, whether coming in the earthy, so-called sweaty saddle style of the Hunter Valley near Sydney, or a richer, riper style from South Australia, were made with Shiraz, *né* Syrah. (This is one grape with two names, a situation that often confuses consumers.) American wine lovers took note of both of these developments, as did the Rhône Rangers, who saw Syrah as a new frontier in the landscape of American wine. To their mind, there was nothing humble about it.

It was in 1980, as a sophomore at Vassar College in New York, that John Alban fell under wine's seductive spell. The son of a Long Beach, California, physician, he expected (and was expected) to become a doctor himself, so his decision to make wine constituted a sort of familial rebellion. "It really was crazy," he admits now, as he describes keeping his plans secret all through college. In his senior year, Alban applied to both medical school and the University of California at Davis program in viticulture and enology. To his chagrin, he was accepted at the former but rejected by the wine faculty (because his transcript lacked necessary prerequisites). Stubbornly determined, he declined the med school acceptance, in the process antagonizing his parents, and enrolled in the undergraduate wine program at Fresno State. The basic courses he took there enabled him to transfer to Davis the next year, but it took longer for the family rift to heal, since his father thought him a daydreamer if not a dilettante. Alban, however, was becoming ever more dedicated, his interest ever more focused. Now he did not want just to make wine. His goal instead was to make new and different wines, special ones that would separate him not only from his family but also from his fellow enology students. "Cabernet and Chardonnay were California's chocolate and vanilla," he remembers. "I decided early on that I wanted to be Baskin Robbins and make other flavors."

Alban was initially drawn to Rhône wines as a student at Fresno. Their forceful secondary aromas and flavors, those that resemble things other than fruit (spice, for example, or leather), proved especially compelling. The whites augmented the taste of summer fruits with echoes of stony minerals and fresh-cut flowers, while the reds tasted of molasses, saddle leather, smoked meat and more. If complexity and completeness distinguish great wine, he thought, then these surely are great wines. When he suggested as much to other wine lovers, no matter whether his professors or fellow students, he invariably was told that Rhône grapes, while potentially interesting, simply were not in the same league as Cabernet and Chardonnay, Pinot Noir, or even Merlot. That is, they were not sufficiently refined or noble.

But the more Alban thought about this, the more he concluded that it made no sense. He knew that some Rhône wines, particularly those made from Syrah in Hermitage, had been valued as highly as first-growth Bordeaux in the nineteenth century. Though they had fallen somewhat out of favor, talk of their lacking vinous pedigree seemed silly.

So he saved up and traveled to the Rhône Valley, where over the course of four summers, he worked in vineyards, befriended vintners, and learned what no one at Davis or Fresno could teach him—the particular character of these grape varieties. When he returned to California, he borrowed money in order to start propagating vines. That proved important, since in order for Rhône-styled wines to become popular, someone needed to do nursery work, making these grape varieties available to would-be growers. Then in late 1989 he went to the bank and borrowed even more money for the down payment on a 220-acre property in the southern Edna Valley near San Luis Obispo. Three years later he made his first wines, which were received with considerable critical acclaim. That acclaim, coupled with his evident seriousness of purpose, helped heal any lingering family wounds, and today his parents are his financial partners, as well as his most fervent fans.

With Syrah, what most excites Alban is an untamed quality that he contends distinguishes any top-notch wine made from it. Alban argues that great Syrah, no matter whether grown in France, Australia, or the United States, always tastes a little wild. "Compare it with Cabernet," he explains: "A first-class Cabernet is like an investment banker, a polished gentleman in a three-piece suit. But Syrah is a cowboy in a tuxedo. It's like Clint Eastwood all dressed up. He looks great, but he's not completely polished. There's always something raw about Syrah." With the top Rhône wines from Côte-Rôtie and Hermitage, that wild element can seem almost feral, while the best Australian Shirazes tend to evidence a more leathery character. Alban's "Reva" falls somewhere between these two, its deep red and black berry fruit being augmented by secondary flavors and aromas reminiscent of bitter chocolate, roast coffee, and, odd as it may sound, freshly laid tar. Those notes hold their own with but do not overwhelm the fruit, giving the wine a truly multifaceted personality.

Named after his mother, "Reva" comes from a six-acre section of Alban's vineyard. He makes two other Syrahs, one named for his wife ("Lorraine"), the other for his father ("Seymour"). Each of the three cuvées reflects a singular location. The "Reva" vineyard block lies at the base of a small hill, is slightly cooler than the other two, and has more clay (as opposed to rock or chalk) in the subsoil. As a result, the wine tends to be full-bodied and richly textured, with firm but not fierce tannins. It displays both ripe, sunny California fruit and earthy depth, and so evidences the sort of complexity that distinguishes any great wine, regardless of variety or geographic origin. Alban produces only about eight hundred cases of "Reva" each year, but that's twice as much as the other two cuvées combined. "It's my standard-bearer," he says; "the wine more people know."

Over the years that Alban has made "Reva," he has refined his winemaking techniques, adapting what he first observed in France to the intrinsic character of grapes grown in California. Like so many American winemakers of his generation, he has learned to do more than mimic practices observed abroad, so as to be able to fashion wines that taste individualistic rather than imitative. The key, he notes, is to respect the distinctive character of the grapes—not just the variety, but the variety grown in a specific place. In the Edna Valley, this has led him to remove more of the woody stems from the grape clusters at crush, to use indigenous yeast during fermentation, and to employ a greater percentage of new wood during barrel aging. "I want the wine to taste powerful but at the same time soft," he explains, "balanced but not astringent." Comparing the wines in a flight of vintages demonstrates that "Reva" has changed subtly but significantly, reflecting both the vines' increased maturity and Alban's evolving understanding of his vineyard. The raw, earthy notes that threatened to dominate the early releases are now held in check by the fruit, and recent vintages impress as much for balance as for brawn.

Alban chose to locate his vineyard in California's South-Central Coast only after careful research. "I came back from France convinced that we had many places suited for Rhône grapes," he says, "but I still needed to figure out where exactly to plant." He knew that the better northern Rhône wines come from warm years in which temperatures stay high throughout the harvest. What is considered hot in Côte-Rôtie, however, is thought cool in most of California, so Alban looked for a temperate area with a long growing season and, most important, a record of sunny autumns. That led him to San Luis Obispo County, with its twin Viticultural Areas of the Arroyo Grande and Edna valleys, where the ocean air moderates the heat, and the ripening period proves exceptionally long. His vineyard lies in the cool southern edge of the Edna Valley. There, vineyard sites are open directly to the Pacific, an orientation that results in moderate temperatures, with little cooling in the fall. "What's exceptional in the Rhône is average here," Alban explains. In the Edna Valley, the ocean influence prevents the grapes from ripening too early, just as the inland warmth allows them to reach full maturity. Alban notes that conditions in other South-Central Coast valleys, particularly Santa Ynez and Santa Maria, also favor Rhône varieties. "This whole area," he says, "seems made for these grapes." Budbreak comes early but harvest late, and there is virtually no chance of rain or frost. Growers thus can let the grapes hang on the vine as long as they need. "Even in a year like 1999, when we essentially had no summer," Alban recalls, "it got hot enough in the fall here for the grapes to ripen."

Along with Alban, vintners such as Bob Lindquist at Qupé and Adam Tolmach at Ojai have helped establish the South-Central Coast as arguably the prime source for contemporary American Rhône-styled wines. Syrahs from this region tend to taste multilayered, with the sort of expressive, earthy, secondary flavors that Alban values so highly. By contrast, wines from other, usually warmer areas in California often seem fleshier and fuller, more akin to Australian Shiraz. But Alban insists that this difference is all to the good. "Syrah grows well in different climates and different soils," he points out, "so it's not surprising that the wines come in different styles." Still, while some excellent Syrahs come from California's North Coast counties, as well as from Washington State, most of the finest to date have hailed from the South-Central Coast. No wonder Alban and other vintners have dubbed the region America's "Rhône zone."

Though the best California Syrahs tend to be made in small lots and carry fairly steep price tags, more and more large-volume, moderately priced wines have emerged over the past few years. As a result, Syrah today is fast becoming a mainstream American varietal. In this regard, Alban notes that the wine market works like a pyramid. "First come us crazies"—he laughs—"making wines no one's heard of. If we're lucky, the cognoscenti want them." Then, after those wines garner praise, other producers follow with clearer profit-making ambitions. "It's a trickle-down process," he says. "We can argue whether trickle-down works with economics, but there's no doubt that it does with wine." More than twenty years after his rebellious, pioneering foray into winemaking, Alban can take considerable satisfaction from Syrah's having become so accepted, with wines selling at all price points and appealing to all segments of the wine-buying public. While few display the nuances of "Reva," a surprisingly large number offer full flavor and genuine complexity. That's because with a newcomer like Syrah, unlike established varietals such as Chardonnay or Merlot, true worth, not hype, drives the market and expands the pyramid's base.

Much as when he made the initial decision to follow the Rhône's siren song, Alban remains motivated by his conviction that diversity is one of the great joys of wine. He argues that the varietal consciousness that characterized the beginnings of the American wine boom back in the 1960s and 1970s led all too quickly to a sort of grape myopia. "For a long time, people would only drink Cabernet and Chardonnay. The emergence of Rhône-style wines, and consumer acceptance of them, signals that this is beginning to change." To date, Syrah is the one Rhône varietal to be widely embraced, but Alban remains convinced that others, Grenache perhaps, or Rousanne, will follow suit. "Look," he jokes, "Syrah is our Tiger Woods. In the same way that watching him got all sorts of people to start taking up golf, drinking Syrah is introducing folks to a whole new set of wines." Such conviction, coupled with evident courage, helps explain why Alban's fellow vintners so willingly acknowledge him as a leader. Others produce more wine, have deeper pockets, or are more publicity-minded, but no one is more committed to broadening the national palate while at the same time elevating standards than this American winemaking rebel—a rebel very much *with* a cause.

A NOTE ON VINTAGES:

"Reva" ages well, although it's difficult to know whether the overtly earthy characteristics in older vintages are due simply to age or also to a winemaking regimen that did not emphasize fruit ripeness as much as John Alban's current practice does. Regardless, it's safe to say that time in the bottle will render the wine less fruity and more leathery. Particularly strong vintages include 1995, 1997, 2000, 2001, and 2002.

THE SUGGESTED PRICE FOR THE CURRENT 2003 RELEASE IS $56.

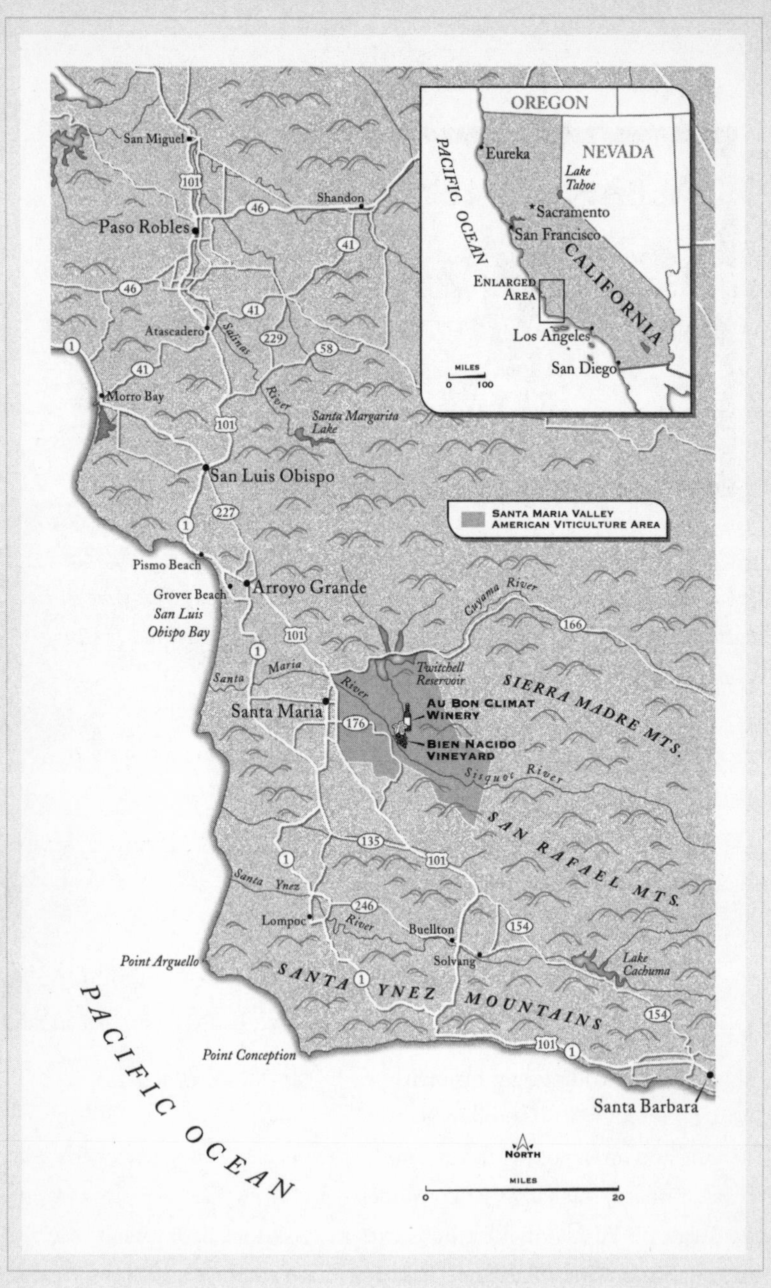

AU BON CLIMAT AND THE SANTA MARIA VALLEY AVA

CHAPTER 2

Au Bon Climat Chardonnay, "Nuits-Blanches au Bouge"

Santa Maria Valley, California

...

Ten years before John Alban made his first Syrah, another rebel vintner opened shop in California's South-Central Coast—this time even farther south, in Santa Barbara County, and this time focusing on grapes native to Burgundy rather than the Rhône Valley. Those grapes, Chardonnay and Pinot Noir, were certainly more mainstream, but Jim Clendenen's approach to them was anything but conventional. A self-confessed eccentric who cultivates something of a wild man image, he has always delighted in going his own way, especially with Chardonnay, defying and often poking fun at California wine wisdom. Clendenen's wit is razor-sharp, so sharp that consumers and critics often miss his jokes. But beneath all his ribaldry, he is extremely serious about what constitutes quality in wine. "Balance," he says. "That's what it's all about." And balance is what he has long argued many California Chardonnays lack, and what he has long labored to express with the wines he makes in Santa Barbara County.

Jim Clendenen

The American public's predilection for big, forward, heavily oaked wines irritates Clendenen. "I hate the taste of wood, and I hate the very concept of Chardonnay tasting like tropical fruit," he declares. Instead, he prefers subtlety and length of flavor, wines with a firm acidic structure and only moderate alcohol—in short, wines like the ones he discovered and fell in love with when he first went to Burgundy nearly thirty years ago. "Except," he admits, "I have to remind myself I'm not there." Santa Barbara County is not Burgundy's celebrated Côte d'Or, and to achieve a true balance, a wine needs to taste of its own origin rather than a foreign model. In this case, the origin is the Santa Maria Valley, a grape-growing region distinguished by a rare confluence of dazzling sunshine and cold ocean air.

Jim Clendenen makes a large number of different wines, including five separate Chardonnay cuvées, reflecting different vineyard sources as well as different stylistic models. The middle ground is occupied by the one he calls "Nuits-Blanches au Bouge" (translated roughly as "Sleepless Nights at a Dive," a perhaps too far inside joke). This wine is French-inspired but at heart Californian, meaning marked by the primary taste of fresh fruit (apples and pears, with additional citrus and white peach flavors, but nothing remotely tropical), and reflecting the presence of all that Golden State sunshine. As such, it represents what Clendenen acknowledges has been an evolution in his winemaking philosophy. Neither as lithe nor as lavish as some of the others he has made, it displays near-perfect balance because it tastes first and foremost of its Santa Maria origin.

Back in 1982, when Clendenen and his partner at the time, Adam Tolmach, founded Au Bon Climat in what was little more than an old shed, their announced goal was to fashion wines on a Burgundian model. Au Bon Climat, a French colloquialism, refers to a good vineyard site, but since the young men owned no land, the name was something of a joke. They set up shop in Santa Barbara County less because of love for any particular vineyards there than because they felt the region as a whole would proved suitable for Chardonnay and Pinot Noir. "Everything up north in California is too hot," Clendenen declares bluntly. "This [the Santa Barbara coastal valleys] is where the Burgundy grapes do best." Growers in Carneros, the Russian River, the Sonoma Coast, the Santa Cruz Mountains, or northern Monterey might beg to differ, but it's worth remembering that in the early 1980s, when Clendenen and Tolmach started making their wines, those areas had not yet established themselves as sources of consistently fine Chardonnay or Pinot Noir. Back then, plenty of vintners still thought that Burgundy varieties belonged in the middle of Napa, right next to the Bordeaux ones that thrive there. Unlike most of their compatriots, Clendenen and Tolmach had traveled in France and worked in French vineyards and wineries. So they understood that these particular grapes benefit from being grown in cooler locales—"not a few degress less than Calistoga in Napa," Clendenen notes derisively, "but *cool*, a place where Cabernet just can't get ripe."

There are three official grape-growing regions in Santa Barbara County: the Santa Rita Hills, the Santa Maria Valley, and the Santa Ynez Valley. These appellations, or AVAs (American Viticultural Areas) in the argot of the trade, rank among the coolest in California. That's because as the Pacific coastline curves inward, the coastal mountains follow suit, allowing ocean air and fog to funnel straight up through the vineyards. The South-Central Coast is the only place on the American West Coast where this geographical phenomenon occurs. Everywhere else the mountains run primarily north/south, forming a barrier between ocean cold and inland heat. The open ocean to the west of Santa Barbara wine country is icy, being the southern edge of a cold Pacific upswell that extends down the California coast each summer. And the inland climate is plenty hot, the Mojave Desert lying due east. The fact that the Santa Barbara vineyards are influenced so much more by ocean than desert is what makes this region so appropriate for Chardonnay and Pinot Noir. As Clendenen puts it, "In Burgundy they have winter. Here we have the Pacific."

But the other thing that Santa Barbara County vintners have, and this is what separates them in important ways from their Burgundian counterparts, is sunshine. Not only does it rarely rain in Santa Maria (while it frequently pours in Beaune), but the sunlight this far south proves intense. That's why the fog burns off quickly most mornings, allowing the grapes to ripen fully, and why those grapes then are capable of yielding wines that taste simultaneously abundant and angular, lush and lean, a beguiling but paradoxical combination. The effect of all the bright California sunshine is sumptuous flavor, while the ocean cool provides high levels of acidity, giving the wines tight, even bracing definition.

Clendenen and Tolmach started with a Burgundy model in part because they admired those French wines so much, but also in part because they thought it was the one winemaking model they could afford. They had worked the 1981 harvest in the Côte d'Or, where they saw dedicated *vignerons* making small lots of high-quality wines without benefit of investment capital or inherited châteaux. They wanted to make wine back home, but at the same time they did not want to be in anyone's debt. As Clendenen puts it, "The concept of thirty-six barrels in a basement in Burgundy seemed very plausible. We figured we could do something like that."

And so they did. Using only the most rudimentary tools, an old press and old-fashioned fermenters, they made wine from purchased grapes in a leased building on the edge of someone else's vineyard. There, they practiced traditional, attention-to-detail winemaking, disdaining the equipment and technology they could not pay for anyway, pressing, fermenting, and aging the wines much as had been done for centuries in small *domaines* and cellars in Burgundy. It worked. Au Bon Climat, or ABC as its fans soon began to call it, quickly developed a reputation for small-production, artisan-styled Pinots and Chardonnays. The former, not surprisingly, were less consistent, sometimes tasting too green or stemmy, but the Chardonnays, particularly the even smaller-production Reserve renditions, drew raves.

The inspiration for the early ABC Reserves, the wines Clendenen and Tolmach designated as their best, came from a 1983 Chardonnay that they had sourced from the first crop off a new vineyard in the cool western edge of the Santa Ynez Valley. Back then, they were often second in line when it came to getting grapes. These, being from very young vines, tasted quite tart, and at first the new wine, even though barrel-fermented, seemed unpleasantly citric and hard. They left it alone, and then they marveled as it softened over time and became wonderfully nuanced, while always retaining structure and definition. "It tasted something like Leflaive," Clendenen says matter-of-factly, alluding to Domaine Leflaive's famed Puligny-Montrachet, one of the most renowned white Burgundies. "It convinced us to go farther down that path." So, starting in 1985, the two partners made a conscious effort to find the highest-acid, lowest-pH, but still ripe grapes available, picking them well before other vintners would deem them ready. They then barrel-fermented the juice, encouraged the wine to go through malolactic fermentation, a bacterial (rather than alcoholic) process that softens wine by transforming harsh malic acid into gentler lactic acid. They also aged it on its lees, the spent yeast and other sediment left over from fermentation, in French oak barrels, for well over a year. Designed for extended cellaring, the ABC Reserve Chardonnays were bottled unfiltered at a time when filtration was standard practice in California wineries. This allowed them to better express regional as well as varietal characteristics, since no subtle, secondary aromas or flavors were removed. When given sufficient time to soften, these wines tasted of citrus and autumn fruits, with a minerally undercurrent much like a *premier cru* from the Côte d'Or. Not everyone appreciated them. Tasters whose palates had been weaned on Napa or Sonoma wines, in which the acid levels were lower and the taste of wood more blatant, thought them odd. But tasters familiar with top-flight Burgundies waxed rhapsodic.

For the first few years of production, the ABC Reserve Chardonnays were sourced from a variety of vineyards, the most prominent being a sprawling one called Los Alamos, right beside the building Clendenen and Tolmach were renting and using as a winery. But in 1988, when that property was sold, the two partners had to look elsewhere—both for grapes to buy and for a place to make wines. Enter brothers Bob and Steve Miller, owners of another large Santa Barbara vineyard, Bien Nacido in Santa Maria.

The Millers had planted Bien Nacido back in 1973. For the first decade or so, they sold most of their grapes to large North Coast wineries, there being little local demand. But by the mid-1980s, interest in Santa Barbara County grapes, especially Chardonnay, was growing, as more and more small, boutique-oriented wineries were opening for business. Most of these new vintners, like Clendenen and Tolmach, bought grapes for their wines, since few had the financial resources to own vineyard land. The Millers presciently recognized that limited-production wines from these small producers, rather than large-volume blends from big wineries located far away, would bring the region renown (and not coincidentally, bring them profit). So, unlike most large-scale grape growers, they sought out individual, often idiosyncratic clients, being happy to sell small lots of grapes and, as important, to farm those lots separately.

Bien Nacido customers could contract to buy grapes in the conventional way—paying by the ton after having had little involvement with the actual viticulture. Or they could purchase by the acre and actively manage the grape growing. This second possibility inspired many of the important Santa Barbara County vintners to begin purchasing grapes from the Millers, as it allowed them to have the same kind of hands-on involvement as vintners who owned their own vineyards. Before long the Bien Nacido name began to be synonymous with quality. The Millers encouraged winemakers to put it on their labels (as Clendenen and Tolmach did with their 1989 and 1990 Au Bon Climat Reserve Chardonnays), and today prestigious producers up and down the California coast offer wines sourced from it. No matter whether located in Santa Barbara or Sonoma, Mendocino or Monterey, many different wineries now make wines with Bien Nacido fruit. But no winery remains more closely associated with Bien Nacido than Au Bon Climat—not only because so many of ABC's top wines have been made with Bien Nacido grapes, but also because this vineyard is where the winery is now located.

That winery is nothing more than a large blue corrugated-metal box that looks like it should store farm machinery. Au Bon Climat shares it primarily with Bob Lindquist's Qupé Cellars, another Santa Barbara boutique producer. In 1989, Bob and Steve Miller built the facility in order to provide these peripatetic wineries with a permanent home. The winemakers were all old friends. Though Adam Tolmach would leave to devote his energies to his own label at the Ojai Vineyard in nearby Ventura County, their friendships deepened, as the place soon became the spiritual heart of Santa Barbara wine country. The ABC/Qupé facility quickly became *the* place to go if you were serious about Santa Barbara wine. And over the past fiftewen years, a whole new generation of vintners have become very serious indeed.

The ABC/Qupé winery is a bare-bones, functional operation, without a hint of tourist appeal. It has no tasting room; there are no tours; no sign even marks the entrance. But scores of winemakers have honed their craft in this windowless, warehouse-feeling building. Jim Clendenen and Bob Lindquist continue to serve as mentors for would-be-winemakers who share their commitment to their craft. And due in no small measure to the quality of the production there (Clendenen's Chardonnays and Pinots, Lindquist's Rhône-styled wines, as well as Italian varietals, Bordeaux blends, and just about anything else one can imagine), the South-Central Coast has rapidly become recognized by critics and consumers alike as one of America's finest wine regions. Unlike many other areas, winemaking there is marked more by camaraderie than competition. No matter, for example, that the Au Bon Climat wines often taste quite different from other Chardonnays or Pinots made with Bien Nacido grapes. The shared goal is ever-improved quality across the stylistic spectrum. "People make all kinds of different wines here," notes Clendenen, with a nod toward a ceiling-high stack of barrels. "That's because we insist that the choice of style is a winemaker's prerogative."

That choice, though, sometimes leads to trouble. When Au Bon Climat became Jim Clendenen's own in 1990, he rededicated himself to what he thought of as his essential style: firmly structured, high-acid, relatively low-alcohol wines. Maybe because he no longer had a partner to rein him in; maybe because he always has enjoyed playing the contrarian; maybe because he just figured he could do it—but at a time when most celebrated California Chardonnays were becoming ever richer, he decided to make what he characterizes as an "even tighter, crisper, more mineral-flavored wine." Not surprisingly, it did not fare as well as some others in the pages of the national press. His "Le Bouge d'à Côté" (the name is a bastardized play on words, meaning the dive next door, but next door to Burgundy) was fermented and aged in new oak, but then racked into older, more neutral barrels so as to mute the taste of wood. It came in at under 13 percent alcohol, with a whopping 8 grams of acid. Clendenen had no trouble selling it, Au Bon Climat having developed a loyal following by then. But the critics (notably Robert Parker, Jim Laube of *The Wine Spectator*, and Norm Roby and Charles Olken of *The Connoisseurs' Guide*) did not accord this wine the sort of praise they had given earlier ABC Chardonnays, the kind of praise they now were lavishing on other California wines.

That was what got Clendenen's goat. "I got fed up when writers told me I was making wines in the wrong style," he recalls. "So I decided to play a joke on them." In 1996, he created a Chardonnay called "Nuits-Blanches" ("Sleepless Nights"). "It took its name from all the time I spent debating whether to make it. I picked the grapes for it weeks later than for my other Chardonnays. It fermented to fifteen degrees alcohol, and I aged it in two hundred percent new oak—racking it from one set of brand-new barrels into another set of new barrels. And I did all that in order to show that I was making a leaner style with 'Le Bouge' because that was my choice, not because I was incompetent."

Of course, no one had ever called Jim Clendenen incompetent. Influential tasters simply preferred other people's wines. And one reason they did was that by the mid-1990s top-end California Chardonnay as a category had improved, so that a winery like Au Bon Climat faced increased competition in the marketplace. But that improvement came in large measure because more vintners were utilizing the very techniques that Clendenen had promoted a decade earlier. If his wines no longer clearly stood out from the crowd, that was because so many others were now following his lead.

Back in the early 1980s, few vintners allowed their Chardonnays to undergo malolactic fermentation. And while new oak was all the rage, most Chardonnays of that era were fermented in stainless steel before being transferred to barrel—that transfer being why so many seemed out of balance and tasted clumsy. By 1996, no matter whether coming from established producers such as Beringer (whose Private Reserve was declared *Wine Spectator*'s wine of the year that December), or more artisanal producers like Chalk Hill, Kistler, Peter Michael, or Newton, most of the state's top Chardonnay producers were consciously utilizing time-honored Burgundian techniques such as fermentation in barrel and minimal filtration before bottling. That most of them were located in Napa and Sonoma meant that they tended to use riper grapes than Clendenen, which in turn meant that what distinguished him—or at least distinguished "Le Bouge"—was austerity as opposed to opulence.

But if one ABC wine, "Nuits-Blanches," was too rich and fat, the other, "Le Bouge," was arguably too lean and tight. The first tasted of bold, blatant fruit, while the second was all sinew and muscle. Neither alone evidenced the combination of tight structure and voluptuous flavor that Clendenen had proved earlier can characterize the finest Santa Barbara wines; that is, neither tasted sufficiently of its origin. Clendenen won't go quite that far, but even he admits that "the joke backfired." So with the 2000 vintage, he pulled back (though he would never use the language of retreat). Instead of making two separate, but each in its own way incomplete wines, he produced what he calls his "reconciliation" wine—"Nuits-Blanches au Bouge." In effect a return to the style of the Au Bon Climat Reserve Chardonnays of a decade earlier, but more complete and more expressive because made with more mature grapes, it tastes sleek and sumptuous all at once. The 2000 was designated as the winery's "Anniversary" cuvée, while the 2001, more expressive still, was called "Harmony." That name could not be more apt.

Make no mistake. "Harmony" does not mean that Jim Clendenen is slowing or calming down. He still makes a numbing number of wines, including some tighter Chardonnays (for example, one sourced from the Sanford and Benedict Vineyard in Santa Ynez), as well as some fresher, fruitier ones (the basic ABC Santa Barbara County cuvée). In addition to using grapes from Bien Nacido, he now makes wines from grapes he grows at his own Le Bon Climat vineyard, as well as from a changing set of sources in Santa Barbara and beyond (including, in some vintages, Oregon). And in addition to Pinot and Chardonnay, he crafts a host of other wines—Bordeaux blends, Italian varietals, a number of specialized bottlings for restaurants, and an intriguing blend of Pinot Blanc and Pinot Gris that he for some reason calls "Hildegard." But the Burgundy varietals remain his standard-bearers, and none tastes more complete and, yes, harmonious, than "Nuits-Blanches au Bouge." That's because, now well into his third decade at Au Bon Climat, he is able to craft a wine that tastes not like an imposed model (whether from Burgundy or elsewhere in California), but truly, deeply, of itself. And that is why, no matter whether one agrees with all of Jim Clendenen's opinions and pronouncements, there can be no arguing the fact that he is one of America's most accomplished winemakers, and "Nuits-Blanches au Bouge" one of the country's finest wines.

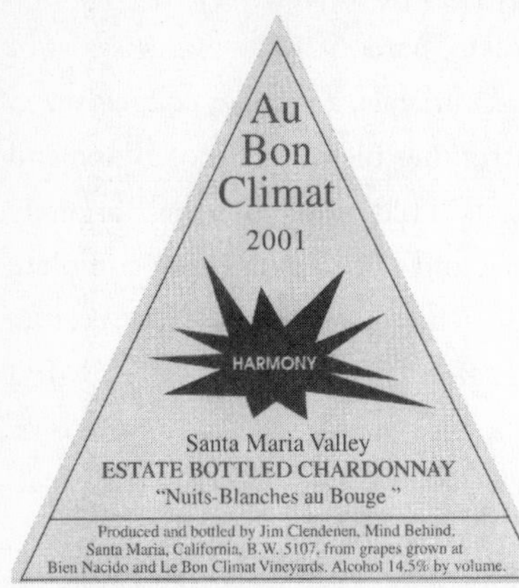

A NOTE ON VINTAGES:

Jim Clendenen has been making Santa Maria Valley Chardonnay at Au Bon Climat for over twenty years, but "Nuits-Blanches au Bouge" only since 2000. Predicting how this wine will age is thus little more than speculation. Since it is neither as opulent as some of his Chardonnay cuvées nor as lean as others, my own guess is that one would do well to drink it within six or seven years of the vintage. The first three vintages—2000, 2001, and 2002—all have been strong.

THE SUGGESTED PRICE FOR THE CURRENT 2002 RELEASE IS $45.

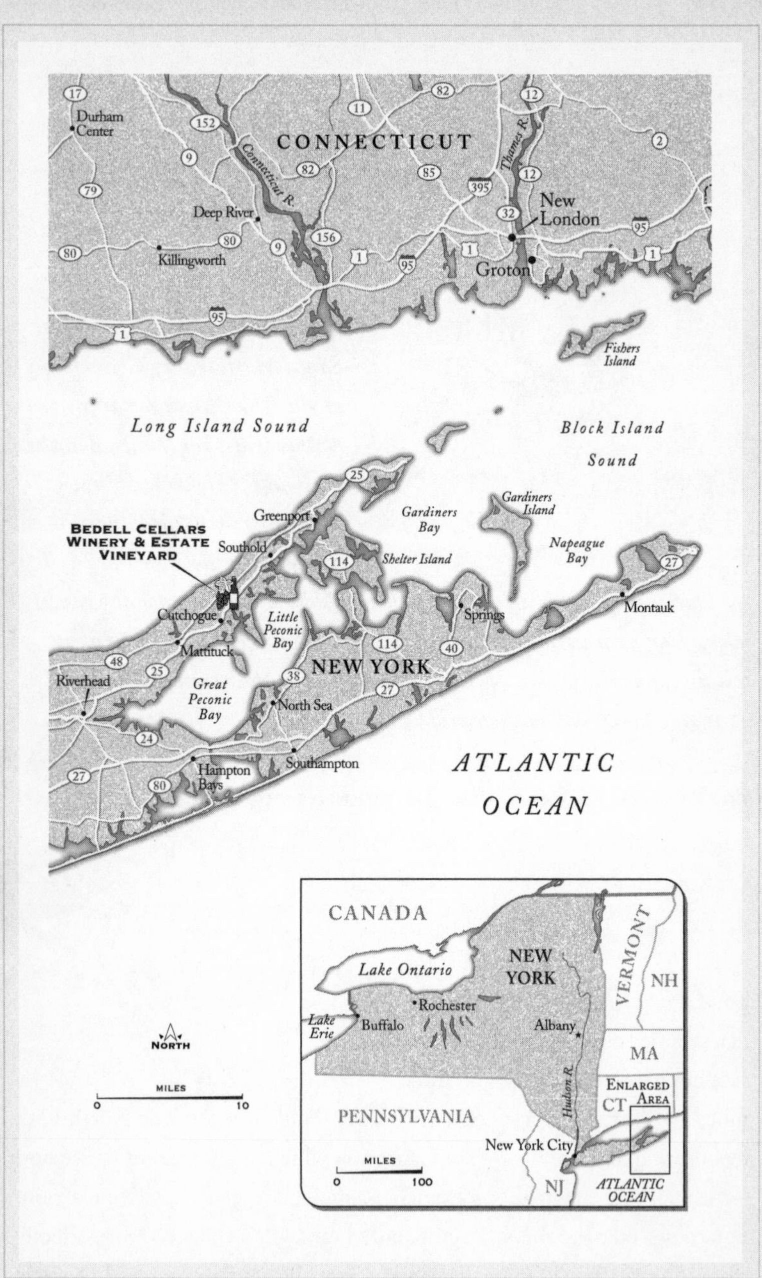

LONG ISLAND WINE COUNTRY

CHAPTER 3

Bedell Cellars Merlot Reserve

North Fork of Long Island, New York

...

Reaching like a gnarled finger into the North Atlantic, the North Fork of Long Island seems an unlikely place to grow wine grapes. A mere twenty-mile spit of a peninsula, this easternmost edge of New York State was settled in the seventeenth century by colonists from Connecticut, and even today the villages of Cutchogue, Southold, and Greenport have a nautical New England air about them. Widow's walks perch atop many of the houses, and restaurants serve chowder, steamed clams, and lobster. The sea, never more than two or three miles away, affects all aspects of life here. While it makes the North Fork feel more like Cape Cod than California wine country, its influence also is the main reason why Long Island has emerged as an exciting wine region. Potatoes used to be the main crop, but grapes, which benefit more directly from the maritime climate, have proved much more profitable. The triple influence of Long Island Sound to the north, the Peconic Bay to the south, and the Atlantic Ocean out east, cools the vineyards in the summer and

Kip Bedell

then warms them in the winter. Because the land is flat, ocean breezes blow continually through the vines, drying the grapes and combating the humidity that proves the bane of many east coast vintners. The soil too is affected by the sea's proximity, being sandy and coarse, with good drainage but few nutrients—exactly what vinifera grape varieties, which inevitably produce better wines with lower yields, need.

To date, one variety in particular has excelled on the North Fork. Merlot, often overshadowed by Cabernet Sauvignon elsewhere, stands proudly on its own here. And for some twenty years, one winery, Bedell Cellars, has produced a Merlot that has served as the touchstone for the variety. Other local winemakers, notably Eric Fry at the Lenz Winery and Russell Hearn at Pelligrini Vineyards, have fashioned equally good wines in various vintages; but no one has outperformed Kip Bedell over the long term. His best Merlot, identified as a reserve, comes primarily from a two-acre plot behind the winery.

For two years, with the 1999 and 2000 vintages, Bedell used only grapes from this plot, "C Block South." Though he now reserves the right to utilize other sources, his focus on this particular site reflects Long Island's development as an important source of fine American wine. As has happened elsewhere in the United States, North Fork winemakers have shifted much of their focus from their wineries to their vineyards. They now think of grapes less as raw material that they mold into a finished product than as an embryonic form of that product itself. In this view, the wine literally is in the ripe fruit, with nature rather than artifice being the primary force that affects the transformation. "The character of a wine like this," Kip Bedell says, holding a glass of his 1995 Reserve, "comes from our land." A soft-spoken, reflective man, he pauses for a moment before continuing: "My job as a winemaker is to maintain that character, which is why over the years I have become such a believer in handling the fruit gently."

In the case of the Reserve Merlot, the result is a wine that has become ever richer and full-bodied. Particularly in vintages such as 1997 and 2001, it displays layered levels of aromas and flavors, with hints of cocoa, tobacco and stony minerals, and none of the herbal, rubber-scented notes that mar some other Long Island reds. The grapes in the C Block South section of the vineyard tend to ripen slowly, and Bedell insists on picking them only when they are completely ready, meaning when the juice has reached the appropriate sugar level and the tannins in the skins and seeds have matured. Because Long Island is susceptible to autumn storms (including the occasional hurricane), variation between vintages is a fact of winemaking life on the North Fork. Many vintners like to point out that the same is true in Bordeaux. Bedell avoids such talk, knowing that it often can become little more than self-promotional hype. Still, there is an important germ of truth here. No matter that the wines may be fashioned quite differently, the best Long Island Merlots evidence the sort of earthy depth that distinguishes good Bordeaux and that has proved so elusive elsewhere in the world. That character comes, quite clearly, from the vineyards.

Wine grapes were first planted in those vineyards back in the eighteenth century, but the story of modern Long Island wine began only in 1973. That was when a young couple, Alex and Louisa Hargrave, purchased a potato farm in Cutchogue and planted seventeen acres with classic European vinifera grapevines. The Hargraves had developed an interest in wine as students in Boston. In tune with the spirit of the times, they fantasized about fashioning their living in nature rather than corporate boardrooms, and their initially quixotic adventure in the wine business was inspired by equal parts counterculture rebellion and romantic idealism. By 1976, they were making and selling wines under their own name. Over the next two decades, the wines from Hargrave Vineyard ran a stylistic and qualitative gamut, reaching an occasional height but never displaying the sort of consistency that distinguishes any top-notch wine, no matter its geographic origin. Nonetheless, Alex and Louisa Hargrave had succeeded in doing something that no one before them had done. They grew classic grapes on Long Island, and they made drinkable, sometimes desirable, wines. That accomplishment turned more than a few heads.

Kip Bedell was one of the people paying attention. A home winemaker who had been producing 100 gallons or so every year in his basement, he had long fantasized about someday owning a vineyard.

Wine was a serious hobby for him, but just a sideline, as he was busy running his family's heating oil business in Garden City, farther west on Long Island. So when he visited a realtor on the North Fork in the spring of 1980 with his wife Susan, he only was thinking about buying a couple of acres at most. "We ended up with fifty," he recalls with a chuckle. "I still don't know how." Over the next few years, the Bedells would drive out to the new property every weekend, slowly and methodically clearing the land and planting vines. By 1983, Kip had transformed nineteen acres of former potato fields into a vineyard. Two years later, in a vintage marred by Hurricane Gloria, he made his first wine from the fruit of those vines—a blend of Cabernet and Merlot that in truth tasted pretty green. He noticed, though, that the ripest and so least vegetal grapes came from the C Block portion of the vineyard a few hundred yards behind the barn that housed his winery.

For the next five years, Bedell worked two jobs—making wine and selling oil. "It was okay for a while," he remembers. "I had good people working for me back in Garden City. Winter was the really busy season there, while summers were busy in the vineyards." Before long, though, he and Susan realized that something had to give way. So, he decided to sell the oil company and became a full-time vintner. "I was still in a business that depends on the weather," he jokes, "and I was still pumping liquid from one container to another. Only now I could drink the product."

In those early years, winemaking at Bedell Cellars was very much a matter of trial and error. There were still only a handful of vintners on Long Island, and while they shared information with one another willingly, there was only one harvest each fall, and so only one opportunity to learn, grow, and improve. What Bedell calls "the first turning point" came in 1988, when he and a group of other North Fork winemakers invited some of Bordeaux's most eminent vintners to visit Long Island. Paul Pontallier from Château Margaux headed the list of guests that July. Joining him in what later became known as the "Bordeaux Symposium" were May de Lencquesaing from Château Pichon-Longueville Comtesse de Lalande; Gérard Séguin from the University of Bordeaux; and Alain Carbonneau, the chief viticultural researcher at the French National Institute of Agronomic Research in Paris. Together, they delivered a series of formal presentations on specific winemaking topics. Virtually all the vintners working on Long Island attended, as did winemakers from throughout the East Coast. The symposium "opened our eyes and got us thinking," Bedell recalls. Specifically, it got him and other Long Island winemakers to begin to shift their focus. They had assumed that the French experts would concentrate primarily on what to do with grapes after they were picked. Instead, most of the conversation concerned what to do in the vineyard, so as to be able to grow the best fruit.

The visitors from Bordeaux talked at length about the need to adapt viticultural techniques to Long Island's climate and soils. The Atlantic's cooling influence on the North Fork during the growing season means that growers need to expose their grapes to as much sunshine as possible; and the fact that Long Island can get a fair share of rain means that drainage is a crucial issue when deciding where to plant vines. Newcomers starting vineyards soon began studying soil compositions, trying to determine which grape varieties would grow best in which sites. At the same time, the already established North Fork vintners started to trim leaves from their vines' canopies so as to expose the maturing fruit to more sunshine. Some even experimented with picking and discarding green grapes in midsummer in order to lower yields at harvest and attain full ripeness. Whatever the technique, the common goal became harvesting more mature fruit, and so evoking more complex flavors in the wines.

At Bedell Cellars, vineyard practices changed dramatically. Kip Bedell started to hedge his vines and thin their canopies so as to get more sunlight on the grapes. He began to experiment with different trellising systems in order to combat humidity. And most important, he did what he would have considered heresy before the symposium, as he cut off about a third of his grapes in August and left them on the ground, aiming for richer flavor from a smaller but more concentrated crop. He remembers that discarding potential income was painful. Two months later, though, when he tasted the young Merlot, he knew he had made the right decision. "I learned," he says "that dropping fruit is necessary here, in terms of quality." Today, yields from the C Block South Vineyard average between 2 and 3 tons of grapes per acre. Back in the mid-1980s, they ran closer to 5.

The most important winemaking lesson that Bedell learned at the Bordeaux Symposium, however, was that Long Island has its own *terroir*, different from Bordeaux just as it is different from California or anyplace else. His rationale for changing vineyard practices was to coax greater distinction from his grapes. His primary goal in the winery, then, had to be to respect that distinction. So he began to question all aspects of his winemaking—how long to ferment, what sort of oak to use, how often to rack or drain the wines out of the barrels, how long to age them before bottling, and so on. He did not experiment for the sake of experimentation, but rather tweaked his techniques, always with an eye toward better expressing the intrinsic character of his fruit. And when he found something that worked, he stuck with it.

Probably Bedell's most controversial decision was to continue the practice of aging his Merlot in American oak barrels. He had first used these simply because they were cheaper than French ones, but he found that he liked the spicy tone they gave his wine. Despite the fact that virtually all the other serious North Fork vintners were switching to French oak, he decided to trust his palate and keep doing what he thought made the most sense for his fruit. "No one can tell me that an American barrel is inferior to a French one," Bedell says. "Is it different? Sure. But not inferior. You have to match the kind of wood you use to your grapes. With my Merlot, American barrels work."

American oak has a tendency to impart an aggressive edge to red wines, particularly in the bouquet, where it often can be identified by a sickly aroma reminiscent of dill pickles or burnt coconut. That jarring note, however, never characterizes the Merlots from the C Block South Vineyard. The explanation seems to be that this and select other sites in Long Island produce grapes of exceptional intensity. Though Merlot often results in soft, fairly low-tannin wines elsewhere, it can yield powerfully concentrated ones on the North Fork, with firm tannins and a tight structure. Kip's colleague, Eric Fry from Lenz, thinks that this intensity is what makes the best North Fork Merlots so special. "Merlot here overpowers Cabernet," he says. "There are only two places in the world where that happens—Peconic on Long Island and Pomerol in Bordeaux." Tasting through a range of the top Long Island wines bears him out. Kip Bedell, for example, makes both a Cabernet and a proprietary blend called "Cupola." Those wines can be very good, but they rarely exhibit the depth or complexity of his best Merlots.

The "second turning point" for Bedell Cellars came with the success of the 1995 vintage. The growing season that year had been exceptionally dry, so the grapes at harvest were fully mature, the most concentrated Bedell had ever seen. By then he already had achieved a good deal of local success. He and Susan were turning a profit, and his own palate told him that his wines were good. That few people beyond Long Island knew or cared did not much matter. He had only to remember what he was doing a decade earlier to feel satisfied. The 1995 Reserve Merlot, however, turned heads far and wide. The British expert, Jancis Robinson, called it Long Island's "benchmark," and went on to include it in a widely reviewed celebratory tasting. The editors of *The Wine Spectator* also were impressed. They placed it in a lineup of world-class Merlots at the New York Wine Experience, an event attended by literally thousands of well-heeled consumers and connoisseurs. And Howard Goldberg of *The New York Times* declared it "a match for top [Merlots] from anywhere."

This acclaim did not much affect sales. Given the size of the vineyard and the low yields, production of Reserve Merlot is small (four to five hundred cases), so the wine always sells out quickly. But the phone at the winery now began to ring more frequently, with people living far away from Cutchogue wanting to know how to get a bottle of the first wine from Long Island to receive national and even international recognition as one of America's finest.

Of all the people taking note of Bedell Cellar's rising renown, the most important was Michael Lynne, president of a New York–based film company. A serious wine collector, Lynne drove out to the North

Fork in the fall of 1999 and shocked the Bedells by offering to buy the property: the farm, vineyards, winery, even the unsold inventory. What clinched the deal was Lynne's insistence that Kip Bedell stay on as the winemaker. "Kip's an icon," he told the press later. "I want to learn from him." The purchase price was $5 million, the highest amount ever paid for a Long Island winery, and Bedell signed a contract to continue to run the operation. "When Michael said he wanted me to stay, well, we just couldn't refuse," he remembers. "He promised me he wants to make the best wines he can." The infusion of new capital has led to renovations in the winery, an expansion of the barrel cellar, and even greater selectivity in the vineyards. It also has allowed Bedell and Lynne to hire a talented associate winemaker, John Irving Levenberg from Napa, and a consulting enologist, Pascal Marty from Bordeaux. As a result, new vintages of Reserve Merlot promise to taste even more exciting than the groundbreaking 1995.

For most of its short history, Bedell Cellars seemed far removed from more celebrated American, mainly California, wineries. There was a distinctly homespun air about the place—a rusted pickup truck often parked outside, the tasting room a bar in an old barn, and the lab little more than a cluttered closet. Now the tasting room gleams with glass and stainless steel, the equipment is state of the art, and the gap between quaint old Cutchogue and glitzy California seems to have narrowed considerably. What hasn't changed is Kip Bedell himself—his dedication to his craft, commitment to ever-improved quality, and faith in his own convictions. Only now he no longer needs to worry so much about balance sheets or bottom lines, and can focus simply on growing the best grapes and making the best wines.

What has happened at Bedell Cellars thus again reflects the evolution of Long Island's young wine industry, as it moves from a local, even parochial enterprise to a business with world-class ambitions. Kip Bedell is not the only person on the North Fork making wines today that can hold their own with the country's finest. But as has happened so often over the past twenty years, he is leading the way.

A NOTE ON VINTAGES:

Because of its firm structure, Kip Bedell's Reserve Merlot needs a few years to open up and reveal its myriad charms. It won't make what the British call "old bones" and be a wine worth drinking after decades of cellaring, but it will taste delicious with five or ten years of bottle age. Strong vintages include 1988, 1993, 1995, 1997, and 2001.

THE SUGGESTED PRICE FOR THE CURRENT 2001 RELEASE IS $30.

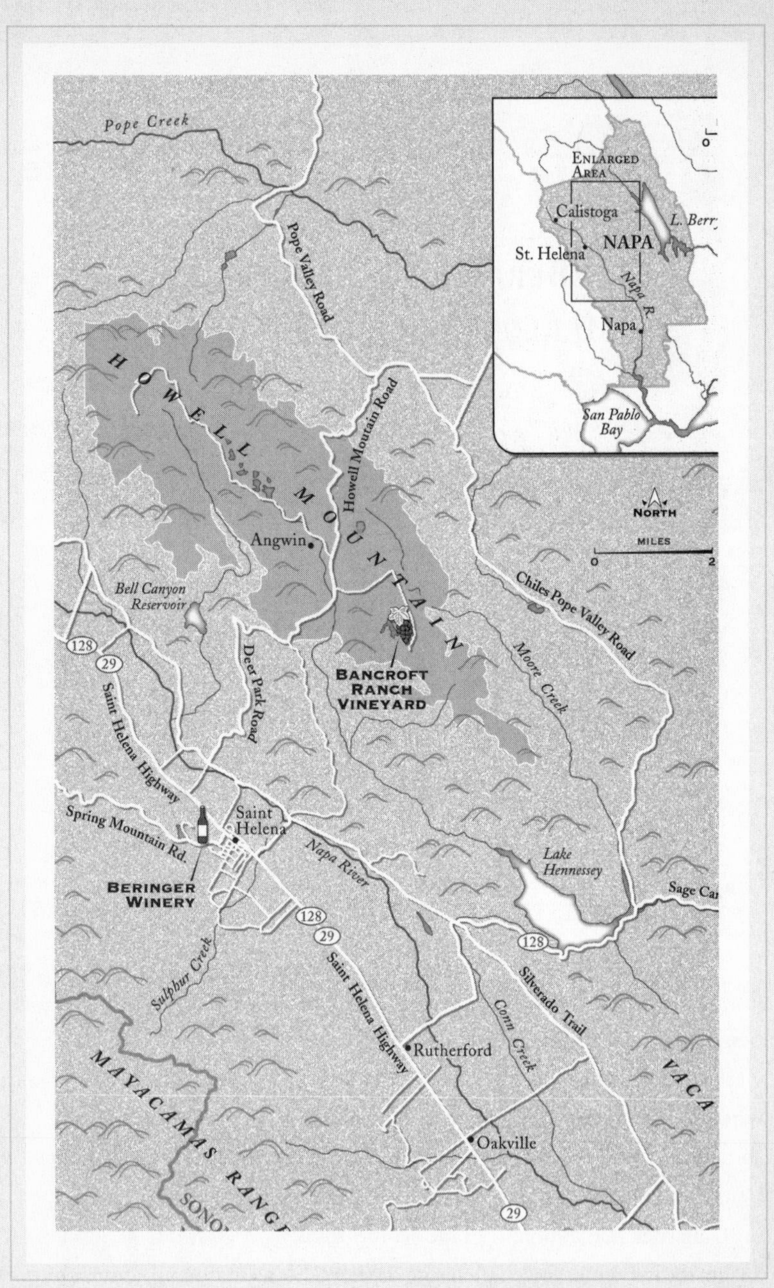

NAPA VALLEY'S HOWELL MOUNTAIN AVA

CHAPTER 4

BERINGER VINEYARDS MERLOT, BANCROFT RANCH

Howell Mountain, Napa Valley, California

...

Ed Sbragia and Myron Nightingale in 1984

Mountain wines are different. Thin ground on steep slopes yields small but concentrated crops, so wines grown in such sites tend to taste firm and fierce, with tight tannins and concentrated flavors. "The culmination of a mysterious miracle of growth," said the much-admired American writer, M. F. K. Fisher, "ripe fruit from stony soil." The Napa Valley lies between two mountain ranges, the Mayacamas to the west, the Vaca to the east, and while it may sound illogical, some of the valley's finest wines come from grapes grown in those mountains. No matter the particular peak, the vast majority of them are based on Cabernet Sauvignon, a grape whose thick skin allows it to produce authoritative wines in challenging *terroirs*. Slow-maturing, unyielding Cabernets from wineries such as Diamond Creek, Dunn, Mayacamas, and Philip Togni display a notably rugged mountain temperament. Other grape varieties are cultivated in the Napa mountains, but as a general rule they lack Cabernet's power and prestige. Beringer Vineyard's Merlot from the Bancroft Ranch, some 1,800 feet up on Howell Mountain, is a striking exception. Deeply colored and tightly structured, this wine tastes nothing like most Merlots grown on the valley floor. Ed Sbragia, Beringer's chief winemaker, takes pride in its power. "I don't want to make a soft wine," he says. "I want something with stuffing." Bancroft Ranch Merlot has stuffing in spades.

Ed Sbragia calls this wine "a Cab-lover's Merlot" because, though sumptuous, it tastes so forceful that even experienced palates often mistake it for that more burly varietal. Its muscle clearly comes from where the grapes are grown. So, while this wine may be atypical for its variety, it nonetheless remains true to type—a mountain wine, defiantly and daringly different. But its preeminence involves more than just locale. Unlike mountain Cabernets that need many years of aging to become palatable, Bancroft Ranch Merlot is deliciously accessible. Sbragia fashions it to be balanced in its youth as well as in its maturity, taming rather than celebrating the tannins. In doing so, he stays true to his own winemaking convictions as well as to the *terroir*. The result is a mesmerizing marriage of vivacity and vigor.

Howell, like Pritchard and Atlas Peak, is an eastern Vaca Range mountain in the Napa Valley. Though the growing conditions are no less severe than on the western side, with comparable elevations, rainfall, and temperatures, wines from the east tend as a general rule to display less earthy flavors and more prominent fruit. Exposure is the most probable explanation. Vineyards facing the valley in the eastern mountains enjoy the benefit of long hours of warm afternoon sunshine, so the grapes are able to ripen fully. "We get all the sugar we want," says Sbragia. "Our challenge comes in getting mature tannins."

That challenge proves important because, no matter east or west, formidable tannin is a hallmark of mountain grapes. Sbragia labors to hold it in check. He wants to craft powerfully flavored wines, not mouth-puckering ones, and so has to be especially conscientious when working with vines that produce small berries, with a high ratio of skins and pips to juice. In addition, low yields on Howell Mountain concentrate phenolics, the chemical compounds largely responsible for intensity in wine. The result can be red wines with firm, at times unyielding structures. Some mountain Cabernets never come into balance, their impenetrable tannins long outlasting their fruit. But Merlot from the Bancroft Ranch retains intensity while at the same time exhibiting vivacity. It tastes dynamic rather than dense.

Tannins are sensed tactilely, not tasted. Many winemakers try to mute their astringent effect after the grapes have been harvested, using techniques such as controlled maceration (the extraction of color, tannin, and other phenolic compounds from the grape skins and seeds), aerated racking (the operation of separating clear wine from its sediment or lees), and gelatin fining (a process of clarification before bottling). Any such intervention, however, has a downside, for the same techniques can rob the finished wines of depth and nuance. For Sbragia, managing tannin in the vineyard is a much more desirable alternative. The key there comes in harvesting the grapes when they are physiologically ripe, not just when they have attained the desired brix or sugar level. Determining physiological maturity, however, is an imprecise science. It involves assessing such factors as skin texture, seed color, and pulp grain, in addition to the standard, measurable variables of sugar, pH, and acidity. In turn, making that sort of assessment entails tasting the fruit and trusting one's own judgment, so not relying—or at least not relying entirely—upon chemical measures.

Sbragia does just that. He lets the grapes be picked only when he literally senses them ready. Invariably, this means that he harvests Bancroft Ranch Merlot at a sugar level of 25 to 26 degrees, two or three degrees higher than traditionally has been prescribed for the variety. "I've found that the Merlot here needs ultimate ripeness to control the tannins," he explains. "If we pick at optimal maturity, then we don't have to manipulate anything afterwards."

Sbragia is a big man who likes big wines, but at the same time wants them seamless and seductive. Texture is as important to him as flavor, and he has earned a reputation as one of America's foremost winemakers by producing a long line of powerful but simultaneously tender wines. A third-generation Italian-Californian, with wine in his blood (his father made homegrown Zinfandel across the mountains in Sonoma County), Sbragia started working for Beringer Vineyards in 1976. Since then, he has honed and championed a recognizable style, one that today is virtually synonymous with this venerable winery. Beringer's best bottlings over the past quarter century invariably have been fruit-forward and sensuously pleasurable. As much as any, they have helped fashion the image of enticingly rich and ripe California wine that has so captivated consumers across the country and indeed the globe.

Sbragia started his career at Beringer as an assistant to Myron Nightingale, one of the post–Prohibition era's premier California vintners. Nightingale had been hired in 1971 to modernize Beringer's cellars and upgrade the quality of its production, a process that included the introduction of the company's "Private Reserve" wines. Sbragia learned at his proverbial knee. "Myron was a great teacher," he recalls. "He understood that winemaking requires subjective input—a feeling, a major preference—just like painting or sculpture."

In 1984, when Nightingale retired, Sbragia was appointed chief winemaker. He is quick to credit his mentor with showing him how to realize a coherent vision. "You've got to make wine that you like yourself," he insists. "Only then can you be consistent. Myron believed that as a winemaker you have to go with your heart." Happily, Sbragia's heart sends him in a direction that American wine drinkers want to go (though it certainly can be argued that he has helped lead them there). Regardless of the grape variety, he aims for wines with bold flavors and a voluptuous mouthfeel. And while Sbragia has made many excellent wines over the years, he has excelled most consistently with Chardonnay and the red Bordeaux varieties, grapes that yield naturally powerful wines and so best suit his style. (His Pinot Noirs and Sauvignon Blancs have tended to be a notch below.) Because Beringer's excellent "Private Reserve" Chardonnays and Cabernets are blended wines, they by definition express a winemaking philosophy more than a specific place. By contrast, Bancroft Ranch Merlot reflects both a human predilection and a natural *terroir*. Given the undistinguished record of many high-priced California Merlots, it may well be Sbragia's most significant accomplishment.

Sbragia and Nightingale first made wines from Merlot grapes in the late 1970s. "Pretty lackluster," Sbragia recalls; "light and not very flavorful." Not surprisingly, Sbragia distrusted the variety at the time, believing that it simply did not fit his then emerging stylistic vision. "After all," he asks rhetorically, "what did most people use it for? To make Cabernet lighter, to take Cabernet down. I never wanted to do that." Then, in 1986, he tasted the mountain-grown grapes from the Bancroft Ranch. There certainly was nothing light about these. Though he could have vinified them and used the resulting wine as a blending component in Beringer's "Private Reserve" Cabernet, he decided to bottle it on its own. This Merlot was just too special—too distinct, too different, too expressive of its mountain origin—to be allowed to play a secondary role in a blend. "I saw," he says, "that this vineyard gives you Merlot to make a wine that's big and rich, and at the same time delicious, a wine that makes you salivate." In other words, Bancroft Ranch Merlot, if grown properly and harvested at the right time, was tailor-made for his and Beringer's style.

The property is named for its owner, Jim Bancroft, a San Francisco businessman, who purchased it, some 300 acres, in 1969, as a weekend getaway. Thirteen years later, having caught the wine bug, he began planning a vineyard. It was an arduous undertaking. "All we did that first summer," he recalls, "is move rocks, some seventeen thousand tons of them." In the spring of 1983, Bancroft planted his first grapes—half white (Chardonnay) and half red (mainly Cabernet, with a little Merlot). A few years later, Mike Moone, Beringer's president, contracted to buy the reds. Moone wanted the Cabernet for Ed Spragia's "Private Reserve" blend, and he took the Merlot almost as an afterthought. Bancroft Ranch Merlot, all of four hundred cases, debuted with the 1987 vintage.

From the outset, this wine's intensity amazed everyone who tasted it. So Mike Moone set about trying to convince Jim Bancroft to graft the Chardonnay on the property over to Merlot. "Mike was very persuasive," Bancroft remembers. "He told me that only a handful of places in the world grow great Merlot, and that this might be one of them." Beringer contributed to the cost of the vineyard conversion, and a few years later the company signed a long term lease to farm the land as well as use the grapes. Today, the Bancroft Ranch vineyard consists of fifty-five acres of Cabernet Sauvignon and five of Cabernet Franc, most of which does go into the "Private Reserve" blend, and thirty acres of Merlot, which ends up in some three thousand cases of this varietally labeled, single-vineyard wine.

Bob Steinhauer, Beringer's long-term vineyard manager, oversees viticulture on the Bancroft Ranch. He supervised the replanting necessary when phylloxera infested the vineyard in the early 1990s, and so knows each dip and swale of the property intimately. "Rock," he says bluntly when asked to explain what makes the site so special. "There's only eighteen inches or so of topsoil here. Then it's just rock." But the rock itself is special, a form of cemented but malleable volcanic ash. Each vine's roots have to thread their way through it in search of nutrients, and the rock goes down so deep that they can't find many. "It checks the vine's vigor," Steinhauer explains. "This vineyard is very low in both nutrition and water capacity. That's why we get a small crop but intense flavors."

These mountain vines would wither without irrigation, so Steinhauer gives them just enough water to let the grapes ripen, but not so much as to swell the berries or increase cluster size. Again, the goal is concentrated, powerful flavor. But achieving that goal in the mountains inevitably means getting potentially offputting tannins. That is why harvesting the grapes when they are physiologically mature proves so important. Though the taste does not change much from 24 to 26 degrees of sugar, the tannins become much suppler, resulting in a far more palatable wine. According to Ed Sbragia, because the Merlot is harvested so late, it has the highest phenolic content of all the red wines he makes—higher even than Cabernet from the same vineyard. Yet even when young, the wine does not feel unpleasantly harsh or tight.

Wine grapes were first grown on Howell Mountain in the 1880s, and by the turn of the last century, the region had earned a reputation for sophisticated reds. A local newspaper opined that it someday "would be to California what Médoc is to France," a prophesy seemingly fulfilled when a Howell Mountain wine won gold at the Paris Exposition of 1900. As happened everywhere in the United States, Prohibition brought things to a halt. Wine growing did not return to Howell Mountain (at least to what is now the appellation or AVA, the official demarcation being land above 1,400 feet) in any serious fashion until the 1980s. Even today, fewer acres are under vine than were cultivated a century ago. That's because mountain viticulture, especially at high altitudes, is arduous work. The land proves difficult to farm. In addition, deer and other predators can wreak havoc, and low yields may result in even lower fiscal returns. The results sometimes prove spectacular, but the risks always remain high. So it helps to have a company with substantial resources on one's side. And despite changes in ownership, Beringer's management teams have never skimped or cut corners at Bancroft Ranch.

Beringer is Napa's oldest continuously operating winery. Founded in 1876 by two German émigré brothers, it was one of the leading players during the valley's first golden age—a roughly twenty-year period beginning about 1890, when Napa wines first proved that they could hold their own with the world's best. Beringer Brothers won medals at all of the important Gilded Age competitions. Their wines were sold as far afield as London, Berlin, and Tokyo, and came to be in demand with connoisseurs on the otherwise Eurocentric East Coast. Andrew Carnegie, who certainly could afford to drink anything he wanted, judged them his personal favorites.

Then came Prohibition. The company struggled through, with an annual production of some 15,000 cases of "altar wine." Its difficulties continued, however, during the decades following Repeal in 1933, and by the 1960s Beringer was producing primarily nondescript, non-vintage wines that undermined its reputation. Then, in 1971, the Beringer family sold the company to Nestlé, which had the resources to finance a return to glory. This giant Swiss corporation purchased new equipment, replanted existing vineyards, acquired additional property, and hired new personnel—including the triad of Nightingale, Sbragia, and Steinhauer. When it sold the company twenty-five years later, the second Napa golden age was well underway, and Beringer once again occupied center stage. Yet another ownership change came a few years later. This time an Australian conglomerate, Fosters Brewing Group, purchased the company. But again, management was committed to high standards, and the best Beringer wines continue today to go from strength to strength. Of the big Napa Valley wineries, none has a higher quality portfolio.

Quality, however, wears all sorts of guises. While other Napa mountain wines can be impressive, they invariably display a different profile from Beringer's Bancroft Ranch Merlot. Randy Dunn's Howell Mountain Cabernet serves as the archetype—brooding, dark and intense, with layers of flavor encased in a hard shell of tannin. It is one of Napa's finest wines—*if* you have the requisite patience to wait for it to soften and settle. Bancroft Ranch Merlot ages well too (the initial 1987 vintage still tastes vibrant), but it is much lusher and hence more attractive when young. The difference is due in part to the grape, Merlot having a thinner skin than Cabernet. But as important is the winemaking, the human vision of Ed Sbragia, Bob Steinhauer, and behind them Myron Nightingale. They share the conviction that, no matter the varietal or the vineyard source, the best wine has to be, as Sbragia puts it, "Yummy—just plain fun to drink, something above all to enjoy." That's very much this very different mountain Merlot.

A NOTE ON VINTAGES:

Beringer's Bancroft Ranch Merlot, lush but at the same time muscular, is at its best anywhere from five to fifteen years after the vintage. Younger wines show more forward fruit, but the wine always displays plenty of ripe berry flavor. Strong vintages for this mountain wine include 1987, 1991, 1994, 1997, and 2001.

THE SUGGESTED PRICE FOR THE CURRENT 2002 RELEASE IS $75.

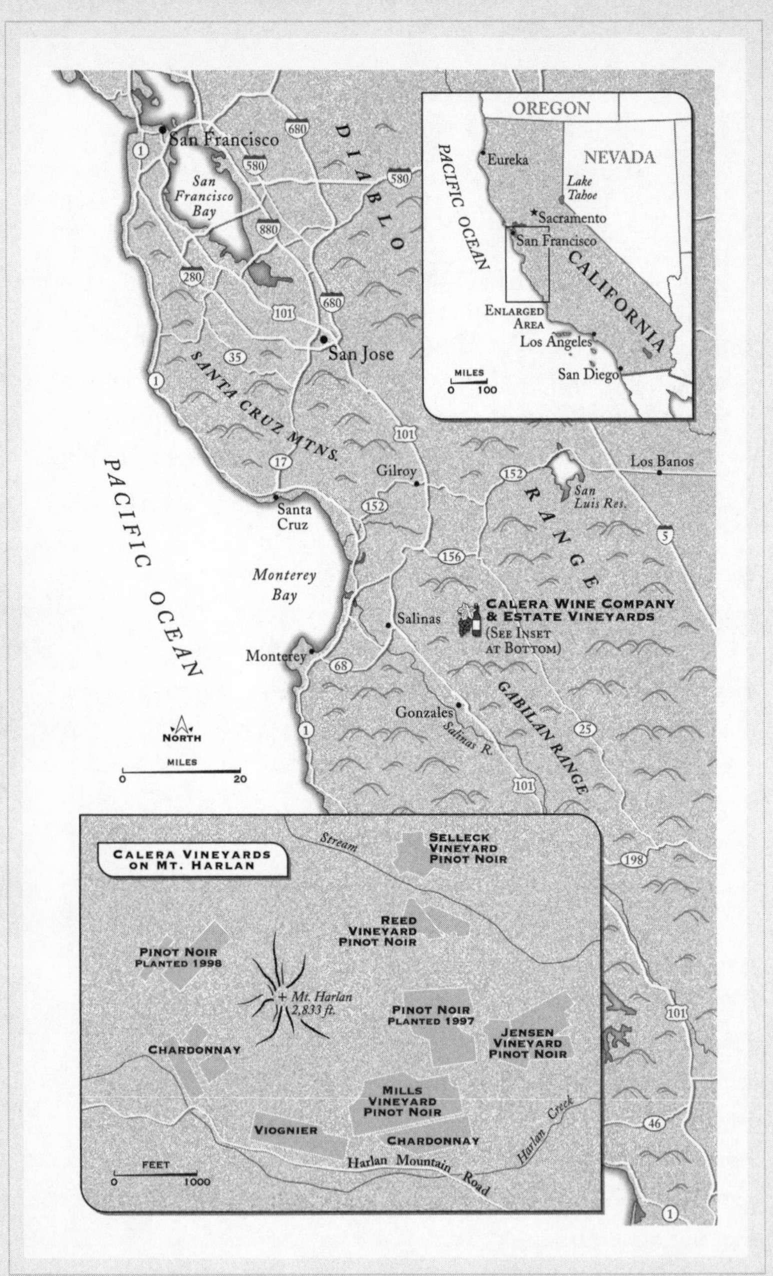

THE CALERA VINEYARDS ON MOUNT HARLAN

CHAPTER 5

Calera Wine Company Pinot Noir, Jensen Vineyard

Mount Harlan, California

...

The theme of the Calera story is fixation, one man's obsessive quest to master the variables of viticulture and vinification that distinguish majestic wines from merely mundane ones. The fixation started literally from the ground up. Because *grand cru* red Burgundies are made with Pinot Noir grapes grown on the limestone slopes of Burgundy's Côte d'Or, Josh Jensen, Calera's owner, began his pursuit of American Pinot perfection by searching for limestone. He found a substantial deposit of it atop a remote mountain in California's San Benito County, far removed from more celebrated (and more comfortable) wine country. So he moved to isolated Mount Harlan in order to grow grapes, to make wine, and to live. But the limestone by itself cannot account for the rich complexity that characterizes his Calera Pinots. As important are all the other aspects of Jensen's fixation: his insistence on extremely low yields in the vineyards, his use of only indigenous yeast for fermentation, and his

Josh Jensen

design of a gravity-flow winery in which each lot of wine receives minimal handling in its passage from press to barrel to bottle. At Calera, wine quality is all that matters. All that Josh Jensen does and does not do to his grapes and his wines provides evidence of his obsession.

Jensen is single-minded in his quest for quality, and the results speak for themselves. Ever since he released his first Pinot Noirs in 1978, he has demonstrated what at the start was thought near impossible—that California can produce world-class wines from this most temperamental and finicky grape variety. His top wines taste distinctive rather than derivative, reflecting the earth and spice of their specific locales as well as more generic California sun and heat. They are a breed apart, and their individuality can be traced back to Jensen's own, his admittedly compulsive fixation on this grape and this wine. His has been a thirty-five-year, at times quixotic quest, but he has done much more than tilt at windmills, for Calera today has an unmatched track record for superlative American Pinot Noir.

The Calera winery, a converted rock crushing plant, is located on a windy road some ten miles south of the town of Hollister, on the eastern flank of the Gabilan Mountain Range. The grapes grow farther up, way up, between 2,200 and 2,500 feet above sea level, making these some of the highest elevation vineyards in the United States. The surrounding landscape is untamed and beautifully rugged, with groves of live oaks and pines surrounding the meticulously tended vines, and scrubby chaparral brush interspersed amidst the white limestone. There are four established Pinot Noir sites, and two newer ones just beginning to come on line. Currently, these young vineyards have not yet been named, but the four older ones all honor people important in Jensen's life. The 14.4-acre Mills, planted in 1984, is named for a former neighbor and friend. The much smaller Reed consists of only 4.4 acres, and pays tribute to one of Calera's original investors; the 5-acre Selleck is named for a man whose passion for wine first sparked Jensen's own; and the larger (13.8-acre) Jensen Vineyard memorializes his father.

These last three vineyards were all planted in 1975, primarily with Burgundy cuttings, though Jensen does contain some bench grafts purchased from a nursery in St. Helena. Each site's contour and exposure is distinct, and the wines reflect as much. Over the years, all four have produced some superb bottlings, but Selleck and Jensen have done so most consistently. They are Calera's two *grand crus*, and the wines from them taste subtly different. Each vintage has its own character, but with time in bottle the Selleck Pinots tend to seem more floral and delicate, the Jensen wines earthier and more muscular. The two are equally good, but because the Jensen Vineyard is larger, and because it carries the owner's family name, the wines from it are somewhat better known.

In addition to these single-vineyard Pinots, Josh Jensen also makes small amounts of Chardonnay and Viognier from Mount Harlan grapes, as well as larger batches of Chardonnay and Pinot Noir from purchased fruit. But the estate Pinot Noirs are what make his heart skip a beat. They—or at least the idea of them—are what brought him to this wild, remote spot, and they are what he has devoted his life's work to producing. That's because for Jensen, then and now, Pinot Noir makes most of the world's finest wines. Greatness does not happen always or often, even with prized *terroirs*; but "when everything is right with Pinot Noir," he says, "when Pinot Noir is in a good mood—well, then it's as good as it gets."

"I like to call Pinot Noir the *especially* grape," Jensen continues, "because almost any generalization you can make about grapes and wine is especially true with Pinot Noir." In both vineyard and winery, this tendency toward the extreme is what renders the variety so temperamental. For example, wine quality will suffer with any grape variety if yields get too large. With Pinot, however, the drop-off is precipitous: half a ton too much and the wine will taste thin and acidic. Similarly, all wines spoil if exposed to too much air. Pinot, though, always flirts with flavors hinting of vinegar, so an extra breath of oxygen can send it over the edge. So, too, any wine will lose color if racked or filtered excessively; but Pinot, being thin-skinned, suffers more than others. And most important, while all grapes are site-specific, Pinot Noir is especially so. As Jensen says emphatically, "With no other variety does it so obviously matter where the vines are."

Jensen learned that lesson as a young man in Burgundy. He had grown up in a fairly affluent San Francisco suburb, where he was introduced to wine by George Selleck, a friend of his father's. But he only began to drink it regularly when he went to Oxford to pursue a graduate degree in anthropology. He lived in England for over two years, had wine with dinner virtually every evening, and fell in love with red Burgundy. So, after Oxford, he decided to visit the source, the Côte d'Or, where he got a job picking grapes at the Domaine de la Romanée-Conti, considered by many to be the world's greatest Pinot producer. This was in 1969. The air was filled with unrest, and Jensen sensed something comforting, something stable, in the rustic simplicity of the Burgundy harvest. He remembers feeling reassured by how basic everything was. As he puts it, "I was enthralled that the greatest wines in the world were made by the most bare-bones methods." That was when he decided to devote his life to wine rather than academics. He spent the next couple of years in France, working part time in wineries, befriending vintners, and reading the relevant texts. Though he found he enjoyed all sorts of wines, the ones that kept thrilling him were the *premier* and *grand cru* Burgundies (still affordable back then for someone on a budget). And when he asked his co-workers what made these so special, he kept getting the same answer: "It's the soil, the limestone soil."

Limestone abounds in the Côte d'Or because the region was once covered by shallow seas. Over millions of years, petrified shells and carbonate of lime from sea water gradually hardened into rock. That rock is now in the subsoil, where a vine's roots will wend through cracks and fissures in search of water and nutrients. No one can say for certain to what degree its presence accounts for the distinctive character of top red Burgundies, their famed *goût de terroir*. On the one hand, the many vineyards located nearby that lack limestone produce notably lesser wines. On the other, many limestone-rich areas elsewhere in the world do not produce good wine at all. Still, when Jensen returned home and assessed the variables involved in the production of the wines he loved, he kept returning to limestone—not as the determining cause, but as an important contributing factor. "I didn't think that I'd necessarily get great wines just by planting on it," he explains. "But I did think that planting on it would increase the odds. And since the whole thing was a gamble anyway, I wanted the best odds I could get."

Back in 1971, when Jensen started looking for property to buy, planting Pinot Noir in California and attempting to make complex, nuanced Burgundy-styled wines was indeed a big gamble. Many people had tried, but very few had succeeded. Most American Pinots at the time were either thin, watery will-o'-the-wisps, or stewy, hot clunkers. Virtually none displayed anything even resembling finesse. The problem was that the vines often were planted in the wrong places—in climates that were too hot, and in soils that were too fertile. Jensen, who had little experience with California wine, instinctively understood as much. So when he looked for potential vineyard land, he looked not just for limestone but also for relatively cool temperatures, which in California means a marine influence. In addition, he wanted hillsides, good drainage, a variety of exposures, and fairly infertile soils, so that the vines wouldn't overcrop. And, since he didn't have a fortune to squander, the property had to be affordable. It took him two full years, but he found all he desired high up on Mount Harlan, in a site that had once been a lime quarry, replete with an old kiln (*calera* in Spanish). The only drawback was that it is in the middle of nowhere.

Being so isolated and so fixated on a single goal would cost Jensen his marriage and in large measure define his life. Calera became his passion, and there is more than a hint of melancholy in his voice when he talks about the choices he made in order to pursue it. "Yes," he admits, "it can get lonely up here." Yet he was not really alone. In fact, he wasn't even first. Around the turn of the last century, a Frenchman, Maurice Tamm, also had gone searching in the Gabilans for limestone. Tamms found it on the western side of the range, up above the Salinas Valley, where he planted grapes—mostly Chenin Blanc. Chardonnay and Pinot Noir went in later, and those low-yielding vines were what compelled another Burgundy fanatic, Richard Graff, to purchase the property in 1969. Graff and his partner, Phil Woodward, called it by its old name, "Chalone," and the Chardonnays and Pinot Noirs they produced there brought them fame. When Jensen first tasted a Chalone Pinot from barrel, he enjoyed a shock of recognition. "It was my eureka moment," he remembers. This wine wasn't what he knew from France, but it shared a certain grace, which was precisely what other California Pinots lacked. Chalone would go on to become part of a publicly held group, and the wines, while often very good, would become for a time quite variable. But Jensen's experience with them was in its own way as important as his earlier experience in Burgundy. "Tasting Dick Graff's wine showed me," he says, "that it could be done here. That I wasn't chasing rainbows."

To get it done, Jensen followed the minimal intervention model he knew from Burgundy. He didn't crush the grapes, use commercial yeast, or pump or filter his wines. Instead, he fermented the whole clusters, including the stems. (Calera doesn't even have a crusher-destemmer, something that Jensen calls "a doomsday machine.") He then allowed nature to follow its own course, overseeing the aging process to prevent spoilage or contamination, but not intervening so as to control or dictate the results. In the early years, when Jensen harvested his Pinot Noir at roughly 22 degrees of brix or sugar in order to yield a wine with a Burgundian level of approximately 12 percent alcohol, the wines seemed thinner than he wanted. He began picking riper fruit in 1982, so that the wines now finish with about 13 percent alcohol, but his old-fashioned, non-interventionist winemaking protocol has remained otherwise unchanged.

This minimalist approach to winemaking is in its own way more difficult than an intrusive one. The vintner needs to have a clear vision, and to know exactly how to pursue it. Jensen soon realized that he needed help with the latter, particularly with the more scientific aspects of winemaking. So in 1976 he advertised for an assistant, someone with training in biochemistry but without preconceived ideas about wine. He found just the right person in Steve Doerner, then a senior at UC Davis. Doerner moved down to Hollister, and for the next sixteen years helped make the wines that established Calera's reputation.

This proved a very good partnership, with Jensen supplying the vision and winemaking direction, Doerner the scientific expertise. Eventually, though, Doerner tired of it—of the isolation and routine, and of not being able to realize his own vision and make his own wines. So in 1992 he left for Oregon, where at Cristom he today crafts one of the very few American Pinot Noirs that can rival Calera's. Since then, Jensen has worked with four assistant winemakers: Sara Steiner, Belinda Gould, Terry Culton, and now Corneliu Dane. A native Romanian, Dane handles the day-to-day winery operation, but the big decisions remain very much Jensen's. As he notes firmly, "I have the final say."

He has the final say in the vineyards, too, but often defers there to the advice and counsel of Jim Ryan, his vineyard manager. Ryan has worked at Calera since 1979, and so knows the property intimately. When asked what makes the Jensen Vineyard special, he points first to the diversity of exposures, noting that the site occupies a small ridge, with slopes that go off in all directions at once. "That's why it takes so long to pick," he explains; "usually a full month from first pass to last." Ryan speculates that the soils play a factor as well. "There's real diversity there too," he says. "It's not just limestone, but the influence of limestone on everything else." Ryan and his crew farm all the estate vineyards organically, and they carefully manage irrigation, the supply of water being limited up in the mountains. Thin, rocky, nutritionally poor soils combined with little water result in pitifully low yields—anywhere from under 1 ton to 3 tons per acre. The average at Jensen is 1.53 tons, or roughly half the amount that in Burgundy is permitted for *premier crus*. When asked if that might be too low a yield, Jensen simply shrugs. "It's what we get here," he says. "To have more, I'd have to go somewhere else."

The Pinot Noir grapes from the Jensen Vineyard are picked ripe enough to be fully flavored (at between 23 and 24 degrees of sugar), but not so ripe as to be raisined. "We've always tried so hard," Jensen explains, "to be sure our wines don't taste pruny." They then are trucked down to the winery, where they ferment in open-top, 2,000-gallon tanks for two weeks. The young wines next go into barrel, all French oak and primarily from the famed François Frères cooperage, where they rest and mature for some sixteen months. All this movement occurs by force of gravity, Jensen having designed the winery so as to minimize the need for handling and potentially bruising the wine. "It's another *especially*," he says. "Pinot Noir especially does not like to be handled roughly. My goal is to be as gentle as possible with it." The 1978 vintage was the first to be made in this facility, and nearly every year since has seen some addition or improvement—a new press or bottling line, new barrel cellars built into the hillside, a new laboratory, a real office. "For fifteen years, our office was a trailer," Jensen notes. "I wanted to get the winery done right first." No surprise there. At Calera, the wine always comes first.

Looking back over more than thirty years of his Pinot Noir fixation, Jensen acknowledges that "we've been around a long time now." So long in fact, "that maybe we don't always get the recognition I think we should. But when people taste our wines, they know how good they are. I think we're hitting the nail squarely on the head now." As with any Pinot producer, even the famed Burgundy *domaines*, not every wine from the Jensen Vineyard is spot on. But tasting a series of vintages reveals far more successes than slips. Taken as a whole, the wines display a consistent style and character, with dark cherry-flavored fruit, herbal secondary notes both in the bouquet and on the palate, a hint of tartness in a long, layered finish, and a firm but not at all astringent structure. Neither as fleshy as most other top American renditions nor as earthy as top Burgundies, they are truly individualistic.

As a varietal, Pinot certainly remains more variable than Cabernet or Chardonnay, but first-rate American versions are no longer the anomalies they were when Josh Jensen first came to Calera. "I like to think," he says, "that we had something to do with that." Though no other obsessive vintner has followed him up the side of Mount Harlan, the principles he has preached and the practices he has followed have been adopted wherever people are serious about Pinot. "My job," he concludes, "is to make the best damned wine I can. With it, I then make converts—one person, one glass at a time."

A NOTE ON VINTAGES:

Most good California Pinot Noirs need a few years of bottle age to begin to express the non-fruit, secondary flavors that can make this varietal so enticing. Calera's Jensen Vineyard Pinot, however, tastes complete and complex virtually from the start. It ages very well, becoming ever more nuanced, but does not need much extra time to be delicious. Strong vintages on Mount Harlan include 1989, 1992, 1996, 1999, and 2000.

THE SUGGESTED PRICE FOR THE CURRENT 2001 RELEASE IS $50.

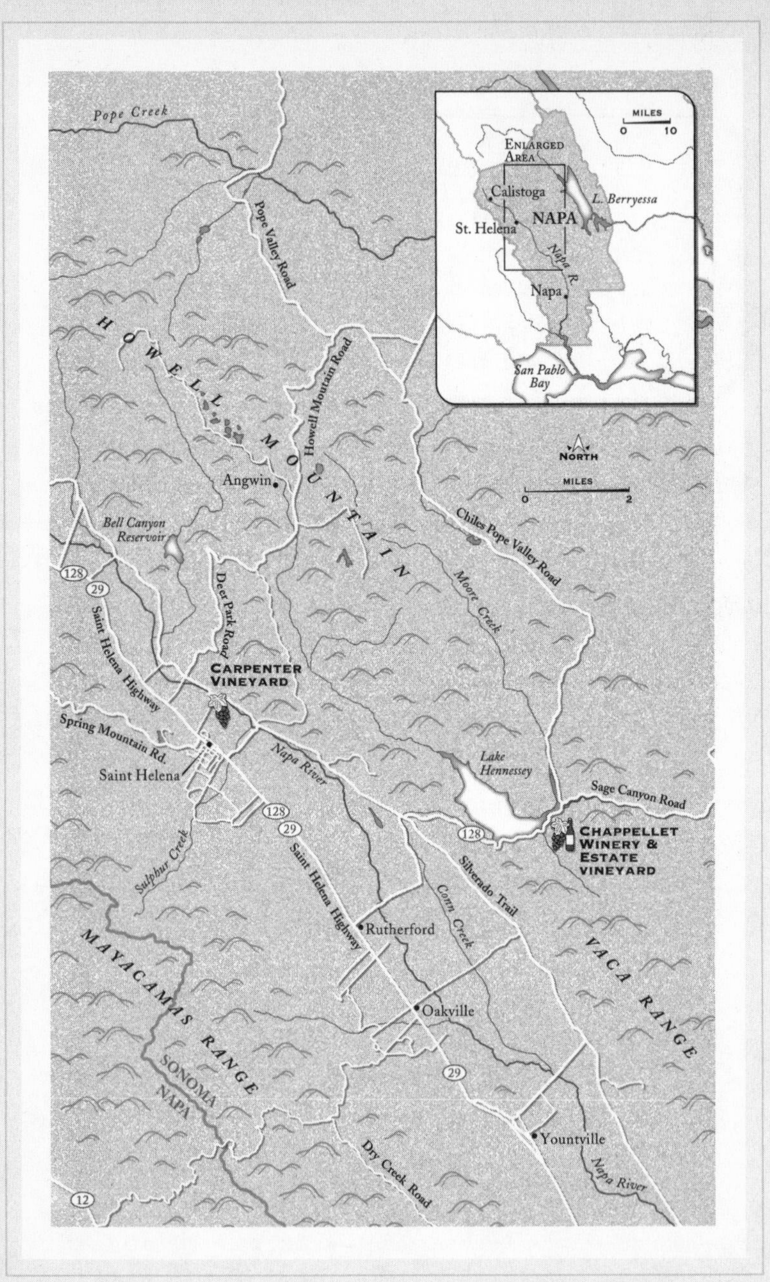

CHAPPELLET'S CURRENT CHENIN BLANC VINEYARDS

CHAPTER 6

Chappellet Dry Chenin Blanc

Napa Valley, California

...

Jon-Mark Chappellet

Wine is much like fashion. Just as hemlines rise and fall, wine styles and types go in and out of vogue. These days, big and powerful wines are in demand, while delicate, lithe ones have to wait their turn. With reds, Cabernet is hot while Gamay is not. And with whites, Chardonnay remains chic while varietals like Gewurztraminer and Riesling are on the outs. But no white grape is more unfashionable than Chenin Blanc. Not all that long ago, it was the most widely planted white wine grape in California. As recently as 1982, some 45,000 acres were under vine, many of them in the Golden State's premier wine-growing regions. The figure today is only about a quarter of that, with virtually all of the vineyards located in the searingly hot Central Valley, where the grape is used primarily to make inexpensive jug blends. Almost no one grows Chenin Blanc in the state's top Viticultural Areas any more. It's easy to understand why. The average price a grower gets for California Chardonnay runs close to $700 a ton, while the average for

Chenin is only about $150. In North Coast appellations, where vineyard land is extremely costly, planting Chenin for wine makes about as much sense as planting Thompson Seedless for raisins. "It's a niche thing," admits Jon-Mark Chappellet, who manages production at the Napa Valley winery his parents founded nearly forty years ago. "Demand is so low that we're an anomaly. Napa Valley Chenin Blanc just doesn't compute anymore."

So why does Chappellet keep making this wine? Jon-Mark shrugs his shoulders when he answers: "Because we like to drink it. Because my mom and dad *love* to drink it." As well they should. Chappellet is one of a small handful of California wineries devoting serious attention to Chenin Blanc, and the results speak, or taste, for themselves. Full of bright, crisp autumn fruit flavors, with plenty of acidity for balance, and surprisingly nuanced complexity, this wine offers what so many American whites (especially wooded Chardonnays) don't—in a word, refreshment. "It doesn't weigh down your palate like Chardonnay," Jon-Mark notes; "even Chardonnay you like, even Chardonnay you make yourself." Chappellet makes a quite good Napa Valley Chardonnay, yet that wine is but one in a sea of comparable others. By contrast, Chappellet's Dry Chenin Blanc is inimitable. Though a victim of contemporary fashion's capricious winds, it is very much an original—an American wine with a character of its own.

Chenin Blanc is the classic white grape of France's central Loire Valley, where in the region of Anjou-Touraine it yields intense, concentrated wines that range from lusciously sweet to numbingly dry. Like virtually all of the important French wine grapes, it has traveled the world. Chenin grows today in almost every significant New World winemaking country. It is a virtual staple in South Africa, where it accounts for nearly a quarter of all grapes harvested. Argentina produces a fair amount as well, as do Australia, Mexico, New Zealand, even Israel. Yet while some vintners in those countries use it to make high-class wines like their French counterparts, more treat it as a workhorse, its ability to retain acidity while delivering high yields being its primary virtue.

That's what most Americans who grow Chenin think as well. This grape came to California under the moniker "White Pineau" soon after the Civil War. H. W. Crabb, who planted the celebrated To-Kalon Vineyard in Napa beginning in 1865, grew it, but for a long time Chenin never gained much of a following. Even after Prohibition, when growers scrambled to find high-yielding varieties they could use to make generic jug wines, it took a backseat to more pedestrian grapes such as Palomino and French Colombard. Why it was neglected for so long is not much of a mystery. Until the 1950s, when the Mondavis at Charles Krug and André Tchelistcheff at Beaulieu pioneered cold fermentation for white wine, resulting in clean, fresh flavors, most California whites were fermented warm, with excessive skin contact. The wines tasted sour and displayed oxidized aromas. Using a so-called noble grape wouldn't have made much of a difference.

As American white winemaking improved, Chenin Blanc started to become popular, both as a component in improved blends and as a stand-alone wine. Charles Krug offered an especially tasty rendition. Slightly sweet, it was one of the first varietally labeled California wines to achieve both critical and mass market success, being a gold medal winner at the California State Fair through the fifties and a consumer favorite. As much as any single wine, its success in the marketplace demonstrated that Americans liked wines that tasted fresh and fruity. As fashion's gods began smiling on Chenin, plantings increased rapidly. In the early 1960s, fewer than 1,500 acres were devoted to it in all of California. By 1972, there were almost 15,000; five years later, nearly 22,000; five years after that, over 43,000.

Many of these new vineyards were in the Central Valley, but some were in the North Coast as well, where the acreage of Chenin Blanc tripled during the 1970s. The grape still was used primarily as a blender, but more than a few well-regarded Napa wineries offered varietal Chenins. These wines tended to be light-bodied and slightly sweet. Charles Krug led the way, with Beringer, Christian Brothers (who marketed it as "Pinot de la Loire"), and others following. But then fickle fashion frowned. As part of the new wave of wine appreciation that started to sweep through the country in the seventies and eighties, light, off-dry wines became *déclassé.* People in the know demanded something allegedly more serious, meaning something weightier, drier, and marked by the taste of wood. Their white wine of choice invariably was made with Chardonnay, not Chenin.

Chardonnay's fortunes in America's vineyards are the mirror opposite of Chenin Blanc's. Just as the one grape fell out of fashion, the other became all the rage. For a long time, neither variety was planted widely or held in high esteem. Then, in the 1960s, the decade in which American vintners began to raise their ambitions and try more explicitly to emulate classic European wines, plantings of both increased significantly. Chardonnay and Chenin each yield renowned wines, the one in Burgundy and the other in the Loire, so this initial interest makes sense. But why Chardonnay eclipsed Chenin so totally twenty years later remains befuddling.

Part of the explanation, surely, lies in the fact that new wine drinkers, those whose palates and purses fueled the American wine boom, came to believe that dry wines must be superior to off-dry ones. Many of the poor wines of the post-Prohibition years, those whose only resemblance to the European standards came in bastardized names like "Chablis" or "Rhine Wine," retained sugar, so the simple fact of dryness became a perceived mark of quality. And while Chenin Blanc in the Loire can produce superlative dry wines, the grape also is used to make delectable off-dry and luscious dessert wines. By contrast, Chardonnay in Burgundy only yields dry table wines. Though few American consumers ever actually tasted them, those wines, the white Burgundies of the Côte d'Or, became by default *the* whites that so many American critics praised and so many American vintners tried to imitate. But it was all just fashion. Nothing about Chardonnay makes it inherently superior to Chenin Blanc—either as a grape or as a wine. So, too, nothing about a glass of Meursault from Burgundy is intrinsically better than a glass of Savennières or Vouvray from the Loire. But in America, where there was virtually no tradition to guide either winemakers or consumers, the force of fashion was felt acutely. It hardly mattered that image did not always match reality, and that many Chardonnays were not in fact dry. Chenin Blanc fell out of favor precisely when Chardonnay became chic.

Donn and Molly Chappellet started the business that carries their family name during Chenin Blanc's all too brief age of American popularity. Having grown Interstate United Corporation into the third largest food service operation in the country, Donn Chappellet sold his shares and used the profits to move his family from Los Angeles to Napa, where in 1967 he purchased a 600-acre estate on the eastern side of the valley. He built a winery there, only the second new one in Napa since World War II. It overlooked a small sub-valley, being located on a rocky, remote slope called Pritchard Hill. The Chappellets moved because they had grown tired of the bustle of business and wanted a different, simpler, more peaceful life. They loved the quiet beauty of their new home, and were intrigued by the possibility that they might grow top-flight grapes and make first-class wines there.

Part of a new breed of Napa Valley vintners, men and women who had made their money in other ventures, the Chappellets had plenty of ambition and passion but no experience making wine. They were, however, avid wine drinkers and collectors. As such, they knew the European standard-bearers well, and from the beginning wanted to emulate them. Donn Chappellet hoped to emphasize Bordeaux-styled reds, and his property included an established seventy-acre dry-farmed, terraced vineyard, with Cabernet and Merlot growing amidst a hodge-podge of varietals—Chardonnay, Gamay, Riesling, and a substantial block of Chenin Blanc. Rather than replant, he decided to expand the vineyard over time while simultaneously playing the hand he was dealt. So, starting with the 1968 vintage, Chappellet made wines from all these grapes. Donn and Molly may not have been as excited about some of them as about the red Bordeaux grapes, but they were familiar with all of them—including Chenin. In keeping with the tenor of the times, they thought of serious wine as dry. And because they knew that Chenin didn't have to be sweet to be good, they made their wine in a dry Loire style.

In doing so, the Chappellets were extremely fortunate in their choice of a winemaker. Irascible and immensely talented, Philip Togni was an Englishman with degrees in enology and viticulture from the Universities of Bordeaux and Montpellier. Before coming to California, he had made wine in Alsace, Beaujolais, and Bordeaux, so knew firsthand what fine French wine was all about. He liked both elegant, long-lived red wines and light, dry whites, and he was given free rein to work in those styles at Chappellet. If Pauillac in Bordeaux was his prototype for Cabernet, Savennières in the central Loire was the model with Chenin.

Togni's primary goal with this grape was a crisp, refreshing wine, with bright fruit aromas supported by secondary notes of minerals and spice. Starting with the very first vintage in 1967, he hit that target. The wine tasted fresh and vibrant, almost steely. No matter that it represented a new style for California Chenin, virtually everyone who tried it liked it—including UC Davis professor Harold Berg, who declared the 1968 Chappellet Chenin Blanc the finest example of the varietal yet made in the state. Although Philip Togni only stayed at Chappellet for five years (eventually moving across the valley to Spring Mountain, where he today makes some of Napa's finest Cabernets under his own name and from his own grapes), he set the house wine style. Subsequent winemakers over the years, including Joe Cafaro, Cathy Corison, Tony Soter, and since 1990 Phillip Corallo-Titus, have stayed true to it. As Corallo-Titus acknowledges, "When I started here, there already was a well-established style. With Dry Chenin, I've tried to follow Philip Togni's and Donn Chappellet's initial vision."

The persistence of that vision does not mean that there hasn't been innovation at Chappellet. "Whatever the variety, a good wine has to stand on its own merits," insists Jon-Mark Chappellet. "We think our Dry Chenin does. Still, we've tried all sorts of things with the grape." The experiments include a 100 percent barrel-fermented Old Vine Cuvée (made for twelve years, beginning in the early 1990s), as well as a few late-harvest, dessert wines (made only in years when nature cooperates with botrytis rather than rot). With Dry Chenin, Corallo-Titius now picks the fruit riper than his predecessors (at approximately 23 degrees of sugar), and he presses the grapes in whole cluster bunches rather than crushing them before fermentation. Otherwise, though, he stays true to established procedure.

The one big change with this wine involves the vineyard. The Chappellets recently planted more Chenin Blanc on Pritchard Hill—"My parents insisted on it," notes Jon-Mark—because the original estate block, over forty years old, had become diseased and unproductive. For a few years now, they have augmented production with grapes purchased from an eight-acre vineyard in St. Helena, the Carpenter Vineyard. But because this site is on the valley floor, near the Napa River, the flavors in recent releases have not been quite as multifaceted as those in wines from earlier vintages. "That's why," Jon-Mark explains, "our goal is to go back to a pure estate wine. We should be able to do that by 2007. But during the transition, as our vineyard comes online, we may have to go a couple of years without any wine." And production, which today averages around four thousand cases, will shrink in the short term to less than half of that.

What renders today's Chappellet Dry Chenin Blanc, sourced almost exclusively from the Carpenter Vineyard, appealing is its balance: vivid fruit set against tingling freshness, the vinous equivalent of biting into a crisp Macintosh apple. To be sure, even when made with old vine fruit from Pritchard Hill, this wine lacks underlying minerality when compared to the best French renditions. But as Phillip Corallo-Titus insists, "the idea never was to make a Loire wine. We can't get the kind of searing acidity that they get there. We have to emphasize the taste of fruit. We have to make our own wine." He and his winemaking predecessors at Chappellet clearly have done just that. The wine tastes first and foremost of apples, with secondary fruit flavors reminiscent of lemons, limes, even pineapple. Though it can acquire an underlying spiciness with bottle age, its complexity reflects those different fruit flavors rather than the flinty, almost metallic notes characteristic of Savennières or Vouvray Sec. Corallo-Titus highlights these flavors with a winemaking regimen that uses wood to provide texture rather than taste. He ferments roughly a quarter of the grapes in used French oak so as to add roundness and softness to the final cuvée, the rest of which is fermented in stainless steel in order to preserve freshness. The wine then rests on its light lees for eight months or so before bottling. Because vivacity is what makes it so appealing, it is very much a wine to drink young, though older vintages sometimes can display a marzipan-tinged charm.

Only a few other American producers—including Dry Creek and Daniel Gehrs in California, Bookwalter in Washington State, and Pheasant Ridge in Texas—treat Chenin Blanc with anything like the respect given it at Chappellet. And virtually all who do make wines in the dry, fruit-driven style that Chappellet pioneered nearly forty years ago. (Some wineries—Beringer most prominently—still make an off-dry Chenin, but those wines are neither promoted by the producers nor perceived by the public as being in the same league.) Although Chappellet has become more of a red wine house in the nearly four decades since grapes first were crushed on Pritchard Hill, Dry Chenin Blanc remains very much a signature statement. "It's what we are," shrugs Jon-Mark. "The fun thing about being up here on Pritchard Hill with Chenin Blanc is that we can do what we want with it. There's no intermediary between this wine and the market. Critics don't matter. *The Wine Spectator* doesn't exist for it. All that counts is what's in the bottle."

And what's in the Chappellet bottle, while woefully out of tune with today' s times, is very, very good. The Chappellets certainly would like to grow and make more Dry Chenin Blanc, but as Jon-Mark explains, "it just doesn't add up economically" when they're also planting Cabernet on Pritchard Hill. "This is very much a niche wine," he continues. "We love it. And our customers love it. So we definitely want to keep making it. But no one else really knows about it." In brief, that's Chenin Blanc's fate—to be both horribly unfashionable and wonderfully delectable. At least that's its fate right now. For just as hemlines never stay up or down, wine vogues invariably change. With American white wine, today is undoubtedly the age of Chardonnay. But tomorrow . . . ?

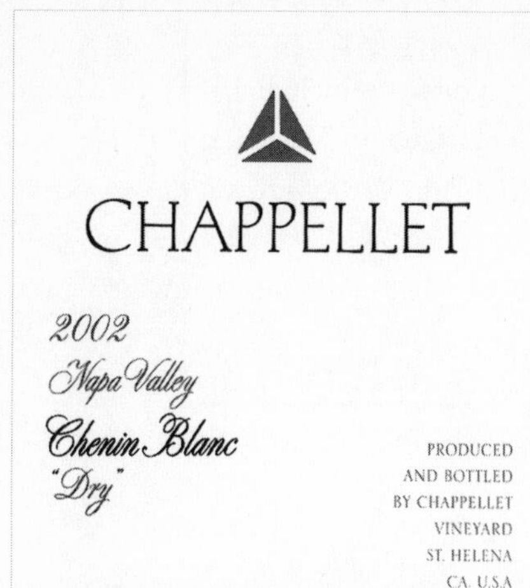

A NOTE ON VINTAGES:

Although the best dry Loire Valley Chenin Blanc wines, especially those from Savennières, can age effortlessly for many years, Chappellet's Napa Valley rendition is best enjoyed when young—within four or five years of the vintage. While it offers a whiff of minerality with time spent in bottle, its charm comes primarily from its fresh fruit flavors, so too much age only detracts from its appeal. Successful recent vintages have included 1999, 2001, 2002, and 2003.

THE SUGGESTED PRICE FOR THE CURRENT 2003 RELEASE IS $15.

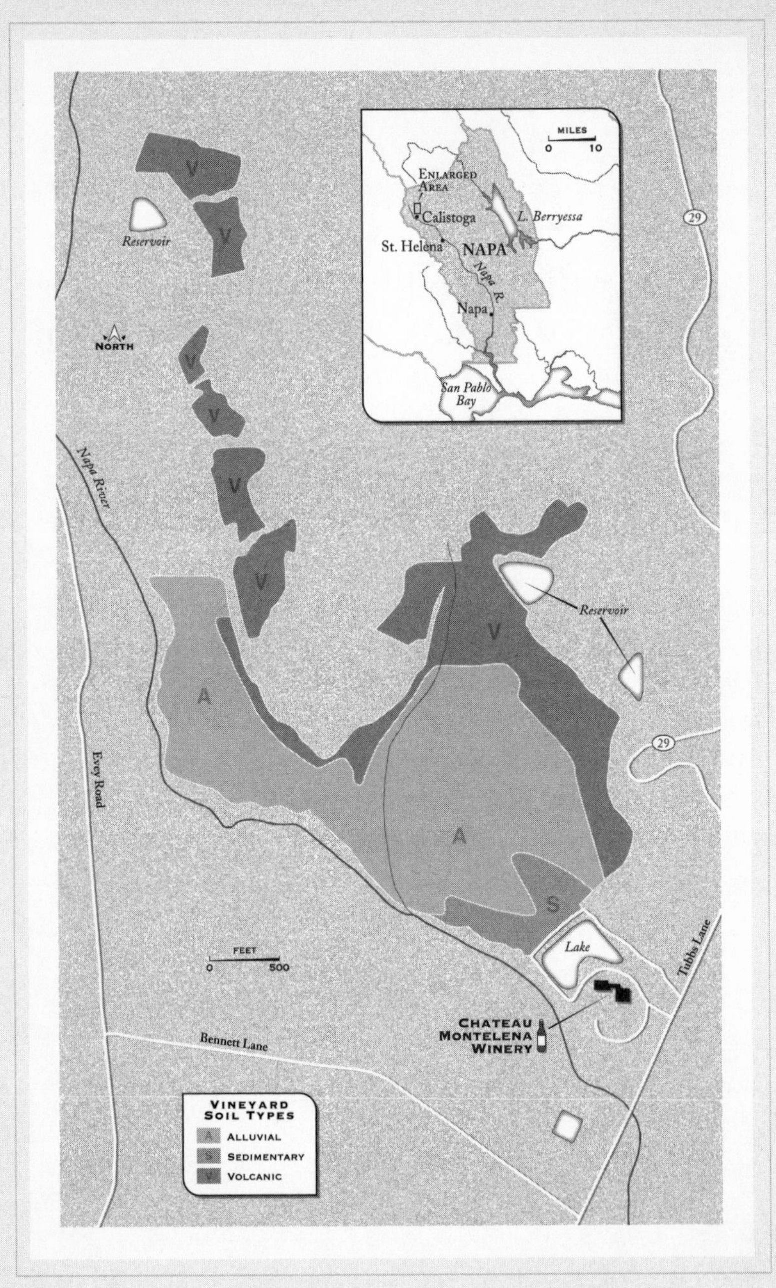

THE CHATEAU MONTELENA ESTATE VINEYARD

CHAPTER 7

Chateau Montelena Cabernet Sauvignon, "Montelena Estate"

Napa Valley, California

...

The American Heritage Dictionary defines a "classic" as an artistic work "of the highest rank or excellence, especially one of enduring significance." But in the canon of great American wine, few consistently top-flight bottlings were produced until the 1970s, the legacy of Prohibition having been so devastating. So can there even be such a thing as an American classic? Do any wines from the United States have the "enduring significance" of the great wines of Europe—Bordeaux's first growths, Burgundy's *grand crus*, the centuries-old estates of the Rheingau and the Mosel?

Bo Barrett

The answer to that question depends on how long one thinks significance has to endure. While there can be little doubt that some individual American wines today occupy as high a rank as any in the world, one vintage does not make a classic. Nor do five, or even ten. But what about twenty-five, a full quarter century of distinction? Since 1978, Chateau Montelena Estate Cabernet Sauvignon, made from grapes grown near

Calistoga at the northern edge of the Napa Valley, has ranked among America's best. Year after year, it has tasted rich, dark, and concentrated, displaying impeccable depth and balance, and with the passage of time, extremely impressive longevity. As important, the wine has exhibited remarkable stylistic consistency, due in part to Montelena's vineyard having escaped the scourge of phylloxera, and even more to a steady winemaking vision that has aimed for excellence from the very start. Over the years, this full-flavored Cabernet has come to serve as a benchmark of quality for the most important American varietal—not only in Napa, but all across the winemaking world. So, if any wine in the country merits being called "classic," this surely is it.

Traditionally, the classics of art and literature came from ancient Greece or Rome, the models to which later artists and writers aspired. Only during the last two centuries has the noun been applied to more modern art, eventually coming to designate excellence no matter the period of production. Today, works like Eliot's *The Waste Land* or Picasso's *Guernica* are "classics" just like *Antigone* or the *Venus de Milo.* So too with wine, though the original models came from post-Renaissance Europe rather than antiquity. Much as Homer and Virgil set the standard for epic verse, the top growths of Bordeaux and Burgundy served as undisputed wine benchmarks, especially for reds. They were the classics, and other wines, no matter their origin or composition, trailed in their wake. Then came the wine revolution of the last fifty years, an essential aspect of which was the challenge issued by wines from less renowned regions—not only in the New World but also in other areas within Europe. Today, wines like Sassicaia from Tuscany and Pesquera from Ribera del Duero certainly can be called classics, for they have become standard-bearers for new styles in previously neglected places. In the United States and the other important New World wine-growing countries, a handful of wines have sustained such high quality and exerted such influence as to fairly earn the designation as well. At the top of the list comes Chateau Montelena Cabernet Sauvignon. Napa Valley Cabernet is America's most celebrated single type of wine, and no Napa Cab has a finer track record—over a quarter century of merit, without a single slip or miss.

"I'll match our record with anyone's," says Bo Barrett, Montelena's winemaker and part owner. He is characteristically blunt when asked whom he has in mind. "I mean *anyone*. Here in California, in France, in Australia. Anyone." His point, made with confidence but without bravado, is well taken. If only because of personnel changes or off vintages, few wineries over the past twenty-five years have managed to avoid qualitative slumps or shifts. But Chateau Montelena's ownership and winemaking team has been in place for almost that whole period, and the winery has produced consistently superlative Cabernets even in years when other top producers have slipped (1998, for example, or 1989 and 1983). "We always stick to our guns," declares Barrett. "After all this time, we've proven that we have staying power."

Bo's father, Jim Barrett, was working as a real estate attorney when, in 1972, he and fellow Southern Californian Ernest Hahn formed a partnership in order to restore what fifty years earlier had been a successful wine-growing estate. Founded in 1882 by a San Francisco entrepreneur, Alfred Tubbs, the property (named for Mount St. Helena, under whose shadow it sits) had been one of the largest wineries in Napa. Its "Finest Old Cabernet Claret," bottled under the Hillcrest label, was particularly popular before Prohibition brought winemaking at the estate to an abrupt halt. Though Tubbs's son, Chapin, started again after Repeal, he ran into personal difficulties, and the property fell into near-total disrepair. The vineyard became overgrown, and both the original wooden winery and Tubbs's home were destroyed by fires.

The estate's revival began twenty years later when Lee Paschich, a Bay Area businessman, bought the abandoned chateau building and then the adjacent vineyard. He renewed the bond and trade name for Chateau Montelena as a working winery, and then sold the reunited property to Hahn and Barrett. From the start, Barrett took the lead in the actual work of renovation. (Hahn would sell him his share in 1977.) He cleaned out the old stone cellars and outfitted the winery with modern equipment. He also replanted the vineyard, removing the old, diseased vines and fumigating the subsoil. "My concept from the get-go," he says, "was to make the best."

To Jim Barrett in 1972, "the best" meant first-growth Bordeaux, the world's most celebrated and, yes, classic wines. He envisioned Montelena's flagship red coming exclusively from its own vineyard, which he planted primarily with Cabernet, the dominant grape in all the top Médoc growths. He wanted this wine to taste rich but at the same time refined. And it had to be age-worthy. "I didn't know all that much about wine," he confesses, "but one thing I did know was that top wines last a long time." To make such a wine, he needed a talented winemaker. Barrett found the man he wanted working down the road for Robert Mondavi. Miljenko "Mike" Grgich had fashioned a Cabernet there that a well-publicized *Los Angeles Times* tasting had decreed California's best. So Barrett wooed him away, and Grgich set out to make the first new wines at Chateau Montelena in over fifty years.

Because the vines on the property were too young to produce a viable crop, all the early wines were made with purchased fruit. And because the initial Cabernets (two separate bottlings, one from Napa vineyards, the other from Sonoma) needed to spend time in barrel, the first releases were white: Riesling and Chardonnay, the second vintage of which went on to triumph at Steven Spurrier's famed 1976 Paris tasting. "Not bad for kids from the sticks," Barrett told a reporter from *Time* magazine when he heard the news.

Yet despite the surprising success with white wines (and Montelena continues to produce a delicious, age-worthy Chardonnay, sourced from vineyards just north of Napa), Barrett kept his eyes fixed firmly on his goal: Cabernet, fashioned like "the best." That, he says, "is what we've always been about." Finally, with the 1978 vintage, the vines were old enough and the grapes good enough to use by themselves. By that point, Grgich had left to start his own winery, and Jerry Luper, assisted by Jim's son (named James but always called Bo), was in charge. The first Chateau Montelena Estate Cabernet was released in 1982, the centennial of Alfred Tubbs's founding of the winery.

The wine received rave reviews right away. Marked by intense concentration and firm tannins, the sort of structure necessary in a red wine designed for aging, it immediately announced itself as a serious contender in the ranks of top Napa wines. At the same time, it clearly was atypical—deep and muscular, more like its French model than its California compatriots. According to Jim Barrett, the style was the result of a conscious choice. "We knew we could soften it up by adding Merlot, or whacking it with oak to make it early drinking, but we didn't want to do that," he says. "We didn't—and don't—want to make that style of wine." But this Cabernet, with its intense varietal character and unabashed richness, did not really taste like Bordeaux. From the very beginning, while nodding to the French archetype, it displayed its own identity. "Our wine is Old World–styled," says Bo Barrett, who took over the winemaking in 1982, "meaning place-driven, not fruit- or oak-driven. But that place is here, in this vineyard. Our vineyard is what drives the wine."

When Jim Barrett first replanted Montelena's vineyard, some sixty-five acres of Cabernet Sauvignon along with about five of Cabernet Franc, he grafted the young vines onto St. George rootstock. At the time, most of his neighbors were following the advice of scientists from UC Davis and using AXR1, a rootstock developed at the university and said to be superior to the old-fashioned St. George, which initially had been planted in response to California's original phylloxera crisis back in the 1890s, when that microscopic root louse first devastated the state's vineyards. Barrett used St. George not because of principled conviction but because all the vineyard expansion in California made it difficult to get enough AXR1. But twenty years later, when other vintners were tearing out their vineyards due to the second phylloxera crisis, Montelena's vines were reaching peak maturity. They never had to be replaced because St. George, being a wholly native rupestris variety, remained resistant to the new biotype of phylloxera infesting California's North Coast. (By contrast, AXR1, being a hybrid or cross between rupestris and vinifera stock, proved susceptible.)

Barrett is too modest when he credits his good fortune solely to "dumb luck." Though he admits that he did not know much about the minutiae of viticulture, he had read enough to understand that AXR1's primary virtue came in its producing higher yields than St. George. And given his focus on "the best," he wanted just the opposite—a small but full-flavored crop. So he was willing to use the unfashionable, seemingly outmoded rootstock. As he puts it, "We were happy to go our own way."

That way involved paying close attention to the different types of soil, as well as the different slopes and exposures, in the vineyard. The initial seventy acres were divided into eleven separate blocks, each delivering fruit with a slightly different personality. By the late 1980s, when fifteen more acres of Cabernet and Cabernet Franc were added, another seven blocks came into the mix. By then, the Barretts had extensively researched the geology of their property, trying to better understand the origin of the diverse flavors in their grapes. The Montelena estate vineyard contains three distinct soil types: a small section of rich, sedimentary loam near the winery; a broad swath of stony alluvial deposits; and a stretch of volcanic soil on the benchland above. Each contributes something distinctive to the finished wine. The grapes from the sedimentary blocks tend to taste rich and fruity, while those from the alluvial ones seem earthier and more complex, and the ones from the volcanic hillsides spicier. Bo Barrett harvests each block separately over a four- to six-week period. Yields average 2 tons per acre, a result of crop thinning and farming without irrigation, in addition to the naturally low-yielding rootstock. The grapes grow loosely clustered, allowing air to circulate and preventing rot, and the berries are small. No matter which block they come from, they inevitably display very concentrated flavors.

Montelena enjoys another advantage: a pattern of warm days and cool nights (with dramatic temperature differences of as much as 50 degrees) that proves ideal for Cabernet Sauvignon. Most vineyards near Calistoga are hotter, the climate overall being the warmest in the Napa Valley. Consequently, Calistoga Cabernet, while inevitably powerful, can sometimes seem excessively alcoholic and jammy. But the Montelena vineyard, bordered on one side by the Napa River and on the other by the benchlands leading up to Mount St. Helena, benefits from a cross-current of cool air. At night and in the early morning, drafts roll down from the 5,000-foot mountain, while in the afternoon breezes from the

Russian River to the west flow across the vineyard and begin the cool-down process. For Cabernet, the result is ample heat for full ripeness, along with sufficient cooling for balance. This unique microclimate, coupled with the diverse soils and low-yielding, fully mature vines, gives the finished wine its distinct personality. As Bo Barrett says, "It's a really remarkable deal to be here."

Like his father, Bo is something of a headstrong character, plainspoken and direct, sure of what he wants and unwilling to suffer fools gladly. When he returned to Montelena in 1982, after a short stint making wine in Paso Robles, he and Jim had to agree on a division of labor, with one man in complete control in the cellar and the other in the business office. That arrangement has worked well for over twenty years, though Bo notes wryly that "Dad still doesn't like it when I go on vacation." Married to another Napa winemaker, Heidi Peterson Barrett (who fashions wines for Grace Family and Screaming Eagle, among others), Bo is certainly one of California's most accomplished vintners. If he receives less publicity than some other winemakers, including at times his wife, that is because he has inherited his father's single-minded drive, which keeps him focused on wine rather than on celebrity. Asked whether he ever feels lost in the shuffle, what with the advent of supertrendy Napa cult wines, he laughs and says: "Not now. That might have bothered me when I was younger, but not now. I'm very happy with what I've got here." As well he should be. No one disputes that Chateau Montelena Cabernet is one of America's best. It so obviously belongs in the top rank of the country's wines that receiving 90+ points from the critics or being included on exclusive restaurant lists no longer raises eyebrows. By now, such recognition is simply expected.

Looking back, Bo Barrett is most proud of how consistent the Montelena Cabernets have been. "Any yokel can make good wine in good years," he says. "It's the tough years that tell the story." A tasting of vintages spanning the estate's revival demonstrates how compelling that story is. The only stylistic difference over time comes in the slightly softer tannins in the more recent wines, the result of the purchase of a machine that separates the grapes from their stems before fermentation, and a reduction in maceration—the amount of time the juice stays in contact with the skins and seeds. Otherwise, this wine's character remains constant year after year—powerful flavors, with the taste of fruit leading the way, subtle secondary notes adding support, and impeccable balance. "That's the key to great wine," says Jim Barrett; "balance, balance, balance." His son agrees. "It's easy to get the power here," he says. "Our work comes in getting something more—an orderly, genteel array of flavors." To that end, he uses only 25 percent new oak, and cycles his barrels through an eight-year rotation, wanting to make sure that no single element in the wine overwhelms the others. "It's naturalist winemaking," he says with a shrug of his shoulders, "letting everything that's here come out."

Chateau Montelena sells approximately nine thousand cases of Estate Cabernet each year, roughly half of which has already been purchased by individual customers as futures. Selling a wine before it has been bottled, many years before it can be drunk, is a common practice in Bordeaux but a quite uncommon one in America. The Barretts first started offering their wine that way with the 1996 vintage. Their goal was not to make money sooner (they charge less than half of what the wine retails for upon release) but to ensure that people who had been enjoying their Cabernet would be able to keep getting it. This prerelease program works because, as Bo Barrett puts it, "People trust us." That trust has been tested recently, with the discovery of TCA, the unpleasant-smelling chemical compound associated with corked wines, in some bottles and so possibly in the winery itself. But the Barretts have promised to correct any problem, and taking them at their word is hardly a gamble. For if past serves as prologue, there will continue to be no more reliably great wine in the United States. Vintage after vintage, Chateau Montelena Estate Cabernet stands out for both excellence and stylistic consistency. That's what makes it an American classic.

A NOTE ON VINTAGES:

If you open a bottle of Chateau Montelana Estate Cabernet immediately upon its release, you'll miss some of the nuances that invariably develop with age; but the wine still will be delicious—big, bold, and beautifully balanced. With time in bottle, it becomes gentler and more refined—yes, more classic. Of the many excellent vintages, 1984, 1991, 1995, 1997, and 2001 stand out as being exceptional.

THE SUGGESTED PRICE FOR THE CURRENT 2002 RELEASE IS $125.

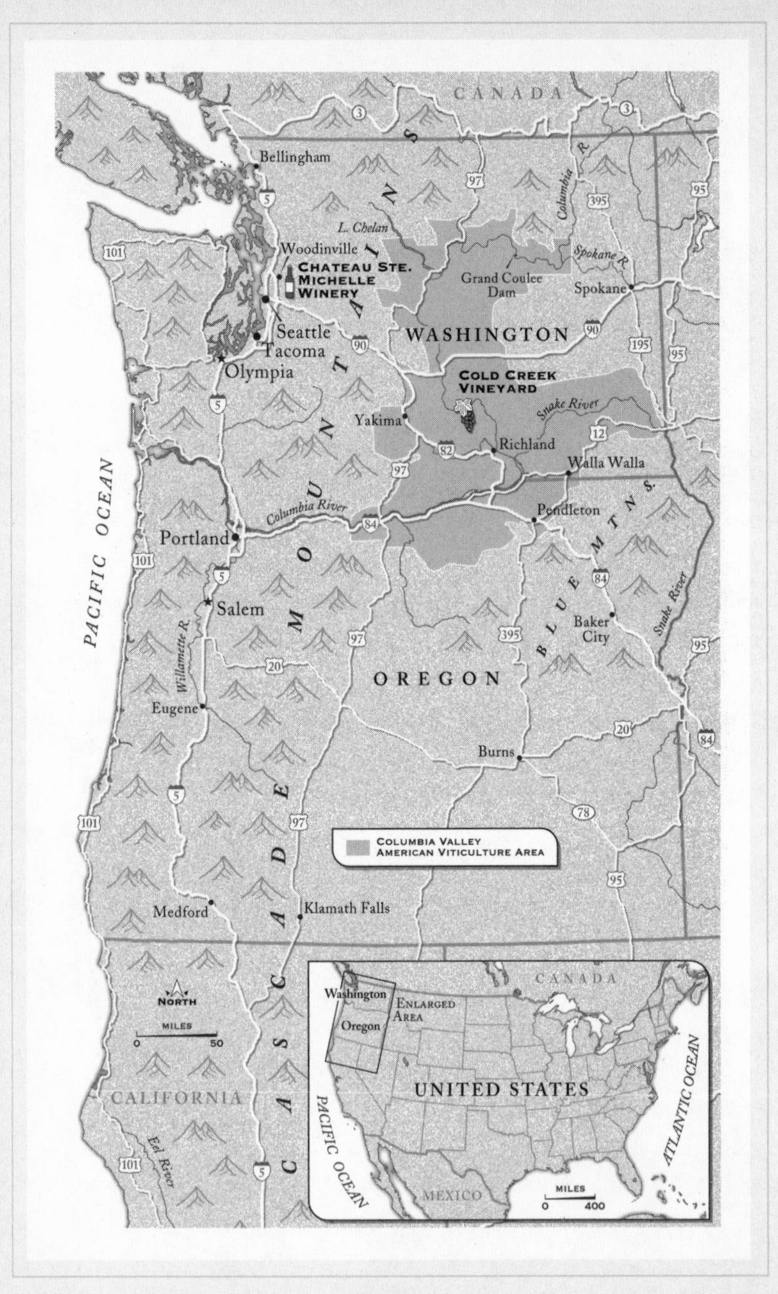

THE COLD CREEK VINEYARD, IN THE MIDDLE OF THE LARGE COLUMBIA VALLEY AVA

CHAPTER 8

CHATEAU STE. MICHELLE CHARDONNAY, COLD CREEK VINEYARD

Columbia Valley, Washington

...

Bob Bertheau

It's a long way from Seattle to Cold Creek—literally some 140 miles due east, but figuratively much farther still. Hip and happening, Seattle bustles, even in the rain. The unofficial capital of the Pacific Northwest, it's a vibrant city full of art, music, and cutting-edge business, home to companies like Microsoft, Nordstrom, Starbucks, and in the suburb of Woodinville, Ste. Michelle Wine Estates. By contrast, and despite its name, Cold Creek is a patch of hot (in summer) near desert. Dry and quiet, it's empty, save for rows of grapevines that stay alive only by virtue of irrigation. Those vines, however, were first planted by someone from Seattle: Wally Opdycke, a big-city financial manager who some thirty-five years ago invested in the future of Washington State wine at a time when hardly anyone else was willing to do so. In 1971, Opdycke organized a few partners to buy the Seattle-based American Wine Growers company. At the time, AWG was selling primarily low-end wine, almost exclusively in state. It operated under a number of brands, only one of which, the small four-year-old Ste. Michelle label, featured premium vinifera varietals. Those, though, were all that Opdycke really cared about. He had faith in what was then largely unproven, the supposition that wine grapes grown across the Cascade Mountains, in the Columbia River Valley, could yield superior wines. And he put his money behind his conviction, two years later buying 500 acres of essentially barren land and planting grapes—Cabernet and Riesling first, then later Chardonnay and more.

This was Cold Creek. The largest Washington vineyard then devoted to quality vinifera vines, it would go on to become the source of many of Ste. Michelle's finest wines. Those wines set the standard to which other Washington vintners aspired, and today a state that once barely merited a footnote in the story of American wine produces more wine than any other save California. Washington wine's rise (in terms of quality as well as quantity) has been remarkably rapid. While there was no exact starting point, Opdycke's 1973 investment in Cold Creek marked a significant point of departure. Other people at the time talked about the state's potential, but he actually got things done. Much has been true ever since at Ste. Michelle. For three decades now, this large-volume company has been Washington's leader, not just in terms of sales but also in terms of vision—and resulting action. Whether growing grapes, fermenting juice, or marketing wine, Ste. Michelle's success has benefited everyone with the ambition to make fine wine in the Evergreen State. Its success is exemplified by the company's headquarters, a large *faux* chateau in Woodinville that has become one of the Seattle area's most visited tourist spots. But it begins far away, in tranquil Cold Creek, where Cabernet, Merlot, Riesling, and Chardonnay yield memorable, sometimes mesmerizing wines.

It's difficult to know which of the Cold Creek wines is best. The Cabernet, being firmly structured and concentrated, ages extremely well. The Merlot, while softer, also excels. And Riesling, particularly the grapes that find their way into "Eroica," a wine made in collaboration with Weingut Dr. Loosen of the Mosel Valley in Germany, balances lush fruit and brisk acidity to near perfection. But when all is said and done, Chardonnay has to be considered the brightest jewel in the Cold Creek crown. That's because it so clearly serves as a benchmark. While other Washington Cabernets, Merlots, and even Rieslings are first rate, no other Chardonnay is as consistently fine.

Much as in California, Washington Chardonnay, the most widely planted grape in the state, often yields monotonously simple wines. Cold Creek Vineyard Chardonnay, however, tastes wonderfully complex. An evocative wine in an explosive style, it exhibits the ripe flavors and full texture so often associated with New World renditions, without seeming heavy or cumbersome. It too is firmly structured, with an acidic frame that gives those flavors shape and definition. Chardonnay makes serviceable, even reliable wines virtually anywhere it's planted, and these days it's planted just about everywhere. But when grown in select sites, and in the hands of top vintners, it can yield truly remarkable wines. Cold Creek is undoubtedly one of those sites. Bob Bertheau has been in charge of the Chardonnay program for the past few years, and he speaks about this wine in exactly those terms: "It's rare to taste the vineyard with Chardonnay, but you can with Chardonnay from Cold Creek. So that's my focus with it—to keep the purity of the vineyard in the wine."

The Columbia Valley is an immense Viticultural Area, stretching 100 miles east to west and 75 miles north to south. Virtually all of the grapes for Washington wine are grown within it, or within its three subappellations—Red Mountain, the Walla Walla Valley, and the Yakima Valley. Vines were first planted there in the mid-1800s—the occasional European vinifera variety but more often North American labrusca grapes such as Concord, Delaware, and Niagara. Growers found that these native grape varieties fared better in harsh winter weather, and for a full century most Washington wine was made with them. Visionary vintners like E. F. Blaine before Prohibition and W. B. Bridgman after Repeal did plant and promote vinifera, but their wines were never much more than local curiosities. Bridgman's Upland Winery in the Yakima Valley opened in 1934, and old-timers recall fondly his

Cabernets, Rieslings, and Zinfandels. But hard freezes in both 1949 and 1950 killed most of the vines. The fact that labrusca varieties growing nearby survived to produce healthy crops helps explain why Concord was by far Washington's most widely planted grape.

But that same time—the post–World War II era—saw the Federal Bureau of Reclamation's Columbia Basin Project near completion. Water then began to be transported from the Grand Coulee Dam in central Washington to more than 600,000 acres of previously arid land. Massive pumping stations and a labyrinth of canals suddenly made large-scale agriculture viable in eastern Washington, a prospect that raised the question of which crops would fare best in the Columbia Valley. Researchers from Washington State University (WSU) took the lead in addressing it. Working at experiment stations throughout the state, they planted test crops and issued reports on what grew well. At the station in Prosser, near Yakima, the faculty of thirty-five included WSU professors as well as U.S. Department of Agriculture scientists. They experimented with apples, beans, cherries, wheat, and more—including grapes.

Dr. Walter Clore was the chief horticulturalist at the Prosser station, and during his long career there, he planted scores of different grape varieties up and down the valley. Over time, he became convinced that, if grown in the right place, and if tended properly (meaning rooted deeply, so as to hold up through the winter), vinifera grapes would not only survive but actually could thrive in Washington. As he testified before the state Commerce and Agricultural Committee: "We have investigated the variety of grapes that are known around the world for their high quality in producing premium wines . . . [and] we have found thus far that many of these varieties seem to be well adapted here from the standpoint of producing good yields and wine of good to excellent quality."

Walter Clore is remembered fondly today as the father of Washington wine. The son of teetotalling Nebraska farmers, he did the pioneering agricultural work that made a large-scale commercial industry possible. That industry can be said to have begun when Wally Opdycke purchased American Wine Growers, but Opdycke only did that after he asked to meet with Clore in Seattle so as to learn what was possible. "We had a great visit," Opdycke remembered years later. "He gave me a lot of information about the potential for investing in grapes and wine. He said, 'Look, someone should really do something here.'" That was in 1970. Only three years later, Opdycke became that someone when he began planting vines at Cold Creek.

Wally Opdycke sold American Wine Growers, which he renamed Ste. Michelle Vintners, for a tidy profit in 1974: to the U.S. Tobacco Company, which still owns it today. He stayed in Seattle, running the business and overseeing its growth, for another decade, at which point he moved on to new, no longer vinous ventures. By then Washington wine had become big business. And no business was bigger than Ste. Michelle, renamed yet again as Stimson Lane Vineyards and Estates (in honor of Seattle lumber baron Frederick Stimson, whose Woodinville summer chateau became the company's chief production facility as well as its corporate headquarters). The company soon expanded to include a number of different wineries, including Columbia Crest, which became Washington's largest. But Chateau Ste. Michelle remained its flagship brand. And regardless of all the growth and expansion, its top wines continued to come from the Cold Creek Vineyard.

The Columbia River flows south for nearly 150 miles in the middle of Washington State before turning west above the Rattlesnake Hills—the northern boundary of the Yakima Valley Viticultural Area, or AVA. The Cold Creek Vineyard lies just below the river and above those hills, so beyond that AVA's border. South-facing, it enjoys one of the longest and warmest growing seasons in the entire Columbia Valley, that warmth being a principal reason why Walter Clore recommended Wally Opdycke first plant vines there. (The other main reason involved water rights, as Opdycke needed a guaranteed source for irrigation.) Because the vineyard is located on a plateau, it receives little cooling from the Columbia. In fact, summer heat spikes ensure that grapes grown there ripen fully every year. At the same time, the silty soils are low in organic matter, and the nights tend to be cool, even in midsummer. As a result, those grapes retain sufficient acidity. With Chardonnay, the result is a wine that manages to taste fat and focused all at once. "It's something of a paradox," admits Bob Bertheau. "Cold Creek Chardonnay tastes like a wine coming from a much colder vineyard." But unlike wines made with grapes that struggle to ripen in low temperatures, this wine displays impressive consistency vintage after vintage, never seeming either too lean or too blowsy. It's a big, powerful Chardonnay, but at the same time a well-defined, precise one. "It doesn't really resemble anything else," says Bertheau. "That's what I mean when I say that it tastes of the vineyard."

Less than a third of the Chardonnay grown at Cold Creek goes into this single-vineyard, 5,000-case production wine. The rest of the crop is used primarily as a classy component in Chateau Ste. Michelle's basic Columbia Valley cuvée, a 250,000-case wine that offers good value. "It's important to use some of our best fruit in wines like that," Bertheau argues. "You can't save it all for the 'special' wines." Making these different wines, though, does require different skills. Or, as Bertheau puts it, "I have to use two different sides of my one head." The multi-vineyard Columbia Valley Chardonnay expresses a coaxed if not imposed style: toasty, vanilla-scented oak atop soft fruit. The challenge with it comes in maintaining that style over time, so not allowing the vagaries of nature to compel change. With the single-vineyard wine, the challenge comes in holding back and allowing nature to express itself. "The first is a wine I have to tweak," Bertheau explains. "The other is a wine I have to leave alone. With Cold Creek, I always need to remember, 'Don't mess it up.'"

Bertheau came to Chateau Ste. Michelle in 2003 to take command of the company's white wine program. His prior winemaking experience all had been in California, and all at wineries that emphasized Chardonnay—including Chalk Hill, Gallo of Sonoma, and Hanzell. Though he since has been promoted to head winemaker at the company, in charge of reds as well as whites, Chardonnay remains a personal passion. "It's unfashionable these days for a winemaker to say he loves Chardonnay," he admits, "but I do. I think it can be a very special wine. Chardonnay is an easy varietal to make, but it's a hard one to make well."

With Cold Creek Chardonnay, Bertheau follows the basic paradigm established by his predecessor, Erik Olsen (who has moved in the opposite direction, to California and Clos du Bois), including fermenting and aging the wine in French oak, compelling it to go through complete malolactic fermentation in barrel, and stirring the lees (the spent yeast and sediment) regularly. At the same time, he has experimented with different yeasts and modified the stirring regime in an effort to better integrate the wood and so evoke even more subtlety. "I'm striving for added complexity," he says. "It's about staying true to the history and style of Chateau Ste. Michelle, while incorporating some individual expression." The 2003 vintage is his first release. While it's too early at this writing to say that this wine is more complex than earlier vintages, it shows every indication of being an extremely worthy successor. Seductively viscous, it and earlier vintages manage to taste simultaneously rich and refined—this vineyard's inimitable signature.

Bertheau's move to Chateau Ste. Michelle constituted a homecoming of sorts. Born in Seattle, he now works nearby. He uses grapes, though, that are grown far away—a fact of geography critical to any understanding of Washington wine. The Seattle region, on the ocean-influenced western side of the Cascades, is simply too cool and damp for quality grape growing. But the irrigated Columbia Valley proves ideal. It does not suffer summer or autumn rain. The northern latitude provides both long, sun-filled summer days and shorter, cooler ones at harvest, giving the maturing grapes all the time they need to ripen. And the diurnal pattern of hot days and chilly nights in midsummer allows for full flavor with sufficient acidity for balance. That's why the best Washington wines, Cold Creek Chardonnay as an exemplar, manage to be both richly fruited and tightly focused.

The Cold Creek Vineyard, though, is a long way from both the winery and the market. In terms of production, that distance poses few problems. Once harvested, the grapes are transported to a leased facility on the Wahluke Slope, only about twenty minutes away. They are pressed there, and then cooled to 40 degrees before being trucked in tankers across the mountains to Woodinville. But in terms of the marketplace, long distance can be a detriment. Columbia Valley wines simply do not carry the consumer cachet of Napa Valley ones, and Seattle, not Cold Creek, is where Washington tourists go. The current success of Washington State wine in the market is thus due wholly to the quality and character of what is in the bottle. And no company has achieved more success with more personality-filled, high-quality wines than Ste. Michelle—universally acknowledged as the state leader.

When talking with vintners at other Washington wineries, both large and small, one hears only admiration, never resentment or jealousy, for Ste. Michelle Wine Estates. That's because for over thirty years now the management at this company has worked to improve the quality and promote the reputation of not only their own wines but also those fashioned by their Washington neighbors and colleagues—even those with whom they compete directly. According to the St. Michelle philosophy, if the state's wine industry as a whole does well, then this one brand will do well—and vice versa. It's an enlightened way of doing business, and without Ste. Michelle's leadership there can be no doubt that Washington wine as a category would not have achieved the success it has today.

Ste. Michelle's own wines, the basic cuvées in addition to the single vineyard and reserve offerings, set high standards, with none higher than that established by the Chardonnay from Cold Creek. It is Washington's finest and one of the country's best, a wine fully capable of holding its own with top wines fashioned from this grape variety anywhere in the world. A generation ago, only a few vintners and entrepreneurs dared guess that wine of this quality might come from the Columbia Valley. Wally Opdycke was one of them, and clearly his investment at Cold Creek has paid very rich rewards.

A NOTE ON VINTAGES:

Chateau Ste. Michelle Cold Creek Chardonnay is capable of evolving and improving in the bottle, but too much time will prove deleterious as the enticing fruit flavors will fade away. Drink it within five to seven years of the vintage. Particularly strong years have included 1995, 1997, 1999, 2002, and the delectable 2003.

THE SUGGESTED PRICE FOR THE CURRENT 2003 RELEASE IS $22.

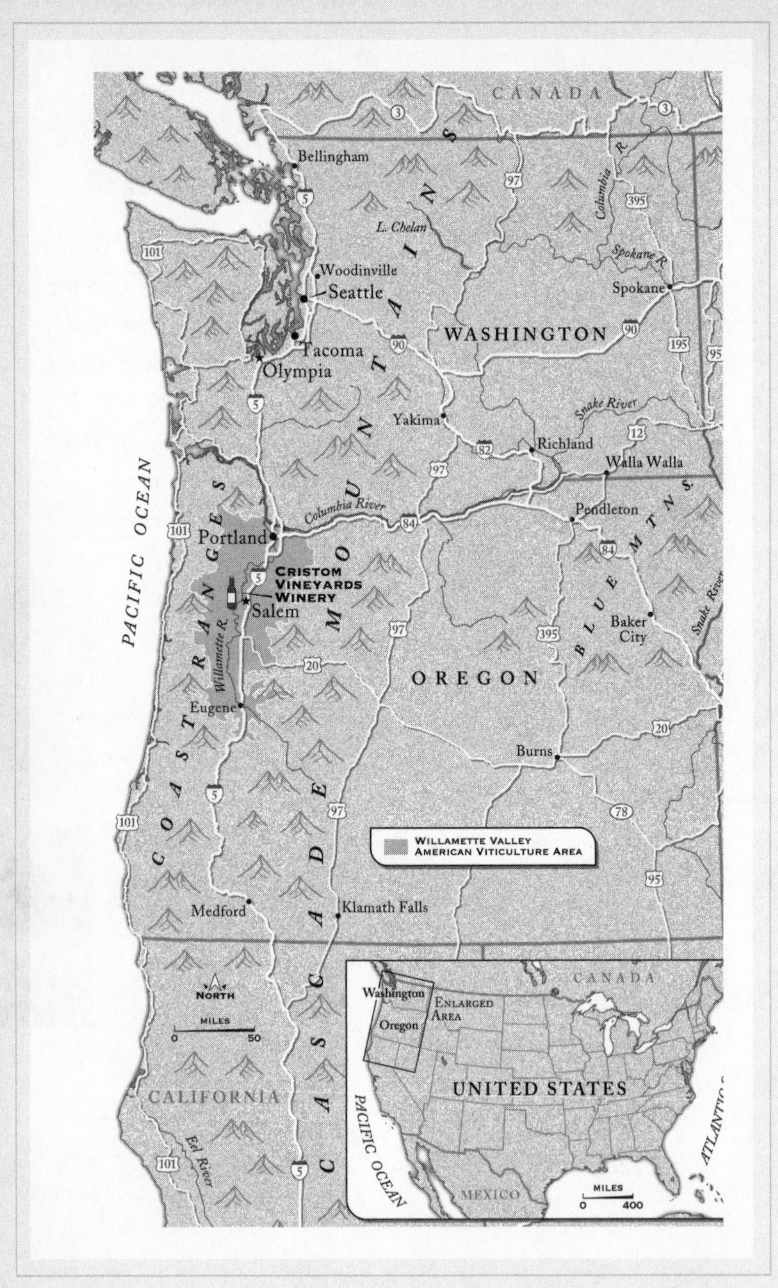

CRISTOM, IN THE HEART OF THE WILLAMETTE VALLEY

CHAPTER 9

Cristom Pinot Noir Reserve

Willamette Valley, Oregon

...

"He's a great talent. Especially as a blender." That's how Paul Gerrie describes Steve Doerner. Gerrie and his wife, Eileen, own Cristom in Oregon's Willamette Valley, and Doerner has made the wines for them since the beginning of their operation, in 1992. Today, their label adorns bottles of Chardonnay, Pinot Gris, and Viognier, but Pinot Noir is the varietal that has won them a devoted following. And the Cristom Pinots that most people know are blends—a basic cuvée incorporating grapes from up to ten different vineyards, and a barrel selection from that cuvée, the Reserve. Doerner also crafts a number of small-production wines from grapes grown on specific blocks at the Cristom estate in the Eola Hills, north of Salem. These rank among the best site-specific bottlings in Oregon. But what sets Cristom apart from the state's other top Pinot producers are the blends. A few fellow Oregon vintners offer equally enticing single-vineyard wines, but their larger production ones often exhibit inferior quality. At Cristom, the blends

Steve Doerner

are every bit as complete as the wines from individual vineyards. In particular, the Reserve Pinot Noir, which spends the same amount of time in barrel as the vineyard designates, offers the advantage of greater consistency while displaying equally nuanced complexity.

"Steve has a real gift as a blender," marvels Paul Gerrie. With characteristic modesty, Doerner demurs, saying, "I just try not to mess up what nature gives me." But his ability to recognize the differences between grapes from those vineyards, and then to envision how those differences will influence what ends up in the bottle, is what makes these blended wines so special. Cristom's multivineyard Pinots, the roughly 3,500-case "Mt. Jefferson" cuvée and the even better 1,250-case Reserve, do not convey a specific *terroir* so much as a rich diversity—of locale as well as plant material. And that diversity, as much as any single soil or site, is what makes top Oregon Pinot Noir so special.

Steve Doerner came to Oregon and Cristom from California, where he had worked with Josh Jensen at Calera for fifteen years, crafting some of America's most respected Pinot Noirs. Doerner's arrival signaled a new stage in Oregon's wine history, as he was the first winemaker with an established track record to leave the Golden State for the opportunity to craft wines up north. Since then, other Californians have followed, including Gary Andrus, Eric Hamacher, and Tony Soter. For Doerner, the primary attraction was viticultural. "I've always thought that the best wines come from places where you're living on the edge because ripeness isn't guaranteed," he says. "That's the Willamette Valley. It was much warmer at Calera. You never had to worry about getting the grapes ripe there." Another attraction was independence, having the freedom to make wines as he wished. That freedom involved something that at Calera was not allowed with the top wines: blending. "I just liked the idea of making something better, something more complete, than any of its components," he remembers. Calera also was extremely isolated, and Doerner felt the pull of a change of pace and lifestyle. So, when Paul Gerrie offered him the job, he never looked back. "Paul and I hit it off right away," he remembers. "We recognized that we had the same ambition, that we both wanted to make really good Pinot Noir."

Thin-skinned and temperamental, Pinot Noir is capricious in both vineyard and winery. One of the oldest cultivated grapes, it remains genetically unstable, and thus is prone to mutation. As a result, different vines planted in different places produce grapes and wines that taste, well, different. Nowhere is this more evident than in Burgundy, where vineyards located literally within yards of one another can yield wines with very different personalities. The issue that has long perplexed Pinot lovers concerns how to account for the differences. There are two schools of thought. On one side, *terroiristes* contend that a grape is primarily a conduit of locale, and that the distinct flavors and textures in one wine as opposed to another reflect where the fruit was grown. While this is true of all grapes, runs the argument, it is especially true of this one, simply because it is so delicate and so mutable. As Aubert de Villaine of the famed Burgundy estate, Domaine de la Romanée-Conti, once put it: "Pinot Noir shows the *terroir* more than any other variety because it has no taste of its own. It is a sort of ghost." But advocates of the other school, the *varietalists*, do not believe in ghosts. Instead, they contend that the character of the grape, as conveyed by both the grower and the winemaker, accounts for the character of the wine. Like any varietal, they argue, Pinot Noir has an identity, so differences between wines are best understood as variations on a common theme—the intrinsic character of the fruit.

Pinot Noir has been grown in Burgundy in northern France for centuries, but it was first planted in the Willamette Valley only forty years ago. Thus, as Doerner points out, making wine in Oregon inevitably means not knowing *terroir* as one might in Burgundy. The vines have not had all that much time to adapt to local growing conditions. Moreover, during the course of those forty years, people have introduced new clones and rootstocks, and they have planted vineyards in all sorts of new sites. Doerner works with grapes and wines that taste distinct, but he is loath to pinpoint any single cause. So, unlike Josh Jensen at Calera, he does not begin by focusing on soil; and unlike Jim Clendenen at Au Bon Climat, he does not focus primarily on climate. Differences between locales, like differences between farming practices and individual vines, "all play a part." No matter its origin, he argues, "Pinot Noir is a subtle grape. That's just the nature of the beast."

When fashioning the Cristom blends, Doerner's primary goal is to express that subtlety. "Optimally, I'd like a wine to have both power and finesse," he explains. "But if I have to sacrifice one of these, I'll always give up power." The Reserve tends to taste of red and black fruits, with a spicy (rather than earthy) undertone. Its seductively silky texture, layered flavors, and expansive finish give it an individuality rarely found in New World Pinots. Perhaps this can be traced to specific elements coming from specific vineyards. But since the wine is a Willamette Valley blend, Doerner's craft surely is the more important factor. He artfully combines Pinot Noir from many different sites in order to fashion a final product in which the whole is superior to the sum of the parts.

In Burgundy, a blend is by definition an ordinary wine. All the *premier* and *grand crus* are defined by vineyard site, not by analysis or evaluation, and so are bottled individually. Only a fool would combine wine from Le Chambertin, for example, with wine from Bonnes Mares, even though the latter tends to be more elegant and the former more muscular. "But Oregon isn't Burgundy," insists Doerner. "Here a blend can be a top wine."

Since Oregon's Willamette Valley vineyards are comparative infants, no one knows for certain what about them accounts for the character of various wines. "I know that the wines from our own vineyards in the Eola Hills are unlike wines from Dundee," Doerner explains, "but I also know that combining the two sometimes gets you something even better." That's the idea behind Cristom Reserve, though Doerner uses many more than two wines when crafting it. He makes sure to distinguish between clones as well as vineyard sites, and he keeps each of up to fifty lots separate during fermentation. In 2000, for example, he worked with thirty-nine batches of wine, representing eight vineyards and five clones. The challenge, he says, is "to do as little as possible to each one," so as not to let winemaking tricks or techniques, involving everything from fermentation to aging, obscure the distinctions between them. Because Pinot is delicate, "you should only do something if you're sure it's an improvement," he explains. "If there's doubt, leave it alone." When he assembles the blend, Doerner tastes each individual lot of wine, mentally projecting how it will develop in barrel, and assessing what it might contribute to the final blend. "I don't agonize over it at that point," he says. "I just try to make the best I can."

Paul Gerrie knows that he was extremely fortunate in hiring Steve Doerner, and so has since made the job even more attractive, giving Doerner a share in the company. "We're in this together," he says, "for the long haul." Gerrie's ambition is for Cristom to produce top-flight, Burgundian-style wines. An engineer by training, he left a successful business and a comfortable home in Pennsylvania to pursue it in Oregon, inspired both by what others had done and by what he intuitively sensed was yet possible to achieve. A serious wine enthusiast with a passion for Pinot, he long had thought that only Burgundy could produce truly top examples. Then, in July 1991, he accompanied some friends to the International Pinot Noir Celebration in McMinnville, Oregon. This annual weekend celebration of wine, food, and good cheer showcases the glory of the grape by bringing together top producers from all over the world, including Burgundy. Attendees mingle with fellow aficionados in what has often been described as a "wine summer camp." Not surprisingly, Gerrie had a good time. Much as he expected, he was impressed by the Burgundies. What he did not expect, though, was to be so intrigued by the Oregon wines. "I remember a tasting with ten or so Burgundies and ten or so Oregon Pinots," he says. "Sure, the French wines were better. But the good Oregon ones had something in common with them, something that other wines, from California, say, didn't have." That something, in a word, was grace—which to his mind was *the* defining characteristic of great Pinot Noir. Gerrie didn't understand why these wines had it, but he knew that other wines lacked it.

Gerrie returned to Pennsylvania excited about his discovery, so much so that he decided to make a career change. A few months later, he went back to Oregon and looked at potential vineyard sites. The property he selected had been planted in the early 1980s, but the owners had abandoned it and the vineyard was overgrown. "It was a mess," he recalls, "but I knew it was the right place—if I could get the right winemaker." The following year, he and his family moved west. By then, he had named the winery after his two children, Christine and Tom, and more important, hired Doerner, who went on to fashion the first Cristom wines, blends made with purchased Willamette Valley grapes, that fall.

"When I came up here," says Doerner, "it seemed to me that Oregon wines were often good but simple. They tasted just of fruit." Gerrie agrees. The wines that had inspired him at the International Pinot Noir Celebration offered tantalizing hints of what might be, but no one was making what he thought was possible. Since then, he says, "we've come a long way." But he then quickly adds: "We still can get better. We're maybe eighty percent there." When asked what accounts for the improvement, Doerner and Gerrie point to a number of factors, including their decision to buy grapes by the acre, regardless of yield, rather than by the ton, improved farming practices throughout the Willamette Valley, and the development of the estate Cristom vineyard. As that vineyard has matured, Doerner has begun to craft site-specific wines from various portions of it, reflecting various soils and exposures, much as he did at Calera. At the same time, he has been able to use a greater percentage of estate fruit in his blends. But neither he nor Gerrie want to produce wine solely from the grapes they grow. They know that, when making the blends, there's advantage in diversity—the diversity of different grapes from different sites and different clones.

Much of the improved quality of the wines up and down the Willamette Valley over the past decade can be traced to the introduction of new and various clones—propagated, virus-free laboratory cuttings with distinct characteristics, chosen because of their suitability to all the variables of *terroir*. The original Oregon plantings in the 1960s and 1970s used material brought north from California, and the selections often proved inappropriate. This was especially true with Chardonnay, as many of the first-generation wines tasted green and aggressively acidic. But it also was true with Pinot Noir, as the use then of only two clones (one, originally French, called "Pommard," and the other, originally Swiss,

"Wadensville," but both propagated at UC Davis) is what rendered many of the early Oregon wines simple and monolithic.

The search for new clonal material began in the mid-1970s, when David Adelsheim of Adelsheim Vineyard in Newberg, just south of Portland, traveled to France and arranged for samples of Burgundian and Alsatian vines to be shipped to Oregon State University, where they were quarantined, evaluated for disease, and then finally propagated. Ten years later, the university began importing so-called Dijon clones of both Chardonnay and Pinot Noir. (These bear that name not because they are old Burgundy selections, but because they were first propagated by viticultural researchers working in Dijon, Burgundy's largest city.) It takes many years before new clones can be released commercially, so these vines did not begin to bear viable fruit in the Willamette Valley until the mid-nineties. Specifically suited to cool climate locales, the Dijon clones tend to produce richer-tasting grapes, and hence potentially more complex wines. Today, growers in Oregon have a wealth of options at their disposal. At Cristom, for instance, five different Dijon clones of Pinot Noir have been planted. "It's made a big difference," says Doerner. "I think the reason that some of the early Pinots tasted simple can be traced to the predominance of the Pommard clone. Sure, primary fruit flavors still define Oregon, but that's not all our wines have to offer anymore."

Doerner insists, however, that no one factor alone is responsible for the character of the wines at Cristom. "The new Dijon clones are important," he says, "but they're just one variable." As important is the fact that each vintage brings increased knowledge about locale, enabling him to better foresee how growing conditions will affect the fruit and in turn the wines. "A winemaker's job," he contends, "is to optimize what nature provides." To that end, his techniques are old-fashioned and non-interventionist. He uses only native yeasts, those on the grapes at harvests, and permits the fermentation to go for up to three weeks, allowing the juice to turn ever so slowly into wine. He destems roughly half of the grapes, fermenting the other half as whole clusters, his theory being that the stems will contribute an attractive non-fruit character to the wine. Doerner's one somewhat untraditional concern is pH level, and he is perfectly willing to acidify or chapitalize if necessary. Because he does not settle the wine before putting it into barrel, it sees lots of lees contact, further contributing to the goal of increased complexity. The Reserve stays in wood for eighteen months, after which it receives a gentle egg-white clarification, or fining, before bottling. "That's it," he says. "Pretty simple." But of course the other critical factor is the blending—choosing which lot, in which proportion, will go into which wine. "My goal with both Mt. Jefferson and the Reserve is consistency," he says. These wines should express less vintage variation than the single-vineyard Pinots. Tasting a succession of the Cristom Reserves, from 1993 through 2000, provides ample evidence that he has succeeded. Though each wine tastes distinct, they share a recognizable common identity, with seductive fruit flavors, nuanced spicy undertones, and above all, remarkable grace.

Such grace may have its source in clones, soils, vineyard management, winemaking, or any combination of these factors. But no matter its origin, it marks the best Pinot Noirs, whether from Burgundy or Oregon, Caifornia or New Zealand. While some of the top Oregon wines come from the pioneering generation of producers (at wineries such as Adelsheim, Erath, Eyrie, and Ponzi), more now come from the next generation. In addition to Cristom, extremely elegant wines are being crafted these days at Bethel Heights, Brick House, Domaine Drouhin, Domaine Serene, Panther Creek, and Ken Wright Cellars—to name my personal favorites. The textural delicacy of these wines resembles that of fine *premier cru* Burgundy, but the aromas and flavors are quite different—with a complexity of bright fruit and spice rather than dark fruit and earth. Cristom's Reserve, with the shared vision of Paul Gerrie and Steve Doerner behind it, exemplifies as much. Its grace and elegance may seem Burgundian, but its flavors do not. As a proud blend, it exhibits unabashed American independence.

CRISTOM

Willamette Valley

Pinot Noir
Reserve
2002

PRODUCED AND BOTTLED BY CRISTOM VINEYARDS, INC., SALEM, OR
ALCOHOL 14.0% BY VOL. PRODUCT OF THE U.S.A. UNFILTERED

A NOTE ON VINTAGES:

Like many top American Pinot Noirs, Cristom Reserve benefits from a few years of bottle age, time in which the wine sheds its baby fat and begins to display more pronounced secondary, non-fruit flavors and aromas. The optimal window for drinking it is probably five to ten years after the vintage. Strong years include 1993, 1996, 1998, 1999, and 2002.

THE SUGGESTED PRICE FOR THE CURRENT 2003 RELEASE IS $35.

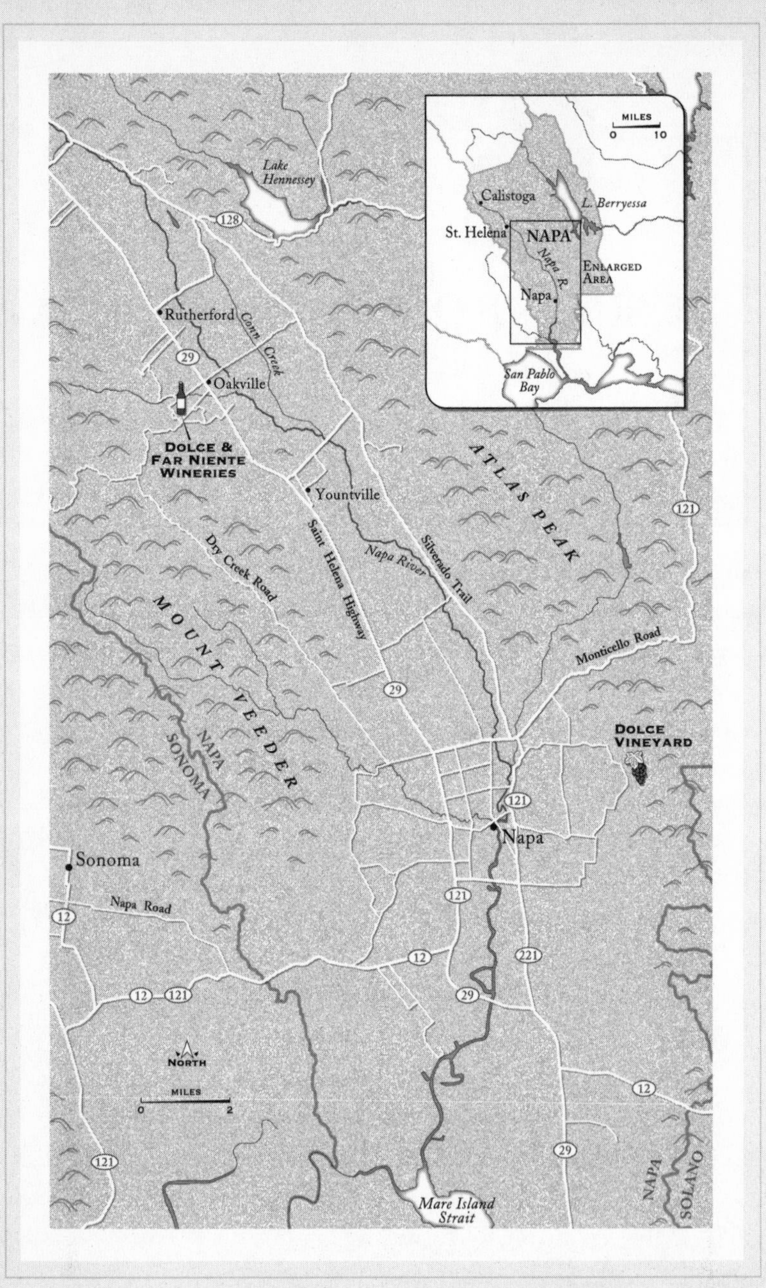

THE DOLCE WINERY AND VINEYARD

CHAPTER 10

Dolce Late Harvest

Napa Valley, California

...

Dirk Hampson

Dirk Hampson, who oversees its production, describes Dolce as "the riskiest wine I know." Because this late harvest nectar, America's finest dessert wine, is made from shriveled, mold-infected grapes, the risks begin in the vineyard, where weather and pests can destroy a vintage. They then extend into the winery, where the juice contains so much sugar that the chance of spoilage is high. "Sometimes," Hampson quips, "I think of Dolce as an exercise in crisis management." Though there is less chance of catastrophe today than in the wine's early years, calamity once proved common—so much so that at a couple of crucial points the enterprise came close to being abandoned. Dolce began as an experiment, and even after the purchase of a vineyard specifically designated for it, failure seemed as likely as success. "It was do or die," Hampson remembers; "luckily, we made it."

Hard-learned lessons ultimately proved more important than luck. Through careful research, Hampson and Dolce's current day-to-day winemaker, Greg Allen, have figured out how to reduce the risk of damage so as to transform shriveled, mold-infected Semillon and Sauvignon Blanc grapes into a clean, lush dessert wine. At first, Hampson thought that they would only be able to make it occasionally. But for well over a decade now, they have produced a superior rendition every year. That record of accomplishment indicates why Dolce is the only non-fortified, late harvest American wine that consistently can hold its own with the great sweet wines of the world. "No one is really trying to go head to head with it," notes Hampson. "That's because the market for this sort of thing is really small. Besides, it's so hard, so tricky to make. We've grabbed the ring—which was why we took the risks."

The Dolce experiment began in 1985. That was when Hampson, then the winemaker at Far Niente (the Napa winery where he continues to manage production as director of winemaking), convinced his boss, an Oklahoma nurseryman turned California vintner named Gil Nickel, to let him try to fashion a wine modeled after Sauternes—the liquid gold from Bordeaux, widely considered the world's best type of dessert wine. "I wanted to do something different," he remembers, "and I always loved dessert wines." Hampson's first challenge involved acquiring the right sort of grapes for this wine—specifically, grapes infected with *Botrytis cinerea*, the fungus sometimes called "noble rot" that imparts a rich, honeyed quality to virtually all of the world's leading late harvest bottlings. Since botrytis is something that the vast majority of California grape growers work diligently to prevent at harvest, sources proved scarce. But Hampson found some infected Napa grapes late in the season, and he went on to make a small batch of wine from them. When it proved promising, Nickel agreed to fund the commercial venture. Since growers would be unable to sell their ripe grapes late in the season if botrytis failed to develop, Hampson had to agree to pay them no matter what happened in their vineyards. And in both 1987 and 1988, no botrytis appeared. Nickel winced at how much this experiment was costing. He winced again when Hampson suggested that he buy land in a more conducive spot and plant his own vineyard there. Because Nickel's primary concern was Far Niente, a winery he was trying to establish as one of Napa's finest, Cabernet and Chardonnay were more important to him than any upstart dessert wine.

Gil Nickel only purchased the new vineyard—some fifty acres in a hollow named Coombsville, where the vines often are blanketed by morning fog—because Hampson convinced him that it would be a good place to grow Chardonnay as well. Indeed, the property has become an important source of fruit for Far Niente's flagship wine, as twenty-five acres are planted to Chardonnay. But since 1991, it also has supplied all the grapes for Dolce. Semillon grows on sixteen acres, Sauvignon Blanc on two, and botrytis makes its presence felt in this vineyard every year. Hampson and Nickel's problems weren't over, however, once they had a more stable fruit source. For along with botrytis came hoards of yellow-jacket wasps, pests that were hungry for sugar at the end of the season. The yellowjackets devastated the vines. Not only did they suck sweet juice from the fruit, they also left pinprick holes in the grapes, inviting decay and bacteria. In 1992, some 80 percent of the crop was ruined, and Nickel issued an ultimatum: Either make Dolce financially viable or stop the project.

Hampson went to work, researching possible solutions. He didn't find many. Spraying with pesticides would damage the fruit; fine mesh nets would cast too much shade; and there were no natural predators he could import. Then he happened upon a scientific article by a Washington State University researcher, who proposed trapping wasps with pheromones. With insects much as with humans, ran the theory, sexual attraction will prove more enticing than sugar. Hampson decided to try with the yellow-jackets, though he admits he thought of it as a long shot. He purchased traps, and the next fall held his breath when the insects returned. Happily, the theory held. The pheromone seduction succeeded, and Dolce's biggest crisis was averted.

Botrytized dessert wines have been made—and prized—since at least the seventeenth century, but their production always has been limited by both geography and economics. The risks and costs involved in making them are so great that only vintners in select regions try to fashion them on any significant scale. In Europe, the first such region was

Tokaj in Hungary, then the Rheingau in Germany, followed finally, and most famously, by Sauternes in Bordeaux. Vintners elsewhere, including America, usually guard against botrytis, knowing that unwanted infection can ruin their crop. Because harvest in California tends to be dry, this is not usually a problem. In fact, botrytis is so limited there that professors at UC Davis have developed a method for artificially infecting harvested grapes in order to facilitate the production of dessert wines. Beringer Vineyard's Myron Nightingale first used this process successfully back in the 1960s, and the wine that today carries his name—Beringer's Semillon-based "Nightingale"—is still made that way. Hampson, however, wanted the botrytis for Dolce's grapes to develop naturally, his goal being to have it spread slowly through the vineyard as the sugar level in the grapes rose.

To reach that goal, Hampson began to talk with growers—grape growers certainly, but also strawberry and other fruit farmers—who employed techniques designed to do just the opposite, prevent botrytis from ever appearing. He then went out of his way to employ contrary methods in the Dolce vineyard. His selection of a foggy, humid spot was only the first in a series of such strategic decisions. Others included irrigating in the fall so as to encourage the fungus with moisture, managing the vines' canopies so as to promote shade, and returning pomace to the vineyard so that botrytis spores can get into the bark of the vines, thus increasing the chance of infection each year. "You have to almost live in the vineyard to get it," he explains. "You can't make botrytis happen, but by learning and executing tons of details, you can help it along."

Botrytis can infect a vineyard at any time, and if the weather becomes inclement, its beneficial presence for dessert wine easily turns injurious, the fungus spreading as gray rot while the crop literally decays on the vine. But when botrytis comes at the right time—that is, late in the harvest, after the grapes have matured—and the weather cooperates by not raining, it will shrivel the grapeskins and dehydrate the pulp, thus reducing the water content and elevating the sugar. The mold literally alters the fruit's chemistry, transforming tartaric acid into gluconic acid and glycerol, giving the resulting wines a seductive viscosity. Botrytis moves across a vineyard slowly and erratically, usually grape by grape rather than cluster by cluster, let alone vine by vine. As a consequence, even when everything goes right, some portion of the crop will remain unaffected. It certainly is possible (in fact, it's common) to make sweet wines from late harvest, non-botrytized grapes. But such wines never taste as ethereally complex as those infected with "noble rot."

The harvest at Dolce takes at least a month, with pickers going through the vineyard and visiting each vine up to six separate times. They need to know precisely which grapes to select and which to leave behind. Because this crop is so different from others, Hampson and Greg Allen, who has been directly responsible for Dolce since 2001, try to use the same crew every year. "Through successive harvests with one group," says Allen, "we've learned, and so can teach them how to recognize the quality we want." They pay the crew, composed of workers who live in Napa year-round, by the hour rather than by weight, encouraging a meticulous selection. During any one vineyard pass, the workers harvest partial clusters and individual grapes—rarely whole bunches. Then the process of selection continues at the winery, as the fruit is sorted for quality, with substandard grapes discarded. This process of *triage* culls the crop even farther, with the result that even in a year with heavy botrytis infection, the Dolce vineyard yields a very small amount of fruit that actually will be used for wine. And because the degree of infection varies vintage by vintage, production levels fluctuate significantly, ranging anywhere between six hundred and thirty-five hundred cases of wine each year.

The different passes through the vineyard produce different batches of juice, each with a slightly different brix, or sugar level, each in turn with slightly different flavors. Allen tests them repeatedly in the laboratory, checking for unwanted bacteria. "That's because they're a microbial zoo," he says, "and we've learned that it's really important to have clean liquid." Rather than make wine directly from these different lots, he first fashions a pre-fermentation blend in order to have a consistent sugar level (usually about 33 degrees brix), and then divides that into a series of small lots. He ferments two-thirds of these separately in French oak barrels, using assorted commercially available yeasts. The other lots are left alone, and eventually ferment by means of the proliferation of yeasts indigenous to the vineyard and winery. This fermentation unfolds ever so slowly, taking up to three months, until the wine reaches the target of 13.5 percent alcohol and 11 to 12 degrees of residual sugar.

At that point, says Allen, Dolce tastes sweet but shrill, "something like hyperactive pineapple juice." It needs time to settle down and harmonize, and so spends two more years in barrel, aging on the spent fermentation lees, gaining nuance and subtlety—specifically, a minerality that supports the sweet fruit and so prevents the wine from tasting sappy. Although Allen conducts tests all through the aging period, he and Hampson do not even begin to think about which barrels contain the wines that will go into the final blend until midway through the second year. "It just changes so much," he says, that until the end, "I just concentrate on making sure it's clean."

Given all the sugar in the wine, plenty still can go wrong, most notably refermentation and bacterial infection. That's why Hampson calls it "the most technically demanding wine," and why Allen insists that a strong foundation in laboratory science is required to make it. A former biomechanical engineer from MIT, Allen has brought to the Dolce team an impressive scientific expertise, but even he admits that he doesn't understand everything that happens to the wine when in barrel. Exactly why it darkens to an almost amber hue, and why it becomes so seductively viscous, and why some barrels turn out just right and others seem slightly off—"I don't have any analytical explanations," he says. "There's really not that much research on this type of wine [even in France]. We're largely on our own in making it."

Even with all the careful selection in the vineyard and then the winery, Allen and Hampson inevitably don't use a significant percentage of the finished wine—usually 25 percent or so. Though they could sell it on the bulk market, they refuse to do so, for they don't want anyone else to be able to bottle a second version of Dolce. The selected barrels then are blended together, filtered, and bottled—the vast majority in 375-ml. half bottles. These, like the occasional larger bottles, sport a distinctive *fin-de-siècle*, Art Nouveau design, made with hand-applied ceramic ink and 22-

karat gold bonded onto the glass. Much as with the liquid gold inside, the packaging process proves laborious and costly; not surprisingly, Dolce is expensive, costing upward of $75 per half bottle. The winery has little difficulty selling it, though, since at least in America it stands alone.

Dolce's competition comes primarily from the wines upon which it's modeled: prestigious, top-growth Sauternes from Bordeaux. Hampson singles out the most prestigious (and expensive) Sauternes when discussing his initial inspiration for Dolce; but both he and Allen are quick to agree that their wine tastes quite different from Château d'Yquem, being bolder and more tropical-scented, with more obvious fruit flavors and fewer secondary, earthy ones. "We're not trying to make d'Yquem in California," Hampson insists. "Our wine certainly derives inspiration from the great sweet whites of Bordeaux, but we are not attempting duplication. Fruit manifests itself differently here." Still, Dolce shares certain characteristics with great Sauternes—a complex interplay of fruit and spice flavors, sufficient acidity to provide structure, and a seductively sumptuous texture. That it tends to seem brighter and more obviously fruit-forward simply reflects its Napa Valley origin, the influence of long, sun-drenched summer days and the overall absence of rain. As Hampson puts it, "You can taste the sunshine in the fruit."

The finest Sauternes, wines from not only d'Yquem but also châteaux such as Climens, Coutet, Lafaurie-Peyraguey and Rieussac, are legendary for their ability to age and evolve in bottle. They gradually darken, becoming golden and then orange-tinted, and their flavors change from fresh to dried fruits, the wines becoming ever more caramel- and molasses-scented as the years go by. Being less than two decades old, Dolce has no real track record, and only time will tell if it will be able to age equally gracefully.

Tasted today, the early vintages of Dolce do seem to have developed additional nuances, their tropical notes having matured into flavors resembling peaches and apricots, with a smoky, spicy, *crème brûlée* character that proves especially enticing in the bouquet. But they are only babies in the rarefied world of age-worthy sweet wines, and the more recent vintages should perform even better, as they reflect all the lessons the winemakers have learned since the Dolce experiment began. Hampson originally thought, for example, that he needed 100 percent botrytized grapes ("because I'd read that about d'Yquem"). He since has learned that the inclusion of some uninfected fruit provides structure and balance. ("When I finally visited d'Yquem," he adds with a smile, "I saw that they do the same thing.") Similarly, the initial blends contained a higher proportion of Sauvignon Blanc than the wines do now. "Five to seven percent is all we need," explains Allen. "More would make the wines less lush." Dolce today certainly tastes lush—supple and smooth, with layers and layers of sweet flavor and an expansive finish. And unlike some Sauternes, it presents those charms early on, tasting delicious even when young. "That's the idea," says Hampson. "Its magic comes in the pleasure of drinking it."

Though Dolce is America's most esteemed late harvest, botrytis-infected wine, it is not the country's only good dessert wine. Delicious, often partially botrytized sweet Rieslings come from wineries such as Arrowood, Freemark Abbey, Navarro, and Joseph Phelps in California, Herman Weimer in New York, and Chateau Ste. Michelle in Washington. Fresh, vibrant Muscats are made by Bonny Doon, Robert Pecota, and Quady. And some East Coast producers, including Anthony Road in the Finger Lakes and Breaux Vineyards in Virginia, fashion superb late harvest wines from French-American hybrid varietals such as Vidal Blanc and Vignoles. But no American dessert wine save Dolce has succeeded in holding its own when pitted against top Sauternes, the world's most admired late harvest wine.

Twenty years ago, Dirk Hampson proposed this wine to his boss as something different, an experiment worth trying. He did not know then what he has learned now—that making it demands "an unbelievable level of perfectionism." Nor did he know that, with lessons learned, he and Greg Allen could succeed so consistently. But succeed they have, and their success explains why Hampson can say with evident pride, "We've created a reputation with Dolce where, at least in this country, we're alone, with no real equal."

A NOTE ON VINTAGES:

A little time helps. Upon release, this wine tastes decadently rich, but then with a few years of bottle age it becomes subtler, more elegant and sophisticated. No one knows if it can age for decades like great Sauternes, but it clearly benefits from cellaring. Rich and balanced vintages include 1990, 1993, 1995, 1999, and 2001.

THE SUGGESTED PRICE FOR THE CURRENT 2001 RELEASE, IN HALF BOTTLE, IS $75.

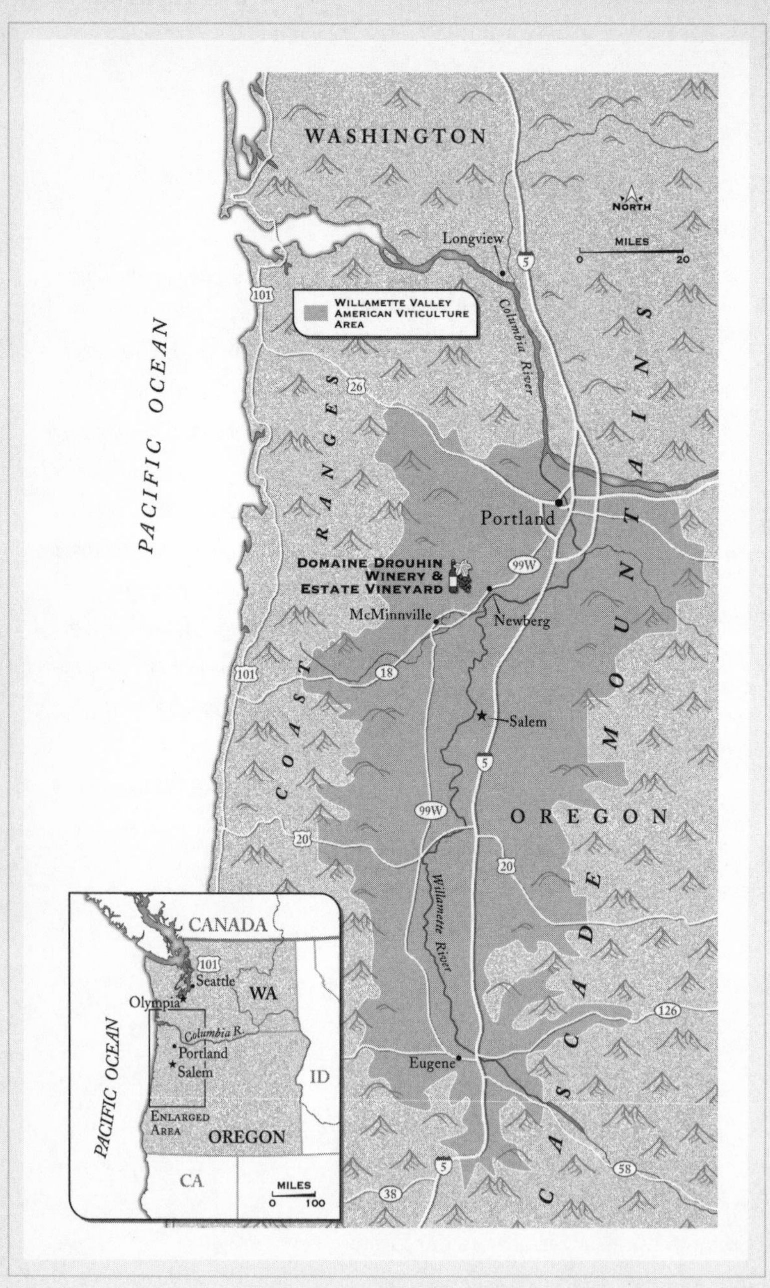

DOMAINE DROUHIN OREGON,
IN THE NORTHERN WILLAMETTE VALLEY

CHAPTER II

DOMAINE DROUHIN OREGON PINOT NOIR, "LAURÈNE"

Willamette Valley, Oregon

...

Robert Drouhin couldn't believe it. The urbane, forty-six-year-old president of Maison Joseph Drouhin, one of Burgundy's most respected wine firms, couldn't believe that a Pinot Noir from Oregon had bested a bevy of *grand* and *premier cru* Burgundies, including a number of Drouhin's own wines, in a tasting sponsored by the French food and wine magazine *Gault-Millau*. The wine in question was David Lett's 1975 Eyrie Vineyards South Block Reserve, and the tasting, held in Paris in 1979, had featured 330 Pinot Noirs from around the world. Surely, Drouhin thought, something was amiss. Perhaps the French bottles had been stored poorly; perhaps bad vintages had been poured; but an Oregon wine simply couldn't be better than a top red Burgundy. So he organized a rematch with wines he handpicked from his company's own cellars. This time the Eyrie Pinot placed second, barely beaten out of the top spot by Drouhin's 1959 Chambolle-Musigny. But French honor wasn't completely restored. After all, the champion was

Veronique Drouhin-Boss

twenty-one years old, and came from a vineyard with an illustrious heritage, centuries of esteemed vintages. By contrast, the upstart challenger was a virtual baby, made with fruit from nine-year-old vines. Robert Drouhin didn't like it, but he had to admit that Oregon's Willamette Valley just might be a good place to grow Pinot Noir.

Drouhin already knew something about Oregon. He had visited the state a few times over the years, so he understood that some ambitious vintners were growing Pinot Noir in the hills south of Portland. He even had befriended some of them, including Eyrie's Lett and David Adelsheim of Adelsheim Vineyard. Before the 1979 and 1980 tastings, Drouhin had been perfectly willing to acknowledge that Oregon showed promise with Pinot Noir. What he couldn't believe was that this promise was being realized so quickly. The proof, though, was on his own palate. So six years later, when Adelsheim told him that an "interesting property" had come on the market, he decided to buy it. The estate, now 225 acres on a south-facing slope in the Red Hills of Dundee, just above the original Eyrie vineyard, was a former Christmas tree farm. It never had been planted to vines.

In addition to being intrigued by the potential high quality of Oregon Pinot Noir, Drouhin had yet another reason to make this purchase. His daughter, Véronique, had just graduated with a degree in enology from the University of Dijon in Burgundy. Now she was ready to begin making wine. But Maison Joseph Drouhin, one of the larger companies in Burgundy, a firm that not only owns vineyards but also buys grapes as a *negociant*, already had a longtime, well-regarded winemaker. Drouhin did not want to saddle him with an assistant who inevitably would be regarded as an heir apparent. Véronique had interned in Oregon when completing her studies, working the 1986 vintage at Adelsheim, Bethel Heights, and Eyrie. She knew something about the Willamette Valley *terroir*, something about the wines. And she liked the Pacific Northwest. Perhaps, then, this is where she could make her mark. Drouhin, a proud father, was more than happy to let his daughter be in control of this new venture, what he thought of as his American "experiment."

Domaine Drouhin Oregon (affectionately abbreviated to DDO by everyone there) was just that from the start—an experiment. As Véronique

Drouhin, now Drouhin-Boss, explains: "It was not possible to expand in Burgundy. Land is too expensive if it is available at all. For us, expanding in Oregon was an experiment, a challenge to make Pinot Noir in a new place." As such, the estate became a locus for trying out grape growing and winemaking practices. Were the conventional Burgundian techniques best? What could be improved? What should be done as it was done in the Drouhin cellars in Beaune? What should be altered? In Burgundy, restrictive regulation coupled with treasured tradition promoted a mind-set in which change inevitably was viewed with distrust. But on the Willamette Valley Christmas tree farm, there were no customs or practices *to* change. When it came to grapes and wine, this domaine was truly virgin ground.

One thing, though, was clear. Robert and Véronique Drouhin were there to grow and make Pinot Noir. Not the Alsatian grape varieties that other Oregonians might be experimenting with—Pinot Blanc, Pinot Gris, or Gewurztraminer. Not Riesling. And certainly not the various Bordeaux varietals. "After all," insists Drouhin-Boss, "coming from Burgundy we knew how to make Pinot Noir, not Merlot!" In the eighteen years since DDO was founded, she has added just one other varietal to the company portfolio. Not surprisingly, it's Chardonnay, the other Burgundian. Drouhin-Boss makes some two thousand cases of estate Chardonnay each year. But she produces six times as much Pinot Noir—the wine that occasioned her and her father's original experiment, the wine they came to Oregon to pursue.

As émigré grapes, Chardonnay and Pinot Noir couldn't be more different. The one seems agreeably adaptable, the other often hopelessly homesick. Although Chardonnay yields very different wines depending upon where it's planted, it grows happily in many places. Cool regions produce leaner wines, warm regions fuller ones. Chalk and limestone soils deliver mineral flavors, alluvial soils tropical ones. But all around the winemaking globe, Chardonnay makes reliable, sometimes remarkable wines. No wonder it's become an almost generic reference for dry white wine.

By contrast, nothing seems remotely generic about Pinot Noir. This grape is notoriously temperamental. It will yield decent wine only if planted in just the right place, and if vinified in just the right way. Even at home in Burgundy, the wines prove irritatingly uneven. But elsewhere, at least until the 1990s, uneven would have to have been considered a compliment. Back then, first-class New World Pinot Noir was such a rare sighting that critics and consumers alike could be forgiven for not believing in its existence. Today, more people in more places (Oregon and California to be sure, but also New Zealand and to a lesser extent Australia) are sometimes succeeding with it, and only the most chauvinistic Burgundian would claim that the Côte d'Or is the sole place where it yields good wine. Still, Pinot remains the most capricious of all the important international grape varieties. So unlike Chardonnay, true achievement with it continues to be defined in terms of the Old World model. That is, red Burgundy provides winemakers everywhere with their stylistic benchmark—red berry or black cherry fruit enhanced by a hint of incense or spice, leather or game, in a red wine that feels sensuously supple and seductive, sip after sumptuous sip.

Véronique Drouhin-Boss knows that model well. As the fourth-generation winemaker in her family, her Burgundian roots go deep—deep in the Côte d'Or soil, deep in Maison Joseph Drouhin's medieval cellars, deep in a wine culture marked by what the author Matt Kramer calls "the mentality of *terroir*." Kramer perceptively defines that mentality as an insistence on distinction: "The greatness of French wines in general—and Burgundy in particular—can be traced to the fact that the French do not ask of one site that it replicate the qualities of another site. . . . It is not that [Burgundy] is the only spot on the planet with remarkable soils or that its climate is superior. . . . It is a matter of the values that are applied to the land." For Drouhin-Boss, those values lead to something of a paradox. Red Burgundy remains her stylistic model, but she can emulate that model in Oregon only by ignoring it. Put another way, to her mind great wine cannot result from a dictated style. Instead, it requires sensitivity, an almost intuitive sensitivity to the peculiarities of place. "When I taste our wines," she says, "I know they could only come from one place. That's the essence of my job, to reflect nature."

Reflection, however, does not mean mirroring. In the case of any wine, but particularly one made with Pinot Noir, effectively reflecting nature necessitates a series of careful, often costly choices, difficult decisions arrived at in both vineyard and winery. Those decisions were what the DDO experiment was all about. And the choices the Drouhins made did not simply echo Burgundian conventions. In 1988, for example, when designing the winery, they decided to build literally into the hillside, creating a completely gravity-fed operation. The idea behind this design (since emulated by a number of Oregon's leading wineries, including Adelsheim, Archery Summit, Domaine Serene, and WillaKenzie Estate) is to handle the grapes, juice, and wine as gently as possible. The young wine is not pumped or otherwise roughed up at any stage of the winemaking process, thus reducing the possibility of unwanted bitterness or astringency. Gravity flow, while theoretically intriguing, is not possible at Maison Joseph Drouhin, where the cellars lie under cobblestone streets and the surrounding hills have long been covered with vineyards. But it was possible on the estate in Oregon. The four-level winery there extends deep back in the hill, so it is cooled naturally. And all during the approximately sixteen months after the grapes leave the vine until the finished wine goes into bottle, everything flows literally downhill. The gravity-feed design does not by itself explain the nuanced character of the DDO Pinots. It is, however, a piece of the puzzle—an un-Burgundian piece that helps result in a decidedly Burgundian-tasting wine.

The first DDO Pinot came from the 1988 vintage. Made with grapes purchased from local growers, and vinified at rented space in a nearby facility (because the estate winery was literally still a plan on a drawing board), it was released in 1991 to considerable acclaim. The critic Robert Parker noted that it had been fashioned "in the Côte de Beaune–like style that Drouhin knows so well." The British wine writer, Clive Cotes, was even more effusive, claiming that it tasted "purer, more cleanly fruity, and certainly more Burgundian" than other Oregon Pinot Noirs. What compelled these and other commentators' attention was the fact that, like many Burgundies, the wine had a silky texture and offered elegant, so not at all chunky, flavors. (True to his own preferences, Parker noted that it was a little less concentrated than he'd like.)

But for Robert and Véronique Drouhin, this wine was little more than a first test. With the 1988 vintage, they were working in neither their own winery nor their own vineyard. And for both father and daughter, the vineyard would be the key to their wine's ultimate success. After all, it contained the nature they aimed to reflect.

The Drouhins had planted their first vines earlier that same year—eight experimental acres, using two commercial clones (Pommard and Wadensville), and as was then conventional in Oregon, planting the vines on their own roots. But the next year, when they began planting on a larger scale, they made big changes, using their experience back home as a guide. For one, they started grafting new vines onto phylloxera-resistant rootstock. That microscopic vine-destroying louse had not yet been found in Oregon, but Robert Drouhin suspected that it would appear soon. (He was right; the first infection was reported in 1990.) Grafting onto resistant rootstock was standard practice in France, and indeed all of Europe. So from 1989 on, all planting at DDO has been with grafted vines, a practice since adopted by many of the better Oregon vintners. For another, the Drouhins were not happy with the Pinot Noir clones they had used, both of which had come to the Pacific Northwest from warm, sunny California. So in 1989, when Oregon State University released the first set of imported French Dijon clones for commercial use, they jumped at the chance to diversify. Inherently low yielding, these new clones, first propagated by Professor Raymond Bernard at the University of Dijon in Burgundy, are better suited to Oregon's cool, sometimes damp climate. Especially when a variety of them are blended together, the resulting wines manage to display concentration and complexity while at the same time remaining elegantly soft and supple.

The most radical development in the vineyard at DDO involved spacing. Rather than plant their vines like their neighbors, with the rows eight feet wide and the plants spaced some six feet apart, they used a high-density template (3.3 feet by 4.25 feet). The result was nearly four times as many vines per acre. High-density planting has since become quite fashionable in California as well as Oregon. The basic idea is to curtail vine vigor by forcing each plant to compete with its neighbors. A high-density vineyard will produce roughly the same amount of fruit as a more conventionally spaced one; the individual vines will just produce fewer clusters. Moreover, the grapes under high-density planting will have smaller berries and hence more concentrated flavor components. High-density spacing is standard practice in Burgundy, and the Drouhins were among the first to employ the practice in the United States. It's an expensive system, but the cost (of yearly pruning as well as initial planting) helps provide another piece in the high-quality puzzle.

The DDO vineyard operation is in many ways now self-contained. All new plantings use cuttings taken from vines growing on the estate. These are grafted onto estate-grown rootstock, so that all the plant material eventually will be unique to the property. The Drouhins thus aim to maintain consistency by propagating what has proven successful in this particular site. Their goal remains to make a wine that tastes of the place rather than the grape—one that announces itself as Drouhin Oregon, not simply as Pinot Noir. Great wine, they insist, cannot merely reflect the grape variety.

Over seventy acres at DDO are now devoted to Pinot Noir, with some forty-five more scheduled to be planted in the future—one or two new blocks each year. In the winery, Drouhin-Boss prefers not to inoculate with cultured yeast but instead lets the fermentations develop naturally with the yeasts indigenous to the site. Once fermentation is complete, the wine flows down one level into the barrel cellar. So as not to overwhelm its delicately nuanced flavors, Drouhin-Boss uses less than 20 percent new wood. Again, the goal is to respect and represent the site. Too much oak, like too much alcohol or too much extract (from overripe grapes), will yield a wine that, though perhaps tasty, reflects the winemaker more than the *terroir*.

Most of the Pinot Noir the Drouhins grow goes into their roughly ten thousand–case Oregon blend. Called "Classique," this wine now includes nearly 95 percent estate fruit, the rest being grapes purchased from other Willamette Valley vineyards. A small number of selected lots, however, are reserved for a prestige bottling—Laurène, named after Véronique Drouhin-Boss's oldest daughter. It is her most successful, most structured and complete wine, because it tastes of so much more than the grape. (So as to prevent sibling rivalry, she fashions two other familial cuvées—Louise, an especially elegant Pinot sold only at the winery and named for her younger daughter, and Arthur, the estate Chardonnay, named after her son.) Laurène reflects the very best of each vintage, and hence the very best of the domaine.

Laurène is a winery not a vineyard selection, as grapes from different vineyard blocks go in it in different years. At DDO, each of the estate's over thirty blocks is harvested, vinified, and aged separately, giving Drouhin-Boss a colorful palette with which to practice her art. Over the course of the wine's roughly year-long aging period, she and her assistants taste each lot repeatedly, noting which ones exhibit the most depth and complexity. These then are reserved for Laurène, production of which averages about two thousand cases each year. While this cuvée does not receive any extra time in barrel, it does benefit from spending nearly two years in bottle before being released onto the market. Laurène clearly is designed to improve with age, and tends to develop secondary, non-fruit aromas and flavors reminiscent of tea, wood smoke, and dried herbs five to seven years after the vintage. Perhaps in time it will become even more site-specific, an expression of certain choice parts of the vineyard. In fact, Drouhin-Boss notes that certain blocks do tend to end up in Laurène—"not always, but usually." These blocks don't make up the whole blend because this vineyard is still in its infancy. She has to trust her present judgment, as there simply isn't enough of a viticultural past on which to rely.

Laurène debuted with the 1992 vintage, and in the years since it has compiled an enviable track record as one of America's finest Pinot Noirs. Neither as rich as some nor as flashy as others, its greatness is a function of structure rather than flesh, whispered understatement rather than shouted force. In this, it resembles what remains the model—fine red Burgundy of the sort long made at Maison Joseph Drouhin in Beaune. With characteristic modesty, Drouhin-Boss resists the comparison. "It's too early," she says. Perhaps. But Laurène already is one of the few New World Pinot Noirs whose appeal comes from secondary subtlety instead of varietal power. And as she well knows, such subtlety quite literally has its roots in a place. Only in this case, the place is a young vineyard in Oregon, not a venerable *grand cru* in the Cote d'Or. Her father once didn't believe that possible. Thanks to her work, he and all who taste this wine now know it is.

A NOTE ON VINTAGES:

This Pinot Noir, tightly wound in its youth, definitely benefits from cellaring. After five years or so, it opens to reveal aromatic subtleties and nuances only hinted at in its youth. In a strong vintage, it will drink well for a good ten to twelve years following harvest. Such vintages include 1993, 1995, 1998, 2000, and 2002.

THE SUGGESTED PRICE FOR THE CURRENT 2002 RELEASE IS $60.

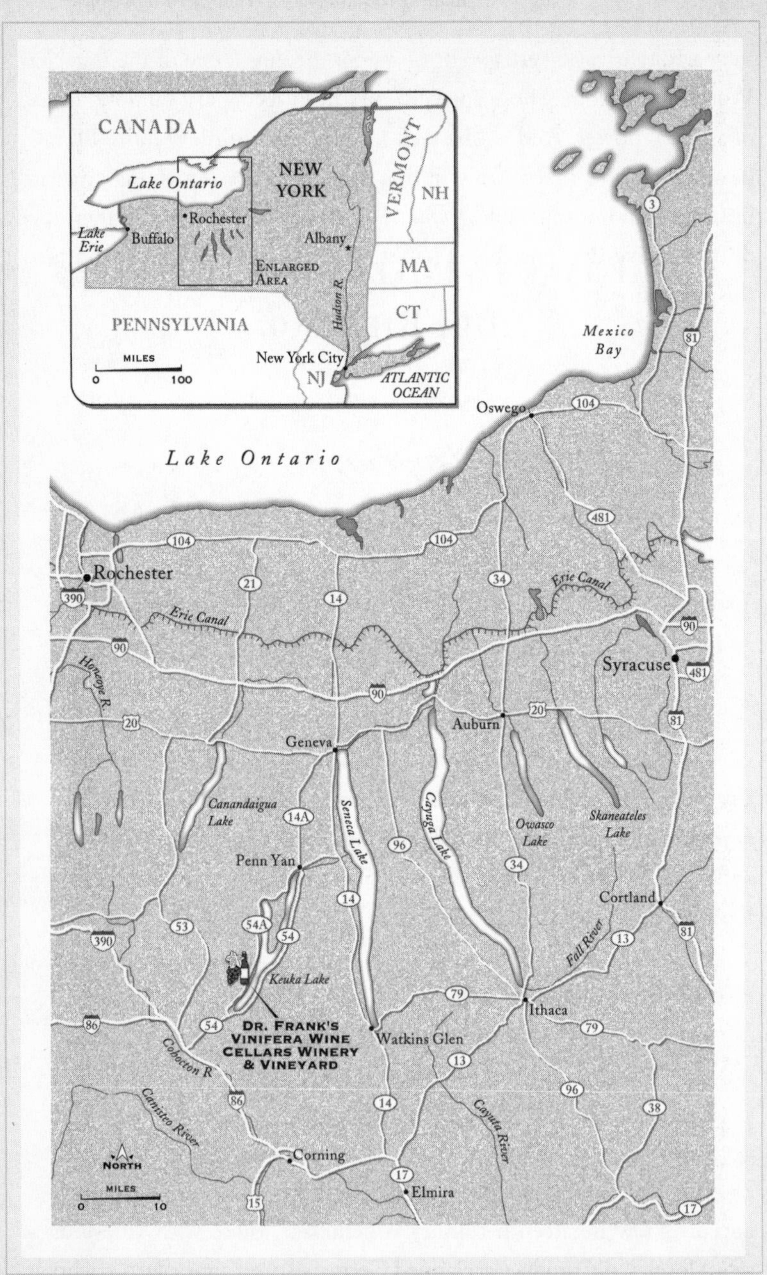

THE FINGER LAKES, IN WESTERN NEW YORK STATE

CHAPTER 12

Dr. Frank's Vinifera Wine Cellars Dry Riesling

Finger Lakes, New York

...

Pity poor Riesling. A hundred years ago, this grape was lauded as the world's finest for white wines, and top German renditions commanded higher prices than the best red Bordeaux. Much as they did with French wines, early American winemakers often tried to emulate the foreign model. Many pioneering vintners were of German descent, and they wanted nothing more than to make wines like those they knew from home. But in eastern states, where European varieties kept dying due to disease, they had to use natives like Catawba or Elvira, grapes that produce wines which taste nothing like Riesling. And in California, where vinifera vines could be cultivated easily, most sites proved too hot, rendering the wines unbalanced. A few nineteenth-century winemakers, those with vineyards in select locales, did produce acclaimed German-styled wines. Jacob Schram, for example, grew Riesling on a hillside near Calistoga, and his was the only Napa Valley white served when President Harrison had dinner in San

Dr. Konstantin Frank

Francisco in 1891. Other Californians occasionally used Riesling as part of blends they called "Hocks," and later, following Prohibition, "Rhine Wines." These usually were off-dry. They tasted sappy and came cheap.

To make matters worse, in the last decades of the twentieth century, just when interest in American wine rose dramatically, Riesling suffered a great fall worldwide. German wine, by dint of the mass production of cheap Liebfraumilch, fell out of favor with all but the most diehard traditionalists. Austrian wine, the victim of a scandal involving unscrupulous producers who diluted their wines with antifreeze, did so as well. Meanwhile, in the United States, where most wine drinkers were new to wine, self-proclaimed experts derided any white with even a hint of sweetness, as the taste of oak rather than fresh fruit became *de rigueur*. No matter that Riesling can yield vibrant, vivacious unwooded wines. No matter, too, that many connoisseurs still consider it the noblest of all white varieties. The grape simply became unfashionable. In California, vineyards were uprooted far and wide, and Golden State Riesling came to be viewed as little more than a pale version of White Zinfandel—something sugary and unworthy of serious attention.

That one state, however, is not the whole of the country, and pity is not the end of Riesling's American story. For at much the same time, in the 1960s, 1970s, and 1980s, first one, then two, then a small band of vintners working a continent away were proving that the United States in fact can produce high-quality Riesling. Led by the example of a hardheaded Ukrainian immigrant, the Finger Lakes region of New York emerged as the source of some of the country's finest cold climate wines, with Riesling its flagship varietal.

Riesling still is not chic on these shores, but quality has become so high today that Finger Lakes vintners profess to see the beginnings of a Riesling renaissance. Though production is small, demand for their wines is high, especially from restaurateurs, as consumers begin to exchange the old stereotype of American Riesling as sweet and sappy for a new image of it as energetic and exciting. More people certainly continue to buy woody, superripe (and superalcoholic) white wines, but a growing minority is looking for crisp, clean, delicate flavors—precisely what Finger

Lakes Rieslings provide. So in the end, this once acclaimed but then neglected grape may yet have the last laugh.

The Finger Lakes resemble the imprint of a thin, bony hand on a map of western New York. Carved by glaciers that left limestone and fractured shale deposits, they are extremely deep, so create distinct microclimates that prove beneficial to grape growers. Though much of this large region (the Fingers Lakes Viticultural Area encompasses some 4,000 square miles) is too cold for grape growing, the lakes themselves rarely freeze, so viticulture is viable near the shores. In winter, the lakes radiate heat to nearby vineyards, protecting the vines from destructively low temperatures. In spring, the water's presence delays budbreak until after the last frost. And in fall, when the lakes stay warm, the growing season lingers into Indian summer, allowing the fruit to ripen completely. This effect is especially pronounced along the banks of the larger lakes—Cayuga, Seneca, Keuka, and Canandaigua. Not surprisingly, grapes long have been an important crop there. In 1900, some 20,000 acres were under vine, and more than fifty Finger Lakes wineries were in business. But none grew Riesling, as vinifera viticulture was thought impossible in the region. Anyone who planted European vines anywhere in the eastern United States saw them die, victims of a harsh climate as well as disease.

Many of the old Finger Lakes wineries folded during Prohibition. After Repeal the few survivors consolidated, and a small set of companies—Canandaigua, Gold Seal, Taylor, and Widmer—came to dominate New York wine production, producing scores of mostly low-end, non-vinifera wines, everything from so-called "Champagne" to kosher Concord. So in 1951, when Dr. Konstantin Frank first came to the Geneva Agricultural Station at the head of Seneca Lake, all commercial Finger Lakes wines were being made with either native grapes or French-American hybrid ones.

At that time, only one person, the author and horticulturalist, Ulysees P. Hedrick, had grown vinifera grapes in the Finger Lakes. Hedrick had succeeded where others failed because he knew to plant on native rootstock (so as to combat phylloxera) and to use fungicides in summer (to prevent rot and mildew). He combated winter cold by mounding earth high on top of his vines each autumn to prevent them from freezing—a costly and time-consuming process. At the end of his career (he died the same year Dr. Frank arrived, at the age of eighty-one), Hedrick was writing primarily for home winemakers, so his achievement went unheeded by the managers at the large New York wineries. Dr. Frank, however, was younger, his voice much louder.

An émigré from Ukraine, Frank had taught viticulture and conducted extensive grape research for the Soviets before World War II. So he knew a good deal about growing grapes in a cold climate, having cultivated vinifera successfully at the former Trubetskoy Estate on the banks of the River Dneper. (Prince Trubetskoy was a nephew of the Russian tsar who had planted wine grapes in Ukraine with the help of German and French *vignerons.*) Frank, whose first jobs in the Finger Lakes consisted of sweeping the floors and hoeing blueberries at the Geneva Station, told anyone who listened that cold-resistant varietals would do fine if planted near the lakes. He had grown such grapes back home, where the temperature fell so low that "when we spit, it froze before it hit the ground." What was needed, he insisted, was hardy rootstock onto which the vines could be grafted. But his words, delivered in halting English, fell on deaf ears. For two years, no one paid the slightest attention. Then in 1953, he met Charles Fournier, the president of Gold Seal. As his grandson, Fred Frank, recalls, both men spoke French, and Dr. Frank "bent Charles' ear," telling this expatriate from Champagne "that he wanted to make wines from the varieties of Europe." Fournier, who remembered cold winters from home, hired him. "Dr. Frank went from floor-sweeper to director of research in one day," Fred explains, "without having yet proved his theory correct."

But the theory held true. Fournier and Frank searched for rootstock all through New York, New England, and eastern Canada, finally finding what they wanted in the garden of a convent in Quebec—vines that bore fruit despite frigid winters. Back at Gold Seal, they grafted Chardonnay, Gewurztraminer, and of course Riesling (the vines sourced from the nursery at UC Davis) onto the Canadian roots. The crucial test came a few years later, when a February cold snap saw temperatures in some of the lakeshore vineyards fall to 25 degrees below zero. Come spring, many of the native labrusca vines growing there bore few if any buds, while Dr. Frank's grafted vinifera vines showed only minimal damage. That fall, when those same vines yielded a nearly full crop, Fournier pronounced himself a convert. He began planting vinifera vines as quickly as he could find rootstock on which to graft them. And in 1961, when the first commercial Gold Seal vinifera wines were released onto the market, Dr. Frank proudly declared the event, "the second discovery of America."

Konstantin Frank started his own winery in 1962. Not surprisingly, he named it Dr. Frank's Vinifera Wine Cellars. From the start he concentrated on Riesling, producing dry, off-dry, and dessert-styled wines. He imported specific German clones (identified as 90-Neustadt and 239-Geisenheim) because, although low-yielding, they produce grapes with especially clean, mineral-laden flavors. And almost immediately, his wines received critical acclaim. They were served at both the White House and Governor Rockefeller's mansion in Albany, and virtually everyone who tasted them praised them. Yet while he profoundly influenced a *Who's Who* of eastern viticulture, not all that many consumers knew his wines. "Dr. Frank was all about the science," explains his grandson. "He wanted to get the message out about vinifera, about what was possible. He was eager to share his knowledge, and he didn't worry about selling or marketing wine."

For over three decades, Dr. Frank kept championing vinifera for the Finger Lakes and indeed the whole East Coast. He battled publicly with the scientists at Geneva, who for a long time kept recommending native and hybrid varieties. "The Genevans say that growers must be experts to grow these grapes here," he fumed to author Leon Adams. "The poor Italian and Russian peasants with their shovels can do it," he asked rhetorically, "but the American farmer with his push-button tools cannot?" Ever so slowly, though, others began to follow his lead. Elizabeth Furness in Virginia, George Mathiesen in Massachusetts, Douglas Moorhead in Pennsylvania—these were just a few of the pioneering, visionary vintners who went to Dr. Frank for cuttings and, more to the point, counsel. He called them his "cooperators," recalls Fred Frank. Today, even though some fine eastern wines, especially late harvest ones, are made with French American hybrid varieties such as Vidal Blanc and Vignoles, the vast majority of wines that merit serious consumer attention are made with vinifera varieties. And the scientists at Geneva, still the principal viticultural research center east of California, are happy to recommend them to growers in appropriate places—like the Finger Lakes.

If Dr. Frank largely disdained the business of wine, his son, Willy, embraced it. "My father is a born salesman," Fred explains with a chuckle. "Willy can sell anything to anyone." Although this only son had inherited a love of wine, he didn't always get along with his headstrong father, and in fact had moved to New York City, where he enjoyed a successful career in the camera business. But in 1984, with Dr. Frank's health failing, Willy came home. In order to make his own mark and not compete with his father's legacy, he not only took over the family business but also purchased a nearby winery with underground cellars for sparkling wine. (He soon planted the first vineyard in the eastern United States containing the three classic French Champagne grapes—Chardonnay, Pinot Meunier, and Pinot Noir.) For twenty years now, Willy Frank has produced wines under two labels—Dr. Frank for still wines, and Chateau Frank for bubblies. The first vintage of Chateau Frank came in 1985, the same year that Dr. Konstantin Frank died.

Willy Frank knows wine well, but he's the first to admit that he's not a winemaker. After his father's death, he needed to find one quickly. Since California schools were the only ones teaching enology at the time, he turned to André Tchelistcheff, the retired master of California wine, for advice. Tchelistcheff, a longtime friend of Dr. Frank's, recommended a young man named Eric Fry, who came east to fashion the first Dr. Frank wines not to be made by its founder. Fry stayed a few years but then moved on. (Today he makes the wines at the successful Lenz Winery on Long Island.) Much the same happened with Peter Bell, a talented Canadian who had studied enology in New Zealand and Australia. (Bell stayed in the Finger Lakes after he left Dr. Frank, and now makes the wines at the highly regarded Fox Run on Seneca Lake.) A series of less talented successor winemakers came and went over the next decade, and with Willy focusing so much on marketing and sales, wine quality started to slip. Some vintages were superb; some tasted a bit off. Meanwhile, other

Finger Lakes producers, including by the mid-1990s Fox Run, Herman Wiemer, Lamoreaux Landing, and Standing Stone, had caught up with Dr. Frank. Their wines, especially their Rieslings, could be riveting.

Stability began to return to Dr. Frank's Vinifera Wine Cellars when Willy's son, Fred, joined the company in 1993. Holding a degree in agriculture from Cornell and having attended Germany's Geisenheim Institute for Enology and Viticulture, he knew the technical aspects of both grape growing and winemaking, so was better able to assess a wine's progress from vineyard to bottle. At the same time, Fred recognized the unique role his family's winery played in the eastern wine industry. "We were, and still are, a sort of incubator for winemakers," he explains. "They come here to learn how to make cool-climate wines, and then we often lose them." To maintain reliability, Fred decided to employ a team of winemakers, with a number of different people sharing responsibilities and working toward a common goal. "I really believe in the team concept," he says. "It helps us keep the style of our wines consistent even when a member of the team leaves." At present, five winemakers craft the Dr. Frank wines. Mark Veraguth, a transplanted Californian with fifteen years experience in the Finger Lakes, and Morten Hallgren, a Dane with an enology degree from the University of Montpellier in southern France, head the team. But they don't manage things dictatorially. "Majority rules," Fred says simply when asked how decisions are made. "We have a very good staff. They're all very professional. And working as part of a team requires everyone to be focused on a common goal—the highest quality possible." Since the late 1990s, stylistic or qualitative variability has not been an issue at Dr. Frank. In fact, the wines are better than ever.

Willy and Fred Frank oversee an operation that makes a wide variety of vinifera wines, everything from Chardonnay to Cabernet Franc and Cabernet Sauvignon, Gewurztraminer and Pinot Noir to Rkatsiteli (a five-thousand-year-old variety from the Caucasus, where the vinifera species probably originated), and of course the Chateau Frank sparklers. They do so in part to honor Konstantin Frank's legacy, his sense of scientific experimentation and adventure. But they do so also because, with vinifera viticulture such a recent development in the Finger Lakes, the jury is still out concerning which varieties grow best in which locales. The one thing they're sure of, though, is that Riesling belongs here. "It's our benchmark varietal," Fred insists, "the one we're most consistent making. There's no question it leads the list, no question it's best adapted to our vineyards."

Riesling vines in the Finger Lakes produce small, golden grapes that develop flavors reminiscent of green apples and tangy citrus fruits, enhanced by intriguing mineral undertones of the sort that characterize the world's finest renditions of this varietal. When made in a dry style, they smell slightly floral but taste crisp and lively, with a clean, refreshing finish. (When vinified slightly sweet or off-dry, their flavors more closely resemble peaches and apricots.) Falling between lighter German wines and weightier Alsatian ones in terms of body, the best Finger Lakes Rieslings gain complexity with age. Like the very finest European Rieslings, they develop a haunting, slightly toasty aroma that British wine writers describe as "petrol," something that may sound unappetizing but is actually seductively sensuous. "Our wine definitely rewards patience," says Fred Frank. "It has tremendous ageability." A tasting in June 1993 proved his point. The younger vintages I sampled were vital and vivacious, but the older ones, going back to the early 1980s, were even more compelling, being nuanced with the patina of age yet still delightfully fresh and alive.

Dr. Frank produces an off-dry Riesling (labeled as Semi-Dry), containing about 3 percent residual sugar. That wine is made primarily with purchased grapes grown in vineyards on Cayuga and Seneca Lakes. The winery also sells a dry Riesling under a second label, Salmon Run, made with purchased fruit as well. But for Dr. Frank's Dry Riesling, the winery's standard-bearer, some 90 percent of the grapes come from the estate vineyard on the shores of Keuka Lake, the same vineyard that Dr. Konstantin Frank planted nearly five decades ago. The old vines there average yields of about 2 tons per acre. Growing in slate and shale soils, they produce wines that are wonderfully evocative because they're so expressive of the mineral-rich site. Willy Frank may be biased, but his insistence that "there's no finer region on earth for growing internationally renowned Riesling" is more than simple salesmanship.

While the market for Dr. Frank's Dry Riesling remains strong locally (in Rochester, Syracuse, and elsewhere in upstate New York), it's growing quickly elsewhere—particularly in the mid-Atlantic, New England, and Manhattan. "We see a real upsurge of interest," says Fred. His father adds: "Twenty years ago I couldn't give it away in New York City. Now it's on allocation because we don't have enough." The wine is sold today in thirty states, and father and son both acknowledge that their biggest problem is no longer marketing but supply. So there's no need for pity. Riesling still isn't especially trendy, but attitudes are changing. Some better wines now come from California (producers like Claiborne & Churchill and Jekel come to mind) as well as from Washington State (where Eroica, a collaboration between Dr. Loosen from Germany and Ste. Michelle Wine Estates sets the pace); but as a category, the best American Rieslings hail from the Finger Lakes—where Dr. Frank's was first and is still on top.

A NOTE ON VINTAGES:

This wine ages quite well, becoming stony and mineral-scented, giving the impression of ever more dryness with time in bottle. And despite significant weather variation, quality has been very consistent over the past few years. Exceptional older vintages include 1979, 1982, and 1988, while 2001, 2002, and 2003 all were strong recently.

THE SUGGESTED PRICE FOR THE CURRENT 2004 RELEASE IS $15.

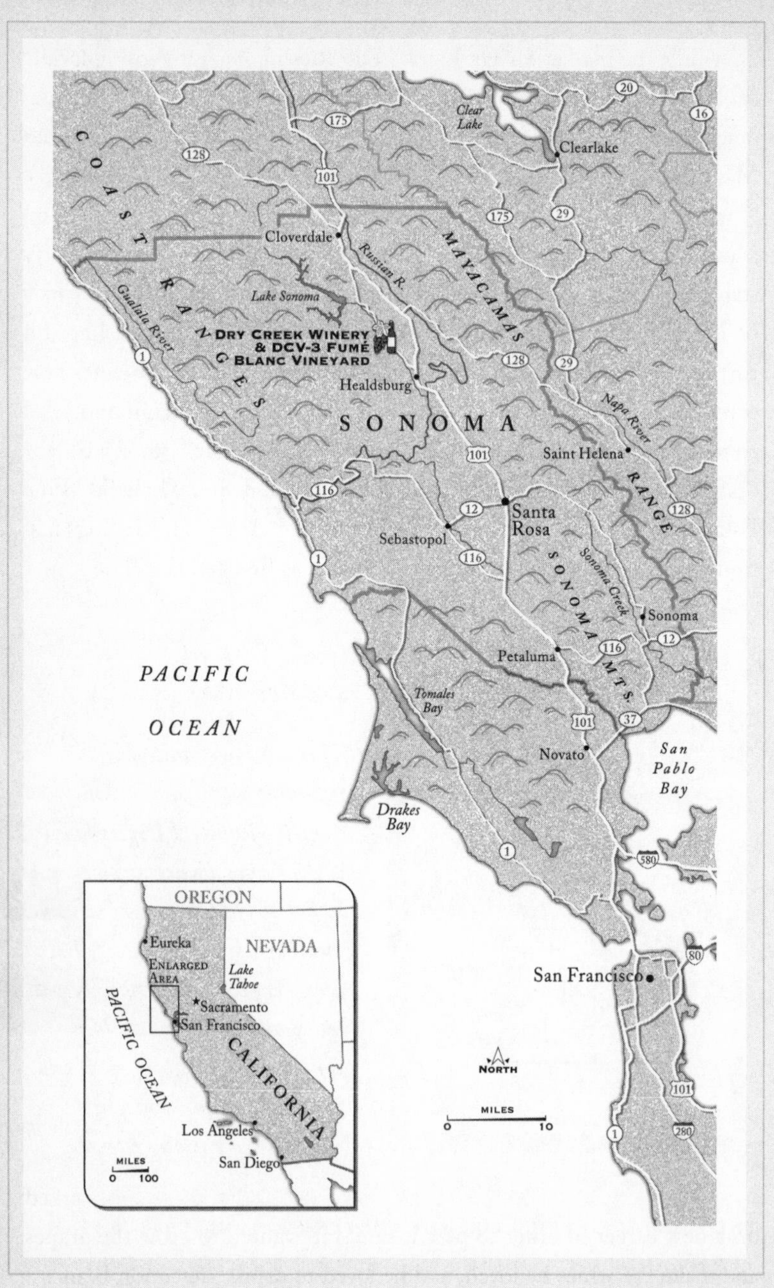

THE DRY CREEK WINERY AND ESTATE VINEYARD, IN NORTHERN SONOMA COUNTY

CHAPTER 13

DRY CREEK VINEYARD FUMÉ BLANC, DCV-3

Dry Creek Valley, California

...

Dave Stare liked it. Back in 1972, when he opened the first post-Prohibition winery in Sonoma County's Dry Creek Valley, he planted Sauvignon Blanc simply because he liked to drink wines made from that grape variety. Not many Americans did at the time. Sauvignon had the reputation of being something cheap and inferior, and few producers sold it as a stand-alone wine. The Sonoma County Farm Adviser whom Stare consulted about his new property recommended against planting it, contending not only that the grape was unpopular but also that the region was too cold for it. Stare didn't care. An engineer from Boston, he hadn't moved his family all the way across the country and embarked on a new career in order to play it safe. He wanted to grow the grapes and make the wines he loved, and he loved to drink Sauvignon Blanc.

Dave Stare in 1980

Stare was particularly fond of wines from the Upper Loire Valley in France—notably those from the twin appellations of Pouilly-Fumé and

Sancerre—so theirs was the style he wanted to pursue. Moreover, he knew that Joe Rochioli was growing a little Sauvignon at his property up the road, so he figured that planting it wouldn't be a complete crapshoot. If no one bought his wine, he'd throw a party and serve it to his guests; then next year he'd sell it in bulk for someone else to use in a blend. "I thought it was worth taking a chance," he says simply.

Dave Stare's gamble paid off, in spades. His Dry Creek Vineyard Fumé Blanc, initially made with purchased fruit, then with more and more estate fruit, was arguably the first modern American wine made from this particular grape variety to actually taste like it. "I wanted that aggressive, herbal grassy flavor," he says. "I like it." In the years since, Stare's winery has had its ups and downs, producing at times too many wines in too many styles at too many different quality levels. For a time, it even lost focus with this, its flagship varietal. But today, under the direction of his daughter, Kim Stare-Wallace, and her husband, Don Wallace, it has regained momentum. Dry Creek's standard Fumé Blanc, which carries a Sonoma County designation, tastes fresh and direct, but the true star of the show is a limited production bottling (one thousand cases or so) made entirely from grapes grown in the original vineyard, unromantically named "DCV-3." This was the first site Stare cleared and planted, and the wine from it exemplifies the style he pioneered in America—full of citrus and green berry flavors, with a racy herbaceous streak cutting all the way through. Other American wineries now make Sauvignon Blanc in this style, but Dry Creek Vineyard came first, and today's DCV-3 tastes as good as any.

Though Stare initially made the wine in the style he liked, paying little attention to alleged consumer preferences, he did make an initial concession to the marketplace: the wine's name. He called it Fumé rather than Sauvignon Blanc on the advice of his friend, Barney Fetzer of Fetzer Vineyards in Mendocino. "I remember Barney saying to me, 'Dave, that name will sell.' I was still learning that my business was selling wine, not just making it." While "Sauvignon" on the label doesn't hurt sales these days, it would have in the 1970s, when those few consumers who could pronounce it associated it with cheap California jug wines. Still, trying to forecast the volatile wine market can be tricky (as Stare would discover later), and the new name provided no guarantee. Don Wallace, who is passionate about the variety, wishes the alias hadn't been necessary, but understands why it was—and why it makes sense to still use it. "When you taste this wine," he says, holding up a glass of DCV-3, "you see that we're not trying to hide its varietal character. Maybe we did once, but these days we're very proud of the Sauvignon Blanc we grow. We still call the wine Fumé simply because we have a thirty-year tradition of doing so."

"Fumé Blanc" is an odd name. It was invented by Robert Mondavi in 1967, when his one-year-old Napa Valley winery was mortgaged to the proverbial hilt. To pay his bills, Mondavi needed to sell his young white wines as profitably and quickly as possible while waiting for his reds to mature. The problem was that he had a lot of Sauvignon Blanc, which few people wanted to buy as a varietal wine. So, with characteristic chutzpah, he decided to make a virtue out of necessity, and fabricated this *faux* French moniker.

Mondavi's barrel-fermented Fumé Blanc surprised even him by selling briskly, and his winery has been making it ever since. Yet while Mondavi deserves credit for helping to turn Sauvignon Blanc into a marketable American wine, his invention had a definite downside. For one, his rationale, while resuscitating the grape, also implicitly damned it. After all, he saw Sauvignon as something to make and sell while waiting for more important wines to develop. For another, the name, while a clever sales tool, was misleading. It sounded reminiscent of Pouilly-Fumé and assertive Loire-styled Sauvignons, but designated a wine made more according to a Bordeaux model, being wood-aged and vanilla-scented, with only moderate acidity and a fleshy rather than a crisp feel. Five years later, when Dave Stare decided to focus on Sauvignon Blanc, he followed suit with the name, but made a wine that tasted very different. It wasn't fermented or aged in wood, so offered no vanilla veneer. Instead, it was sharp and racy, a wine designed to wake the palate and enliven the senses. And that's what's strange about the name. "Fumé Blanc" has never designated a distinct style or a winemaking philosophy. It remains nothing more (and nothing less) than a marketing gimmick.

Whatever it's called, wine made with Sauvignon Blanc has a checkered American history. The grape first came to the United States in the nineteenth century. During the decades before Prohibition, California "Sauterne," misnamed in homage to wines from Bordeaux, proved quite popular. After Repeal, American "Sauterne," often with other grapes in the blend, tended increasingly to be vinified off-dry. It tasted sappy and sweet, and was disdained by consumers with a preference for dry wine. A revival of sorts started in the seventies and eighties, when the American wine boom exploded. At that point, some dry Sauvignon-based wines tasted soft and supple, like Mondavi's. A few others, like Stare's, tasted clean and fresh. But far more were vegetal and unpleasant. With flavors resembling canned peas or asparagus, they inevitably reflected vineyards in which yields had been allowed to get too high and foliage too abundant.

To be fair, most growers at the time did not truly understand this grape variety's idiosyncrasies and so did not know how best to trellis the vines and thin the canopies. But the wines also proved disappointing because so many vintners continued to regard Sauvignon Blanc as a cash cow. They thought of it as a wine they could make in large volume and sell quickly, so they wanted big yields and fast profits. When their wines tasted disagreeable, many then tried to tame the grape by treating it like Chardonnay, overwhelming its varietal character with oak. Though vintners (and some easily influenced writers) talked about flavors resembling melons and figs—descriptors used nowhere else in the world for Sauvignon Blanc—the wines in truth tasted predominantly of sappy vanilla and spice, the telltale sign of overexposure to wood.

Dry Creek Vineyards was not immune to these stylistic shifts. As production grew at the winery, so did pressure to follow the crowd and move away from the original style, one that had never been easy to market. Much as had happened years before at Robert Mondavi, Dave Stare wanted to sell his young white wines quickly in order to finance other aspects of the business. So, beginning in the late eighties, he and Larry Levine, his winemaker at the time, started aging some of their Sauvignon Blanc in wood, all because they thought that the sweet, smoky taste of oak would give the wine mass appeal.

For about seven years, Dry Creek's Sonoma County Fumé Blanc veered off its original course. It lost its tart citrus edge and became softer, sweeter, and significantly less distinctive. "Looking back," admits Don Wallace, "I think we sold out to the devil. The shift was all driven by marketing, and had nothing to do with wine quality." Paradoxically, though, the marketing turned out to be wrong. The 1990s saw a worldwide revival of interest in unmasked Sauvignon Blanc, led in large measure by the evident quality of wines made in that style coming from New Zealand. Before long, Wallace, Stare, and everyone else at Dry Creek realized their mistake. "So we went back to the future," says Wallace, "back to the wine we knew how to make, the wine we were passionate about." But they didn't go all the way back. Dry Creek continues to ferment a small amount of Fumé Blanc in French oak, resulting in a wine that to me seems as vapid as DCV-3 seems vivacious. And in 2004, the winery introduced a small-volume cuvée made from the perfumed Musqué clone—a wine that smells and tastes good but generic.

The DCV-3 Fumé Blanc debuted with the 1998 vintage as part of Dry Creek's stylistic revival. When Stare and the rest of the winemaking team decided to restore the basic Sonoma cuvée to its original, edgy, Loire-inspired self, Wallace began arguing that they should go a step further and demonstrate their renewed commitment with a single-vineyard version. His idea was to take only the best grapes from the original site, vinify them separately, and make a wine wholly expressive of its varietal character. "It's the purest form of Sauvignon Blanc we can make," he says. "It reflects both Dave's initial passion and our current one, because it tastes entirely of the grape."

But the grape has to come from somewhere, and DCV-3 tastes even more specifically of Dry Creek Valley Sauvignon Blanc. Neither as minerally as its original Loire Valley models nor as uncompromising as its contemporary New Zealand counterparts, it is fruit-forward, tasting first and foremost of lemons, limes, and grapefruit. A grassy, herbal (fresh thyme) vein remains evident but secondary, and the wine impresses most for its balance, being neither soft nor shrill. As such, it avoids the dual excesses that still mar so many California renditions, no matter which name adorns their labels. Having erred with the varietal once, Wallace is determined not to do so again. "We want this wine to taste as ripe and balanced as possible," he says. "That means making sure that nothing—not acid, not alcohol, not any one flavor—sticks out. It's like a star. All the points have to be equidistant. None should be bigger than the others."

The Dry Creek Valley is for the most part red wine country, notable in particular for Zinfandel, a variety that matures to near perfection on the western hillsides. Increasingly, however, growers are planting Sauvignon Blanc on the valley floor. Unlike Chardonnay, which performs much better in the cooler Russian River AVA, the variety can attain full ripeness without losing acidity and structure. "We're seeing a renaissance of Sauvignon in Dry Creek," notes Wallace. "More and more people are figuring out that it's *the* white grape to grow here." In addition to Dry Creek, Lambert Bridge, Preston, and Quivira do especially well with it, each producing a wine with true varietal character and plenty of charm.

"Sauvignon is the chameleon of white wines," Wallace says. "Depending on where it's grown, and what the winemaker does, it can be many different things." As long as those things don't involve covering up or hiding the grape's naturally expressive personality, that versatility is all to the good. After decades of largely dreary wines, American vintners finally are beginning to produce more than the occasionally good Sauvignon Blanc. The wines come in different styles. Some, like DCV-3, taste lean and racy. Others seem softer and more sinuous. But no matter the style, the key to success comes in getting the grapes ripe, and so avoiding the excessively vegetal aromas and flavors that marred so many earlier efforts. "But not too ripe," Wallace cautions. "If it gets too ripe, it won't taste like Sauvignon Blanc."

Harvesting this variety can be tricky. Pick the grapes too late, and the wine will end up hot, heavy, and excessively alcoholic, having lost aroma, harmony, and balance. Pick them too early, and the wine will taste harsh and weedy. In DCV-3, a relatively small (nineteen-acre) vineyard, the vines are monitored closely all summer long, the fruit evaluated for optimal maturity. The trick involves more than observation, for the vines need to be managed carefully through the growing season so as to restrain vigor. This entails thinning the canopies so that sunlight will hit the maturing fruit, but not so much so that the grapes will become sunburned. As much if not more than other varietals, quality Sauvignon Blanc comes primarily from decisions made in the vineyard, not the winery. Particularly with tank-fermented, early-bottled renditions like DCV-3, the winemaker's task is to retain what nature provides, not to enhance or add to it. "That's why it's so important to plant Sauvignon in the right place," argues Wallace, "and to take care of it properly there. Dave was right on the money with the location. Now we're getting better and better with the farming."

As that comment suggests, DCV-3 is still a wine in evolution. Because the vineyard was becoming tired and diseased, a multiyear replanting project began in late 2003. In order to ensure production of the wine, blocks are being cleared and replaced gradually, using cuttings from the best and healthiest original selections in addition to clean nursery stock. Viticulturalists today know much more about Sauvignon than they did thirty years ago, so the spacing, trellising, and training are all being changed. In time, then, the wine should become even more expressive and exuberant. "We're rededicating ourselves to it," Wallace says. "It's our passion."

That rededication is a hopeful sign—not only for Dry Creek Vineyard but also for American Sauvignon Blanc at large. With over 12,000 acres under vine, Sauvignon is the second most widely cultivated white vinifera variety in the country. The vast majority of the vineyards are in California, but growers have planted it, if only experimentally, in most of the other serious wine-producing states. Yet whether in California or Washington, New York, Texas, or Virginia, many vintners seem almost afraid of it. As a result, though hundreds of American Sauvignon Blancs come onto the market every year, surprisingly few taste distinctive. Dave Stare contends that there's a bias against the varietal in the press, so that when compared with Chardonnay, it inevitably gets relegated to a supporting role. "The *[Wine] Spectator* never gives a Sauvignon Blanc ninety-five points," he laments. "It's always presented as a second-choice wine." But surely more problematic than critics' comments are the puzzling attitudes of many American winemakers, those who mistakenly believe that barrel fermentation and oak aging distinguish all top white wines, no matter the grape variety or the vineyard site.

At revitalized Dry Creek, the winemaking team, now led by Bill Knuttel, avoids that mistake by deliberately following a traditional Loire Valley model. In particular, they look to the Sancerres from Henri Bourgeois for inspiration. That family-owned French firm purchases fruit for its basic cuvée from contract growers while making smaller lots of wine from grapes grown in individual, estate vineyards. That's the model that Dry Creek follows, and the wine from DCV-3 is very much patterned on Bourgeois's celebrated "La Bourgeoise."

A small but growing group of American vintners are embracing this pure style of Sauvignon Blanc. Some listen to a Loire muse while others look to New Zealand, but whatever the motivation, wines from the likes of Mason, St. Supéry, Philip Togni, and Voss are helping revive interest in Sauvignon as a first-class varietal. Still, far more wines continue to disappoint, as do many American white wines made from other aromatic grapes. The paucity of superior Sauvignon Blancs, Rieslings, Gewurztraminers, and Muscats in the United States can be traced directly to the misguided but prevalent notion that one winemaking model is inherently superior to others. As the example of the improved quality of American Pinot Noir demonstrates, red wine vintners are learning the value of taking different approaches to different varieties in different places. Surely it's time for more white wine winemakers to follow suit. The story of Fumé Blanc at Dry Creek Vineyard provides both a cautionary and an exemplary illustration of why.

A NOTE ON VINTAGES:

DCV-3 Fumé Blanc is very much a wine to drink young, when its bright, vibrant flavors have not been dimmed by the passage of time. The wine has tasted true to form every year since its initial release in 1998, but I'd advise drinking only the youngest, hence freshest vintage.

THE SUGGESTED PRICE FOR THE CURRENT 2004 RELEASE IS $25.

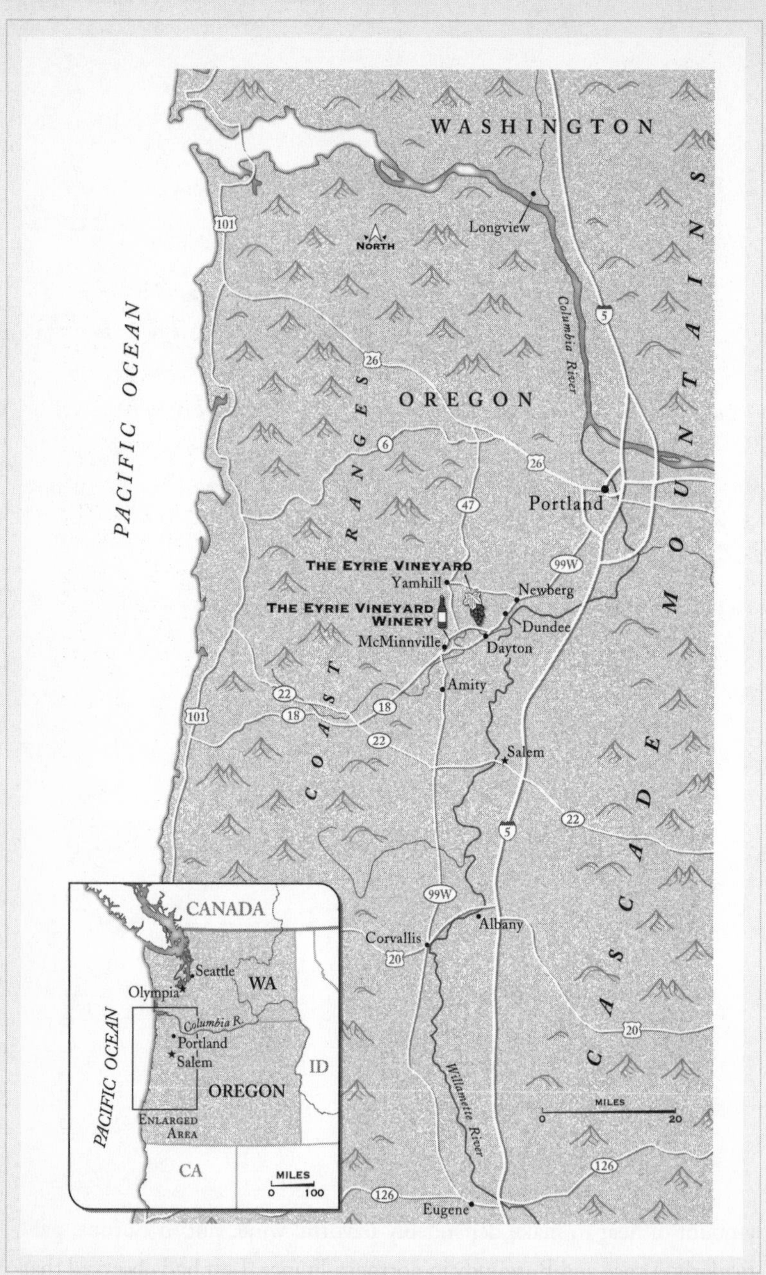

THE EYRIE VINEYARD AND WINERY

CHAPTER 14

The Eyrie Vineyards Pinot Gris

Willamette Valley, Oregon

...

David Lett is a contrarian. "Always have been," he grins. Back in 1965, when the California wine renaissance was just beginning, Lett, who had earned a master's degree in viticulture at UC Davis, moved to Oregon, a state with such a limited history of wine growing that renewal or rebirth was never at issue. No one knew whether the state could produce decent wine, and most of the admittedly few people pondering the question had doubts. Lett's professors at Davis, for instance, thought he was crazy. But Lett had just returned from an eye-opening trip to Europe, and his was the craziness of the converted. The Davis professors preached the gospel of warmth, declaring that grapes need to receive a comfortable amount of heat to make dependably flavorful wine. But in Europe, particularly Alsace and Burgundy in northern France, Lett had observed that many of the best wines come from regions in which grapes struggle to ripen, the absence of heat being as important as its presence. "I discov-

David Lett

ered," he says, "that in order for a wine to express the true flavor of the grape, you have to plant the vine in just the right place."

California, at least the California Lett knew, was simply too hot for many grape varieties, so he went where it was cooler—the Willamette Valley, some thirty miles south of Portland. There, he approached what to plant by using grapes from the coolest French wine-growing regions—Alsace, Burgundy, and Champagne. His was the first planting of Pinot Noir and Chardonnay in the Willamette Valley, the first of Pinot Gris in all the United States. In 1966, Lett and his wife, Diana, founded the Eyrie Vineyards, naming it for the red-tailed hawks who made their nest in the fir trees at the top of the vineyard. In the years since, two generations of Oregon vintners have followed him, and the vast majority have planted the varieties he pioneered. Today, western Oregon produces some of America's finest Pinot Noirs, as well as the country's very best Pinot Gris. Lett, or "Papa Pinot," as he is affectionately known in the wine-growing community, continues to make wines from both grapes. His Noir—light, lithe, and more delicate than most American renditions—ages remarkably well. And his Gris, bright and bracing, is marked by a mineral-tinged complexity rarely found in dry wines made from this variety. The first successful American version, it sets a quality standard—in Oregon and beyond. "It's a wine with class," says Lett proudly.

Pinot Gris is something of a contrarian itself. Though it can produce a very light, almost colorless white wine, it actually is a genetic mutation of dark-skinned Pinot Noir. Like Noir, it is a historic variety, and so prone to clonal instability. Also like Noir, it was first cultivated seriously in Burgundy, where under the name "Beurot," it was traditionally used to soften red wines. These two members of the Pinot family are so closely related that it is nearly impossible to tell them apart in the vineyard. Only after veraison, the stage of grape development when the berries begin to soften and change color—Noir to purple and Gris to pinkish gray—do their disparate identities become apparent. Pinot Gris grows under a multitude of monikers throughout Europe—as Malvoisie in Switzerland, Szurkebarát in Hungary, Rulandac Sivi in the Balkans, and both Rulander and Grauburgunder in Germany. But it is in Alsace, where for a long time it was called Tokay, and Italy, where the name is Pinot Grigio, that it makes the wines most people know.

These two could not be more different. In Alsace, Pinot Gris is rich and lush, with a musky, honeyed, succulent character. Even when vinified completely dry (and most examples are not), it conveys a fecund impression of ripeness. By contrast, northern Italian Pinot Grigio tastes crisp and light. A good version may offer a faint suggestion of minerality or spice, but its chief virtue is invigorating acidity. The fact that one grape can yield two such contrary styles demonstrates that it's a variety, and a wine, of many surprises.

Eyrie Pinot Gris surprises yet again because it fits neither profile. Though it offers a somewhat honeyed bouquet, becoming more expressive with time in the bottle, it does not reach an Alsatian level of richness, and so finishes deliciously dry, with nary a hint of sugar. And while it tastes refreshing, like its Italian counterparts, it offers much more flavor—a mélange of apple, citrus, and most notably pear fruit, along with marked mineral undertones, and a faintly floral scent. Its distinction surely comes from the fact that the cool Willamette Valley limits yields and allows the different Pinot grapes to express their varietal personalities. Whether red or white, the good wines here taste first and foremost of the grape, their complexity reflecting an interplay of fruit flavors rather than added ones from vinification or barrel aging. As David Lett puts it, "There's absolutely no reason to grow grapes here except for their amazing varietal flavors."

The Willamette Valley stretches some 150 miles from the Portland suburbs south past Eugene. The vineyards lie scattered in the foothills of the Coast Range, and though grapes are cultivated up and down the eastern side of the Willamette River, the most valuable sites almost all lie in the northern end of the valley. That's because the climate gradually warms as you head south, and most Oregon vintners, being Pinot devotees, want their vines to receive just enough, but not too much, heat. That is a difficult balance to achieve, particularly since weather patterns can change significantly from year to year, meaning that vintage variation becomes more of an issue in Oregon than in California or Washington. Still, the best wines tend to come from vineyards and wineries located in three northern Willamette subregions: the Eola Hills near Salem; the Chehalem Ridge near Portland; and the Red Hills of Dundee, midway between. The difference between these three is less climatic than geological, as each has a distinct soil type (or types). In the Dundee Hills, home to The Eyrie Vineyards, the predominant soil is called "jory." It has a dark red color, due to high iron content, and is fairly deep, with excellent water-holding capability. As Lett tells it, he chose to locate his vineyard there when he drilled down with an auger and, unlike other places he tried, didn't immediately hit rock. The elevation, high enough so as not to be plagued by spring frost, and the exposure, primarily southeast, seemed good, but Lett had no way of knowing that this ruddy-colored soil would turn out to be so well suited to Pinot Gris and Noir. "I just guessed right," he admits. "This place is what gives the wines their finesse."

Understatement and finesse are Eyrie trademarks, so much so that Lett's Pinot Noir can get overlooked by critics in comparative tastings, where "bigger is better" often rules. But it is difficult to disregard his Pinot Gris, since the wine's subtle flavors are supported by just the right degree of acidity to ensure nearly ideal balance. The crucial factor with the Pinot varieties, Lett contends, comes in knowing when to pick the grapes. Harvest too early, and the wine will taste sour; too late, and it will be unfocused and blowsy. "I've made all the mistakes," he says, laughing, "but I think I know what I'm doing now." Many vintners in Alsace, as well as plenty in the Willamette Valley, let their grapes hang long on the vine, their goal being a wine with textural weight and richness. "But if you let the grapes get overripe," Lett scoffs, "you lose varietal character." So he harvests earlier than many of his neighbors. In the winery, he both ferments and ages the wine in stainless steel, never allowing it to come into contact with wood and unwanted oxidation. The wine stays on its lees (the spent yeast and sediment) until bottling (usually nine months or so after harvest), enhancing complexity, but unlike wines in barrel, not introducing any new or foreign flavors. "I've reinvented the wheel with Pinot Gris a bunch of times," Lett notes. "I've tried everything with it over the years. But I've got to say, I think the wine I'm making now is pretty darn good."

When he planted the original Eyrie vineyard, Lett only put in 160 vines of Pinot Gris. That's because he was experimenting with all sorts of early maturing grapes—Gewurztraminer, Riesling, Muscat Ottonel, and more—all in an effort to learn which varieties were best suited to the Willamette Valley. "But my heart was always in the Pinots," he recalls. "As for the rest of them, it was a question of what would and what wouldn't work." His first commercial vintage came in 1970. "I have to admit, I didn't much like the Pinot Gris," he confesses, "but the Pinot Noir was even worse." Back then, Lett practiced seat of the pants viticulture and trial by error winemaking. But he was a quick study. His fortunes improved noticeably nine years later, when a bottle of Eyrie 1975 South Block Pinot Noir bested a number of Burgundies in a grand tasting held in Paris. The international press picked up the story, which proved critical in putting Oregon on the world wine map.

Perhaps not surprisingly, Oregon Pinot Noir was all that the American market cared about at the time. "I couldn't sell the Gris," Lett remembers. "I literally had to give it away to restaurants. If people got it on their lips, they loved it. But it was hell getting them to try it." Further complicating matters, when consumers thought about white wine, they usually wanted Chardonnay. After all, since Oregon had demonstrated that it could produce Burgundian-styled reds, logic suggested that it could do the same with whites. Perhaps someday it will, and today's wines can be quite good, but the vast majority of Chardonnay vineyards in Oregon in the 1970s and 1980s consisted of inappropriate clones, and most of the wines tasted tart and unappealing. And having experienced a sour mouthful of one Oregon white, few people wanted to try another, especially since Pinot Gris was a varietal that hardly any consumers knew at the time. As late as the early eighties, nearly twenty years after his move to Oregon, Lett was producing only five hundred or so cases of Gris, and struggling to sell them. "I'd trade bottles of the wine to salmon fishermen on the coast," he remembers. "It's a wine that goes great with salmon."

That food and wine match, coupled with the interest in Gris then being expressed by a few other Oregon winemakers, helped lead to the varietal's eventual success in the marketplace. By the mid-1980s, when "I finally got it through my thick skull that I had to work to make this a successful wine," Lett decided to try to expand the local production. To that end, he supplied cuttings from his vineyard to anyone interested in planting them, including two fellow Oregon wine pioneers, David Adelsheim and Dick Ponzi. Before long these three friends embarked on what Lett calls their "Three Musketeers' marketing trips," going across the country, introducing consumers and wine professionals alike to Oregon Pinot Gris—invariably poured with salmon. It worked. And as consumers began to pay attention, so did a new wave of winemakers.

The most important of this second generation of Oregon vintners was Ed King III, who in 1992 released the first wines from King Estate, a large (75,000-case-production) winery located near Eugene. Inspired in large measure by the Eyrie wines, King focused primarily on Pinot Noir and Gris, making significantly more of the latter. Though the King Estate vineyards today yield an increasingly large percentage of the grapes for the wines, he began his operation in the early nineties by purchasing fruit and blending wines. His expressed need for Gris led growers throughout Oregon to devote more acreage to it, so that supply and demand grew apace. And most important, King's wine tasted good. Though it was neither as complex nor as subtle as Eyrie's, it was much more widely available, and soon started showing up on restaurant lists and retail shelves all across the country. So, after David Lett pioneered Oregon Pinot Gris and made the wine that convinced his compatriots to grow it, King Estate's success with it brought it to wider attention.

Today, that attention is not exclusive to Oregon. Good Pinot Gris is being grown and produced in cool regions here and there across the country—in California's Russian River Valley, for example, as well as the Shenandoah Valley in Virginia, and Michigan's Old Mission Peninsula. And though not from the United States, the wines grown in the

Okanagan Valley in British Columbia can be stunning. Vintners in all these places, like their Oregon colleagues, owe Lett their gratitude. He led the way that they followed.

Pinot Gris today is firmly established as a significant Oregon varietal, the top white wine grape grown and produced in the state. Still, production at Eyrie remains small. Lett makes roughly five thousand cases of Gris each year, an amount that accounts for about half his total production. (Pinot Noir takes up about another 2,500 cases, with Chardonnay, Pinot Meunier, Pinot Blanc, and Muscat accounting for the rest.) "I've never wanted to grow too big," he says, "too big" being defined as when one person no longer can oversee all aspects of both the viticulture and the winemaking. Most Oregon wineries are similarly sized—in part because vintners are conscious of the Burgundy parallel, but even more due to the fact that yields in the Willamette Valley are naturally low.

Lett gets approximately 3 tons per acre of Pinot Gris from his vineyards (he now owns four separate sites), and though some growers do harvest more, the region remains unsuited to large-scale viticulture. There are few large swaths of land appropriate to grapes, and the climate restrains vigor. As a result, even large Oregon wineries, like King Estate, are small when compared to those in California or Washington, and Oregon wines remain the province more of the cognoscenti than of casual consumers. Though their work often gets them enthusiastic international recognition, Oregon vintners tend to eschew celebrity, thinking of themselves primarily as farmers, thus reinforcing their (sometimes cultivated) image of homespun charm. That may explain why so many of them practice sustainable agriculture. Only a handful of Oregon vineyards are certified as organic, but a significant number of growers employ organic principles and techniques. As with so many things, David Lett did so first. "I've been growing grapes organically since day one," he declares. "But I have no interest in getting involved with some bureaucracy to get a certificate. I just grow grapes the right way, and I always have."

Ever the individual and, yes, the contrarian, Lett continues to do things his own way. "I make atypical wines even here," he says, with more than a hint of pride in his voice. He mocks the international trend toward heady wines that "just taste of alcohol," and bemoans what he sees as an increased standardization and homogenization in the marketplace. Closer to home, he contends that too many of his Oregon compatriots have succumbed to the pressure of that marketplace, producing wines designed to garner high scores from influential critics rather than provide personal pleasure. "Look," he says, "there are only a few places in the world where you can grow grapes and make wines that have the true flavors of the Pinot varieties. This is one of them, and that's what I do."

It is difficult to know what will happen to The Eyrie Vineyards in the years to come. Lett still has plenty of drive and energy, but after nearly forty years of growing grapes and making wine, retirement cannot be too far away. As of now, no successor is waiting to take the helm when he steps down. Yet in a sense, all the other Oregon vintners are his heirs, and Oregon wine as a whole is his legacy. Lett's contemporary compatriots do not necessarily make wines in his style. Like all offspring, they struggle to assert their own identity. But a trace of his idiosyncratic spirit can be sensed in most of the better Willamette Valley wineries, where varietal choice is dictated not by marketing trends or strategies but by the reality of vineyard *terroir*. In their devotion to Pinot, both Gris and Noir, today's best Oregon vintners build upon the foundation laid at Eyrie. And at least for now, Lett continues to produce wines that, in their elegance and grace, set a difficult standard to reach. "Mine is a simple philosophy," he says. "I like to drink what I grow. I'm fortunate that I found a good place to grow Pinots. They're the wines I most like to drink."

A NOTE ON VINTAGES:

This wine ages surprisingly well, becoming leaner and stonier as its primary fruit flavors fade, but staying focused and balanced for many years. A bottle of 1983, tasted in 2003, was remarkably lively. Strong recent vintages include 1990, 1999, 2000, 2002, and 2003.

THE SUGGESTED PRICE FOR THE CURRENT 2003 VINTAGE IS $16.

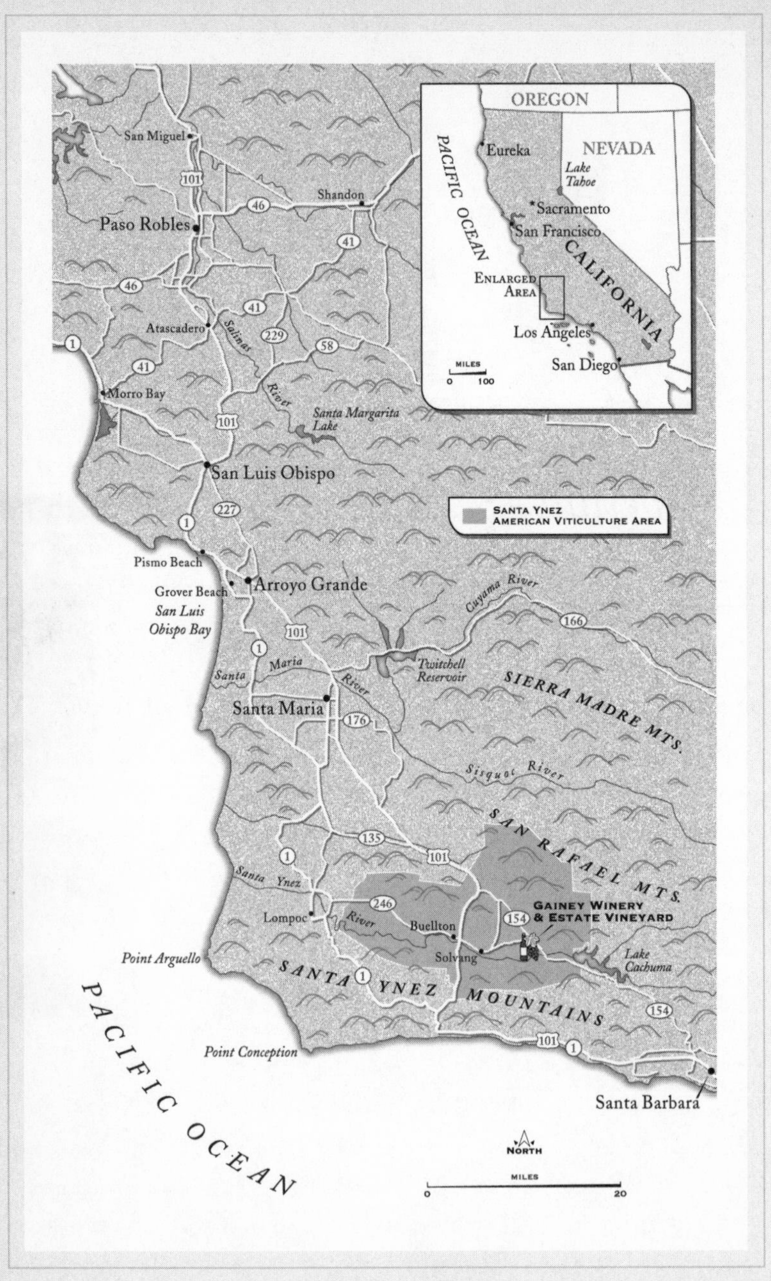

THE GAINEY WINERY AND HOME VINEYARD,

IN THE SANTA YNEZ AVA

CHAPTER 15

GAINEY VINEYARD SAUVIGNON BLANC, LIMITED SELECTION

Santa Ynez Valley, California

...

On the eastern edge of California's Santa Ynez Valley, roughly thirty miles north of Santa Barbara, the winemaking team at Gainey Vineyard produces one of the few American Sauvignon Blancs with a stylistic identity all its own. Most consistently good examples of this varietal echo foreign models. For example, Dry Creek Vineyard's DCV-3 Fumé Blanc, the only other Sauvignon included in this book, is deliberately fashioned to resemble a Loire Valley wine. It tastes delicious but to some degree derivative. Much the same is true of the Sauvignon Blancs from producers such as Napa's Duckhorn and Spottswoode that are fashioned more in line with a Bordeaux paradigm. But Kirby Anderson, the energetic young winemaker at Gainey, insists that any wine he makes must taste first and foremost of the grapes grown in Santa Ynez. "I love Sancerre," he admits, "and I'd love to make a wine like it. But I can't do that here. My objective with Sauvignon has to be to make a fruit-filled, varietally true *California* wine."

Dan H. Gainey

That Anderson is succeeding is a testament not only to his own talent but also to his and the Gainey family's commitment to Sauvignon Blanc. They consider it a legitimately noble grape, one capable of producing elegant, graceful wines marked by finesse and flair. Only a handful of American vintners share that view. Most others treat Sauvignon more like a workhorse, a competent grape yielding primarily second-class wine, especially when compared to Chardonnay. Anderson and the Gaineys make a quite impressive rendition of that more popular white variety, a Limited Selection Chardonnay that critics regularly praise. But they justifiably are no less proud of their Sauvignon Blanc.

Does the fact that the general qualitative level of California Chardonnay is higher than California Sauvignon mean that the latter is the more difficult grape to grow and wine to make? "They're so different," says Anderson diplomatically, when contemplating that suggestion. "I don't think it makes sense to compare them." At the same time, he argues that "it also doesn't make sense to say that one's better than the other. Both can make really good wine." And boring wine, as so much American Sauvignon Blanc regrettably is these days. Gainey's Limited Selection Sauvignon stands out because it tastes genuinely exciting—fresh and aromatic, yet at the same time rich and substantial. It is not clearly superior to the small number of other top-notch American Sauvignons, but it is conspicuous for its distinctively homegrown character. Its zesty but polished personality demonstrates that Sauvignon Blanc in the United States need not speak with a foreign accent.

Like all vinifera grape varieties, Sauvignon Blanc came to the United States from Europe, and vintners here inevitably make their wines with foreign archetypes in mind. What complicates matters with this variety, and surely has contributed to the confusion surrounding it, is the fact that Sauvignon is used to make two very different but equally distinguished styles of wine abroad. The first emphasizes, even accentuates, the grape's naturally aggressive character, while the second tries to tame it, both by blending Sauvignon with other varieties and by aging the wine in oak. Wines from the Graves and Pessac-Léognan appellations in Bordeaux exemplify this softer style. Customarily barrel-aged and blended with

Semillon (sometimes Muscadelle as well), the best examples exhibit nutty, custardy, occasionally even slightly honeyed flavors. By contrast, wines made in the sharper style taste of green berries and tart grapefruit, with a grassy, herbal edge. The Upper Loire Valley in France is the original European home of this style, but wines from New Zealand, especially the Marlborough region of the South Island, have taken it to a new level of intensity. The best examples display a startling clarity of fruit flavor. They seem razor-sharp.

Though Dry Creek Vineyard and a handful of other producers do make first-rate unmasked Sauvignon Blancs, most American vintners prefer to fashion softer, rounder wines. In doing so, they often use the white Bordeaux model as a rationale if not an excuse. This has been true for a long time. Whether sweet or dry, pre-Prohibition California whites that included Sauvignon in the blend tended to be sold under Bordeaux-inspired generic names such as "Sauterne" or "Haut Sauterne." More recently, when the supposed predilection of consumers for the aroma and taste of wood led many winemakers to begin aging Sauvignon in barrel, producers (or their marketing agents) often invoked Bordeaux as a model. But since the climate in southwestern France is both wetter and cooler than in most American Sauvignon Blanc vineyards, similar winemaking techniques often can yield markedly different results. Especially in the hotter California Viticultural Areas, this grape variety can develop so fast that it will attain technical ripeness without full maturity and aromatic development. The result all too frequently is a wine high in alcohol but lacking fruit flavor. Not surprisingly, exposure to wood, particularly if the wine first has been fermented in tank, can obliterate what little varietal character the vineyard has provided. Moreover, as the Dry Creek example illustrates, even vintners who respect the grape's inherent grassy temperament can be seduced by market pressures into trying to mute it. As a result, the number of American producers with anything resembling a track record of achievement with Sauvignon Blanc is remarkably small.

Even though the Gainey Limited Selection Sauvignon is partially barrel-fermented and then barrel-aged (for ten months, with about 10 percent of the wood new), it does not display the pronounced vanilla and caramel flavors that characterize so many renditions made in this fashion. That's because its fruit flavors prove extremely focused and pronounced. "I want to use the wood to help bring out that fruit character, not to compete with it," insists Kirby Anderson. Oak and Sauvignon Blanc certainly can integrate happily, but a successful marriage can be difficult to attain. This grape's acidity often clashes with the wood tannin, leaving the wine unfocused, its components at odds with one another. Even in Bordeaux, the wood can prove too strong. "You've got to be really careful with it," Anderson admits. "Just a little too much exposure and the wine becomes unbalanced." At Gainey, the barrel influence is evident in the wine's texture much more than the taste. Medium-bodied, the Limited Selection Sauvignon Blanc feels seductively creamy, conveying an impression of richness that enhances its exciting citrus flavors, making it brighter than most Bordeaux, but lusher than most Loire or New Zealand Sauvignons.

Kirby Anderson never refers to foreign stylistic models when discussing this wine. That's in part because he finds most white Bordeaux varietally indistinct. "Any wine I make," he insists, "has to taste of the grape. That's what distinguishes good California wine, no matter the varietal." At the same time, he does not look to more fruit-forward Loire or New Zealand Sauvignons for inspiration. He considers many Kiwi wines too showy, and while he certainly admires good Loire wines from Pouilly-Fumé and Sancerre, he knows that the Santa Ynez *terroir* does not yield the sort of minerality that makes those wines so special. "All those styles are not our style," he says. "We don't have the high acids here. Or the secondary, non-fruit flavors. And we don't keep the residual sugar." Instead of looking abroad, Anderson focuses on what the Gainey home vineyard gives him—in his words, "so much juicy fruit that the wood just can't take over." His goal is to craft a wine that is neither too aggressive nor too tame, one that may echo the foreign standard-bearers but that has its own sumptuous style. "We've done that successfully in California with Cabernet, Chardonnay, and other varietals," he says. "So why shouldn't we do it with this one?"

Anderson is the third winemaker at Gainey, a winery that forms part of a large, diversified Santa Barbara farming and ranching operation. Father and son proprietors Dan J. and Dan H. Gainey grow vegetables, raise cattle, and breed Arabian horses; but grapes, while occupying only 85 acres of their 1,800-acre estate, receive their most sustained attention. The Gainey wines, red as well as white, have garnered awards and critical acclaim for nearly twenty years, and wine growing is the family's largest source of income. Their home vineyard, first planted in 1983, lies in the warm eastern end of the Santa Ynez Valley. It is devoted largely to Bordeaux varieties, since this upstream area receives sufficient heat to ripen those varieties. The family also owns a vineyard on the cooler, Pacific-influenced side of the Viticultural Area. This narrow funnel introduces the AVA. Called the Santa Rita Hills, it is a prime area for cool-climate grapes, and the Gaineys grow their Chardonnay, Pinot Noir, and Syrah there.

As these different vineyard plantings suggest, the Gaineys are acutely aware that different grapes should be cultivated in different sites. This is a lesson that many American vintners have learned painfully, but perhaps because of their farming background, the Gaineys understood it instinctively from the very beginning of their winegrowing operation. They continually have urged their winemakers—first Hugo Oswald, then Rick Longoria, and now Anderson—to craft wines that reflect the character of the fruit that comes from their land. Although their Sauvignon Blancs have seen subtle stylistic shifts over the years, the best examples always have tasted primarily of the Gainey home vineyard grapes, with a pronounced citrus (lime and grapefruit) charm, a supple texture, and a firm core of acidity to provide balance.

When Dan H. Gainey first suggested to his father that they put in a vineyard beside the grazing fields on the family's home ranch, no one was growing grapes or making wine in the eastern half of the Santa Ynez Valley. "We really didn't know what to plant," he recalls with a laugh. The UC Davis heat summation system identified the property as Region III, meaning that it was judged warm enough for Bordeaux grapes, so the Gaineys dutifully planted Cabernet Sauvignon, Merlot, Sauvignon

Blanc, and a little Semillon. As time passed, it became clear that the Davis scale, while a fair general indicator, did not take into account the particularities of their property. Rick Longoria was the winemaker for twelve of the winery's first thirteen years, and try as he might, he was never able to craft a Cabernet that did not taste green and undeveloped. Yet from the start, the Sauvignon Blancs he made tasted delicious. This particular place apparently was well suited to this particular variety, as the accumulation of relatively even summer heat allowed the grapes to become mature without becoming overripe and hence losing either aroma or acidity. "It didn't take long," Gainey remembers, "to see that wines made from these grapes could be really special."

So, even though most California producers viewed Sauvignon Blanc as a bit player, the Gaineys decided to treat it as a star. Doing so involved making careful selections after the harvest, keeping individual lots separate after fermentation, and sparing no expense in the winery. Even more important was the attention devoted to the vineyard, where yields were kept relatively low—roughly 3 tons per acre. More than most vinifera varieties, Sauvignon vines need to be tended extremely carefully, as excessive vigor can lead to the vegetative flavors that make some Sauvignon Blancs taste unappealing. Little viticultural research on the variety was available when the Gaineys first planted their vineyard, so they farmed through trial and error. The vineyard team was not always successful with every block, and in the early days some lots of wine did taste coarse and green. But since Sauvignon Blanc was valued so highly at Gainey, these were separated out, and the bottled wines rarely exhibited harsh flavors.

At first, those wines came in separate styles, reflecting Sauvignon Blanc's dual heritage. Rick Longoria fashioned two quite different Sauvignons: a fairly assertive, stainless-steel-tank–fermented, Loire-styled one; and a richer, rounder, barrel-fermented, Bordeaux-fashioned selection. Over the years, both wines sold well, but because Gainey presented the varietal to the public in these two separate guises, the first an Oak Leaf selection, the second the Limited Selection, its commitment to the grape was to some degree divided against itself.

When Kirby Anderson came aboard in 1996, he and the Gaineys agreed to narrow the gap between these two wines. To do so, Anderson took it as his goal to find a stylistic middle ground that would function as an assertion of particularity. In pursuing that objective, he focused on the Gainey wines themselves, not on distant paradigms. For the Limited Selection Sauvignon, he shortened the amount of time the wine spends in oak, reduced the number of new barrels, blocked malolactic fermentation, and stirred the lees less often—all in order to preserve the grapes' natural flavors and aromas. And for the leaner Oak Leaf offering, he introduced some barrel fermentation in order to make the wine feel richer and rounder, thus approaching the stylistic midpoint from two directions simultaneously.

Similar changes came in the vineyard. The Gainey crew began cutting off more vertical shoots from the maturing vines and pulling leaves that might shield the grapes from light, again aiming for full fruit rather than vegetal flavor. At the same time, Anderson asked them to farm one block of vines differently, so that the grapes there would attain a pronounced herbaceous character that he could use in different proportions to enhance the two final blends. "We had to go slowly," he acknowledges, "because we didn't want to alienate customers. In fact, the transition is still ongoing." That transition has affected both bottlings, and tasting a vertical series of vintages demonstrates how close the two wines have become. The winery produces roughly equal amounts of them (about 4,000 total cases), and Anderson acknowledges that the day may well arrive when Gainey will make just one Sauvignon Blanc in one homegrown style.

At present, the Limited Selection Sauvignon is still the more nuanced, complete wine. It displays superior balance, with vibrant fruit flavors poised against a firm refreshing backdrop of acidity. Crisp and lively, it also seems supple and multilayered, in part as a result of Anderson's use of about 10 percent Semillon in the final blend. "Semillon in other places adds weight and width to a wine," he says. "But here in Santa Ynez, it contributes lift. I have no idea why that happens, but it does." That lift or extra level of complexity gives this wine individuality, making it seem simultaneously light and lush, an admittedly paradoxical but clearly compelling combination found in few Sauvignon Blancs grown anywhere.

Dan H. Gainey's and Kirby Anderson's focus on the particularities of the grapes grown in the Gainey estate vineyard helps explain what makes this particular wine so distinctive. In the particulars of body, aroma, and flavor, it very much goes its own way, and so reflects a deep-seated respect for the varietal as cultivated in California and even more specifically in Santa Ynez. "We want both of our Sauvignon Blancs to taste lively and fresh," Anderson notes. "The Limited Selection comes from our best vines, so it may taste fuller. But it still has to have clear varietal character. In California, the taste of fruit always has to come first."

Although such respect for Sauvignon Blanc has been notably absent from most American wineries' programs, it is heartening to observe that over the past decade the team at Gainey has been joined by a number of other producers aiming to make equally distinguished wines. These include relative newcomers like Mason, Selene, and Voss in California, as well as Linden in Virginia, and more established producers such as Dry Creek and Rochioli in Sonoma, Cain in Napa, Chateau Ste. Michelle in Washington, and Gainey's neighbors in Santa Ynez, Babcock, and Brander, all of whom are displaying considerable enthusiasm for the variety. Their combined efforts mark a step in a journey American vintners and wine drinkers alike are taking toward at long last accepting Sauvignon Blanc for what it is—a grape capable of producing truly complex, riveting wines. But then, the folks at Gainey have known that for a long time. Their deep-seated respect for this grape as a grape, rather than simply for imported wines made from it, accounts for their wine's superiority. In that, they and their wine stand alone.

A NOTE ON VINTAGES:

Like virtually all New World Sauvignon Blancs, this wine's charm comes from its vibrant spring-like flavors. Time in bottle only dulls that appeal, so it's a wine to drink young—as young, in fact, as possible. The older vintages I sampled when visiting at Gainey Vineyard were fine but nowhere near as exciting as the youngest, freshest one (at that point, from 2002).

THE SUGGESTED PRICE FOR THE CURRENT 2003 VINTAGE IS $18.

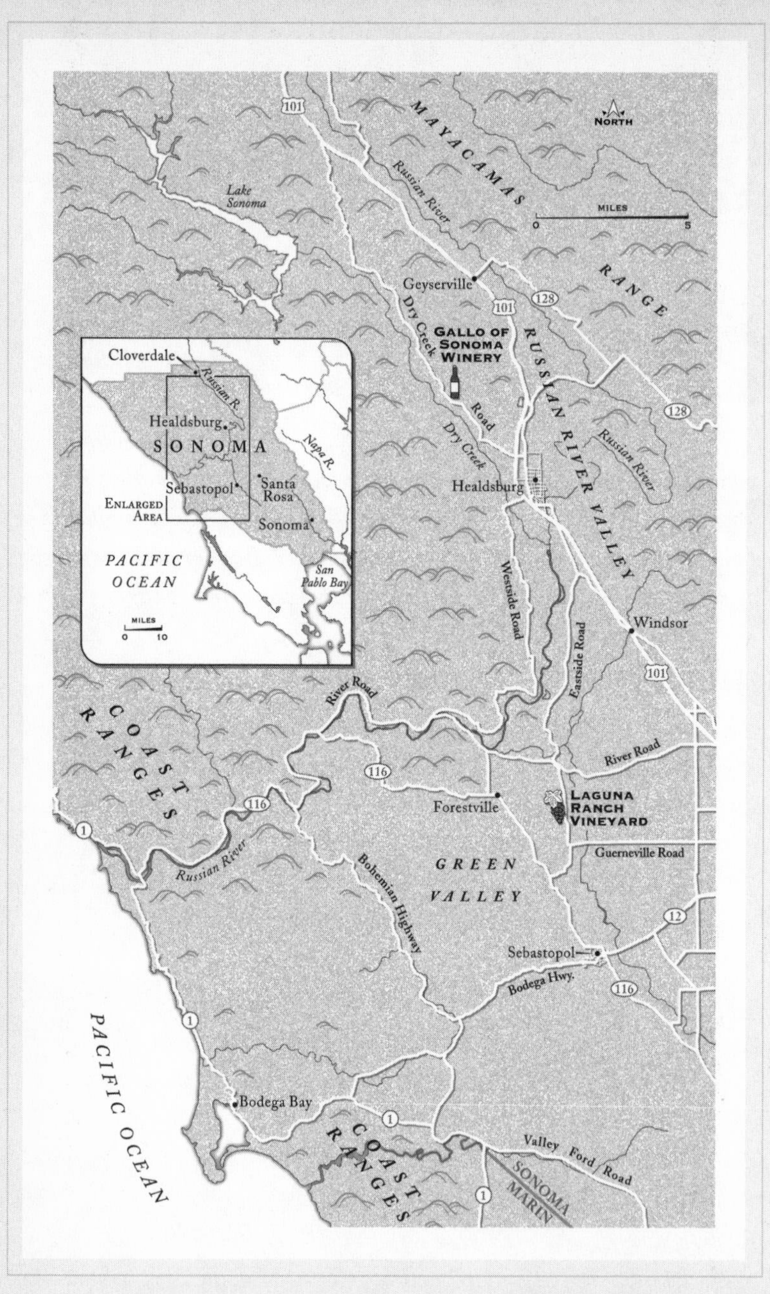

GALLO OF SONOMA'S LAGUNA RANCH VINEYARD,
IN SONOMA COUNTY'S RUSSIAN RIVER VALLEY

CHAPTER 16

GALLO OF SONOMA CHARDONNAY, LAGUNA RANCH VINEYARD

Russian River Valley, California

...

Gina Gallo

The Russian River traverses multiple *terroirs* as it wends its way across California's northern Sonoma County. Entering from Mendocino County, it meanders south through the broad, open Alexander Valley, winds past the town of Healdsburg, and then cuts west, flowing through groves of dense pines and redwoods, until finally emptying into the Pacific. When the river turns toward the setting sun, the surrounding valley narrows and grows cooler. Sites near the coast, where heavy fog covers the ground each morning, can get downright chilly. The soils change as well, with sand and gravel replacing clay and loam near the ocean. The Russian River American Viticultural Area (AVA) covers only the last leg of this journey, but its political boundaries extend far, and there are marked variations within it. Though grapes grow all over, the more vigorous eastern side is Zinfandel and hearty red wine country, while the foggier west is renowned for the more delicate Burgundy varietals, with Russian River Chardonnay having an especially illustrious track record. Sonoma-Cutrer first brought Chardonnay from this area fame in the 1970s, and today boutique producers such as Steve Kistler make some of America's most avidly collected wines from grapes grown there. Their best Chardonnays convey a vivid sense of fruit—sometimes tropical, but more frequently reminiscent of tart lemon peel or crisp, juicy apples.

Because Russian River Chardonnays display a sumptuously lush texture, they are quintessentially Californian, meaning that they entice less with elegance than with enthusiasm. Kistler's Vine Hill Chardonnay, a wine that fairly overfills with flavor, might well be considered the regional archetype. Made in small volume, much like the top wines from other renowned Russian River boutique producers such as Dehlinger, Gary Farrell, Martinelli, and Walter Hansell, it offers concentrated fruit in a full-bodied, sumptuous, and yes, sexy package.

Small-volume vintners, however, are not the only people crafting ebullient Russian River wines nowadays. A number of larger producers make excellent wines sourced from vineyards there, and the largest privately owned winery of all—Gallo—owns the AVA's largest single Chardonnay vineyard. Named for the Laguna de Santa Rosa, a historic wetland that feeds the river's final rush to the sea, this vineyard yields wines that are as focused and expressive as any in the region, no matter the size or supposed standing of the producer. Marked by forward fruit, racy acidity, and smoky, spicy oak, Gallo's Laguna Ranch Chardonnay tastes exciting because so exuberant and full-flavored. While connoisseurs and cult collectors may not always acknowledge as much, that exuberance explains why it deserves to be ranked among the very best.

Gallo has introduced more Americans to more wines than any other company. For many years, those wines were mostly blended generics, often sold in jugs. Now, though the blends have not disappeared, the more important wines are varietals linked to a place—most often to Sonoma County, which is why the company's premium division is named Gallo of Sonoma. The Gallo family fashions good, sometimes superb wines from multiple sites throughout the county. For Cabernet and Zinfandel, they particularly prize vineyards in the Alexander and Dry Creek valleys. For Chardonnay (and more recently Pinot Noir), they especially esteem the Russian River Valley. "When deciding what and where to plant, we have the great advantage of experience," says Matt Gallo, one of the G-3, or third Gallo generation that is playing an increasingly prominent role in the company.

Although the Gallo headquarters are in Modesto in the Central Valley, Gallo's founders, the brothers Ernest and Julio, knew Sonoma well. They purchased Sonoma grapes for decades, at one point buying just about half of everything grown there. That points to Gallo's other advantage: size. Matt directs grape growing for Gallo of Sonoma, and he acknowledges that the company's substantial resources enable him to do things that would be inconceivable at other wineries. At the Frei Ranch in Dry Creek and the Barrelli Creek property in the Alexander Valley, the Gallos literally reshaped the vineyards, using surplus bulldozers and earth movers they purchased from the Alaska Pipeline project to turn steep hillsides into gently rolling slopes, with precisely the exposures they wanted. And a recent extensive redesign and replanting project at Laguna has cost them a pretty penny. "We've changed a lot of things," Matt explains, "all in order to get better wines. Here [at Laguna], we've altered the spacing, the trellising, even the clonal material we're using. It's an opportunity to improve quality. We want the wines to make a statement, a statement about this place."

As with many things the Gallos do, grape growing at Laguna is a large-scale operation. The property encompasses over 400 acres, nearly 350 of which are under vine. Some of the vineyard blocks are devoted to varietal and clonal trials, and there is a substantial harvest of Sauvignon Blanc every year, but Chardonnay comprises some 85 percent of the grapes grown there. "We're convinced," Matt says emphatically, "that it's a perfect marriage, the right variety in just the right place." A great deal of the harvest goes into Gallo's moderately priced "County Series" Chardonnay; but about 10 percent of the crop, mostly from the higher benchland blocks, is reserved for the company's top whites—the quite limited Estate Chardonnay, and the 8,500-case Laguna Ranch vineyard wine. Made to express a stylistic model more than a specific *terroir*, the Estate tastes deliciously refined. By contrast, the lavish Laguna Ranch Chardonnay seems unbridled. Its rich, spicy flavors and seductively lush texture emphatically make a statement about the place.

For most of its history, Gallo did not want to make statement wines. Only in the late 1970s did Ernest and Julio begin producing premium varietals in addition to "Hearty Burgundy," "Chablis Blanc," and the various blends (including skid row fortifieds like "Thunderbird") that had made them their fortune. For a long time, they actively resisted change. Ernest, who was in charge of sales, bristled at anything even hinting of wine snobbery or pretension, and Julio, the winemaker, was such an advocate of blending that he long opposed even vintage dating. Gallo's first vintage varietal wine, a Sonoma County Cabernet, didn't come until 1978. But it was a harbinger of things to come. For when the brothers finally decided to change, they did so in a big way. They had spent fifty years building their company to be the biggest. Now, beginning in the early 1980s, they decided to try to make it the best.

Ernest and Julio always had paid careful attention to market trends, and by 1980, though they may not have completely understood why, they recognized that the American wine market was changing. A new generation of drinkers—including their own grandchildren—wanted better wines. As important, these new consumers were willing to pay top dollar for wine. When the Gallo brothers realized as much, they also realized that they needed to do something to meet the emerging demand. Their company had long been the biggest buyer of wine grapes in California, so they could have made the move to premium varietals simply by purchasing better fruit. The brothers, however, presciently perceived that they needed to have more control over their products. So they decided to purchase land—again, on a large scale. They concentrated on Sonoma because Julio insisted that fruit quality was nowhere higher in California. Their purchases were huge. In addition to Laguna, they bought 900 acres at two properties in Dry Creek and 800 acres at three in the Alexander Valley—all in a matter of months. Some of this land was already planted to grapes, but plenty more was not.

Laguna, owned at the time by the Frei family, was a Gravenstein apple orchard, and the taste of those apples is what convinced Julio to buy it. "Julio used to say that wherever you saw apples growing, you knew you could do okay with grapes," recounts Matt Gallo. "Grandpa had the natural instincts of a farmer," adds his sister, Gina, the G-3 family member who now plays a key role in the winemaking at Gallo of Sonoma. "He had such trust in this land. He just knew that grapes would do well here. I remember too how much he loved the apple pie that Grandma would make with these apples. He used to say it was the best he ever had." Julio Gallo died in 1993, and his wife, Aileen, in 1999. But the Gallo family still holds on to that pie recipe, and a row of apple trees still abuts the vineyard. "It really is the best pie you'll ever have," says Gina.

The connection between apples and wine grapes involves more than instinct. What they share is acidity, and a resulting impression of crispness underlying the sweet taste of ripe fruit. That impression certainly characterizes Laguna Ranch Chardonnay. Marked by richly expressive fruit flavors, augmented by plenty of spicy, smoky oak, the wine nonetheless tastes bright and focused. Gina, working with longtime Gallo winemaking guru Marcello Monticelli, gives it a no-holds-barred contemporary California Chardonnay treatment. Fermentation, using about half wild yeast, lasts for two weeks, after which the wine goes directly into barrel—100 percent new, heavily toasted French oak—where it ages on its lees for a full year. Meanwhile, it undergoes a complete malolactic fermentation, softening the aggressive acids and so making the wine taste even rounder and richer. Certainly an opulent Chardonnay, it overflows with fruit flavor, a showy, smoky bouquet, and a lush, luxuriant texture. But beneath all that abundance lurks the acid—tight and lean, holding everything in check, giving the wine superior balance. The combination of intense flavor, from both fruit and wood, and racy acidity is what makes it so special—and so true to its Russian River origins.

Julio Gallo first planted Riesling and Gewurztraminer at Laguna, aiming to make off-dry wines that would satisfy the American consumer's sweet tooth. If he did not initially foresee the rapid growth in consumer demand for Chardonnay, especially wines with a sweet vanillin veneer from oak aging, he was keenly attuned to the winds of change. So it did not take him long to start concentrating on the varietal—at first in small lots, then more and more, until by 1989 the vineyard was planted predominantly to it.

Those same winds were blowing across the entire Russian River AVA during the 1980s. Brice Jones and Bill Bonetti had pioneered high-end Sonoma Chardonnay in the 1970s at Sonoma-Cutrer, and they were followed all during the next decade by a host of artisan vintners who brought new renown to the region. By 1993, when the first Gallo of Sonoma wines appeared, the Russian River, particularly the western side of the AVA, was becoming acknowledged by connoisseurs and collectors as the source of some of America's finest wines.

The new Gallo line, Julio declared shortly before he died, "will dispel the idea that fine wines can't be made by companies that put out volume." Three years later, the Laguna Ranch Chardonnay took top prize at the San Francisco International Wine Competition. Then, in 1998, it was named best white wine at the London International Wine Challenge; and in 2001, it won the Gran Menzione at Vin Italy in Verona. Still, some consumers persist in equating high quality with small size, and cannot believe that Gallo of Sonoma's wines are in the same league as those from the boutiques. "Changing people's minds takes time," admits Gina Gallo. "But we're staying very focused. Grandpa didn't start out making these kinds of wines, but he saw the possibilities. We want to stay true to his vision."

Gina started working for the family company in sales, but her heart was never in that job. Reticent, almost shy, she felt more at home amidst tanks and barrels in a winery than out on the road making sales calls. When she confessed as much to her grandfather, he was "super-supportive. He didn't tell me it wasn't a woman's job. Instead, he said, 'Gina, if you're serious, I want you to learn from the best we have.'" So for three years, she worked in the Gallo experimental winery in Modesto—conducting clonal and varietal trials, making small batches of wine under the tutelage of George

Thoukis, Julio's right-hand man in the winery. Then, in 1993, she started working alongside Marcello Monticelli, a thirty-five-year company veteran. "Marcello is one of the most talented winemakers in the world," Gina declares. "I learn from him all the time." For his part, Monticelli notes that while a lot has changed at Gallo, the company has always cared about quality. It just has a higher standard in Sonoma than in Modesto. That standard is evident in the winery—in the state-of-the-art equipment, the ongoing trials and experiments, and the commitment to treating each batch of wine as a separate entity. "Sure we're big," says Gina, "but we approach each wine as if we were small." Paradoxically, the company's size, and the resources that come with it, enables them to do so.

Since moving to Sonoma in 1996, Gina has become the public face of Gallo—in advertisements and press releases, as well as public appearances, media events, and the like. She at first was not all that comfortable in the role, but says that playing it has gotten easier. "I'm definitely happier at home and in the winery, but it's okay now on the road. It's just talking with people, taking time, letting them know what we're doing." Her brother feels much the same way. He'll do what he's told he has to do to market Gallo of Sonoma, but he'd rather get back to work—in the vineyards, where he insists lots of jobs still need to be done.

The most recent big job at Laguna has involved replanting. The vines, with root systems nearly thirty years old, were slowing down and becoming diseased, so in 1991 Matt and his crew began to replace them. In the process, they completely redesigned the vineyard. Instead of the widely spaced vines with sprawling canopies that Julio had planted (that being the conventional system at the time), they introduced a vertically trained trellising system and tight, high-density spacing. The idea is to produce fewer but better grapes per plant. "We're going tighter and tighter," Matt says, "especially up on the higher benchland blocks. Those are the least vigorous soils and so the most thrifty vines. They're also the ones that give the best wine." Jim Collins, who directs grape growing at all the company properties, explains that Gallo designs vineyards based on soil fertility, using infrared aerial photography to map every parcel of land. "It's really sub-block farming," he notes. Again, deep pockets permit a very large winery to operate like a small, artisanal one—only arguably better because of the benefit of so much more experience and expertise.

"Everything we're doing," says Matt Gallo firmly, "is to improve quality." His sister echoes that sentiment: "Our philosophy is to make wines that are unique to the vineyard." It just so happens that this gorilla of a company owns a lot of vineyards, and that none of them are small. The Gallo winery in Dry Creek produces 1 million cases of wine a year, under a host of different labels, including Frei Brothers, MacMurray Ranch, and Rancho Zabaco. Some 440,000 cases carry the family name, and of these only 20,000 are the top, vineyard-designated wines. The line includes some excellent reds, particularly Cabernet and Zinfandel from the Frei Ranch in Dry Creek, and Cabernet from Barrelli Creek. There are now two single-vineyard Chardonnays—Two Rock from the Sonoma Coast, and Laguna.

At this level, the very top of the Gallo portfolio, each wine tastes distinct. Each has its own personality. Each makes a statement. In the case of Laguna, arguably the most consistently successful Gallo wine, that statement is all about the Russian River Valley—or more precisely, the AVA's cool, damp western fringe, where Chardonnay performs so well. There, in the hands of the region's top producers, Gallo very much included, the best wines taste truly riveting. Simultaneously opulent and focused, they are as good as this varietal gets in the United States.

A NOTE ON VINTAGES:

Though the cool Russian River Valley location provides this wine with plenty of acid, which inevitably benefits aging, the allure here comes from the aroma and taste of fresh, ripe fruit—along with the lush, sensuous impression the wine makes on your palate. More than a few years of cellaring will dull that luster, so it's a wine to drink fairly young—within five years of harvest. Older wines will taste interesting, just not as exciting. Strong years have included 1995, 1996, 2001, 2002, and 2003.

THE SUGGESTED PRICE FOR THE CURRENT 2003 RELEASE IS $25.

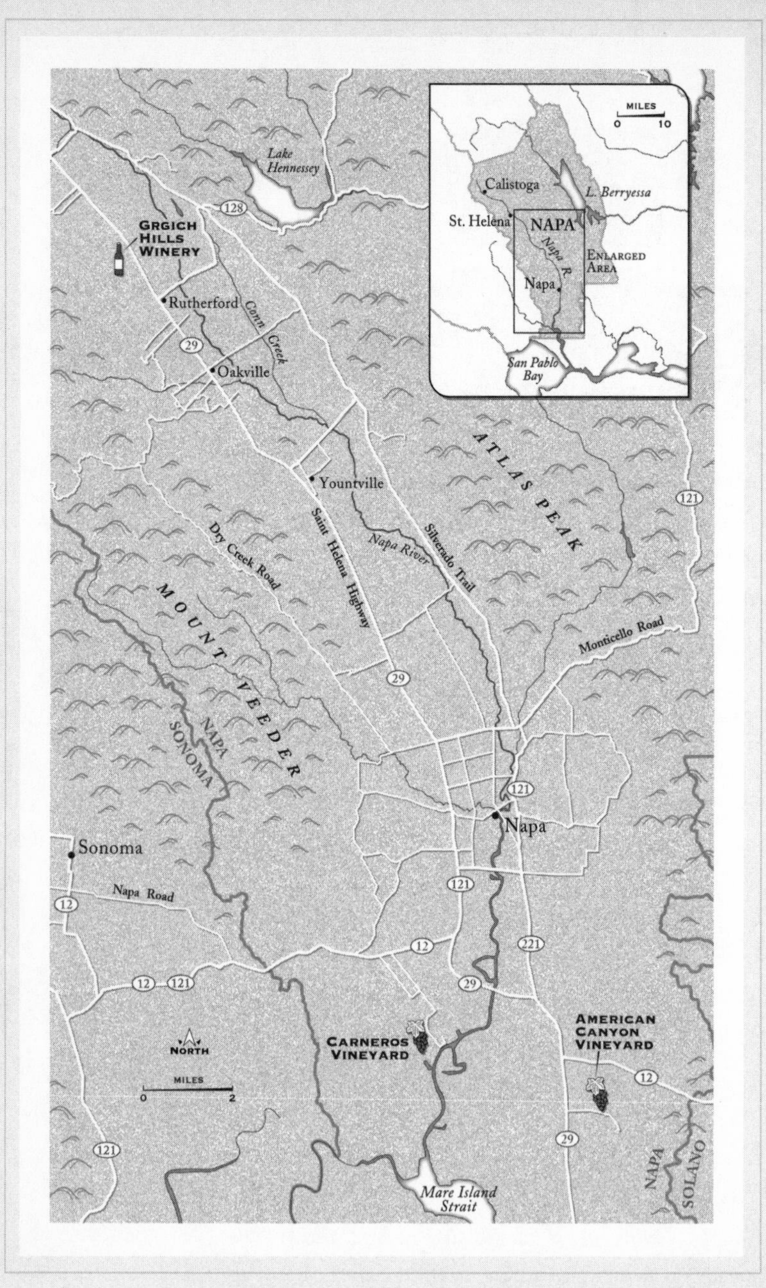

THE GRGICH HILLS WINERY AND
TWO ESTATE CHARDONNAY VINEYARDS

CHAPTER 17

Grgich Hills Cellar Chardonnay

Napa Valley, California

...

Grgich Hills Chardonnay is an anomaly. One of California's most historically important white wines, it tastes neither like most current Golden State renditions nor like this varietal's original French model, white Burgundy. Fruit-driven but firm, and capable of developing remarkable complexity with age, it sets its own style, to the evident satisfaction of its many admirers. In doing so, the wine resembles its creator, the diminutive but stubbornly principled Miljenko "Mike" Grgich. Back in 1976, Grgich brought international acclaim to California Chardonnay with his triumph in Steven Spurrier's famed Paris tasting, where two Golden State wines bested a set of white Burgundies and red Bordeaux. Since then he has swum steadfastly against the current of intensely concentrated, oaky wines that has swept up so many vintners, both in America and abroad. The Chardonnays that Grgich and his grandnephew, Ivo Jeramaz, fashion taste elegant,

Miljenko "Mike" Grgich

balanced, and round. "Round like a bowl, so nothing stands out but the pleasure," he says. "That's my goal."

Grgich initially identified that goal as a student in his native Croatia in the 1950s. He then began to strive actively toward it when he emigrated to California in 1958. For nearly two decades, he worked in Napa as an assistant, honing his skills beside some of the Valley's most celebrated vintners. So when he started his own winery in 1977, he was able to identify exactly the sort of wine he wanted to make. It would be marked by rich California fruit, with sufficient acidity for balance and longevity. Most important, it would taste neither angular nor blowsy, but instead would be subtle and sophisticated. The inaugural Chardonnay from Grgich Hills Cellar was all that and more. In 1980, at a celebrated tasting in Chicago, it was ranked first among 221 Chardonnays from across the globe, and named the world's very best. Almost immediately it had to be put on allocation, with individual consumers given a three-case-per-year limit. (It took fifteen years for production to grow sufficiently to meet demand.) While other American vintners have gone on to garner considerable acclaim with more full-blown wines, Mike Grgich was the first to be recognized internationally as a master of the varietal. And though critical preferences have shifted somewhat in favor of more opulent, powerful wines, the style at Grgich Hills has not changed. "For Ivo and me," he says, "the goal is still to make a harmonized wine. Not too much oak, not too much alcohol. A whole wine." A wine, that is, that remains above all a pleasure to drink. "Maybe I'm lucky," he adds with a smile, "that I'm what some people call bullheaded."

More than anything else, Mike Grgich's European sensibility is responsible for his Chardonnay's impressive consistency. "In Europe," he argues, "a house develops a style. That's what I've tried to do here. There's a tremendous benefit from knowing the style." That benefit is in part financial, as consumers tend to buy wines they think they can trust, but it also is philosophical, since it necessitates being true to oneself rather than to the vagaries of the marketplace. Grgich and Jeramaz strive each year to make better wines, but the wines they want to improve are their own. They do not look to their competition for motivation, but rather find inspiration in their own work, in those places where they have succeeded as well as those where they may have missed the proverbial mark. Consequently, change comes cautiously at Grgich Hills. Though today's wines are crafted with grapes from different vineyards, they do not taste substantially different from those made twenty-five years ago. Few American wineries can or even would want to claim as much, innovation frequently being considered more desirable than constancy. But at Grgich Hills, novelty is viewed with suspicion, and other wines, no matter how popular, have little to do with the house style. "I'm only going to compare my style with my wines," Grgich says, "so that we stay not in the style of someone else but in our own."

The youngest of eleven children, Miljenko Grgić (he anglicized the spelling when he immigrated) grew up in a farming community in the village of Desne on Croatia's Dalmatian coast. His family owned a small vineyard, and young Mike stomped the grapes each fall. "I don't think I would have been born if my father didn't need my feet," he quips. "Ever since I was three or four, every year, I've never missed harvest." Grgich's upbringing influenced him in many ways, personally as well as professionally. He remembers his father telling him, "Do what you are doing today better than yesterday, and a little better tomorrow, and every day forward." He has tried to follow that advice all through his life.

Grgich went to college in then-Communist Yugoslavia, attending the University of Zagreb, where he studied agriculture, graduating in 1954 with a degree in viticulture and enology. He made the difficult decision to leave his family and emigrate to the United States because, after publicly protesting the firing of a favorite professor, he found himself being followed by the secret police. After nearly two years in Germany as an exchange student and another two in Canada, he arrived via Greyhound bus in the sleepy town of St. Helena, California, having posted a "position wanted" advertisement in an industry newsletter, ready and eager for a job in his chosen field.

J. Leland "Lee" Stewart answered that ad, and Stewart's Souverain winery is where Mike Grgich first fermented grapes in the Napa Valley. It was not easy. Stewart, famously tightfisted and driven, proved a demanding boss. Though the winery should have had four or five full-time employees in order to be run properly, there were just two, Stewart and his new assistant, which meant that Grgich had to work long, back-breaking hours, doing more than a little bit of just about everything. Yet Stewart toiled just as hard, being utterly devoted to his wines. "He was a very special man," Grgich remembers. "He asked for perfection. I was lucky to find him."

Some twenty years ahead of his time, Lee Stewart, who had purchased his mountain property in 1943, was convinced that if people cared enough, California could produce truly great wines. And Stewart cared passionately. Never satisfied with the status quo, he paid little attention to what other winemakers did or what they thought about him, focusing exclusively on the quality of his very small production. All through the 1950s, the Cabernets, Rieslings, and other wines from tiny Souverain piled up heaps of medals in competitions, regularly outperforming bigger, better-known producers. And according to Grgich, Stewart's single-minded drive is what gave those wines their distinctive character. "Everything at Souverain had to be done in a particular way," he recalls. Consequently, "every wine had special style."

Grgich's second California mentor, André Tchelistcheff, operated on a larger scale but was equally committed to high standards. For nine years these two like-minded European émigrés oversaw production at Beaulieu Vineyard in Rutherford, then widely considered Napa's leading commercial winery. Together, they introduced controlled malolactic fermentation for BV's red wines and cold fermentation for its whites, two techniques that helped raise the bar for American wine as a whole. They pioneered sterile bottling and filtration, processes that prevented bacterial spoilage and stabilized the finished products. They also experimented in the vineyard (with frost protection projects, for example), always with an eye toward making something good even better. "André and I established quality control," Grgich recalls, noting that his time at Beaulieu taught him the value of overseeing a wine all the way from the vine to the bottle. "I controlled the whole circle," he says, "and that gave me experience that I have used since then to make better wines year after year." Tchelistcheff insisted that top-notch wines could be made only if the people responsible for them devoted the necessary attention to them. This involved being willing to try new things, never cutting corners, and meticulously monitoring each aspect of grape growing and winemaking. "André Tchelistcheff made superior wines," his former assistant remembers, "because nobody else knew how to do it better."

Grgich accepted a new job at the new Robert Mondavi winery in 1968. He left Beaulieu because he knew that he would always play second fiddle there, and his new boss promised him greater control of the day-to-day winemaking. At Mondavi, though, he found a different business philosophy. Growth was the buzzword, with production doubling nearly every year. Grgich helped make many of the wines that established Mondavi's reputation as an industry leader, but the constant pressure to expand made his head spin. So, in the spring of 1972, when two Southern California businessmen, Jim Barrett and Ernest Hahn, offered him a financial stake in their fledgling Calistoga winery, he had no trouble making up his mind. Nonetheless, much as with his time at Souverain and Beaulieu, he experienced something important at Mondavi, something that again reinforced lessons first learned back home. "That was a winery of action," he says, the action coming from Mondavi himself, a man who channeled all his energy into one overarching ambition—to make exceptional wines. "I was proud," Grgich recalls, "that I came to the place where my energy was meeting his." So Lee Stewart's dedication, André Tchelistcheff's vision, and Bob Mondavi's energy all left their mark. The lessons the immigrant winemaker learned gave him the confidence to lead rather than follow, no longer an apprentice because now an artisan. As he put it years later, "I felt a little artistic blood in my veins, so wanted to do it my own way."

At their newly restored Chateau Montelena, Barrett and Hahn promised Grgich that he could control all aspects of production. Being Bordeaux drinkers, they wanted him to focus primarily on red wines, particularly Cabernet. But Grgich told them that they were unrealistic, since it would take at least five years before the first bottle of red would be ready to sell. "Start with white wines," he advised them, "wines which you can make and sell and have cash flow until your Cabernet comes into the market." So the initial emphasis at Montelena was on two white wines, Johannisberg Riesling and Chardonnay. Both almost immediately received considerable critical acclaim, the Riesling being named "best of California" by the *Los Angeles Times*, and the Chardonnay outscoring a Bâtard-Montrachet in a well-publicized San Diego tasting. That acclaim turned to crescendo when the second release of Chateau Montelena Chardonnay, from the 1973 vintage, triumphed in Paris, outperforming Domaine Roulot's Meursault-Charmes, Joseph Drouhin's Beaune Clos des Mouches, Ramonet-Prudhon's Bâtard-Montrachet, and Domaine Leflaive's Puligny-Montrachet Les Pucelles (as well as Chardonnays from Chalone, David Bruce, Freemark Abbey, Spring Mountain, and Veedercrest in California). Suddenly Mike Grgich was the king of American Chardonnay.

The news from France thrilled Grgich, but it did not change his view of his work. "I knew I had a good wine," he says. What happened simply "affirmed my own sense of what I had done." That affirmation brought him new attention, though, and he soon began thinking about starting his own winery. The problem was money. So later that year, when Austin Hills of the Hills Brothers Coffee family began talking to him about yet another new job, he was in a position to propose a partnership, one in which Hills would supply the finances and Grgich the manpower and winemaking expertise. Their agreement became official early in 1977, and ground was broken at Grgich Hills Cellar on the Fourth of July, signaling independence. For Mike Grgich, this was "the culmination of my lifelong dream . . . to be on my own and be able to learn what I want and to create what I want." More than anything else, what he wanted was to craft wines that set their own standard. And while that goal applied to all the wines he would make, it was most clearly articulated with Grgich Hills Chardonnay, the varietal that he already had shown the world he could master.

With Chardonnay, Mike Grgich emphasizes balance above all else, a balance of fruit, oak, and acid, resulting in a wine distinguished by a firm structure that guarantees longevity. According to Grgich, a vintner's primary task is to "balance the wine to achieve complexity." That begins with the selection of grapes in the vineyard—specifically, choosing the best clones, planting in optimal locales, and harvesting at the correct moment. Grgich Hills today only uses grapes from its two estate Chardonnay vineyards in the cool Carneros and American Canyon sections of the Napa Valley, but for most of its history it used a combination of purchased and estate fruit. Even then, Grgich monitored the harvest, insisting that the grapes be picked when they were fully ripe, the seeds soft, the skins supple, and the juice appropriately sweet.

This emphasis on complete maturity has become widespread; but back in the 1970s and 1980s, when most California vintners made picking decisions based solely on sugar levels, Grgich was something of a contrarian. "I've never thought," he says, "that sugar by itself is all that matters." To his mind, acidity is equally important, and he insists that his Chardonnay maintain the grape's natural acids. "Pick it ripe," he says, "but not too ripe." If the grape tastes in balance, so too will the wine.

Although Mike Grgich helped introduce Napa, and by extension America, to the process of controlled malolactic fermentation during his days working with André Tchelistcheff at Beaulieu, he scrupulously prevents it with Chardonnay at Grgich Hills Cellar. This process employs bacteria to convert crisp malic acid into softer lactic acid. It is widely practiced in Burgundy, as it can make wines seem rich and buttery. "It makes sense there," argues Grgich, since the French grapes taste tart at harvest. "But in Napa, the total acid is either at a normal or below normal level, so in my opinion it's wrong to reduce it. I don't want my wine to taste like butterscotch!" The vast majority of contemporary California Chardonnay producers induce malolactic fermentation in at least some portion of their blend. "That's their style," Grgich says. "It's not ours." In a similar vein, the Grgich Hills style calls for a judicious use of oak, with only one third of the barrels each year being new, so that the taste of wood never overwhelms the fruit. Again, the goal is balance, with the winemaker neither adding nor subtracting too much. "Wine is like a long chain, from the vine to the glass," Mike Grgich insists. "Every link is important. If one or two are missing, or don't hold together, the whole thing falls apart."

Though still very much involved in his winery's operation, Mike Grgich works these days in semi-retirement. His daughter, Violet, manages the business, while his great-nephew is responsible for the daily decisions that keep all the links in the winemaking chain firmly together. Grgich brought Ivo Jeramaz to California from Croatia in 1986, and since then has instructed him in every aspect of production, helping a new generation learn to make wine much as he learned himself, as an apprentice under a tutor's watchful eye. Asked to reveal the secret of Grgich Hills Chardonnay, Jeramaz says, "There is none. The only secret is having good grapes and working hard to make good wine." Grgich nods in agreement. "Yes," he adds, "making wine is half art and half science, and then half again hard work."

After nearly fifty years in the Napa Valley, Mike Grgich, the immigrant winemaker who arrived with virtually nothing, takes considerable pride in everything he has achieved. Grgich Hills Cellar today produces roughly 80,000 cases of wine each year, all made with estate fruit. "We now own all our own land," he says when asked about the winery's future. "Everything is paid off. I feel safe going into an era where we do not need to buy another vineyard or pay off another loan. The ship has been built, and now we just need to navigate it." Grgich came to America as an apprentice, then became a master, and now is a mentor. And he knows well the lessons he needs to impart—to his grandnephew and daughter at the winery, but even more to winemakers and wine lovers everywhere. "Stay true to yourself," he says simply. In that regard, his goal with Chardonnay remains what it was when he founded Grgich Hills—to strive for ever better wines within the framework of an established style, one that resembles but does not replicate anyone else's, one that stays true to both what nature provides and what he as a vintner desires. Grgich's Chardonnay has bucked trends and fads for over a quarter century now. That it tastes neither as rich as some other top California examples nor as earthy as some Burgundies means simply that it tastes of itself. Now as then, its greatness is evident in the glass.

A NOTE ON VINTAGES:

Few American Chardonnays age as well as Grgich Hills's. After five or so years in bottle, the fresh autumnal fruit flavors begin to fade, and secondary notes echoing smoked nuts and dried herbs begin to emerge. But if well-stored, the wine will not seem oxidized or tired. Deciding when to drink it, then, is a matter of personal preference (though I wouldn't advise holding on to it for decades). Especially strong vintages include 1990, 1994, 1996, 2001, and 2002.

THE SUGGESTED PRICE FOR THE CURRENT 2002 RELEASE IS $45.

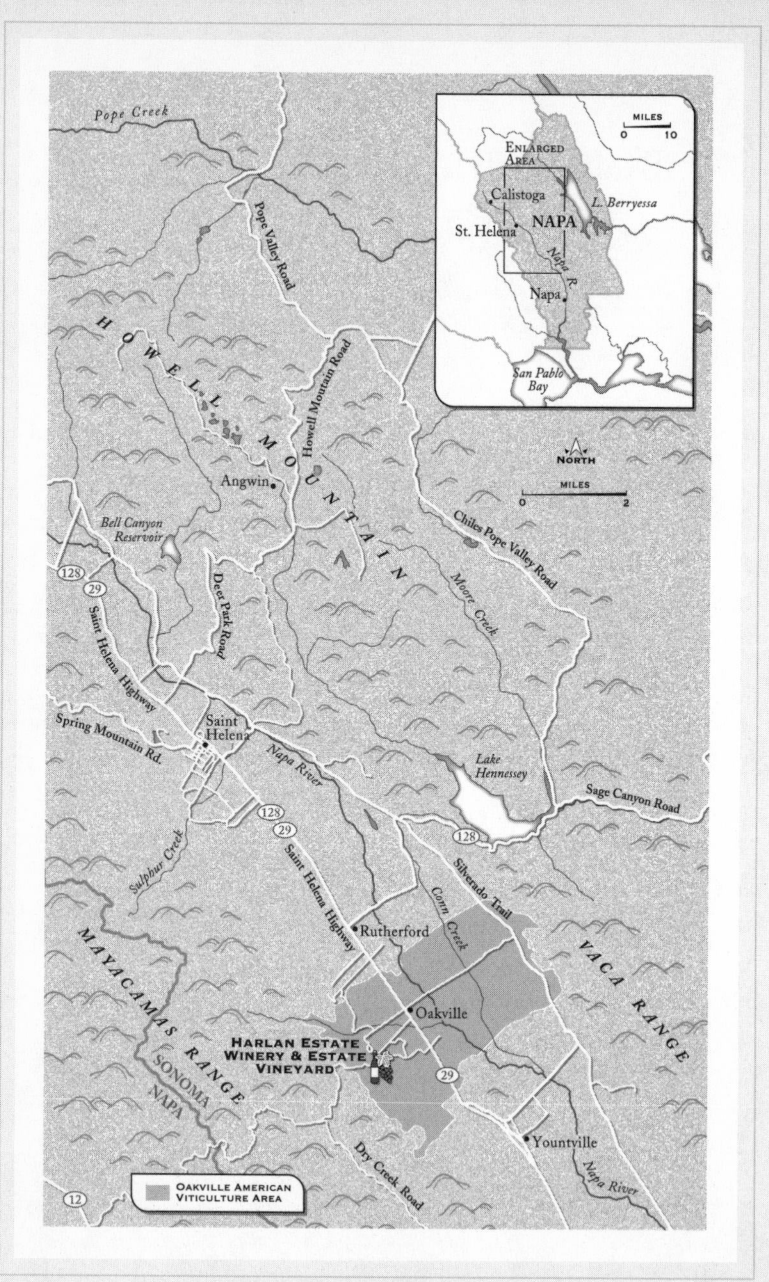

HARLAN ESTATE AND THE OAKVILLE AVA

CHAPTER 18

HARLAN ESTATE PROPRIETARY RED WINE

Oakville, Napa Valley, California

...

Harlan Estate is something of a paradox. Founded by Bill Harlan, a California real estate entrepreneur, both the wine and the property were conceived to endure. Harlan's goal was to create something "with a certain permanence," a wine-growing tradition that "might last for generations." Yet Harlan Estate's eponymous wine, designated simply as a proprietary red (in case the winemaker decides to use less than the legally mandated 75 percent of Cabernet required for varietal identification), has exploded on the scene to become one of California's hottest cult wines. Produced commercially only since 1990, it is far too new to have anything to do with tradition. So collectors pursue it feverishly not because of its track record or demonstrated ability to improve over time, but because owning a bottle or two has become extremely trendy—and extremely profitable.

Bill Harlan

Bill Harlan enjoys the glowing reviews his wine has received, but he is uncomfortable with its cult status. He knows that many people buy it only to resell it, with profits ranging from 100 to 1,000 percent. He knows too that trends rarely last. "Things tend to go down just as fast as they go up," he says, "so being part of a cult is not what we want." Nonetheless, Harlan Estate is a central player in the California cult craze. Bill Harlan sells his wine, at prices that rise significantly just about every year, some eighteen months before its release. Hence he permits supply to become depleted well before anyone has an opportunity to assess the finished product, which inevitably inflates demand if that product turns out to be good. And at least as evaluated by the critics, Harlan Estate's proprietary red wine has turned out to be very good. James Laube of *The Wine Spectator* has called it "the best Cabernet in Napa Valley"; Robert Parker of *The Wine Advocate* has gone even further, declaring that "Harlan Estate might be the single most profound red wine . . . in the world." These influential commentators praise the wine because they find it compelling, not chic, but their plaudits, usually directed at barrel samples rather than finished bottlings, have made owning or ordering it ultra-fashionable. Hence the paradox. The way in which Harlan Estate is marketed and sold helps fuel the cult craze, even though its achievement ultimately has more to do with careful, long-term planning.

The rise of upstart cult wines, both in the United States and abroad, can be traced directly to the correspondent rise of the autonomous wine press, specifically the handful of journalists whose reviews and ratings so demonstrably affect sales. Twenty-five years ago, most critics were part of the wine trade, their recommendations influenced as much by their knowledge of the market as by their sense of inherent quality. Today, virtually all the important American commentators work independently and so attempt to evaluate wine impartially. They pay little or no attention to context—market inventory, the producer's track record, when and where a particular wine might best be drunk, even their own personal biases. This sort of supposedly objective analysis tends to emphasize bold rather than delicate flavors, since these are what stand out when wines are tasted in peer groups. And because the critics no longer care about market issues of supply and demand, they are perfectly happy to heap lavish praise on wines that few consumers can locate, let alone purchase. So it has been with California cult wines. Though Harlan maintains that his wine is fashioned on a classic model, it clearly fits this stylistic profile. Firmly structured but lushly textured, it is packed with rich, sweet flavors, and exemplifies the contemporary vogue for succulent, fruit-forward, vigorous red wines.

The cult wine phenomenon caught Bill Harlan, and just about everyone else, by surprise. California had a small history of producing exclusive collectibles, but no one a generation ago imagined that a new set of elite bottlings could fetch such outlandish prices or inspire such passions. Historic Golden State gems had included Beaulieu's Georges de Latour and Inglenook's Cask Cabernet Sauvignons in the 1940s and 1950s, wines made by Martin Ray in the 1950s and 1960s, Stony Hill Chardonnay and Heitz Martha's Vineyard Cabernet in the 1970s, and then in the 1980s, Williams Selyem Pinot Noirs from Sonoma County, as well as Napa Cabernets such as Caymus Special Select, Diamond Mountain Lake Vineyard, and Dunn Howell Mountain. Expensive for their day, these all were in high demand. None, though, was ever in as high demand with collectors and connoisseurs as the top growths from Bordeaux and Burgundy, traditionally the world's most desirable wines.

But when New World wines started to become as popular as European ones, the criteria for desirability began to shift. Traditionally, people would spend significant amounts of money only on wines with established track records, meaning both a long series of successful vintages and the demonstrated ability to improve with time spent in the bottle. What few new wines came onto the market had to wait their turn. Now, with a bevy of potentially exciting innovators showing up every year (from the Old World as well as the New, including "Super Tuscans" from Italy and so-called garage wines from Bordeaux), consumers began to replace the traditional criterion of pedigree, meaning an estate's record of storied vintages, with critics' snapshot judgments. A score of 95+ in *The Wine Spectator* or *The Wine Advocate* became as important as (if not more important than) a wine's history, particularly when a wine like Harlan Estate had such little history.

Bill Harlan insists that his goal is to develop a record of sustained excellence, not to make a fashion statement. He argues that a triad of "quality, consistency, and character" distinguishes the world's finest wines, and that it will take time to realize all three. "That combination is what we're after," he says frankly, "and what we have not yet achieved." For nearly two decades, he and his team have remained focused on one thing, the creation of what they call "an American first-growth wine-growing estate." That they have become successful so quickly, in a way they could not have predicted, in no way changes their approach. Nor does it change Harlan's conviction that his goal cannot be realized fully until many more years have passed, years in which his wine can demonstrate its ability to satisfy every criterion of excellence—the current emphasis on ripe flavor coupled with the traditional insistence on pedigree.

Harlan started Harlan Estate only after meticulous study and deliberation. Having first become interested in wine as a college student at Berkeley in the late 1950s, he visited the Napa Valley frequently during the early days of American wine's renaissance. By the 1970s, he had become involved in a number of real estate ventures there, including Meadowood, the area's premier resort. Not surprisingly, he soon began thinking about purchasing land and making wine. Yet, unlike so many of his compatriots who bought vineyards and began bottling wine as quickly as possible, Harlan took his time—over a decade to be exact, years filled with analysis, study, and investigation. "It gradually became clear to me that I didn't just want to be in the wine business," he recalls. "My ultimate objective was to produce one of the very best wines. In order to meet it, I then had to learn what was involved."

To that end, Harlan talked extensively with the winemakers who gathered at Meadowood for meetings of the Napa Valley Vintners Association. He also became a founding partner in Merryvale Vineyards, a high-quality winery in St. Helena, in order to gain hands-on experience. In addition, he traveled extensively in Europe, particularly France, in an effort to discern what the world's great wines shared. Gradually it became clear to him that the very best wines have certain characteristics in common: an extremely high level of intrinsic quality, a clear record of consistency, and an individual personality that distinguishes one from another. He knew that the first of these was within his reach. All he had to do was spend the money to buy the best equipment and hire the most talented staff. The other two, however, might prove problematic. He was not sure that he or anyone else really understood the source of a wine's personality. And in California, all the money in the world could not get him a track record.

"The riskiest part of my strategy back then," Harlan freely confesses, "was deciding to buy land that had never been planted to grapes." He hedged his bets with research. While he admired wines made in other parts of the state, he chose to look only at hillside plots in Napa, the region with the most illustrious lineage. And he decided to concentrate on Cabernet Sauvignon because it had the richest history there. In the fall of 1983, an Oakville property on the hilly western side of the valley came up for sale. Heavily wooded, with an undulating terrain and steep slopes, it lacked a viticultural heritage but lay near two sites with as impressive records as any in Napa—Robert Mondavi's To-Kalon Vineyard and the May family's Martha's Vineyard, both distinguished primarily for their impressive Cabernets. So Harlan bought it, an estate consisting of some 230 acres of land above the valley floor but below the fog belt. The next year he started clearing the parcels that he hoped to turn into his vineyard.

The Harlan Estate property ranges from 200 to 1,200 feet in elevation, but grapes are planted only on the band or "tenderloin" between 300 and 500 feet, where there is good drainage, proper sun exposure, and little risk of frost. The vineyard comprises some thirty-five acres, roughly two thirds devoted to Cabernet Sauvignon and the rest to Merlot, Cabernet Franc, and a tiny proportion of Petit Verdot. In the beginning, a few of these acres contained vines on AXR1 rootstock and so proved susceptible to phylloxera. They had to be replanted, but the rest of the vineyard remains today much as it was when first designed twenty years ago, which means that many of the vines are now at an optimal age for high-quality wine production.

Bill Harlan feels confident that this stunningly beautiful site has the potential to produce consistently great wines—by which he means wines whose personality is rooted in the land's evolving history. "I have come to believe," he says, "that what makes a great wine distinctive is its ability to express the character of a place." At the same time, he recognizes that such character can be neither conveyed nor identified quickly. "The *history* of the land is all-important," he insists. "We're still developing that here. I feel we've gotten off to a good start, but it will take a long time to get where we want to go."

This farsighted approach applies to the winemaking as well. Bob Levy crafted the first wines at Harlan Estate in 1987. In part because the vines were young, and in part because it was too early to have a secure grasp of the estate's character, this and the next three vintages were never released commercially. The wines did not taste bad, but they also did not taste special, or at least special enough. In the midst of this unsatisfactory series of vintages, Harlan decided that he and Levy needed help. To that end, he sought out Michel Rolland, the world's preeminent consulting enologist today, but at the time relatively unknown outside his native Bordeaux. Rolland now owns or is a partner in a number of esteemed properties there, most notably Château Bon Pasteur in Pomerol. He also is a globe-trotter who helps some of the most prestigious producers in Argentina, Chile, Italy, Spain, and the United States turn out prodigious wines. Harlan hired him, and in 1996—some twelve years after the estate was founded, nine years after the first grapes had been crushed—Harlan Estate finally released its first wine, less than five hundred cases of the 1990 vintage.

One of the keys to Harlan Estate's achievement has been Bob Levy's willingness to keep his ego in check. Many winemakers, especially those working at such a high-profile winery, would take exception to a foreign consultant breezing into town three or four times a year, full of counsel and opinion. But Levy's considerable talent, innate sense of curiosity, and acceptance of Bill Harlan's farsighted goal, allows him to think of the wines he fashions as living things to be nurtured rather than as products of his individual craft. He has come to understand that the physiological maturity of grapes is as important as sugar levels at harvest, and that the best wines can virtually make themselves if left alone to do so. Michel Rolland's philosophy emphasizes ripe fruit, supple tannins, and minimal manipulation. As a consultant, he serves more as a stylist than a full-fledged winemaker, so he advises and suggests, but never actually commands. While his signature style can be detected in virtually all the wines he works with, he tries not to impose a template onto any one winery's style. Thus, as a consultant, he too is always learning—not how to make wine, but how to make wine in a particular place. Levy and Rolland worked together for a while at Merryvale, when Bill Harlan was a partner there. The fact that the wines they produced then, though often extremely good, never displayed Harlan Estate's multiple layers of aroma and flavor belies any suggestion that they are working by preordained design now.

In the vineyard, where yields average less than 2.5 tons per acre, the grapes for Harlan Estate are handpicked, cluster by cluster, with workers making as many as three or four passes through the blocks. The fruit then gets sorted literally grape by grape, so that every piece of stem, sliver of wood, or fragment of leaf can be discarded. Each lot—defined by vineyard block, grape variety, and even day of harvest—stays separate. The grapes are fermented in small batches, some in stainless steel and some in wood fermenters, and the wine then is aged in new French oak barrels (from some five or six different coopers). This sort of care, extending from field to cellar, though not unprecedented, is extremely rare, and Michel Rolland notes that no other estate at which he works displays such meticulous attention to detail. The resulting wines, deeply colored, tend to display seamless but complex flavors, supported by fine-grained tannins and marked by exceptional length. Though large-scaled and definitely New World styled, they offer nary a hint of coarseness or alcoholic heat, and temper their abundant vigor with grace. As the vineyard has matured, production has increased, to nearly 2,000 cases in an abundant, high-quality vintage (along with about six hundred cases of a second wine, named "The Maiden"). Demand, however, has increased faster, as every year sees more and more names added to the already lengthy waiting list.

That demand, fueled by critics' praise, is what makes Harlan Estate such a cult wine. And the plaudits keep coming. Both *The Wine Spectator* and *The Wine Advocate* continue to assign it top marks each year. Robert Parker awarded two of the first seven vintages (1994 and 1997) perfect scores of 100 points. And the British wine writer Jancis Robinson included the 1995 Harlan Estate among her lineup of the ten best wines of the twentieth century (the only American wine to be included in what was an overwhelmingly French list). Consumer demand, coupled with what remains very small supply, means that even for many well-heeled connoisseurs, the wine is virtually unobtainable. In turn, lack of availability causes prices to surge, especially at auctions, where a case of as yet unreleased Harlan Estate can fetch as much as $7,000. That sort of mind-boggling figure defines what the cult wine phenomenon is all about—the pursuit of a scarce but chic commodity, no matter the cost.

Scarcity, however, is not Bill Harlan's goal. "I'd make more wine if I could," he stresses, "but I can't at the level I want." (He and Bob Levy are now making wines under the Bond label, a series of single-vineyard Cabernets from other vineyards in Napa.) Nor is Harlan much concerned about money. "Remember," he says, "it took twelve years before we saw a nickel of revenue." No, his aim is much more forward-looking. In business terms, he wants to create a multi-generational company, family-owned and free of debt, and so thinks of Harlan Estate as a legacy he will leave to his children's children. In terms of the wine itself, his objective is greatness as he has defined it, something that he knows also will take years to achieve. Harlan's vision for his wine-growing estate is thus based upon a desire to achieve something comparable to the greatest achievements of the past. His sense of simultaneously following in historic footsteps and treading new paths for others to follow explains why, no matter that he has reaped considerable benefit from it, Harlan dislikes all talk of cults or fads. When asked if there is any danger that the accolades and acclaim his wine has received will go to his head, he insists, "Absolutely not," and then adds reflectively, "That's just not what we're about."

In its short history, Harlan Estate already has become one of

America's finest contemporary wines. For Bill Harlan, who speaks of it with a paradoxical mix of humility and pride, that is not good enough. "Unlike anything else I've done," he says, "there is a chance that this will last for many generations." So his eye remains firmly fixed on the long term, on the history he intends to make and the standards he intends to set. In that sense, Harlan Estate may only be hinting at what it may yet become.

A NOTE ON VINTAGES:

Opaque in color and densely flavored, this wine is delicious when young. It's even better, though, after five to seven years of cellaring, when its complexity becomes as compelling as its concentration. (And it shows every indication of being able to age well for a good two decades or more.) Every vintage to date at Harlan Estate has been strong, but the wines I've tasted from 1994, 1995, 1997, and 1999 were extraordinary.

THE CURRENT 2001 RELEASE SOLD AS A FUTURE TO CUSTOMERS ON THE WINERY'S MAILING LIST FOR $235.

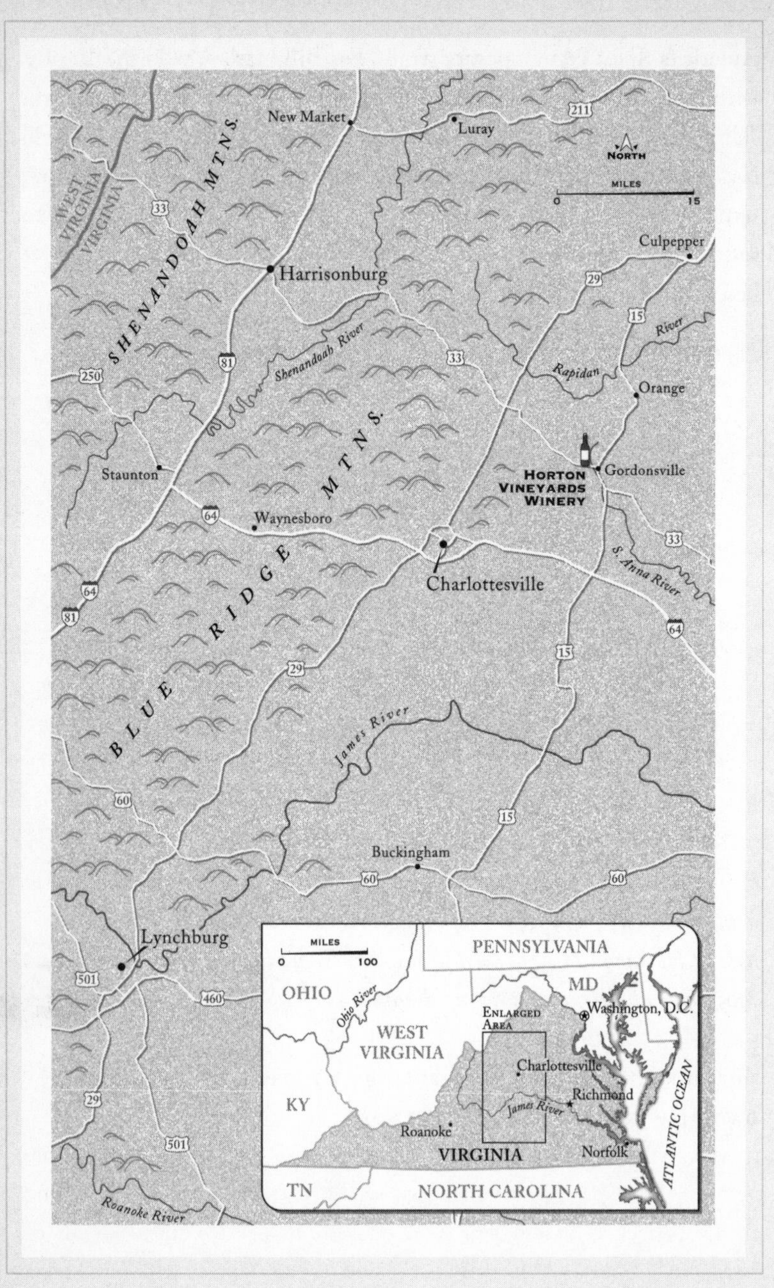

HORTON VINEYARDS, IN CENTRAL VIRGINIA'S WINE COUNTRY

CHAPTER 19

Horton Vineyards Viognier

Orange County, Virginia

...

Imagine peaches and honeysuckle, apricots and jasmine, aromas reminiscent of sweet spring flowers and flavors redolent of succulent summer fruits. Imagine all that in a rich, almost creamy white wine, and you will understand the attraction of Viognier, a relatively obscure grape that until twenty-five years ago grew only in the small appellations of Condrieu and Château Grillet in France's northern Rhône Valley. Today, inspired in large measure by the search for alternatives to Chardonnay, vintners in many of the world's important wine countries are cultivating it, with the United States ranking second to France in overall production. California leads the way in terms of volume, but exciting wines increasingly are being made elsewhere. Some of the most exciting come from Virginia, where in superior vintages Dennis Horton of Horton Vineyards produces an especially fine rendition of this varietal, a seductive wine that tastes for all the world like a bright June morning in a glass.

Dennis Horton

Viognier appears to have a natural affinity for the growing conditions of central Virginia, being not much bothered by steamy summer humidity, autumn rain, or winter cold. Horton first took a chance on it back in 1991, betting that it could yield a well-structured wine in the Old Dominion. Even he, however, did not expect it to turn out as good as it has. "It's better to be lucky than smart," he says with a chuckle, "and I was mighty lucky with Viognier." That luck first became apparent with the 1993 vintage—only the winery's second release, and still probably the single best wine Horton has made. Critics swooned over it, declaring it the equal (if not the better) of the finest from France, and consumers started clamoring for it. Horton planted more, and he soon began selling his Viognier all across the country, with California becoming his biggest out-of-state market. Featured in some of the country's toniest restaurants, including Rubicon in San Francisco and Jean Georges in Manhattan, Horton Vineyards Viognier became the first wine from Virginia to win serious acclaim outside the state.

Viticulture, however, is nothing new in Virginia. Grapes have been cultivated there since 1619, when Lord Delaware imported both French vines and French *vignerons* to the fledgling colony in hopes of making a "fruitful vintage in no time." It never happened. Delaware's vines died within only a few years, as did all the imported European vines planted by would-be Virginia vintners for the next two centuries. The problem was that these vinifera varieties proved highly vulnerable to the pests and diseases to which native vines had developed immunity over time. And unfortunately, native Virginia grapes made foxy-tasting, virtually unpalatable wines. In the nineteenth century, growers experimented with hybrids, both natural crosses such as Alexander and Catawba, and cultivated native ones such as Norton, all of which produced at least drinkable wines. A native blend called "Virginia Claret" was for a time a big seller, and by 1890 the state ranked fifth in the country in wine production. Then came Prohibition, which devastated Virginia viticulture. Not until the 1970s did serious winemaking return to the state.

As happened throughout the East, the growers who spearheaded Virginia's wine revival focused initially on French-American hybrid varieties, grapes with both a vinifera and a native North American parentage, and a proven ability to survive in harsh climates. Yet before long, growers began to experiment with pure vinifera varieties. Advances in viticulture, including improved disease management, the evolution of winter-hardy vines, and new forms of trellising and pruning, had at last made it possible to grow European grapes on the eastern seaboard. Much like their colleagues in New York, Pennsylvania, and other states, Virginia vintners were eager to find out which grapes would make the best wines.

Virginians enjoy an advantage over most other eastern vintners because an enlightened state government keeps encouraging them. In part as a response to the depressed market for tobacco, long a staple crop in the state, Virginia's legislators actively support the wine industry. Led most recently by Governors Jim Gilmore and Mark Warner, they provide tax advantages to wineries, fund enological and viticultural research, and energetically market wine tourism. As a result, the number of acres under vine keeps increasing each year, and the quality of the wine has taken a quantum leap forward. Today, over eighty commercial wineries call Virginia home. They almost all make wines with vinifera grapes.

Because Virginia is still very much an emerging wine state, the question of which grapes to plant in which sites remains open. Many producers concentrate on varietals with mass market appeal, and some have succeeded brilliantly. Wines such as Linden's vineyard-designated Cabernets, White Hall's Reserve Chardonnay, and Rockbridge Vineyard's Merlot can outperform all but a small handful of bottlings made from these popular grapes elsewhere in the country. Other producers, however, choose to take a different approach. They cultivate less familiar varietals in an effort to appeal to more of a niche market, hoping to bring renown to Virginia with new wines and flavors. No one has traveled farther down that path than Dennis Horton, who today makes nearly forty different wines, and who just about every year replaces a block or two in his vineyards with something new. "If my claim to fame is anything," he says, "it's probably that I've ripped out more vines than most people have put in." Horton, who thinks of himself as a wine grower more than a winemaker, concentrates on how well a variety performs on the vine before beginning to worry about how the resulting wine will taste. He insists that, no matter the specific variety, "we can make good wines in Virginia only if we grow good fruit." To his mind, the fact that consumers might not recognize the name of one of his wines makes little difference. All that matters is the quality of the grapes.

Horton helped tend vineyards as a teenager in his native Missouri, and when a business opportunity brought him to Virginia in 1969, he planted vines behind his house. He initially grew native grapes like Catawba, Concord, and Niagara, and then tried French-American hybrids such as Chambourcin and Seyval Blanc. Later, he began testing vinifera varieties, thus mirroring in a span of little more than a decade the nearly four hundred–year history of commercial East Coast viticulture. When he found grapes he liked, he kept growing them, but he more often was just as happy to take a stab at something new. So, in 1988, when he and his business partner, Joan Bieda, decided to start a commercial winery, he planted an eclectic mix of one native grape (Norton), one French-American hybrid (Vidal Blanc), and five different vinifera varieties—Cabernet Franc, Marsanne, Mourvèdre, Syrah, and Viognier. Horton recalls consulting Jancis Robinson's *Vines, Grapes and Wines* when trying to decide which grapes to plant. "I kept asking myself, what can I grow here that can make wines that might compete nationally and internationally?" Of those initial choices, only Syrah was a flop, as too many vines died during winter freezes. Viognier, though, turned out to be a star.

Horton selected Viognier in large measure because of its thick skin and loose clusters, both of which he accurately foresaw would enable it to survive Virginia's hot, humid summers. "In this climate," he says, "I needed an acidic, rot-resistant little sugar machine." Viognier's ability to tolerate rain turned out to be an added bonus. More often than not, autumn in central Virginia (Horton's vineyards are located roughly twenty miles north of Charlottesville) sees abundant rainfall, so a big question when deciding what to plant there has to be whether the particular variety will be able to maintain flavor. Viognier turns out to do so exceptionally well. "I didn't know that when we planted it," Horton admits, "and even now I haven't a clue why. But it gets fifty percent less rot than Chardonnay, holds its acid better, and sugars up a lot better." Even in a year like 2000, when a hurricane swept through in September, his Viognier made good wine. "It was the only fruit we picked that year that was clean and had nice sugars. All the other grapes—forget it!"

Horton also chose Viognier because he is happiest when going his own way, tilting at windmills in search of something new and better. When it comes to white wine, he loves to challenge Chardonnay. Though he has fashioned credible wines from that variety, he does not much like it—in part because it grows poorly in his vineyards, but in part also because so many other people do. Horton contends that diversity is what makes wine, both its production and its consumption, interesting; and he argues that when too many vintners make too many versions of a single varietal, that interest inevitably becomes dulled. "I've always liked wines that taste different," he admits. Dennis Horton's quest for unusual grapes led him at first to Rhône varieties, and even now he sometimes is lumped together with California "Rhône Rangers" such as John Alban and Matt Garretson, who are giving grapes like Mourvèdre, Rousanne, Syrah, and, yes, Viognier vivid new American expression. Horton, however, quips that he is a "Lone Ranger," since he has moved beyond his West Coast colleagues. Today he makes wine from a slew of offbeat grapes, including Rkatsiteli from Russia, Tinta Cão and Tourica Nacional from Portugal, and his current passion, Petit Manseng, a spicy green-skinned variety from Jurançon in southwestern France. In addition, he makes a host of fruit wines and ports, various blends, a sparkler, and a number of non-vinifera wines. Why such a range of products at a relatively small winery, where production hovers around 35,000 cases a year? "Because," he says bluntly, "I can." Many of these wines are quite good, but one suspects that overall quality at Horton Vineyards would be improved if he were to narrow his focus somewhat. Still, without the spirit of iconoclastic experimentation that pervades his enterprise, Horton's wines probably would never be all that special. And the best of them are very special indeed.

Sharon Horton, Dennis's wife, manages the four Horton vineyards—Berry Hill, Elly, Gibson Mountain, and the home plot in front of the winery. She grows Viognier only on the first two of these, since trial and error has shown her that the variety benefits from the higher elevations there. A former registered nurse, Sharon is her husband's confessed "secret weapon," a quiet, unassuming woman who now tends to "thousands of patients," as she sometimes refers to the vines in her care. Over the past decade, she has become one of the East Coast's most accomplished grape growers. Her calm demeanor serves as a counterpoint to Dennis's penchant for bluster, while her knowledge of their vineyards keeps his affinity for experimentation in focus. As she likes to remind him, their shared quest has to be for grape varieties that can thrive (rather than just survive) in Virginia's often trying climate. In this regard, no vinifera variety planted to date outperforms Viognier.

The success of Horton Viognier results not only from the couple's accomplishments in the vineyards but also from the attention they and their winemaking staff devote to it in the winery. About half of the juice goes into the varietally labeled bottling, the rest being declassified and used as a component in less expensive blends. As a result, Horton Vineyards only produces between two thousand and three thousand cases of this flagship wine each year. "We're really picky with it," Dennis Horton insists. Mike Heny, the current day-to-day winemaker, helps him keep a watchful eye. Together, they oversee the harvested grapes, refrigerating the fruit for a full day before crush. Whole clusters of grapes are then pressed and divided into two cuts, only the first of which gets used in the Viognier. In all stages of the winemaking process, Horton and Heny's goal is to maintain varietal character. To that end, they only allow a percentage (the number changes depending on the vintage) of the wine to undergo malolactic fermentation, and they age it for seven months in a combination of stainless-steel tanks and oak barrels. None of the barrels is new, for Horton and Heny insist that they don't want to make a vanilla-scented, tropical-tasting white wine, or as they put it, "a pseudo-Chardonnay." Instead, they want their Viognier to taste of Viognier, or more precisely, of Viognier grown in Virginia. "Our style is different than the French or California styles," Horton argues. "It's our own."

Virginia's short history of quality vinifera wine production means that this style is still evolving. Nonetheless, as evidenced by Horton and the state's other leading Viognier producers—including Barboursville, Breaux, Chrysallis, and Michael Shaps—the wines present a common profile. Richly perfumed, with a fairly full body, they balance their lascivious charm with subtlety and elegance. Like their French cousins from Condrieu, Virginia Viogniers tend to display the sort of minerality that accompanies most of the world's finest white wines, without bitterness or heat to mar the finish. And while they offer rich, lush flavors like their California counterparts, these wines rarely seem blowsy or fat, a trait that too often characterizes West Coast renditions. This stylistic combination of ripe primary flavors and steely secondary ones makes the wines both delicately complex and supremely refreshing. It also bespeaks great promise for the future, since the French experience suggests that the finest Viogniers come from vines that are at least fifteen or twenty years old. As good as the best Virginia versions taste now, odds are strong that the wines will get better as the vineyards mature.

"We in Virginia have come a millennium in no time," says Dennis Horton, "but we have so much more to do." While he acknowledges that some Virginia producers have fashioned excellent wines from Cabernet, Chardonnay, and Merlot, he remains perplexed why more haven't pursued Viognier and other so-called alternative varietals. Yes, exotic wines can be difficult to sell, he argues, but they also can help distinguish a largely unknown wine region. This debate goes on today throughout the winemaking world, in all the Old and New World regions that are making exciting wines but do not have a long lineage of successful vintages behind them. The question is simple: Should vintners in these areas concentrate on varietals that already sell well, or should they make wines that will set them apart? Of course, these objectives need not be mutually exclusive. One reason for the international popularity of Chardonnay, for example, is that it grows successfully in many different places. And despite its ubiquitous global presence, the best examples do stand out within an extremely crowded field.

For Virginia wines, the jury is still out, and probably will remain so for a good while. The finest of the state's Cabernets and Chardonnays are certainly impressive, but so too are many wines made from less familiar varieties. Viognier sets the pace, but ambitious winemakers have done well with everything from Barbera to Vidal. The only thing that seems clear is that after centuries of failure, Virginia vintners now finally are able to make genuinely top-flight wines. Thus perhaps more important than the choice of grape is the level of commitment to wine growing itself. Horton agrees. "We need more people in the wine business really to be in it," he says, "not just growing grapes as a glorified hobby." In that respect, the future looks bright. State government assistance, coupled with a slow but steady influx of new capital, promises that quality Virginia wine will be no passing fad. More and more investors are buying land and planting vineyards with the dream of making first-class wines. And each year, the number who reach that goal increases, even if only by one or two at a time. Virginia today is arguably the most promising wine state east of the Rockies. Its best producers stand poised on the edge of sustained success.

Dennis Horton as much as anyone else has brought them there. His Viognier makes its mark in part because it has less high-quality national competition than do wines made from more popular grape varieties. But it also stands out because of its inherent quality. A number of California and Washington winemakers have pursued this varietal just as ardently as he has over the last decade. Their wines tend to get more press than Horton's, but only a handful (Alban's, Calera's, and McCrea's come to mind) have proven themselves to be real rivals.

Given the variables of an East Coast climate, vintage variation always will be a factor in Virginia. Yet when nature cooperates, no Viognier made anywhere in the United States proves better than Horton's. Dennis Horton's competitors acknowledge as much all the time, calling and writing him for advice on everything from how to grow their grapes to how to vinify their wines. Though he sometimes chafes at being identified so closely with this one variety, his achievement with it has helped bring unprecedented renown to the grape as well as to his adopted home state. Viognier is not the only variety capable of excelling in Virginia, but to date it has proven itself the most distinctive as well as the most distinguished. And that never would have happened were it not for this one man's quest for new and different vines, and more important, new and better wines.

A NOTE ON VINTAGES:

Like virtually all wines made with Viognier, this one should be drunk within a couple of years of the harvest. The varietal's seductive allure comes from its floral bouquet and fresh summer fruit flavors. Time in no sense enhances it.

THE SUGGESTED PRICE FOR THE CURRENT 2004 RELEASE IS $20.

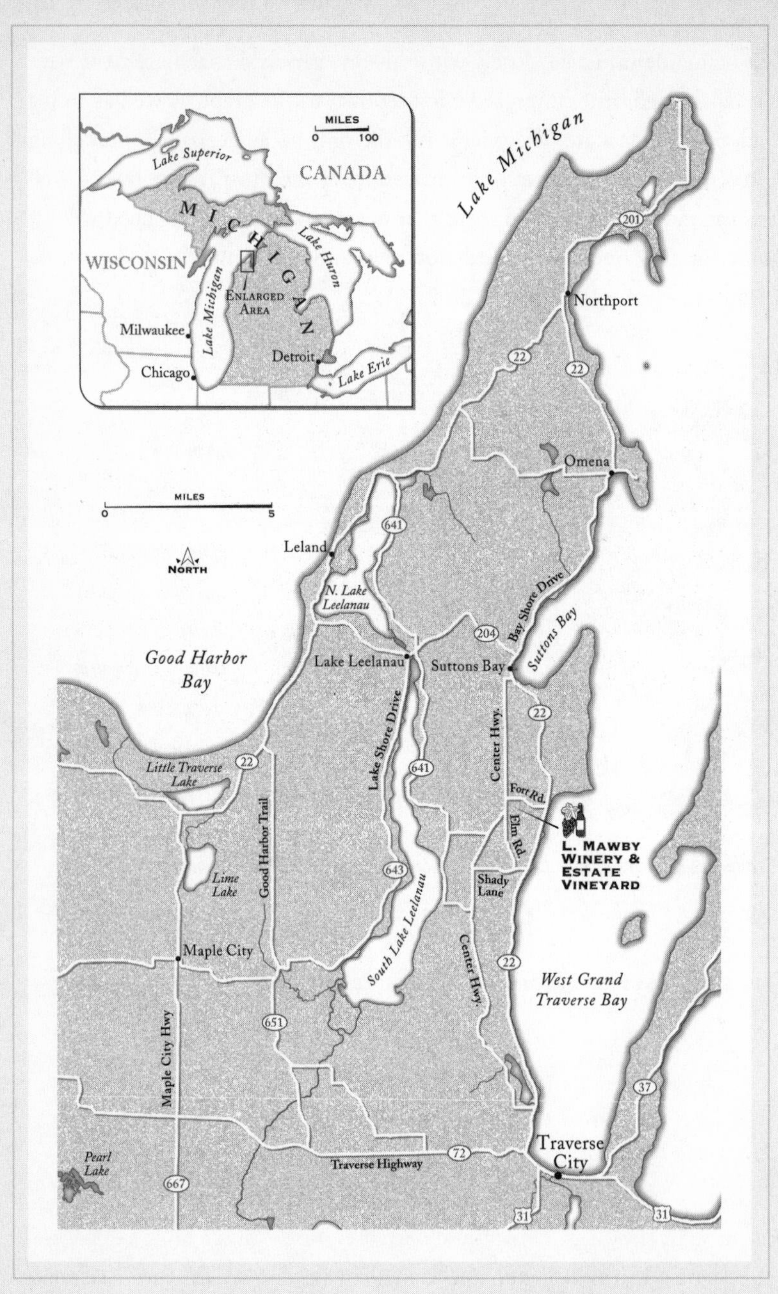

L. MAWBY'S VINEYARD AND WINERY,
IN NORTHERN MICHIGAN'S LEELANAU PENINSULA

CHAPTER 20

L. Mawby Talismon Brut

Leelanau Peninsula, Michigan

...

Larry Mawby is a man on a mission. He grows wine grapes in Michigan's Leelanau County, and he believes passionately in the region's viticultural promise. Though few American wine drinkers have heard of this cool, northern district, Mawby insists that the Leelanau and Old Mission peninsulas, both of which border Grand Traverse Bay, contain some of the potentially finest sites in the country in which to cultivate sparkling wine grapes. His self-imposed mission, then, is to compel consumers to think of Michigan when they think of classy, elegant American bubbly.

Larry Mawby

That's not as far-fetched as it sounds. Unlike grapes grown in warmer climes, the Chardonnay, Pinot Gris, Pinot Noir, and Vignoles in Mawby's vineyard ripen very slowly, attaining physiological maturity at a low level of potential alcohol but a high level of acidity. In this, they clearly resemble the grapes grown in Champagne. Less than 150 miles from the Canadian border, Michigan's Leelanau Peninsula lies right at the geographical edge of viable viticulture. The midwestern winters tend to be severe, but much as in northern France, the temperate summers provide near-perfect ripening conditions for sparkling wine, grapes for which always need to be harvested with less sugar than those designated for table wine. Mawby, an energetic, ebullient man whose passion for his craft proves contagious, made still wines for many years. "The acids always were a little too high and the sugars a little too low," he recalls. "One day it dawned on me that this fruit might be just right for sparkling."

Mawby made his first bubbly in 1984, and every year since he has become more ardently committed to it. Since 2000, he has made nothing else. While some of his wines, now marketed under the "M. Lawrence" label, are tank-fermented (using purchased fruit and juice, including some base wine shipped from California), his *méthode champenoise* L. Mawby wines are crafted exclusively with grapes grown in the Leelanau Peninsula. He makes up to seven different cuvées, including a Blanc de Blancs, a Cremant, and a dark rosé called Redd; but he reserves his best grapes from his own vineyard for a brut blend he calls Talismon. Displaying both finesse and full flavor, this wine tastes of baked apples and pears, with a toasty, brioche-scented bouquet, and a long, satisfying finish. In exceptional years, Mawby has saved the very best lots for a vintage estate brut called "Mille," but he confesses he's not sure that either he or Michigan really needs such a rarity. "We still have to prove ourselves," he says. "This place has the potential for great wine, but we're just beginning." As he sees it, his job is to craft wines that will bring Michigan, specifically Michigan sparkling wine, to the attention of wine lovers elsewhere. Though he only makes some three hundred cases of it each year, Talismon tastes so good that it already is doing just that.

Michigan is the fourth largest grape-growing state in the country, but the great majority of the crop goes into jellies and juices. Serious wine growing is confined mainly to two spits of land that form a wishbone above Traverse City—Leelanau to the west and Old Mission to the east. Viticulture in these twin Viticultural Areas is defined and indeed enabled by their proximity to Grand Traverse Bay, itself an appendage of Lake Michigan. Because the bay stores summer heat, lingering warmth helps stave off early autumn frosts, giving the grapes extra time to ripen. Conversely, the frigid water in spring helps prevent early budbreak, thus serving as a natural form of frost protection. And in winter, heavy lake-effect snow insulates and protects the vines.

The climate this far north is almost always cool, so many grapes will never get ripe. Not surprisingly, the vinifera varieties that to date have fared best for still wines are the Alsatian trio of Pinot Gris, Riesling, and Gewurztraminer. Quality varies by vintage, some years being just too cold, but in the hands of talented winemakers such as Bryan Ulbrich at Peninsula Cellars, the wines can be very good. Larry Mawby applauds those efforts, while at the same time arguing that the growing conditions that make table wine production difficult prove ideal for sparkling wine grapes—specifically Chardonnay, Pinot Gris, Pinot Noir, and Vignoles—just about every year. That no one has yet followed him and made more than the occasional bottle of northern Michigan bubbly has more to do with temerity than *terroir*. Sparklers are both difficult and costly to make. They require continual diligence on the part of the winemaker, and, especially if made by the *méthode champenoise* (with the second fermentation in the bottle), a significant expenditure of capital. Particularly if working in a relatively obscure region, it takes money and courage to devote oneself to them. Mawby doesn't have all that much of the one, but he makes up for it with an abundance of the other—the courage of his heartfelt conviction.

In most New World wine-growing regions, grapes for sparkling wine are grown right alongside those for still wine, there being no equivalent of Champagne in France—a viticultural area devoted almost exclusively to bubbly because the grapes grown there simply can't ripen sufficiently for table wine. Many New World vintners thus feel compelled to harvest unripe grapes for their sparkling wines. Since they need the sugars to be low and the acids high, they have no real alternative. But according to Larry Mawby, this approach has a definite downside. "No matter what kind of wine you're making, unripe grapes will always taste wrong," he argues. "A winemaker always wants grapes that are ripe. But you have to understand that ripe means different things in different places." In most American wine-growing regions, the vast majority of which are significantly warmer than the Leelanau Peninsula, ripeness entails rich, juicy, even opulent flavors. By contrast, ripe fruit in northern Michigan tastes much sharper and crisper. As Mawby notes, he can harvest grapes evidencing that sort of vibrant, vivacious character virtually every year. "That," he says, "is what makes this place special."

Though the Leelanau Peninsula is not (yet) well known for wine grapes, it long has been celebrated for another fruit: cherries. And cherries are what first brought the Mawby family there. Larry's father was a downstate apple farmer who presciently realized back in the 1950s that he needed to diversify to stay in business. In 1953, he bought a Leelanau cherry orchard near the resort town of Suttons Bay. Ten years later, he moved his family north. Mawby spent such an idyllic adolescence in Suttons Bay that after graduating from Michigan State in 1972, he knew he wanted to make his home there. But he also knew that he wanted to do something different from his father. "Like my Dad, I liked the idea of making my living off the land," he remembers, "but I wasn't really interested in a large-scale, commercial business. Instead, I wanted something smaller, something aesthetically pleasing. I liked the idea of taking a crop to the table, of being connected to the consumer."

Like so many of his generation, he had developed an interest in wine as a student during a trip to Europe—"where I couldn't afford to drink Coke," he laughs. Boutique wines were just then becoming trendy, and Suttons Bay was a fashionable summer vacation destination. Mawby figured that if he could grow grapes and make decent wine, he'd have an audience for it. So, with his father's blessing, he planted a few experimental acres with a score of different hybrid varieties. Though a couple of adventuresome Leelanau home winemakers already had demonstrated that wine grapes could ripen this far north, no one had systematically studied which varieties would grow best. "We just didn't know," says Mawby, speaking not only of himself but also of the era's other pioneers—Bernie Rink, who grew the first grapes in the area; and Edward O'Keefe, who planted the first vinifera varieties at his Chateau Grand Traverse winery. "We just didn't know which plants would be productive, which would survive the winters." When he saw that some of his vines were thriving, Mawby took the plunge. He purchased thirty-two acres of primarily southwest-sloping hillsides, and in 1976 planted his own vineyard, using the two hybrid varieties that had fared best at his father's farm next door: Seyval Blanc and Vignoles. Over the years, the composition of this vineyard would change, as vinifera grapes would become dominant, but the Mawby mission was well underway. "I had become convinced," he says, "that this is a good place to grow wine grapes. And nothing that's happened since has changed my mind. We have seventeen thousand acres planted to cherries up here. Of those, at least twelve thousand are suitable for grapes, especially grapes for sparkling wine. Maybe I'm nuts, but I really do see the future of agriculture in this area being largely wine grapes."

Mawby admits that he didn't really know what he was doing when he made his first sparkling wine. "I made it like still wine—crushing the grapes, skin contact, barrel fermentation, the whole nine yards. It didn't really work." Yet, while the wine tasted heavy and coarse, it was not unpleasantly tart or shrill. "I knew the problem was me, not the grapes," he acknowledges. So he went to work, reading everything he could find, asking questions, gaining experience and expertise. Three years later he made a sparkler that he thought tasted something like Champagne, the first L. Mawby wine to really express Leelanau's potential. Disgorged and offered for sale in 1990, it attracted considerable attention. "People who tasted it kept telling me, 'If you can do that here, you should do more.' That was my first eureka moment."

From that point on, Mawby became more serious about bubbly. He started making sparklers on a custom basis for other wineries—one hundred cases here, two hundred there—an experience that enabled him to hone his craft, giving him multiple cuvées each year. And he began grooming his own vineyard specifically for sparklers. In 1996, following a bout with colon cancer, he decided to make the commitment complete. "Back when I started, I had promised to give myself twenty years, enough time to see if this business would work," he explains. "Well, at the twenty-year mark, the business was fine. But when I took stock, I realized that I wasn't. I was still making more still wine than sparkling, and I didn't really have the right equipment to make the best sparkling. So I told myself to stop fooling around." It was a big gamble, bigger than the one he took when he first opened his winery for business. L. Mawby had become an established local brand with loyal customers. The decision to make only bubbly meant that many favorite wines would disappear. "But I had to do it," Mawby says firmly. "I wanted to make the best I could, and sparkling was the best I made."

Over the next few years, Mawby spent a small fortune on equipment—a French gyropalette to riddle or turn the bottles and settle the sediment, a disgorging machine and corker, a used tank press, then a brand-new tank press, bottles imported from Champagne, a whole new building for storage, and more. "Lots of capital went out"—he laughs—"while not much income came in." He needed to age the wine on its lees for three years or so before releasing it, so for a time had little inventory to sell but plenty of bills to pay. It was all part of the gamble—which after a few lean years began to pay off. By the start of the new millennium, L. Mawby was attracting new customers as well as keeping old local ones, as word of this surprising, even remarkable wine began to seep out ever so slowly. Johnny Apple of *The New York Times* praised it, as did Tom Stevenson, the British Champagne and sparkling wine expert, who would soon become a friend. And Mawby kept fine-tuning it, experimenting with different blends. "It was a steep learning curve," he says, "and I'm still on it." Though he arguably makes too many different cuvées, all his experimentation is clearly necessary. No one else in northern Michigan can show or teach him what to do.

Mawby recognizes that he is very much a pioneer, and as such is eager for others to follow him on the path he has trod. "I very much want other people to come here," he says. "If I don't have credible competition, then I'll just be a freak." He contends that, with the possible exception of Mendocino County, virtually all of California is too hot for good bubbly, so wonders why the French Champagne houses that invested so heavily in California back in the 1970s and 1980s did not seriously investigate Michigan—where the climate is so much more like

Reims in Champagne than Yountville in Napa, and where the grapes evidence a similar lean, angular profile.

At the same time, Mawby recognizes that sparkling wine remains a difficult sell in America, as too many consumers think of it solely as a celebration beverage—something to lift in toast at a wedding or on New Year's, but not a serious wine. With characteristic enthusiasm, he describes these marketing problems as opportunities, not obstacles. "I think there is a huge untapped market in this country," he insists. "We don't always do a good job selling sparkling wine to Americans, but that doesn't mean that people don't like it when they taste it." Many people, including the Champagne executives who invested so heavily in California, have made that same argument for decades now. That they have not yet succeeded in changing the country's palate in no way dims Larry Mawby's enthusiasm—for his wine and for his pioneering mission.

Part of that mission involves introducing sometimes skeptical consumers not only to Michigan wine, and not only to Michigan wine with bubbles, but to sparkling wine itself—a beverage worth savoring and sipping no matter the occasion. "It's fun," he exclaims. "Drinking this stuff is just plain fun!" His tank-fermented M. Lawrence line of bubbly is designed to promote just that sense of pleasure. Moderately priced, these wines sport lighthearted names so as to demystify the category. The most popular, a slightly off-dry, simple but tasty rosé, is called "Sex," a name that Mawby never believed the authorities would accept. "But they did," he says, laughing, "and let me tell you, Sex sells!" His plan is to grow the line and eventually sell it, and then to use the profits to further improve his estate vineyard. M. Lawrence bubbly doesn't have to come from Michigan, but L. Mawby sparklers do. And Michigan is where his heart lies. "Passion even more than money is what we need here," he says thoughtfully. "Those of us who started in Michigan thirty years ago were nuts, but we had passion. We need more of that now."

While Mawby's infectious zeal can prove inspirational, the quality of his wine is ultimately what will compel other vintners to invest their dollars and their passions in Michigan. Talismon tastes rich and full but at the same time finely balanced, with a seductively creamy texture and plenty of zesty acidity for support. At present, it is a blend of four grape varieties: three vinifera (Chardonnay, Pinot Gris, and Pinot Noir) and one hybrid (Vignoles). Mawby makes no apologies for using a hybrid grape, as Vignoles contributes depth to the wine, but he acknowledges that his best blends to date have been those in which it has played only a supporting role. "The trick," he says, "is to keep it in check," his goal being a harmonious mélange of flavors, with no one variety dominating the others.

To that end, Mawby recognizes that he needs to plant more Chardonnay and Pinot Noir, and envisions slowly increasing production as he narrows his focus, concentrating on what he and his Leelanau vineyard do best—Talismøn, which as its name suggests, is something extraordinary if not actually magical. (Mawby initially called it Talisman, switching to the ø after he discovered that Talisman Cellars in California has exclusive rights to the name.) "You don't really need tons of money to make sparkling wine," he insists, "and you don't need to work on a big scale. But you do need that passion in order to stay focused." Outside of California, the only other notable American winery that focuses exclusively on sparklers is Gruet in New Mexico, and perhaps not surprisingly that Champagne family outpost makes some excellent *méthode champenoise* bubbly. Even within the Golden State, the finest sparklers tend to be those coming from producers that don't get distracted with still wines, Roederer Estate being the leading example. As Larry Mawby argues, bubbly is different—to make, to grow, and to appreciate. "It's not just still wine with bubbles," he says simply. "It's a completely different animal. And to make it, you really need that focus." Though Mawby now is single-minded in his pursuit of high quality, Champagne-inspired sparklers, he also is alone in that quest in northern Michigan. But the excellence of Talismøn suggests that he may not be so for all that long.

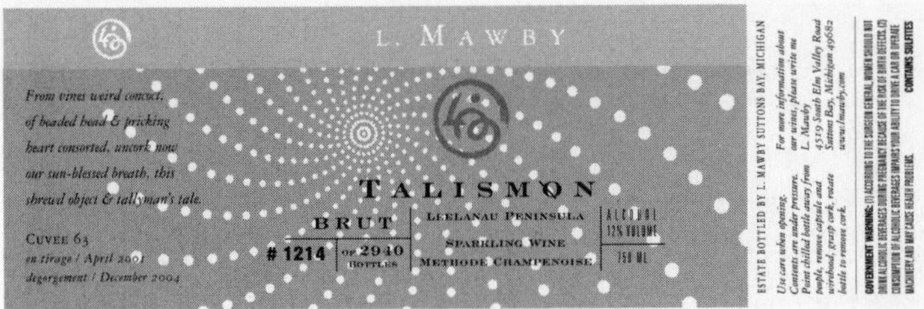

A NOTE ON VINTAGES:

A non-vintage blend, Talismon is delicious when first offered for sale. It does have the requisite acidity for successful cellaring; but since I have not tasted older cuvées (Larry had sold out when I visited), I don't know how long it will stay fresh and vibrant.

THE SUGGESTED PRICE FOR THE CURRENT RELEASE IS $27.

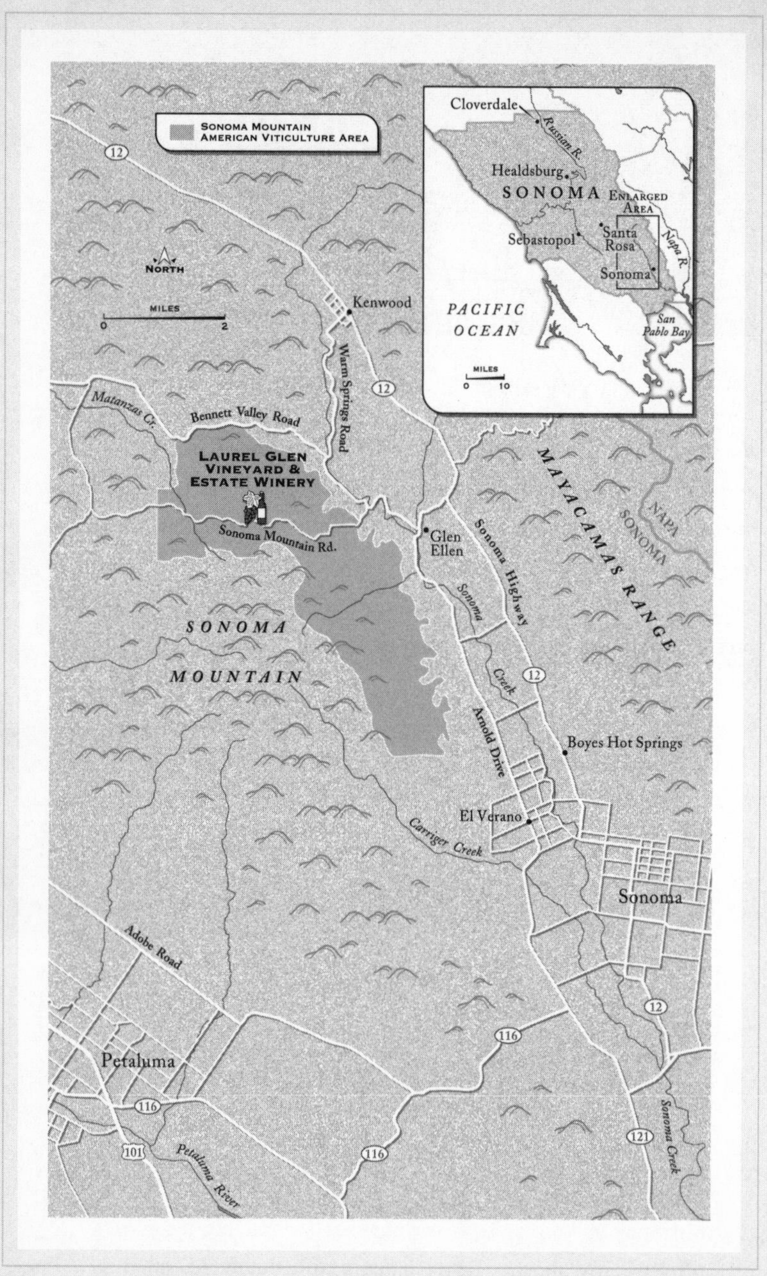

LAUREL GLEN AND THE SONOMA MOUNTAIN AVA

CHAPTER 21

Laurel Glen Cabernet Sauvignon

Sonoma Mountain, California

...

Patrick Campbell

It can be easy to overlook Laurel Glen Cabernet Sauvignon. The grapes come from an estate vineyard on Sonoma Mountain, an appellation with a long history of wine growing, but one that is not especially well known. The winery sits at the end of a long, private dirt road, and production is small, usually less than one thousand cases. There is no tasting room, not even a road sign. The owner and winemaker, Patrick Campbell, lives next door, and he values his family's privacy. Very much a man of principle, Campbell does not spend much time marketing Laurel Glen. He used to go on the road with it, but now, with more than a quarter century of vintages under his belt, he lets the wine sell itself. Thus Campbell does not send samples to critics, advertise his wine in glossy magazines, or otherwise court the press. And because he pays little attention to the whims of fashion, he refuses to adapt his winemaking style to anyone's preferences but his own.

Laurel Glen Cabernet tastes elegant and nuanced, much as it has ever since the first commercial release back in 1981. Firmly structured, it inevitably benefits from a few years of aging, after which it displays grace and finesse much more than muscle or brawn. In that, it echoes its origin, both the rugged serenity of the vineyard and the gentle strength of the man. At a time when many supposedly elite wines are distinguished more by hype than merit, their styles having been adjusted to get points from pundits, this wine's distinction comes completely from what is in the bottle. Despite its occasional obscurity, there is no better Cabernet grown in Sonoma County, and only a handful elsewhere in the country over the past two decades have proven to be its equal. Wine lovers overlook it, then, at their own loss.

Sonoma Mountain has a rich tradition of viticulture. The first vineyards were planted in the 1860s, and no area in California was more highly regarded for red varieties at the turn of the last century. Yet few nineteenth-century wineries actually were located there, roads being rare and the terrain rugged. Instead, growers tended to sell their fruit to winemakers elsewhere. That helps explain why, despite the region's earlier renown, post-Prohibition viticulture did not take off until four full decades after Repeal. Even today, most of the grapes are trucked down to the valleys below—either on the east side, where wineries such as Benziger and Kenwood use the fruit, or to the west, toward the city of Santa Rosa. Only a few vintners make wine on Sonoma Mountain itself. Of these, Campbell, who purchased the original thirteen-acre Laurel Glen vineyard in 1977, is the clear leader. He now farms thirty-five contiguous acres, twenty-four of which he owns, all planted to Cabernet. The wines he makes from the grapes there set a qualitative as well as stylistic standard for the region. Put simply, they define what Sonoma Mountain Cabernet is, and can be.

For a wine fashioned from mountain grapes, Laurel Glen Cabernet tastes unexpectedly supple rather than strapping. Campbell credits the vineyard for his wine's elegant character. He specifically points to its eastern exposure, arguing that the west-facing mountain vineyards across the way receive the full brunt of afternoon sunshine, resulting in grapes with thicker skins and higher levels of astringent tannin. By contrast, the Laurel Glen vineyard only receives direct sun during the cool morning hours, so the wines are texturally softer. It's an interesting theory, one that seems to hold up in the Sonoma Valley (though not as well across the way in Napa). In addition to Laurel Glen's, the top Cabernets from Sonoma Mountain include Kenwood's from the Jack London Vineyard, Benziger's Estate bottling, and Ravenswood's Pickberry blend, and they do seem more lithe and fragrant than wines from the west-facing Mayacamas side of the valley.

For Laurel Glen, other aspects of the *terroir* are probably just as important as exposure. Elevation, for example, is critical, since the vineyard sits just above the fogline, a position that allows the grape clusters to ripen evenly. Soils, too, play a crucial role. "The great difficulty here, and the great benefit, is the variety of soils," says Campbell. "We have distinct types, all volcanic, and depending on the depth, very different when it comes to vigor and growth. A vineyard like this is difficult to farm, but it gives complexity to the wine." The difficulty comes from the separate sections of the property ripening grapes at their own pace, so that harvest at Laurel Glen typically takes from four to five weeks (as opposed to only a few days at many wineries), even with just the one variety planted. Other vintners might save time and trouble by picking at two or three intervals. But Campbell and his vineyard manager, Valente Rodriguez, go through the vineyard up to eighteen times, harvesting the ripe fruit not only block by block but often row by row within each block, and sometimes even vine by vine. Their goal is full maturity, meaning, in Campbell's words, "the appropriate balance of all the components of the grape."

"Balance" is a word that comes up frequently when talking with Patrick Campbell—both when referring to wine and when discussing other aspects of life, especially life on Sonoma Mountain. That may be because religion and meditation, not viticulture, first brought him there. In January 1973, then twenty-five years old and looking for direction—not because he had none, but because he felt pulled in so many different ones—Campbell joined a lay community of Zen Buddhists on Sonoma Mountain Road. He had become acquainted with Buddhism as a graduate student at Harvard, and was drawn to Zen because of what he calls "its cerebral quality," the opportunity that life in a contemplative community might provide for achieving inner harmony. The son of a university history professor, Campbell had earned his master's degree in the philosophy of religion, but felt too restless to follow his father up the ivory tower; a musician, he played the viola professionally, but was unsure whether he had the talent or drive to make a career of it. Already something of a Renaissance man, he had lots of interests but no one consuming passion. During his time at the Genjo Ji Zen Center, he found just that, though it certainly was not anything he imagined when he first arrived.

The Zen community owned a three-acre vineyard, and one of Campbell's first tasks as a resident was to take care of it. "I discovered that I really liked doing that," he says, "being outside, working in the elements, being part of them." Over the course of his three years there, he continued to play music, then got married and began a family, practiced daily meditation, and became ever more fascinated with wine growing. "By the time I left," he remembers, "I knew that I was going to dedicate myself completely to viticulture."

Campbell left the Zen Center because he grew restless with the ascetic, communal life, but he is quick to credit his time there with giving him the opportunity to find the direction he sought. "Zen taught me balance, discipline, and control," he says succinctly. The balance that he found in wine growing involved the juxtaposition of manual labor with intellectual insight, working with mind as well as body, and being in control of both. Campbell is very much an intellectual vintner, a sort of Wendell Berry of grapes, concerned not just with harvesting a crop but with treating his vineyard as a living entity. He believes in working with rather than simply on it, so as to respect its individuality and character. "This is a special place," he says. "I feel privileged, and humbled, to be here."

Viticulture first fascinated this self-confessed "generalist" because he saw it incorporating so many different interests—everything from chemistry and mechanics to natural history and aesthetics. But Campbell also was attracted by the physical challenge involved. One of the remarkable things about the man is that, as a victim of childhood polio, he is paralyzed in both legs, yet insists on working every aspect of the vineyard and winery himself. He swings along on crutches, hoists himself onto a tractor equipped with handles that allow him to work it manually, and even manages to make it to the tops of tanks of fermenting wine in order to punch down the caps. It sounds clichéd to say that he has refused to succumb to adversity, but it's difficult to convey exactly how strong Campbell is—both physically and mentally. An ardent kayaker, he has an extremely fit upper body, evident in his muscled arms and firm handshake. An independent thinker, he looks you straight in the eye, and has no qualms about expressing an opinion—on wine, politics, or pretty much anything else. At the same time, there is nothing brash or aggressive about him. As the British wine writer Oz Clarke has observed admiringly, "Gentleness, utmost gentleness, is his creed."

Laurel Glen Cabernet thus expresses Campbell's character as much as his vineyard's *terroir*. "I like wines with acid and not too much alcohol, wines in balance," he says. "That's what this vineyard, which is cool for Cabernet, gives. That's what I make." His wine displays blackcurrant fruit flavors, tinged with mint and bitter chocolate undertones, as well as a wisp of earth. Though rich, it seems above all tender, with nary a component—acid, fruit, tannin—out of place. Its admirers sometimes cite its balance when they compare it to Bordeaux, but in truth it's very much a California wine, with a sunny disposition and a lingering sweetness.

But Laurel Glen Cabernet does not taste much like the over-extracted, highly alcoholic Golden State wines that are so in vogue today. Campbell calls those "Parker wines." While he certainly respects the noted critic (who championed early releases, but has only occasionally reviewed Laurel Glen Cabernet recently), he disparages what he considers the one man's excessive influence on contemporary American wine. He is particularly critical of the 100-point scale. "Numerical scores work fine for dog races, math tests, and fruit fly populations," he argues, "but not for wine!" He contends that the use of this scale, particularly in *The Wine Advocate* and *The Wine Spectator*, has led to homogeneity, with many contemporary wines fashioned to earn high scores, and so tasting alike. "Too many California wines are boring now," he says. "The scale discourages regional character and winemaker individuality. It suggests a fixed truth. But wine is alive, so never fixed. It ages and changes, just as we change." That Laurel Glen Cabernet never tastes boring is easy to understand. The man and the site together give it integrity.

Although Campbell took a few courses here and there, he was largely self-taught as a vintner. And having found methods early on that work, he sees no reason to change them now. Along with Ray Kaufman, his right-hand man in the winery, he vinifies his Cabernet unconventionally, treating it much as many people treat Pinot Noir, using squat, open-top fermenting tanks, and laboriously punching down the cap of skins rather than pumping juice over the top. That's how he fermented homemade wine when he first bought the Laurel Glen vineyard—in a plastic garbage can, pushing the cap down so as to bring oxygen to the must. Working on a larger scale now, his rationale is that pumping would extract extra tannin from the grapeskins and pips, and that Sonoma Mountain fruit has sufficient tannin all by itself.

Campbell wants a gentle wine, so he treats it gently in the winery, trying to retain all the subtleties and nuances that come from the separate soil types and vineyard blocks. He does not leave the young wine on the skins in an extended maceration to gain color and grip, again because he thinks his fruit has plenty already. Instead, right after fermentation, he presses the wine into French oak barrels, where it stays for nearly two years. About halfway through that period, he and Kaufman begin to make a selection of the best lots, which they blend together to form that vintage's edition of Laurel Glen. The remaining lots, often well over half the production, go into a second label called "Counterpoint."

"Not much has changed over the years," Campbell says when reviewing his production methods. "I might pick the grapes a little riper now, but that's only because the vineyard's older and I want to keep the acid down and the wine in balance. It's not to get the flavor up." The first wine he made that truly impressed him came in 1978. Never released commercially, it still ranks among his favorites and still tastes delicious—deeply flavored and in near perfect balance. "I hope what I make is still at that level," he says modestly.

When Campbell left the Zen Center in 1976, he used a small inheritance to buy Laurel Glen, which had been named by its owner, Carmen Taylor, for a grove of trees on the property. The purchase consisted of thirteen acres, three of which already were planted to Cabernet. Gradually, he expanded the vineyard, clearing and planting an acre the next year, two the year after, and so on. Taylor had sold her grapes to Chateau St. Jean, which for a couple of years bottled a Laurel Glen vineyard designate. Campbell did the same, and then added Kenwood as a buyer. But before long, the idea of keeping the fruit and making wine began to take hold. He saw the prices that the wines made from his grapes fetched, and quickly realized that while small-scale grape growing brought meager profits, high-quality winemaking could supply his young family with an adequate income. He knew that his homemade wine was good, so had faith in his ability to fashion a reputable commercial cuvée. His first Cabernet went to market in 1984, as did Campbell himself, who beat the proverbial bushes bringing it to the attention of restaurateurs and retailers across the country. From the very beginning, the wine attracted curious, then loyal customers. His fifth release, from the 1985 vintage, cemented its reputation, and from that point on, Campbell no longer needed to work to sell it.

Not one to rest, let alone rest on laurels, Campbell soon turned his attention to other winemaking endeavors. The Laurel Glen vineyard yields only about 2 tons per acre, and the cost of farming it is high. As a result, the wine is expensive. (Recent releases sell for roughly $50 a bottle.) Campbell decided that he wanted to make another wine, one "that ordinary people could afford." This new wine wouldn't come from Sonoma Mountain, but rather from purchased grapes, sourced primarily from Napa and Sonoma counties. Called "Terra Rosa," it debuted in 1992 and sold for $10. A few years later, the California grape market dried up, but Campbell had already moved on—to South America, first Chile and then Argentina, where he contracted to buy grapes and wine for import. Today, he makes roughly 18,000 cases of value-priced South American wine, as well as a comparable amount sourced from Lodi (under the REDS and ZaZin labels). He's made money from these ventures; but to his mind as important is the fact that he has offered consumers good wines at reasonable prices. "Look," he says, "wine shouldn't be thought of as a luxury. It's something to drink. Wines like Laurel Glen are special, but they're not everything."

As that statement indicates, Campbell is at heart a realist. Or, as he puts it, a skeptic. "A skeptic keeps an open mind," he explains. "You have to do that when you're working in a medium that changes from year to year. If you ever get into a rut, start making wine by a formula and stop asking questions, then you might as well give up." Happy at home on remote, isolated Sonoma Mountain, he pays little regard to talk of glamorous "wine country," just as he has little patience for claims that winemaking is an ethereal art. "There's nothing glamorous about pruning in the rain, or breathing sulfur dioxide in the winery for ten hours," he says. "And it would be nice to think I'm some great 'artiste,' but that's just not the case."

Making wine, Campbell insists, is nothing more, and nothing less, than a reputable, honorable craft—one in which a human being works with what nature provides in order to purvey pleasure. Many well-known contemporary winemakers try to add to what nature gives them by making wines in a predetermined mold. Such wines can taste fine, but the pleasure they give is inevitably one-dimensional. Laurel Glen Cabernet does much more, as its subtleties and nuances—the secondary notes reminiscent of spice and dried herbs that augment the rich taste of dark fruit—give it true distinction. That distinction comes from the vineyard, but the vineyard as lived and worked by the man. As Campbell himself admits: "I'm really a vineyard guy. After all these years, I think I understand this place pretty well."

A NOTE ON VINTAGES:

This wine's well-defined structure and rich but restrained fruit flavors make it an excellent candidate for cellaring. It simply gets better, meaning more complex and multilayered, with time. The 1978, a wine not even released commercially, was still vibrant and vital when tasted in 2003, so strong vintages should last a good twenty years. These include 1986, 1990, 1992, 1999, and 2001.

THE SUGGESTED PRICE FOR THE CURRENT 2002 RELEASE IS $50.

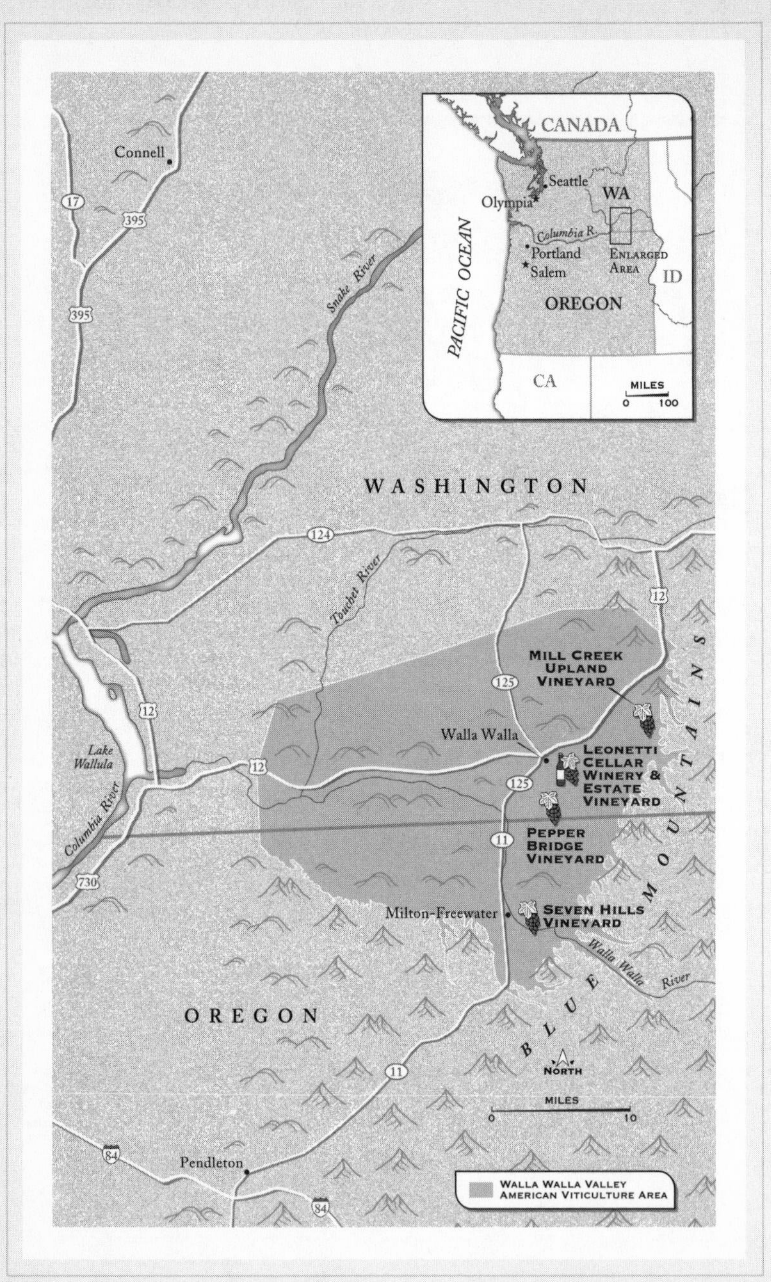

LEONETTI CELLAR'S WALLA WALLA VINEYARDS

CHAPTER 22

Leonetti Cellar Merlot

Columbia Valley, Washington

...

"We just can't rest on our collective thumbs," argues Gary Figgins, when asked what the future might hold for Leonetti Cellar and the other wineries in Washington State's Walla Walla Valley—the source of an increasing number of superb, long-lived American red wines. "If we stop making dust, we'll end up eating it." Figgins has been the wine pacesetter in Walla Walla for a long time. His Cabernets and Merlots helped bring the region early acclaim back in the 1970s and 1980s, winning so many plaudits that fellow Evergreen State producers felt compelled to try to emulate them. And in the 1990s, when Figgins started using ever more local grapes, other vintners followed—buying land, planting vineyards, and setting up shop in this isolated corner of the Pacific Northwest. Walla Walla, previously known primarily for onions, suddenly became the source of some of the country's most coveted because compelling wines.

Chris and Gary Figgins

No wine made in Walla Walla is more sought after than Leonetti Cellar Merlot. Some twenty years ago, it became the first Washington wine to achieve cult status, with demand outpacing supply and sales allocated to clients on a waiting list. That list is longer than ever today, and not surprisingly, many of Washington's best red wines echo Leonetti's style—opulently rich and ripe but at the same time clearly shaped and structured. Though Figgins does not use only local grapes, Walla Walla fruit dominates his Merlot blend. "I started making wine here because I lived here," he explains. "But over the years I've come to believe that the soils and climate of Walla Walla make this one of the best places on earth to grow red wine grapes." As late as 1995, only six wineries called Walla Walla home. Today, there are nearly forty, with over 1,000 acres under vine. When asked what accounts for this phenomenal growth, Figgins answers quickly. "Wines here," he says, "taste like our own." Leonetti Cellar Cabernet and Merlot have demonstrated as much for nearly three decades now. That's why they're Walla Walla's benchmarks, and why Figgins continues to make plenty of dust.

Walla Walla is nothing if not remote. Located just north of the Oregon border (the AVA in fact includes vineyards there), and some 100 miles from the Idaho line, it has a long farming history but a relatively short record of grape growing. Isolation and distance, however, not inherent fruit character, account for the fact that commercial viticulture came to it later than to other parts of Washington's Columbia Valley. For a long time, wheat, alfalfa, peas, and of course onions were the big crops, with grapes an afterthought—if a thought at all.

Gary Figgins was one of the few who pondered them. His maternal grandfather, Frank Leonetti, had grown a variety he called "Black Prince" (most probably Cinsault) on a Walla Walla hillside, and Figgins remembers being served small portions of homemade wine, diluted with plenty of water, as a child. He liked it, but even more than the taste, the process of fermentation is what intrigued him. "I loved to watch the stuff bubble away," he says with a laugh. Later, as a young man, he tried his hand at it, fermenting local apples, cherries, elderberries, and more. But it was only when he began making trips to California as an Army Reservist that his hobby started to turn into a passion. He sampled wines there unlike any he knew from home, wines that augmented their forward taste of fruit with unexpected nuances and subtleties. And he became fascinated by wines that resembled one another but at the same time seemed individualistic—the similarities and differences, for instance, in a series of Napa Valley Cabernets. "I got hooked," he says simply. So, back home in Walla Walla, he started reading everything he could find about wines, and hatching plans. By then he was married, with a young child, and working as a machinist in a local can-manufacturing plant. He knew it would take time, but he was determined to become a winemaker.

Figgins made his first wine in 1975, a Pinot Noir from purchased California grapes that he aged in an old whiskey barrel. But from the start he wanted to use Washington, especially Walla Walla, fruit. So the year before, with the help of his uncles, he had cleared and planted his initial vineyard, a small plot on the hill just above the original Leonetti homestead. Dry-farmed, it contained mostly Cabernet, with a few rows of Riesling. A few years later, as soon as his bank account allowed, he planted another vineyard, this time beside his home, and this time with Merlot. At that point he bonded his winery—a former tackroom next to his house (his basement provided storage). Leonetti Cellar wines, the first to be produced commercially in the Walla Walla Valley, began flowing with the 1978 vintage.

Although the idea of making fine wine in Walla Walla was certainly unconventional at the time, Figgins was not entirely alone. His wife, Nancy, who believed in the project from the start, ran the business side of the enterprise. And his good friend Rick Small, who lived just outside of town, shared his enthusiasm for fine wine. Small had been in the Army Reserve with Figgins, and the two men had toured California wine country together, learning, sampling, and becoming ever more fascinated. Now, in Walla Walla, Small was making small lots of experimental wine, and the two men constantly talked and tasted together, trying each other's wines and comparing them with those they remembered from their travels. "It was great to have someone to bounce ideas off of," Figgins remembers. "It didn't take all that long for us to become pretty sure that our wines were good."

Rick Small would go on to start his own winery—Woodward

Canyon in Lowden, a few miles west of Walla Walla, where his barrel-fermented Chardonnay, toasty Cabernet, and rich Merlot have earned him a strong following. But back in town, Figgins and Leonetti Cellar already were pioneering a Walla Walla identity—"fruit like California," he says, "in a wine that has acid and structure like Bordeaux." The 1978 Leonetti Cabernet, released in 1981, exemplified as much, and was named "best in America" by *Wine and Spirits* magazine. By that point Figgins had set himself a new goal: to grow the business so that he could quit his machinist job and devote himself fully to wine.

"We had to move slowly," Figgins insists, "and we needed to stay focused." Neither he nor Nancy had money to invest in the winery, so growth had to be funded entirely from sales. At first, they longed for orders, and they can remember racing each other to answer the phone. Before long, however, it seemed as though the phone was ringing all the time, as few Leonetti Cellar customers failed to call back and reorder. Figgins liked the idea of making a number of different wines, but decided that staying focused meant concentrating on the reds. "I found they were my forte," he says. "I made a Gewurztraminer in 1978, and Chardonnay and Riesling up until 1983, but I then kicked out the whites to have more space and equipment for the reds." Cabernet got most of his attention until, as he puts it, "events focused things on Merlot."

Those events occurred in the marketplace as well as in the vineyard. The grapes grown in the Leonetti Estate vineyard proved richly concentrated, and when Figgins began offering Merlot for sale (the first vintage was 1981), consumer demand began to skyrocket. It wasn't just for his wine. As a category, Washington State Merlot boomed in popularity all through the 1980s. Led both by moderately priced, large-production wines like Columbia Crest and by expensive, small-volume ones like Leonetti and Woodward Canyon, Washington Merlot offered suppleness with structure, a combination that few elsewhere could match. To be sure, some wines missed the mark, but when compared to Merlots of the time from California, Washington's tended to have higher acids and more tannins, so seemed less flabby or candied. These wines were fully fruited, with black rather than red berry flavors. At the same time, they seemed soft and inviting, with little astringency. Though the Merlot boom of that era was not led primarily by Washington State, Washington's renditions were more consistently successful than most—both in terms of intrinsic quality and in terms of consumer demand. The varietal soon became the state's flagship, as it put Washington on the proverbial radar screen for wine lovers living far away. And though only a small number of them ever tasted Leonetti Cellar Merlot, this one wine was the category's unquestioned standard-bearer. As Figgins acknowledges, "it's the wine of ours that more people know."

From the very beginning, Leonetti Cellar Merlot was a rich, extroverted wine. Figgins insists that he has toned things down a bit over the years, aiming for a more polished style than he did at first, but the wines he is making today remain extremely opulent. Lavishly oaked, they are even more lavishly fruited. Especially when young, they seem about as seductive and, yes, sexy as any red wine can possibly be. Though they age well, developing a smoky character after eight to ten years in bottle, they become less distinctive because tamer and more restrained over time. Chris Figgins, Gary's son, who works alongside him in both the vineyard and the cellar these days, describes the Leonetti style perfectly. "We love the flash and flesh of Merlot," he says. "That's what we want our wine to express. And that's why it's so good when it's young." At a tasting at the winery in January 2003, featuring wines going back to the 1980s, the most exciting I sampled were those four to eight years old. While they had lost any grapey, baby-fat character, they were still lush and luxurious—mouth-watering and unquestionably hedonistic. The Rubenesque 1998 in particular stood out that day, being concentrated and complex but not at all weighty or brooding, a seductive delight to sip.

Part of the pleasure provided by Leonetti Merlot comes from its marriage of wine and wood. Gary Figgins is an unabashed fan of new oak barrels. While he acknowledges that some wines from other producers can seem over-wooded, he insists that the culprit in such cases isn't the barrel so much as the juice. "If there's too much oak flavor in a wine," Figgins argues, "then there's not enough fruit flavor. We make sure to use the best grapes as well as the best barrels." To get top oak barrels, he buys from different coopers in different places—France, to be sure, but also the United States and Hungary. He has even gone so far as to select oak logs himself, air-dry them at the winery, and then send them off to the cooperage. "I want the best," he says simply. To that end, he built a new winery in 2000, replete with an underground cave for barrel aging. That is where Leonetti Merlot rests, the barrels never stacked more than two high (so as to allow air to circulate evenly), for some thirteen months, during which period the wood and fruit flavors integrate and become harmonious—a happy marriage indeed. As Chris Figgins puts it, "Something magical happens when you put the best components together."

The search for the best grapes begins in Walla Walla, as some 75 percent of the Leonetti Cellar Merlot blend now comes from vineyards within the valley. In addition to the home vineyard, Figgins uses grapes from three other Walla Walla sites. Mill Creek, which his family owns outright, sits at the northern edge of the AVA. Pepper Bridge, a vineyard long respected as a source of some of Washington's finest grapes, lies just north of the Oregon border. And Seven Hills, an equally renowned vineyard that Figgins owns in partnership with a number of other vintners, actually is in Oregon. These four sites provide him with the fruit that forms the backbone of his Merlot blend. But roughly a quarter of the *cuvée* still comes from two vineyards farther west in the Columbia Valley—Sagemoor Farms near Pasco, and Conner-Lee on the Wahluke Slope near the town of Othello. "I've used fruit from there for a long time," he says simply. "It's as good as ever, so I see no reason to change."

Yields are kept low in all of these vineyards (from 1.5 to 3.5 tons per acre), no matter whether Gary and Chris Figgins manage the site themselves or contract with others to do it. And deficit irrigation, a time-consuming procedure in which the vines are monitored so as to receive less water than they want (but enough for what they actually need) is practiced in all the vineyards, the result being less vegetative growth and more intense flavors in small berries. "Our goal," says Chris, "is really ripe and really concentrated fruit"—again, the best. "We don't cut corners," insists his father. "Our whole focus is to have the best wine possible in the glass. If you don't strain every nerve to be first, you don't become second. You inevitably become last."

Production at Leonetti Cellar is small—some six thousand cases of wine a year, almost three thousand of which contain Merlot. Demand far outpaces that supply. Nancy Figgins sells roughly half the wine to distributors for restaurant purchase and half to individual customers on a mailing list. (There's a second list of more than 1,500 names, folks wanting to be able to place an order.) Despite this backlog, no one at Leonetti wants to increase production. "I've seen people in this business become successful, try to make two or three times as much wine, and then compromise themselves," says Gary Figgins. "We don't want that." Chris amplifies: "At this size, Dad and I can do all the wine work ourselves. That's what we like." But most of the profits at Leonetti Cellar still go back into the business—into the new winery and aging caves, for example, or into vineyard land. Up until 1997, Figgins had to buy most of the grapes for his wines. Now 85 percent of his total production comes from vineyards he and his family own. And all of those are at home, in the Walla Walla Valley.

A long growing season, marked by a succession of warm days and cool nights, coupled with fertile but well-drained soils, accounts for Walla Walla's ascendancy as a premium grape-growing region. Serious frost does not usually appear until late November, giving the grapes extra time to ripen physiologically—not so much gaining sugar as becoming completely supple. Chris Figgins argues that those final weeks before harvest are when Walla Walla fruit begins to reveal its true character. Since the nights turn chilly in the fall, acid levels stay high while the flavors become ever more rich and sumptuous. The only viticultural drawback in Walla Walla is an occasional winter freeze so severe that it can wipe out a vintage. The most recent hit in 1996. Gary Figgins purchased grapes that year from a grower in California's Dry Creek Valley to blend with what little quality Washington fruit he could find, and then put "Appellation America" on the label of his wines. Still, for

Figgins the advantages involved in growing grapes and making wine in this isolated corner of Washington State far outweigh that disadvantage. "We're fortunate to be here," he insists.

Others clearly agree. It's hard to keep up with wine in Walla Walla these days, as new vintners are arriving and new wineries opening all the time. With them come journalists and curious tourists, and this sleepy town is quickly waking up—with cozy bed and breakfasts, chic restaurants, and trendy boutiques now lining its streets. "It's fun being here these days," says Chris Figgins, "though it is harder to park downtown." Most of the Walla Walla winemakers have followed Leonetti Cellar's lead and so focus primarily on Cabernet and Merlot. Notable names include L'Ecole 41, Pepper Bridge, Seven Hills, and Tamarack Cellars. A few others, though, including Christophe Baron at Cayuse and Eric Dunham at Dunham Cellars, both of whom produce excellent Syrah, have gone their own way. Even they, though, acknowledge that they wouldn't be in Walla Walla were it not for Gary Figgins.

This enthusiastic, ebullient Washingtonian was the first to demonstrate that wine made in Walla Walla could compete qualitatively with top wines made elsewhere. At first, he could only use a small percentage of local fruit. As time passed and his fortunes improved, he has been able to use more and more—much of which he has planted himself. "But my goal today is the same as it was when I started," Figgins insists—"to make only ultra-high-quality, handcrafted wines." To the degree that his fellow Walla Walla winemakers share that ambition, they very much follow in his footsteps.

A NOTE ON VINTAGES:

There's no doubt that Leonetti Merlot can age, but increased secondary subtlety comes with a loss of vibrancy. And since bold, vibrant flavor is what makes this wine so special, I think it shows its best within a decade of harvest. Especially strong past vintages have included 1989, 1990, and 1994; stellar recent ones include 1998 and 2003.

THE SUGGESTED PRICE FROM THE WINERY FOR THE CURRENT 2003 RELEASE IS $60, THOUGH THE WINE OFTEN RETAILS FOR CONSIDERABLY MORE.

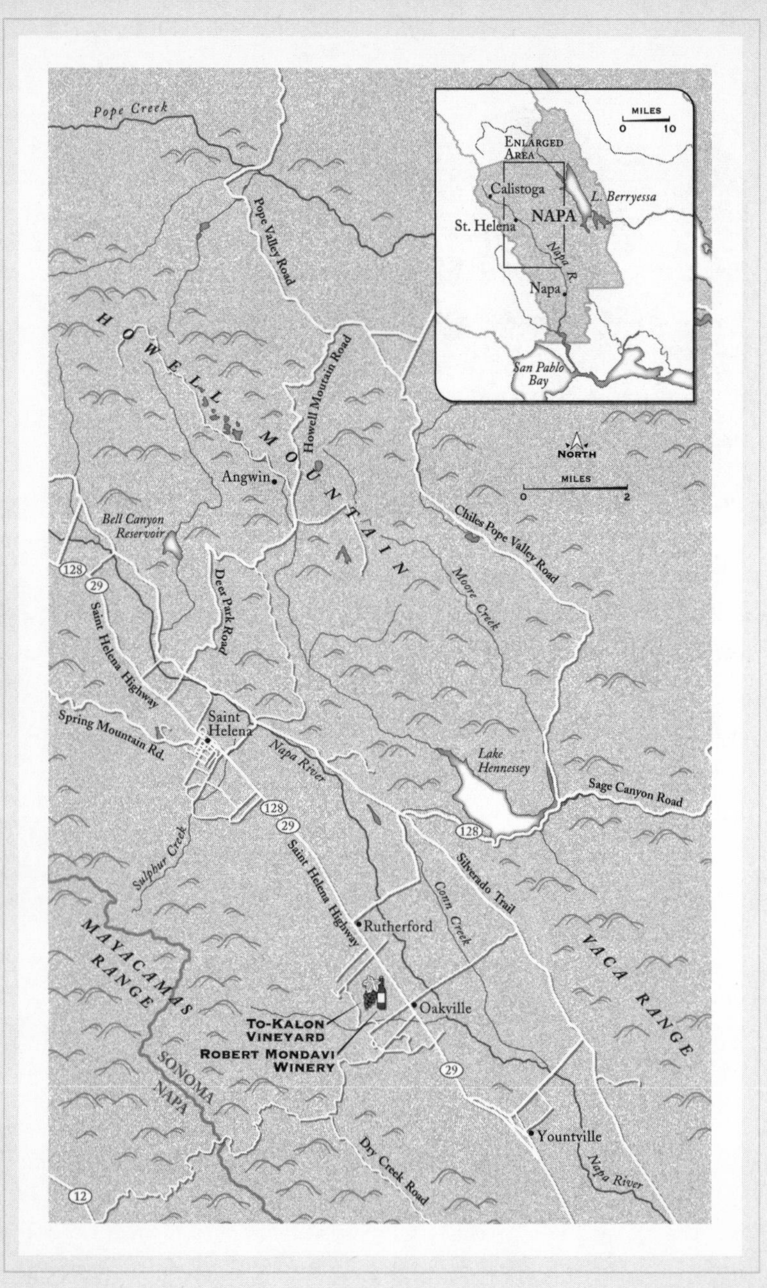

THE ROBERT MONDAVI WINERY AND THE TO-KALON VINEYARD

CHAPTER 23

Robert Mondavi Winery Cabernet Sauvignon Reserve

Napa Valley, California

...

Genevieve Janssens

Everything is in flux at the Robert Mondavi Winery in Oakville, in the very heart of the Napa Valley. Everything, that is, except the wine. Cabernet Sauvignon has long been Mondavi's best wine, and the young Mondavi Cabernets aging peacefully in French oak barrels are oblivious to all the changes whirling around them. Those changes involve management and ownership. Although this iconic Napa winery began as a family business and often was viewed as such by consumers, Mondavi in fact was for a long time part of a much larger public corporation; and a series of poor management decisions over the past decade produced increasingly unmanageable debt. So in December 2004, the corporation's board of directors, which included Robert Mondavi's son Tim and daughter Marcia, had no choice but to vote unanimously to accept an offer ($1.03 billion in cash and $325 million in assumed debt) from Constellation Brands, the world's largest wine company and a leading producer and marketer of spirits and beer. "Wearing my shareholder hat, this is a good day," Tim Mondavi told the press when the sale was announced. He then added, "wearing my family hat, it's a sad day."

If the Mondavi sale was inspired by financial need, its purchase was motivated by perceived opportunity—the opportunity it gave Constellation Brands to become *the* major player in American wine. In turn, much of that opportunity involved potential profits that would come from the sale of the Mondavi Corporation's non-Napa wines. But equally important was perception, the opportunity to be viewed by the wine trade and consumers alike as being an elite producer of elite wines. According to Jon Moramarco, president of the Constellation division devoted to fine wines, the top Mondavi Cabernets played an integral part in the Mondavi brand's public image: "For Constellation, this purchase was attractive because of the incredible power and recognition the Robert Mondavi brand has in the marketplace. The Reserve wines have been among the very best wines produced in the Napa Valley. They mean very much to the overall quality image and reputation of the Robert Mondavi legacy."

Constellation Brands, then named Canandaigua, was founded in 1945 by Marvin Sands in the Finger Lakes region of New York. For decades, the company made a steady profit through the sale of low-end wines, including J. Roget "Champagne," kosher Manischewitz, and Richard's Wild Irish Rose. That last wine, sweet and cheap, was named after Marvin's son Richard, who today serves as Constellation's chief executive. And it is Richard Sands who has orchestrated the company's recent rapid growth through acquisition. He has bought many wine and liquor companies—including Barton Brands, a large beer and spirits line, and such mass market California wine brands as Almaden, Inglenook, Paul Masson, and Taylor California Cellar. Perceiving that the market had changed, with fewer people buying jug wines and more willing to spend money on premium and ultra-premium varietals, Sands then got into the fine-wine business in 1999 with the purchase of Franciscan Estates in Napa. (Along with Franciscan, this acquisition included such plums as Simi in Sonoma and Veramonte in Chile.) Five years later, he plucked the ripest plum of all—Robert Mondavi.

In an interview a month after the sale was announced, Richard

Sands explained why he decided to purchase the Mondavi Corporation. Much of his rationale certainly centered on the less expensive, mass-market brands that share a name (but not much else) with the prestigious Napa winery—"Private Selection by Robert Mondavi," a line composed of wines that sell for about $10 and are sourced from coastal California vineyards, and "Woodbridge by Robert Mondavi," a set of wines costing about $7 and made from grapes grown primarily in the hot but fertile Central Valley. But Sands's first explanation focused on the Napa operation. "In our opinion," he said simply, "the Robert Mondavi Winery is the pre-eminent Napa Valley winery."

Some critics, particularly those who favor unabashedly powerful, heady wines, might differ with that assessment today, but there can be no arguing the fact that Mondavi was Napa's flagship winery for many decades. And Cabernet Sauvignon was always its flagship wine. It still is. The winery's reputation undoubtedly has lost some luster recently, but when it comes to quality in the glass, Mondavi still shines brightly with Napa Valley Cabernet, particularly with its Reserve. First produced in 1971, this wine signals the very best of the vintage. Rich and fruit-driven, but also harmonious and balanced, it continues to give more than a passing nod to Bordeaux while always reflecting its sunny California origin. Its identifiable style—forward cassis fruit flavor with a hint of mint in a firm but pliant structure, a wine of finesse rather than brawn—helped define Napa Cabernet when the valley first rose to international prominence a generation ago. That style is a bit anomalous now, as the contemporary vogue prefers more muscular wines, but this Cabernet remains true to its origins—both its primary vineyard source and its illustrious heritage. As Genevieve Janssens, who has helped craft it since 1997 and is now in charge of production, explains, Mondavi is "perhaps the only American winery that can give a winemaker a vision of tradition and the future together." Indeed, substantial past accomplishment, coupled with significant present achievement, explains why, despite all the current change, Robert Mondavi Reserve Cabernet deserves to remain ranked as one of America's finest wines.

The accomplishment began in 1966 with the opening of the winery—

the first wholly new Napa facility to be built since Prohibition, notable for its stylish pseudo-Mission architecture, and even more for its owner's audacious ambitions. Robert Mondavi was the eldest son of an Italian immigrant. His father, Cesare, had come to California (the Lodi area, south of Sacramento) to buy and sell grapes, having run a successful grocery business in Minnesota. That business included the material for home winemaking during Prohibition, and Cesare always thought of wine as something wholesome but simple, an unexceptional part of everyday life. His son, however, built this new winery with a different goal. He wanted to make wines that could compete with the world's best—specifically, Cabernet Sauvignon that could compete with red Bordeaux. No matter who has crafted the wines at Robert Mondavi over the years, that goal has never been forgotten.

Robert had moved to the Napa Valley in 1943 when he and his brother, Peter, convinced their father to purchase the historic but dilapidated Charles Krug property in St. Helena. In subsequent years, with Peter as the winemaker and Robert in charge of sales, they transformed that property into one of Napa's most successful operations. Under their direction, Charles Krug in the 1950s produced a small number of varietal wines that regularly won medals at the California State Fair, and a far larger number of generic jug wines that brought the family considerable profit. (This split, between wines designed to compete at a high-quality level and wines made for mass market consumption, would be reenacted years later at the Mondavi Corporation.) Then, in the early 1960s, following an eye-opening trip to France, Robert began to dream of bigger things—not agricultural fairs but *haute cuisine* and *haute couture*, fine wine as part of what he liked to called "the civilized life." When he tried to convince his family that they could make American first growths and *grand crus* in Napa, they thought he was putting on airs, his ego having spun out of control. The more he talked, the more their resistance hardened. So following a fistfight with his brother, he set off on his own, naming his new venture after himself. Napa, California, and American wine at large would never be the same.

What distinguished the Robert Mondavi Winery in its early years was less the superiority of the wines (after all, Beaulieu, Inglenook, and to a lesser extent Charles Krug already produced high-quality Napa wines, and a host of ambitious innovators were about to open shop) than the aspirations they embodied—not simply to be good, or even very good, but to compete with the best in the world. As Robert explains in his autobiography, *Harvests of Joy*, such competition involved "several interlocking layers of ambition." He wanted to make "great world-class wines," to marry "European craft and tradition with the latest in American technology," and, most important, to "help [Americans] learn how to appreciate fine food and wine."

That last ambition was what set Mondavi apart from the era's other American vintners, some of whom made equally good wines. In the mid-1960s, there simply was no national market for world-class American wine. Some West Coast connoisseurs and a few East Coast eccentrics bought the wines that aimed to compete qualitatively on the world stage; but there were just a handful of such wines, and the audience for them remained very small. Bob Mondavi, however, was determined to create a new market and attract a new audience. He would do so with his wines, and, as important, with his own chutzpah. For he took it as his mission to show people—restaurateurs, retailers, and individual consumers all over the country—that American wine could be as good as the best from Europe.

All during his first decades in business, this consummate salesman cajoled cynics into comparing his wines with top French cuvées. If they liked his wines (and they usually did), he sold them not simply a case labeled Robert Mondavi but a whole new way of thinking about American wine. Before long, others joined him, as comparative tastings became *de rigeur* when selling top-end domestic wine. And gradually, a new market emerged. More high-quality, European-inspired wines appeared, and more and more customers wanted them. What began as a trickle turned into a stream, and then a flood. To be fair, the work of an entire generation of vintners changed the face of American wine—both the quality in the bottle and the perception in the marketplace. But Robert Mondavi undoubtedly was that generation's visionary leader. In his own words, people needed "to compare [in order] to see the quality we were able to achieve."

This emphasis on comparison meant that the Mondavi wines always were crafted with European, particularly French, models in mind. With the two most important varietals, the prototypes were clear—Côte d'Or Burgundy for Chardonnay, and classified growth Bordeaux for Cabernet. Thinking in terms of such models did not entail blind imitation but rather respect—specifically, respect for the qualities that set those wines apart from others. Put another way, at Mondavi, *quality*, meaning excellence, was always defined in terms of specific *qualities* or characteristics. And those qualities were the ones traditionally found in top French wines.

In the case of Chardonnay, texture, a rich, almost lush mouthfeel, was one such quality; minerality, or secondary earthiness, another. (The former proved easy to attain in California, the latter much more elusive.) With Cabernet, Mondavi and his winemakers wanted to express nuanced subtlety. Mondavi's travels in France had showed him that, unlike the good California Cabernets of the 1950s and 1960s, wines from the top Bordeaux châteaux tasted nuanced and complex rather than big and bold. And that, he declared from the start, was what he wanted in wines with his name on the label. So he told his winemaking staff to give him wines with, in his words, "grace and style, harmony and balance," wines "as soft as a baby's bottom."

Mondavi issued that stylistic directive to Mike Grgich, Zelma Long, and all the winemakers who worked for him during the winery's early years. He then repeated it over and over again to his son, Tim, who became the head winemaker in 1976. Tim Mondavi stayed in charge of production until the sale of the company in 2004. He recalls his "first role" as "interpreting for my father"—all because "my father always spoke in visionary terms." Over time, as his own vision evolved, that role changed and Tim became somewhat more self-reliant. Yet he readily acknowledges that any and all stylistic changes came "with my father's support." He insists that theirs was a shared philosophy, one that never changed significantly. "We always wanted to avoid overly oaky or heavy wines," he explains, "wines that are over the top, wines that might shout rather than whisper or seduce." In short, father and son both wanted "wines of elegance, character, and finesse."

Genevieve Janssens shares that goal today. "We are trying to stay very true to Robert Mondavi's vision," she says. "It is too early to know the impact of the new management. But in the vineyard and in the winery, we continue to focus on making rich yet elegant wines." Rich wines come with the territory in Napa. The combination of sunshine, warmth, and minimal rain during the growing season produces fruit that tastes concentrated and forthright. The wines thus inevitably assert varietal identity. Elegant wines, however, wines that do more than simply declare their fruit and so taste of more than just the grape, come from calculated choices made in both the vineyard and the winery. Those choices, invariably French-informed if not -inspired, are what set Mondavi Reserve Cabernet apart.

Mondavi Reserve Cabernet is a blend of grapes from a number of different sites—one in the Stags Leap District, another on the western edge of the town of Napa, still another up against the Mayacamas foothills—but the dominant source (some 70 percent of the blend) is the famed home To-Kalon vineyard in Oakville. Robert Mondavi first purchased 12 acres of this large estate back when he built his winery, another 250 a few years later, and the remaining portion in 1978—for a total of 770 acres, some three quarters of which are under vine today. Though a number of different grapes are cultivated at To-Kalon, Cabernet is by far the most widely grown variety. Some of the Cabernet vines, those planted on St. George rootstock, escaped the phylloxera infection of the 1990s, but the majority of the acreage was gradually replanted during that decade in a then-radical (for the Napa Valley) Bordeaux-style, high-density format. Mondavi was one of the first American wineries to shift from the then-standard eight-foot by twelve-foot format to a tighter (in this case, four-foot by four-foot) system, and on a large scale—some 250 acres of Cabernet Sauvignon at To-Kalon. The rationale came from the realization that dense spacing forces the vines to compete with each other for sustenance, resulting in lower yields per plant, smaller berries, more vivid secondary flavors, and a greater expression of site. But that realization only came after the Mondavis compared their vineyards with those in Bordeaux—specifically, with the one at Château Mouton-Rothschild—and acknowledged that they could do better.

The joint venture between Robert Mondavi and Mouton's Baron Phillippe de Rothschild that led to the creation of Opus One, for a time Napa's most expensive and highly publicized wine, brought the Mondavi winemaking and grape-growing teams into direct contact with their French counterparts. Part of that contact involved transatlantic exchange. In 1989, Genevieve Janssens, born in Morocco but raised in France, began working as director of production at Opus One. Janssens holds a National Diploma of Enology from the University of Bordeaux. Before coming to California, she owned her own wine laboratory in Provence and served as a consulting enologist to many French châteaux. At Opus One and now Robert Mondavi, she brings what she acknowledges is "a different sensibility and culture" to Napa Valley winemaking, one that values restraint as much as power. That sensibility is definitely in accord with Robert Mondavi 's initial insistence on wines marked by grace and harmony, elegance and finesse.

Not everything at Mondavi is modeled directly on French practice. In the winery, which was completely renovated and redesigned for the 2000 harvest, the Cabernet grapes ferment in large, 16-ton oak tanks rather than neutral, stainless-steel ones—no matter that, back in the 1970s, Robert Mondavi himself helped pioneer the use of stainless steel in California (and no matter that few Bordeaux producers use wood-fermentation vessels anymore). "The oak adds depth to the wine's structure and brings texture to the tannins," insists Janssens, when asked to defend the practice. Being porous, wood allows a slow micro-oxidation during fermentation, softening tannins and invoking delicacy. At least so goes the theory. The jury is still out, as the wines made from the new method are too young to compare fairly with those made previously. Still, the winery redesign, much like the vineyard reconfiguration, is all part of the same overarching effort—to make wines marked by subtlety rather than just vigor.

Even with the emphasis placed on qualities such as grace and harmony, refinement and polish, Robert Mondavi Reserve Cabernet does not taste light or delicate. After all, Cabernet Sauvignon is a naturally muscular grape variety, with rough skins so tough tannins, and plenty of weight. When grown in Napa, with so much more heat and sunshine than Bordeaux, it tends inevitably toward richness, the sugar and potential alcohol levels being high at harvest. For Janssens, the goal is not to block Cabernet's natural exuberance, but rather to hold it in check—"Like teaching a young child manners," she says.

Such instruction entails being sure to handle the fruit gently—letting the juice flow by means of gravity rather than pumping it, for instance, and not filtering the wine before bottling. It also involves blending, as small percentages of all the other traditional red Bordeaux varietals (Cabernet Franc, Malbec, Merlot, and Petit Verdot) can find their way into the finished wine. California Cabernet's expressive fruit character is thus very much present, but unlike so many contemporary examples, the extract does not seem overwhelming. Tasting a set of vintages demonstrates that this wine is nuanced and complex, but that the specifics of its complexity are very much its own—not so much Bordeaux echoes of pencil shavings or cigar boxes as notes reminiscent of sweet spice, cedar, and, above all, mint. Most impressive of all is the wine's body—rich without being heavy, so luxurious and multilayered. Despite the presence of Bordeaux as a model, it seems clearly Californian and hence true to itself. In this, it outperforms Opus One, its sibling rival, a wine that while always tasty, too often seems formulaic rather than individualistic.

The harmony that Robert Mondavi always declared he wanted in his wines and that Genevieve Janssens works to express is a delicate balancing act, with traditional European-styled delicacy set against hedonistic Golden State richness. Janssens and her winemaking predecessors have not achieved it with all of their wines. Reserve Pinot Noir at Mondavi can taste jammy, and the company's Reserve Fumé Blanc has swung from tart to woody. Chardonnay has been more successful, though as with so many North Coast versions, secondary subtlety has proved an elusive target. But, save for a slight misstep at the close of the 1990s, Mondavi Reserve Cabernet Sauvignon has consistently hit the bull's-eye. Janssens acknowledges that slip when she admits that the wines she and Tim Mondavi made in 1998 and 1999 were perhaps too restrained. They "showed more structure than texture," she says. But subsequent vintages have returned to form. "They show more richness but stay very elegant."

Richard Sands, Jon Moramarco, and the rest of the Constellation Brands management team have important plans for their new purchase. First and foremost, they want to restore profitability—in part by more clearly distinguishing the mass market Private Selection and Woodbridge wines from the Napa Valley ones. This is in large measure a matter of sales and marketing, but it also involves image and reputation. The Mondavi name has suffered somewhat in recent years from being associated with these large-volume brands, and consumers and critics alike have sometimes forgotten to focus on the Napa Valley wines. That, Sands says emphatically, will have to change.

Robert Mondavi Reserve Cabernet Sauvignon, however, does not need to change. It continues to represent the realization of its ambitious creator's initial vision—a Napa Valley wine that belongs front and center on the world stage, with the same qualities, and hence quality, as the Bordeaux first-growths. Robert Mondavi today is a big business, producing nearly 10 million cases of wine a year under various labels. Not surprisingly, not every wine with the Mondavi name on the bottle proves exciting, not even every one from Napa. But year in and year out, the Reserve Cabernet Sauvignon most definitely does.

A NOTE ON VINTAGES:

At its best, this wine marries power and elegance as well as any Napa Valley Cabernet. It ages well, reaching a plateau of maturity after about a decade, and resting there for a good ten years more. Past glories still drinking well include wines from 1986 and 1987. More recent stellar vintages include 1990, 1991, 1997, 2001, and 2002.

THE SUGGESTED PRICE FOR THE CURRENT 2002 RELEASE IS $125.

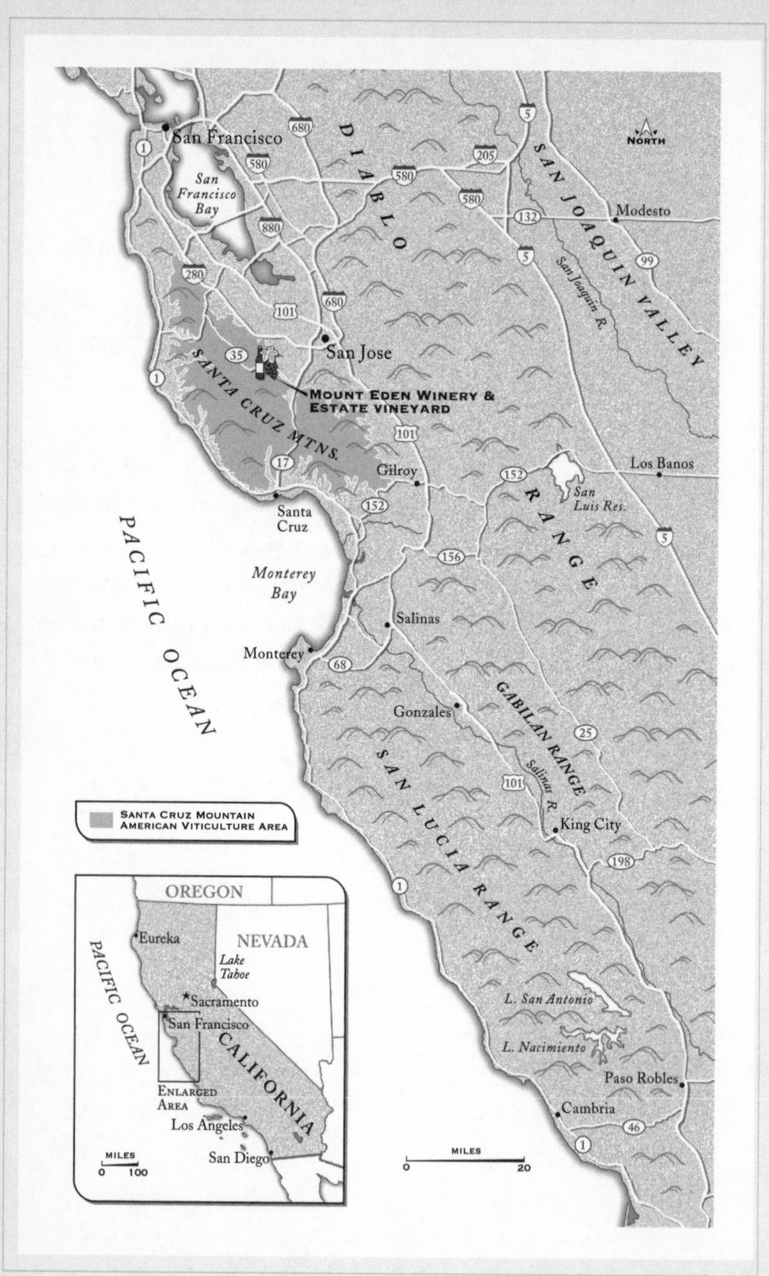

MOUNT EDEN, HIGH IN THE SANTA CRUZ MOUNTAINS

CHAPTER 24

Mount Eden Vineyards Estate Chardonnay

Santa Cruz Mountains, California

...

The aptly named Mount Eden Vineyard sits high atop a ridge in the Santa Cruz Mountains, some 2,000 feet above the Silicon Valley town of Saratoga. The Pacific Ocean lies only some twenty miles to the west, but because the mountains block the way, the dominant impression is one of insular beauty and seclusion. This vineyard-in-the-sky was first planted over sixty years ago by stockbroker turned vintner Martin Ray. He used cuttings from vines that his mentor, Paul Masson, had imported from Burgundy back in the 1880s, the Chardonnay allegedly coming from the famed hill of Corton. Today, Mount Eden's winemaker, Jeffrey Patterson, uses fruit from descendants of those same vines to fashion a Chardonnay that is marked by virtually every attribute one might ask for in a dry white wine—a complex bouquet, vivid fruit, clearly defined secondary flavors, superior length and depth, and demonstrated ageability. But the vines by themselves cannot account for this wine's greatness. As important is Patterson's reverence for the place, with its stony Franciscan shale soils, cool but temperate climate, naturally low yields, and stunning beauty.

Jeffrey and Ellie Patterson

This paradisiacal site, so isolated from all the bustle below, resists any winemaker's attempt to impose rather than invoke character, and its history bespeaks a long legacy of distinctive vintages. That legacy has been passed from owner to owner and winemaker to winemaker, all of whom have valued the place and its products to the point of veneration. While the wines may have changed stylistically, they always have been inspired more by personal, artistic ambitions than overtly commercial ones. That makes Mount Eden the quintessential California boutique winery, meaning not simply a small facility, but one in which wine is an avocation more than a trade. Patterson and his wife Ellie have made their home on this ridge for almost twenty-five years now, crafting the wines, running the business, and raising their family. For them, as for Paul Masson and Martin Ray, wine at Mount Eden is a labor of love and a way of life.

Though small wineries have existed for as long as people have made and sold wine, boutique wines are a relatively new phenomenon. As recently as a generation ago, only someone independently wealthy could afford to take a truly artistic approach to winemaking. This was true even in Burgundy, where the vineyards long have been divided between a multitude of growers, some of whom farm only a few acres and make only a few hundred cases. But as fine wine became a sought-after global commodity during the last quarter of the twentieth century, independent wineries found an expanding, often international market. That market could support small-volume wines selling at high prices. In turn, those prices were what allowed vintners to enjoy the luxury of focusing on quality to the exclusion of other concerns. And extreme high quality, coupled with ultra-premium pricing, is what distinguishes the boutiques from the more old-fashioned farm wineries, *garagistes* from traditional small-scale winemakers—no matter whether in Burgundy or Bordeaux, Priorat or Piedmont, South Australia, Stellenbosch, or the Santa Cruz Mountains.

Some people dislike the term "boutique," as it suggests to them a certain degree of snobbery or pretension. Yet maintaining an unwavering focus on excellence necessitates making distinctions; and drawing distinctions in matters of taste inevitably indicates that one person's judgment may be superior to another's. Such discriminations characterize the boutique movement, and they are nowhere more prevalent than in otherwise democratic, egalitarian America, where the overall rise in both the quality and the prestige of wine has in large measure been inspired by the work of dedicated, passionate avocational vintners, often laboring in isolation if not obscurity. Though they may define it differently, depending upon their knowledge, judgment, and taste, excellence has been their shared but sole goal.

There certainly is nothing pretentious about Jeffrey Patterson. Tall and lean, customarily clad in bluejeans and T-shirts, he earns his living by the sweat of his brow. Making wine on top of a mountain entails doing a little bit of everything, and Patterson is as much at home tinkering with tractor engines or digging fenceposts as tasting barrel samples. Only when it comes to assessing the quality of the wine in those barrels does he evidence the sort of aesthetic discrimination that can sometimes be mistaken for snobbery. "Mount Eden has an elitist, purist reputation," he acknowledges. "It goes way back, and I have to say, it's deserved." That reputation can be traced to the winery's earliest days, when Martin Ray first dared to make wines to rival the finest imports. "Ray was a maverick and a visionary," says Patterson. "He was far ahead of his time. My constant goal and motivation is to honor and build on his legacy."

The father of America's boutique movement, Martin "Rusty" Ray approached winemaking with an intensity and passion that some people attributed to arrogance and others to genius. A native Californian, he first became interested in wine as a boy when, after his own father died, he found a surrogate in the French émigré Paul Masson, who crafted wines that at the time were considered "the pride of California." Masson cut a dashing figure in the decades before Prohibition. Strong and imposing, he was a cultured man of the world who never shrank from physical labor. Whether working in a vineyard or hosting an elegant dinner party at his La Cresta estate, he conveyed an infectious *joie de vivre*. Young Ray revered him.

Although Ray would have liked to make wine with Paul Masson, Prohibition was in full swing when he came of age. So he became a stockbroker instead, eventually opening his own firm in San Francisco, where he managed to make a substantial amount of money during the bull market of the 1920s. Then in 1936, when Masson retired, Ray used his savings to purchase the La Cresta estate and follow in his mentor's footsteps. Five years later, after the Frenchman's death, he gave up on big-time, commercial winemaking and sold the business to Joseph Seagram, the Canadian spirits conglomerate. He took the profits and purchased a mountaintop property at the end of a road named Mount Eden.

After clearing the land, Ray planted a vineyard with Chardonnay and Pinot Noir, and settled down to make what he confidently proclaimed would be America's finest wines. All through the 1950s and 1960s, his Martin Ray Vineyards produced tiny quantities of those two varietals (and later Cabernet Sauvignon), along with blanc de blancs and blanc de noirs sparklers, all of which developed a devoted following despite carrying astronomical price tags. They were America's first boutique wines.

Ray made and marketed his wines by hand, advertising them in a newsletter he wrote himself and selling them via mail order. He bottled them in thick, Champagne-style bottles, securing the corks with wire cages, and charged outrageous prices: $12 per bottle in 1952, then $24 ten years later for a Chardonnay that he proclaimed was "the world's greatest white wine." Visionary but also defensive, he took affront at even the slightest hint of criticism. Because he inexplicably refused to use sulfur in his cellar, his wines sometimes oxidized and spoiled. If a customer complained, he declared that the customer did not appreciate great wine and simply deleted his or her name from the mailing list. Yet Ray also could be remarkably principled. He insisted on cultivating grapes and making wines in his own meticulous, hands-on fashion. And he refused to grow or make anything but the very best. He railed against other producers who valued quantity over quality and settled readily for mediocrity. He disparaged the then standard practice of blending inferior grapes with premium varietals, and he declaimed strenuously against the custom of using generic monikers like "chablis," "burgundy," and "rhine wine," insisting that such names reduced American wines to mere copies of foreign originals.

In making these and other arguments, Ray, who died in 1976, was indeed well ahead of his time. Had he lived only a decade or so longer, he would have seen virtually everything he advocated come to pass. In the 1970s and 1980s, the widespread emergence of genuinely world-class American wine was led in large measure by small, independent boutique producers like himself. Though not inured to the pressures of the mass market, these vintners, like Ray, had the resources to resist them. And through their resistance, they in the long run changed the very face of the American wine market. Sales of jug and generic wines declined precisely as sales of premium and ultra-premium wines rose, and before long all the large-volume producers started to offer reserve or single-vineyard wines of their own. Ray had predicted as much. Virtually alone in his generation, he understood that expensive, exceptional wines would be the ones to lead American wine out of its post-Prohibition hangover. "The market for fine wines is limited," he wrote presciently in 1955. "Yet the market for all other wines is supported by it."

The last decade of his life saw Martin Ray become ever more cantankerous and contentious. In an effort to expand his vineyard, he organized a group of investors to provide financing. But when his relations with them soured, he ended up in court, where he lost virtually everything he had. At his death, he owned only five acres at the very top of the mountain. The rest of the property, now a separate legal entity with new owners, had a new name: Mount Eden Vineyards.

As an independent entity, Mount Eden had a somewhat rocky start. Absentee owners micromanaged the estate without a clear sense of direction, changing winemakers every year or two. Dick Graff from Chalone made the first Mount Eden wines, including a couple of super-ripe, quite woody Chardonnays. Then Merry Edwards, one of California's pioneering female winemakers, signed on, followed in rapid succession by Bill Anderson, Rick White, and Fred Peterson. The resulting wines varied considerably in style and character. In 1981, Jeffrey Patterson, fresh from the enology program at UC Davis, came aboard. Perhaps because he had so little winemaking experience, his vision of the wines he wanted to make came less from himself than from his sense of the vineyard's history. "Like everyone else," he says, "I knew about Martin Ray. I thought my job was to continue what had been started before me." A rift in the ownership group a few years later led to buyouts and consolidation. When the dust settled, the majority of shares belonged to a Sacramento businessman named Neil Hagen. Very much a silent partner, he was (and still is) content to let the Pattersons, who now own a considerable number of shares themselves, run the business as they see fit. "We care for the place as if it were all our own," Jeffrey explains. "No one tells us what to do or when to do it." Ellie amplifies: "The land and its history are the heroes here. Our job is simply to let them speak through our wines."

Mount Eden's vineyard is planted to Cabernet, Chardonnay, and Pinot Noir. All three wines taste good, but the Chardonnay is the most complex and consistent. Perhaps surprisingly, it more than the other two needs bottle age after release in order to reveal its true character. Unlike all but a handful of California Chardonnays, it improves notably over time, with many vintages fresh and vibrant after more than a decade. At a vertical tasting in the summer of 2002, the most impressive wines turned out to be from 1990 and 1984, with the latter displaying a stony, mineral-scented bouquet and multilayered citrus flavors, still full of verve and vigor. "I've always thought that how a wine ages is more important than how it tastes right away," argues Patterson. "That's the key to this wine. It always needs a few years to come together, but then it holds on for years."

When asked what accounts for this remarkable longevity, Patterson identifies two things: the vineyard, specifically the high level of acidity that distinguishes grapes grown there; and his non-interventionist philosophy. "I've learned," he says, "to make the wine clean, let it settle, and then leave it alone." Mount Eden Chardonnay undergoes complete malolactic fermentation. It spends two months or so on the gross lees, with minimal stirring, then about eight more months in wood (French oak, half new and half one year old). Patterson used to play with it more, stirring it frequently and exposing it for a longer period to the spent yeast. All that added something to the wine, he acknowledges, as the Chardonnay tasted quite rich, but it removed something too—specifically, vitality and ageability. So, these days, he's content to let the wine develop at its own pace. After bottling, he lets it rest in storage for almost twenty months before offering it to the public. "I wish we could hold on to it longer," he says with a shrug of his shoulders. "It always tastes better after a couple more years."

Martin Ray originally planted four acres of Chardonnay below his house. Gradually, Patterson has expanded that vineyard, so that it now includes twenty steep, hillside acres. Though he replanted (and redesigned) it during the 1980s, the vines themselves, which now average nearly twenty years of age, have never been worked on or cleaned in a nursery. As a result, the Mount Eden Chardonnay selection, cuttings of which often are sought by vintners elsewhere, is inherently low-yielding. This mountain vineyard averages roughly 2 tons per acre. Patterson and his crew rarely have to cut off green grapes to reduce yield, as the combination of spring damage and meager production per vine keeps the crop level low and the fruit concentrated.

The resulting wines exhibit a discrete flavor profile. Unlike North Coast California Chardonnays, which tend to display orchard fruit flavors, or Central Coast ones that taste more tropical, the Mount Eden wines have a lemony, citrus character, with nutty, herbal secondary notes, and a noticeably mineral-infused undertone. In short, the combination of these particular vines in this particular site yields a wine that tastes distinctive as well as delicious. "That's priority number one," Patterson notes, "to capture the flavors that this place produces." He makes between 1,200 and 2,500 cases each year, depending on the vagaries of the vintage, far less than the market wants. "That's all the vineyard gives us," he says simply.

Low yields are a fact of life throughout the Santa Cruz Mountains, particularly in the higher elevations. As a result, many of the wineries there need to augment production with grapes brought in from elsewhere in California. Mount Eden is no exception. Patterson makes over 8,000 cases each year of Chardonnay sourced from the Edna Valley in San Luis Obispo, and he's perfectly honest about why he does, noting simply, "If we didn't make that wine, we couldn't afford to make our Estate Chardonnay." Unlike Martin Ray, who thumbed his nose at the business of wine (and as a result lost most everything he had), the Pattersons pay close attention to the bottom line. After all, they run a company that is not entirely or even mainly their own. Yet, like Ray, the estate is their passion.

Such devotion to a place and its products characterizes the best boutique producers, those for whom pursuing excellence is less a sign of snobbery than a mark of heartfelt commitment. The Santa Cruz Mountains, home to over forty small, mostly family-owned wineries, has long inspired such devotion. From Paul Masson to Martin Ray, and then such vintners as David Bruce, Tom Mudd at Cinnabar, Martin Mathis at Kathryn Kennedy, and Ken Burnap at Santa Cruz Mountain, the area continues to attract individuals who consider their finest wines to be expressions of a place they love.

One has only to taste the two Mount Eden Chardonnays side by side to understand what distinguishes a true boutique wine. The Edna Valley rendition, lush and luxuriant, performs quite well when compared to most other California Chardonnays, many of which cost considerably more. It pales in comparison, however, to the far more refined, ageworthy, and multifaceted estate bottling. That wine—full of flavors resembling lemon curd, tangerines, smoked almonds, and so much more—tastes truly individualistic. It bespeaks a place, but even more a deep-seated respect for that place. As such, it exemplifies why Jeffrey and Ellie Patterson feel so at home atop their Santa Cruz mountain. Mount Eden is where their hearts are.

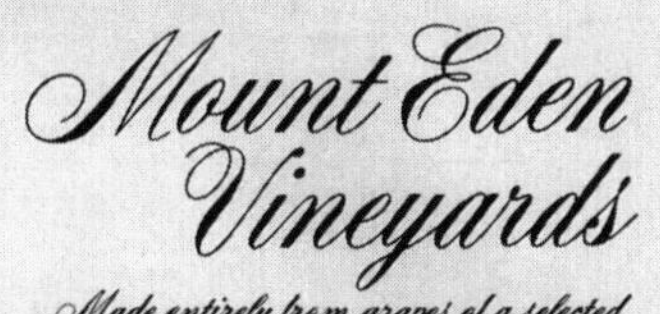

A NOTE ON VINTAGES:

Mount Eden Chardonnay tastes nutty and slightly honeyed once its primary fruit flavors fade into the background, and in a strong vintage it can stay in balance for many, many years. I personally prefer it, though, at about eight to ten years after the harvest, when it shows both fresh fruit and nuanced, secondary subtlety. Particularly strong vintages include 1984, 1988, 1990, 1991, 1996, and 2000.

THE SUGGESTED PRICE FOR THE CURRENT 2002 RELEASE IS $35.

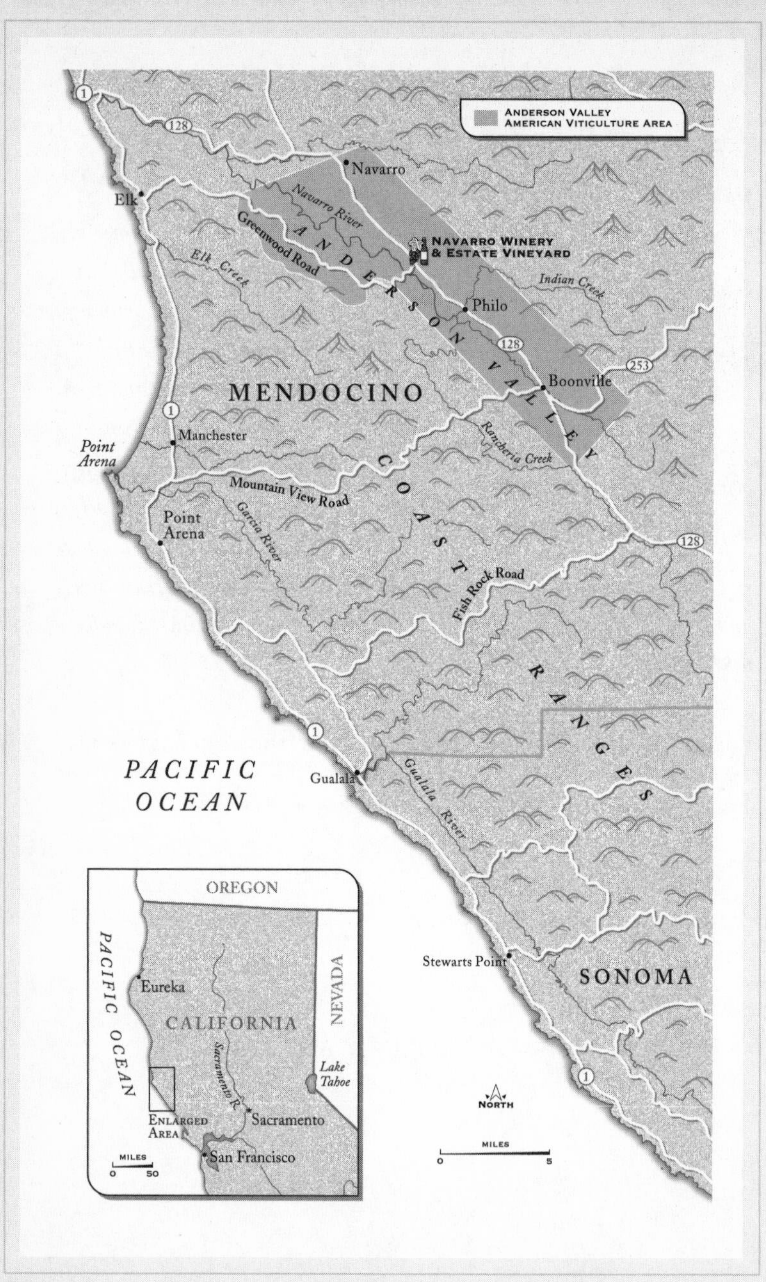

NAVARRO AND THE ANDERSON VALLEY AVA

CHAPTER 25

NAVARRO VINEYARDS DRY GEWURZTRAMINER

Anderson Valley, California

...

"Our idea was to do something different," says Ted Bennett, who along with his wife, Deborah Cahn, owns Navarro Vineyards in Northern California's bucolic Anderson Valley. Back in 1973, Bennett gave up a lucrative career as an executive with CBS Records in order to grow grapes and make wine. But the impulse to go their own way characterizes everything the couple has done at Navarro—from their choice of locale, through the varietals they make, to the way they run their business. They certainly were not the only people to catch the wine bug and start a new life in California's vineyards. But in their determination to move to a remote spot in Mendocino County, some 125 miles north of San Francisco, specialize in often-overlooked grapes, and then to eschew normal distribution channels, they swam against the American wine industry's main current. And they continue to do so today, especially in the ways they manage both their vineyard and their payroll. "Yeah," Bennett admits with a laugh, "we're still counter-culture."

Deborah Cahn, Ted Bennett, and their dachshund, Simon

Bennett and Cahn moved to the Anderson Valley from Berkeley, where, as she puts it, "we were part of the whole back-to-the-land movement" of the late 1960s. "We knew we couldn't control the whole world," she explains, "but thought we could control our little corner of it." That corner turned out to be a 900-acre sheep ranch, 90 of which they planted with vines. (They raised sheep as well, paying the obstetrician with lambs when their first child was born.) Navarro Vineyards now produces some of America's most exciting wines from those vines, including an exquisite dry Gewurztraminer, redolent with the floral spiciness and delicately layered flavors that characterize the world's finest expressions of this varietal. Bennett and Cahn's commitment to excellence, coupled with an idealism that they put into daily practice, separates Navarro from the vast majority of American wineries. Because they in fact have succeeded in controlling their bucolic little corner of the world, they indeed are different. And their wines are very special.

The Navarro difference begins with the land, a site just north of the small town of Philo. It first attracted Bennett and Cahn because they hoped (correctly, it turns out) that its gravelly clay soils and cool coastal climate would prove beneficial for the type of wines they wanted to make. True to form, they were unconventional wine drinkers. "We liked mainly French wines," Bennett remembers, "and we especially loved the whites from Alsace." So, while most California vintners were planting Cabernet and Chardonnay, they decided to specialize in Alsatian grape varieties: Riesling, Pinot Gris, Muscat, and especially Gewurztraminer. At the time, there were only four other vineyards in the Anderson Valley: an old, pre-Prohibition block of Zinfandel high in the Greenwood Ridge Hills; the remnants of an Italian Swiss Colony project from the 1940s; and two newer ventures, twenty-four acres owned by Dr. Donald Edmeades, and twenty-one recently planted by Tony Husch. Both of these contained small, experimental blocks of Gewurztraminer.

In September 1972, with the idea of changing careers already in the back of his head, Bennett drove up from Berkeley to help Dr. Edmeades harvest the vintage. Doing so reinforced his sense that wine growing could be more rewarding than corporate management. It also showed him that Gewurztraminer in this locale could get ripe and at the same time maintain balance. Though still very much a neophyte vintner, he knew that most California Gewurztraminers tasted blowsy and unbalanced, due in large measure to their low acids. No matter where this particular grape variety is cultivated, it is naturally low in acidity. Bennett understood that Golden State heat and sunshine can only exacerbate the problem. But in the cool, ocean-influenced Anderson Valley, the Edmeades grapes (Husch's vines had not yet produced a crop) showed real promise. So when Bennett and Cahn made their move the next year, they did so in large measure for Gewurztraminer. "It's the wine," Bennett says, "that I came here to make."

Gewurztraminer is a tricky grape to grow. Naturally vigorous and early ripening, it almost seems to want to make bad wine, for the difficulties with balance and structure become heightened if yields become high and sugar levels rise too early—which is exactly what happens without the proper human intervention. This variety's great attraction is its perfume, a heady mix of rose petals, lychee, orange peel, and exotic spice. If the sugars develop too rapidly, potential alcohol levels will shoot up while the potentially fragrant skins remain immature, so the seductive scent won't develop. And even if the grapes ripen fully, the bouquet will become faint if yields are allowed to increase, so the wine will have lost its appeal.

In Alsace, this variety's homeland (though not its birthplace, since it originated in the Alto Adige region of northern Italy), Gewurztraminer benefits from a relatively long growing season, with plenty of sunshine but a generally cool climate—ideal conditions for these aromatic grapes to ripen while maintaining their acids. The Anderson Valley offers similar advantages. With chilly evenings, foggy mornings, and sun-drenched afternoons, it is classified as Region I (the coolest of five zones) on the UC Davis Scale. Though Cabernet and Zinfandel are cultivated up above the fogline in the Mendocino Ridge Viticultural Area, only cool climate varieties ripen down on the valley floor. A pattern of warm days and cold nights explains why Chardonnay and Pinot Noir for sparkling wine do well there, and why Anderson Valley Gewurztraminer manages to stay in balance and offer such enticing aromas.

As a wine, Gewurztraminer has a small but devoted following. Many of its admirers prefer it off-dry, and even contemporary Alsatian renditions often taste a tad sweet. In the United States, most Gewurztraminers contain significant residual sugar, in part because vintners in warm regions need to retain sweetness in order to keep the alcohol down. When nature cooperates, Navarro makes a botrytised, late harvest version, but the winery's benchmark offering is its dry Gewurztraminer. In fact, over the years the wine has gotten slightly but steadily drier ("Like our humor," Ted Bennett quips), so that it today exhibits a faint peppery edge, much like the finest renditions from traditional producers in Alsace. Although some other American wineries—notably Edmeades and Lazy Creek in the Anderson Valley, Peninsula Cellars in northern Michigan, and Herman Weimer on Seneca Lake in upstate New York—also succeed with dry Gewurztraminer, only Navarro makes a wine from this variety that consistently can hold its own in the company of the world's finest.

Navarro was not the first winery to plant Gewurztraminer in the Anderson Valley, but Bennett and Cahn's stable ownership and commitment to the varietal have made them its standard-bearers. "We've learned a lot," Bennett admits, "mostly through trial and error." In the vineyard, pruning is a big issue, since the vines need to be trellised so as to allow sufficient sunshine for ripening but not so much as to bake away the grapes' natural spiciness. Back in the 1970s, Bennett came up with a system in which the vines are bent up over the grapes so as to even growth. (He was proud of his invention, until he took a trip to Alsace and discovered that growers there had been using a similar method for decades.) Controlling vigor is another important concern. Over the years, Bennett has learned to thin the potential crop at two separate points: in the spring right after flowering, and then in summer at veraison when the grapes begin their transformation from hard, green pellets to soft, succulent berries. That way, overcropping rarely proves a problem, as each vine produces a desired amount of fruit. But perhaps the most important viticultural decision involves deciding when to pick. According to Bennett, color is the critical indicator. Mature Gewurz-traminer grapes turn russet-red, a sure sign of the terpenes, or floral-flavor compounds, that account for the rich perfume. At Navarro, workers return to each vineyard block several times during the harvest, cluster-selecting the fruit only when it has become completely red. And it will turn red only if it has received neither too much sunlight (which would make the grapes yellow) nor too little (which would leave them green). All this attention to detail in the vineyard finds expression in the finished wine. As Bennett says, "We've learned that the more you manipulate the grapes, the less you have to manipulate the wine afterwards."

At Navarro, manipulating the grapes involves *not* doing things in the vineyard as well—not fumigating for insects, for example, and not using commercial fertilizers. Eco-friendly farming practices include employing an integrated pest management system, planting cover crops for compost, and using the least toxic antifungal sprays available. Bennett and Cahn's respect for the land extends to a respect for their employees, more than 95 percent of whom work for Navarro full time and receive full benefits, including medical and dental insurance and participation in a pension plan. Theirs is an atypical but extremely principled way of doing business, especially in an agricultural industry that relies heavily on migrant labor. To make it work, Navarro's employees have to be able to do different jobs. Members of the tasting-room staff, for instance, go outside to help during crush, and vineyard workers later come inside to assist with bottling and packaging. "We structure work so as not to have to lay anyone off," says Bennett. "We make sure to take care of the people who have helped us get where we are."

Yet another difference involves sales, for Navarro is one of the few wineries of any significant size (production averages about 40,000 cases a year) that markets and sells the majority of its wines directly to consumers. "I didn't make that decision," Bennett explains. "The stores did it for me." He recalls that he initially intended to sell his wines conventionally, through wholesalers and retailers, and recounts making a sales trip to Corti Brothers in Sacramento, then as now one of the most important shops in California. "Darrell Corti liked our wine," he remembers, "but he told me he wasn't going to buy it, because no one had heard of Navarro and no one much liked Gewurztraminer. I drove away angry. But then it occurred to me that I couldn't really blame him. So I turned around and went home, and we came up with a different way of selling wine."

That way was mail order. Navarro Vineyards ships some 25,000 cases of wine to its customers every year. In addition, it sends out 60,000 copies of a roughly twenty-page newsletter, a new edition every four months. Handsomely illustrated and entertainingly written, it tells a story, replete with a photograph or two, for each wine offered. Direct sales allow Navarro to charge full markup; but since printing, mailing, and shipping add to their expenses, Bennett and Cahn figure that their costs (and profits) are about the same as they would be if they sold their wines to wholesalers. The advantage, they argue, is that they can personally serve their customers, many of whom purchase their wine year after year, and so can better monitor what people think of their work. In addition, without middlemen, they can keep prices reasonable. (The dry Gewurztraminer sells for under $20 a bottle.) The disadvantage with selling exclusively off a mailing list is that wine lovers who live in states that do not allow interstate sales—at present, there are seventeen—cannot buy Navarro wines. But Bennett and Cahn argue that a winery of Navarro's size cannot satisfy everyone. They do sell roughly 20 percent of their production to restaurants, directly in California and through wholesalers in New York and a few other states. But when they sign a contract with a wholesaler, they request that no wine be made available to retail shops. That's because they do not want to do anything to alienate their loyal and devoted mail-order customers.

Gewurztraminer is Navarro's most renowned wine, but the winery produces a host of different varietals: the other Alsatians—Muscat, Pinot Gris, and Riesling—as well as Chardonnay, Pinot Noir, Sauvignon Blanc, and Zinfandel. Estate grapes account for roughly 65 percent of the total production; purchased fruit, mostly from Mendocino County, makes up the rest. Since 1992, Jim Klein has been the winemaker. He came to Mendocino from Israel, where he made wine for Yarden, one of that country's premier producers, and Napa, where he worked for

Charles Krug. "This place," he says modestly, "produces lovely, crisp white wines. I just help them along." Yet just as Gewurztraminer is tricky to grow, it can be quite difficult to make, or at least to make well, and Klein's talent is evident in the wine's passage from vine to bottle. Much of the distinctive flavor and aroma comes from the skins, so pressing needs to be handled slowly and gently. At the same time, in order for the wine to taste fresh and lively, Klein needs to extract as little tannin as possible.

Navarro's grapes are hand-harvested at night or early in the morning, when the grapes are cold, so as to minimize the effect of tannin and other phenols. Both fermentation (which lasts roughly a month) and aging (six months) occur in seasoned French and German wood casks that have been outfitted with steel cooling panels in order to keep the wine at just the right temperature. The idea is not to extract flavor from the wood, but to allow the introduction of a small amount of oxygen, thus enhancing flavor intensity. Because he wants to retain as much acidity as possible, Klein does not induce malolactic fermentation; and because he wants complexity, he leaves the wine in contact with the spent yeast lees until it is ready to bottle and blend. His meticulous care for this and the other wines he makes can literally be tasted in the glass, and in 2002 the *San Francisco Chronicle* named him "winemaker of the year"—quite an achievement considering that the newspaper's readers cannot go to a wineshop and buy Navarro's wines.

Klein, along with Bennett, Cahn, and others on the Navarro staff, tastes the Gewurztraminer from cask as it ages through the winter, and then again when the final blend is put together in the spring. Klein contends that "*terroir* is a winemaking tool, not an end in itself," so the vineyard lots that go into the premium, estate-bottled wine can change significantly from year to year. Sunlight, temperature, and wind may favor one site one year, another the following year. Typically, only about 65 percent of the cask wine makes the final cut, the rest being either downgraded to a house wine or sold on the bulk market. "We've learned there's a lot of vintage variation with this grape," notes Bennett. "We now have a pretty good idea of how to process it, but plenty still doesn't make the cut."

A lot doesn't make the cut at Navarro that would at other wineries. After thirty years, Ted Bennett and Deborah Cahn continue to do things their own way, guided by their aesthetic and gustatory values as well as by their ethical ones. They still make the wines they like to drink, and they still grow grapes and run the company with an eye to things they consider more important than the bottom line. They may not farm their land, or handle their payroll, or make and market their wines conventionally, but in all these endeavors they clearly are successful. And the key to their success is, in a word, *control*. As Cahn puts it, they control their little corner, meaning that they do not have to answer to anyone—corporate managers, distributors, shareholders—other than themselves. And because the end result proves so tasty, customers are willing to go the proverbial extra mile to come to them—literally, when people make their way up to Navarro's cute but remote tasting room, and figuratively when they go to the trouble to order Navarro's wines.

"We're like an English garden," Ted Bennett says, looking back over thirty years of wine growing in the Anderson Valley. "It just all happened." But of course an English garden only looks that way, its beauty being in actuality the result of careful planning and hard work, not happenstance. So too at Navarro. Bennett and Cahn knew exactly what they wanted to create when they first moved to Mendocino—a refuge from corporate life in an enclave where they would not have to answer to anything other than their own convictions. They have spent three decades working diligently to ensure that this is what they have there. And as part of their work, they have fashioned one of America's top wines. It succeeds where so many other Gewurztraminers fail both because they chose an appropriate locale and because they are so in control of it—all the way from the vineyard to the winery and then the final bottled product. But more important, they are in control of their lives. No—neither their business nor their wine just happened.

A NOTE ON VINTAGES:

Gewurztraminer, being opulently perfumed and relatively low in acid, is a wine to drink young. This is particularly true of dry versions, as their balance can be precarious. Ted Bennett and Jim Klein at Navarro invariably get the balance right, but their wine's aromatic allure will only weaken with time. So drink it; don't save it.

THE SUGGESTED PRICE FOR THE CURRENT 2004 RELEASE IS $18.

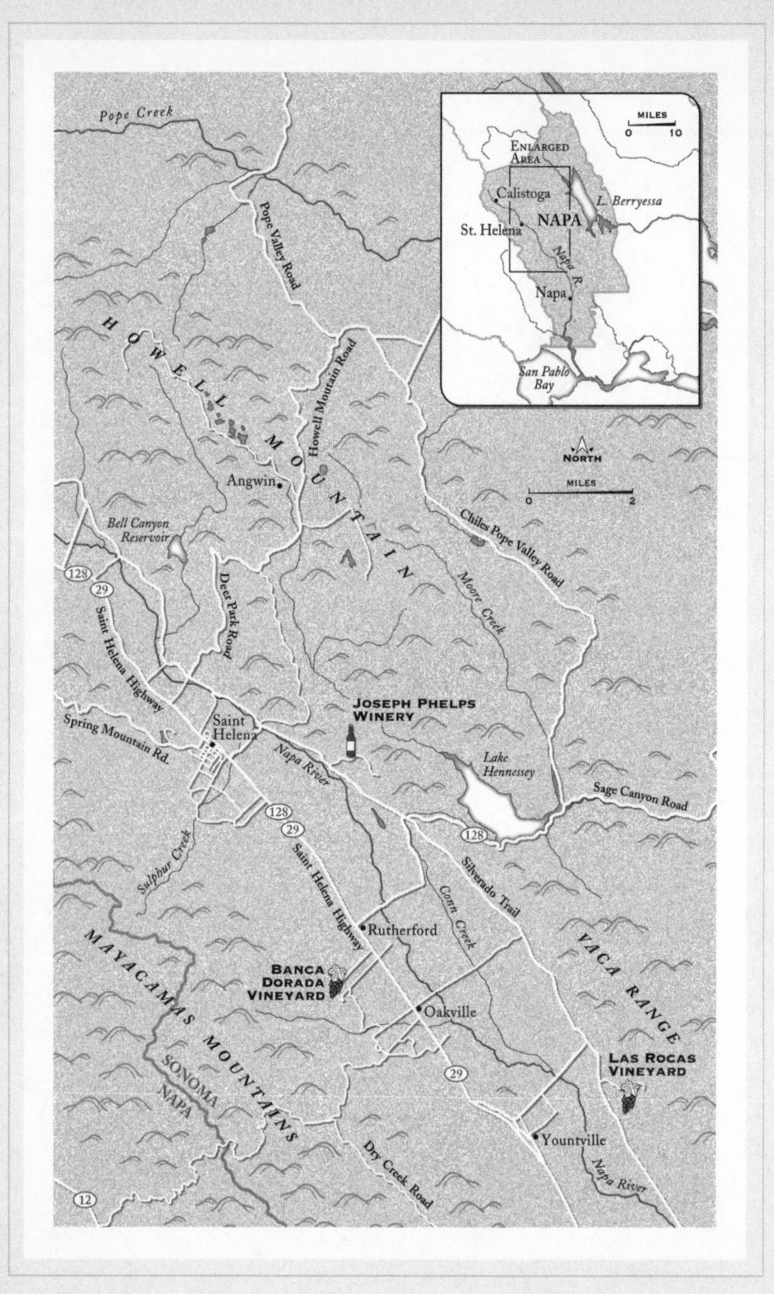

THE JOSEPH PHELPS WINERY AND THE INSIGNIA VINEYARDS

CHAPTER 26

Joseph Phelps Vineyards Insignia

Napa Valley, California

...

"The name came to me one morning while I was shaving," recalls Joseph Phelps, the retired patriarch of the Napa Valley winery that carries his name, "but I'd had the idea for a long time." The idea was to use only the best grapes, no matter the specific varieties or vineyard sites, in order to produce the very best wine possible. And the name was Insignia, from the Latin *insigne*, meaning an emblem or distinguishing sign. In 1974, when he experienced this sudsy moment of epiphany, Joe Phelps's winery was barely a year old, and he hoped that his idea might distinguish it as a rising star. Napa back then was just waking from its post-Prohibition slumber, its revival financed in large measure by newcomers. Phelps was one of them. He first had come to the valley as a general contractor from Colorado, having been hired to build the Rutherford Hill and Chateau Souverain wineries. When he caught the wine bug and decided to open his own facility, his outsider's perspective allowed him to see that, despite all its promise, most of Napa was still virgin ground in terms of fine wine production. He hoped that his idea would prove good

Joe Phelps in the mid-1970s

as well as novel, and that his new wine might elevate his winery to the top rank of Napa producers.

Because Joe Phelps did not want to be hamstrung by anyone's past choices, he immediately committed himself to experimentation and innovation. In keeping with this pioneering spirit, he decided not to designate his flagship wine as a "Reserve," but instead gave his winemakers license to use different grape varieties in different proportions depending on the vintage. At the time, federal government regulations required that at least 51 percent of a wine come from a single grape variety in order for the wine to be labeled varietally—as Cabernet Sauvignon, for example, or Merlot. But Phelps insisted that his winemakers should have the freedom to use whatever percentages they judged would make the best wine. (In 1983, the federal requirement was raised to 75 percent; Phelps didn't change his mind.) The 1974 Insignia released in March 1978, was California's first proprietary-named blend. A sensation with critics and consumers alike, it brought immediate renown to the young winery. That initial release was followed over the years by a series of often stunning vintages, and before long the wine was being echoed by new proprietary blends, many excellent but none better. Today, more than a quarter century after its introduction, Insignia continues to set a stylistic and qualitative standard, demonstrating that scrupulous selection yields superior wine.

While Insignia undoubtedly was a significant innovation, it also constituted a bow to tradition. The tradition, however, was French rather than Californian. "My idea was to produce a Napa Valley wine following a top-growth Bordeaux model," Joe Phelps explains, "to follow the Bordelais approach to making a *grand vin*." That approach has at its heart the principle of *assemblage*. A Bordeaux château's best wine, the one that carries its name, will be composed of a selection of only the best lots, wines coming from different vineyard sites and often different grape varieties. Once the winemaker has identified those lots, the challenge lies in blending them so as to produce a harmonious whole, one with a stylistic identity that reflects its geographic origin as well as its history. Fashioning just such an *assemblage*, using grapes harvested from vineyards up and down the valley, was precisely the challenge Joe Phelps and his winemakers faced with Insignia. The idea was simple: to pay more attention to overall composition than to individual components, in the process fashioning a wine in which the whole would be greater than the proverbial sum of its parts.

Although blending wines was nothing new in California, most vintners with fine wine ambitions in the 1970s tended to frown upon the practice. They associated it with generic jug wines, the sort of screw-capped bottles labeled as "burgundy" or "chablis" that composed about 75 percent of the state's table wine production at the time. Many of these wines were blends of grapes grown in vineyards throughout the state, and many included high proportions of undistinguished varieties such as Burger, Colombard, and Thompson Seedless. These wines were precisely what the new wave of Napa Valley vintners wanted *not* to make. Their ambitions focused instead on premium production, and they inevitably identified their wines varietally. The radical aspect of Joe Phelps's idea, then, was not the blending itself, but rather blending with only the finest grapes from the finest vineyards. He believed that overall quality was more important than varietal character.

The initial vintage of Insignia included 94 percent Cabernet Sauvignon and 6 percent Merlot. The next year's rendition combined 14 percent Cabernet with 86 percent Merlot, the reversal coming simply because the Phelps winemakers thought this the best *assemblage*. After a return to a Cabernet-dominated wine in 1976, the 1977 blend introduced a new element: 20 percent Cabernet Franc (along with 50 percent Cabernet Sauvignon and 30 percent Merlot). The vineyard sources varied, too. Although always from Napa, the grapes for Insignia came from seven separate vineyards in Calistoga, Oakville, Stag's Leap, and Spring Valley, with different sites contributing different percentages, depending upon the vintage's particular strengths. On it went in this manner for some fifteen years—varying proportions of these classic red Bordeaux varieties sourced from separate vineyards. Only a small proportion of the blend ever came from grapes grown on the Phelps home ranch. Instead, independent Napa Valley growers, including Milt Eisele,

John Stanton, and John Tench, contributed the vast majority of the fruit. Their grapes, always of high quality, expressed different sites as well. And since the Insignia blends themselves differed from year to year, the wines inevitably bespoke a series of shifting origins.

Given the differences in varietal composition and vineyard sourcing, it is not surprising that this first generation of Insignia vintages included wines that tasted quite distinct from each other. Some displayed secondary mint flavors while others seemed spicy; some, especially those with higher percentages of Merlot in the blend, tasted of cherries and red fruits, while others evidenced cassis and blackcurrant flavors. During the late 1970s and 1980s, Insignia almost always received laudatory reviews, and was regularly ranked as one of Napa's top wines. Soon other vintners began to flatter it by imitating it, and before long Bordeaux-styled blends, including the Mondavi-Rothschild Opus One, became fairly common in Napa. Yet the different vintages of Insignia still varied stylistically. Precisely because the original intent was for this to be the finest wine Phelps produced, regardless of variety or locale, Insignia at this point did not have an identity beyond that of the individual year's blend. So even as it began to acquire a reputation for quality, it lacked consistency. Its first rush of success had proved that *assemblage* could produce a very good American wine. But the nagging question remained as to whether *assemblage*, as the dominant principle, was sufficient to produce a great wine.

More than anyone else at Joseph Phelps Vineyards, Craig Williams analyzed and even agonized over that question. Williams had come to the winery in 1976, a year after graduating from UC Davis, to work with Walter Schug, the estate's first winemaker. Schug, a German émigré who had studied enology at the famed Geisenheim Institute in the Rheingau, made his mark mostly with white wines, particularly late harvest dessert wines in a German style, and he soon assigned his young assistant oversight of the reds. From the start, Williams was intrigued by the idea of creating a premium blend that tasted better than any of its components. "It was so new," he recalls. "Back then, there were no blended wines at the high end. We were all learning as we went along." In 1983, when

Schug left to run his own winery in Carneros, Joe Phelps promoted Williams. Responsible from that point on for a host of different wines, Williams never forgot that this *assemblage* was his boss's special project. Gradually, it became his as well, as he slowly improved the wine by aiming for (and attaining) stylistic consistency, in the process elevating Insignia to its current rarefied status.

In his early days at the winery, Williams concentrated primarily on cellar techniques. With his degree in fermentation science, he was well versed in the technology of vinification, but like many Davis graduates at the time, not much concerned with viticulture. As he worked with Insignia, however, he started to think differently about his job as a winemaker. The shift was inspired by Joe Phelps's continued insistence that the blend should be based on a Bordeaux model. The great Bordeaux châteaux, Williams recognized, produce wines that, despite the vagaries of fortune or vintage, taste individualistic as well as good. That is, they display a recognizable personality year after year. Williams started to think that Insignia could not attain that sort of identity without a more stable supply of grapes. At the same time, he worried about limiting potential sources, thus changing the wine from a variable but always delicious blend to something site dependent and hence potentially more uneven in terms of quality.

Williams and Joe Phelps talked at length about this dilemma. Gradually, both men agreed that Insignia needed to become more identifiable. And in order to do that, it had to be defined more narrowly, so that it could evolve into a wine with a specific history of Napa Valley vineyard sourcing. So, in 1983, Phelps purchased thirty-five acres off Manley Lane in Rutherford. Named Banca Dorada or "Golden Bench," this vineyard was planted primarily to Cabernet Sauvignon and Cabernet Franc. He then bought forty acres in the Stags Leap District, the Las Rocas vineyard, planted to Cabernet Sauvignon and Merlot. Under Williams's direction, these two vineyards would become the backbone of the Insignia program, the new goal being to have estate fruit dominate the blend.

"It seems so obvious now to say that wine quality is directly related to where and how the grapes are grown," Williams says, "but believe me, in the late 1970s and early 1980s, the idea was revolutionary. At least it was in this country." American vintners back then certainly understood that vineyard location mattered. For the most part, though, they conceived of differences between vineyard sites simply in terms of climate, or even more simply, heat. Davis graduates in particular relied almost exclusively on a "degree-day" system, devised by two esteemed professors at the university, Maynard Amerine and Albert Julius Winkler, that measures the temperature in a particular region in terms of the number of hours in which grapes will ripen. When he started working at Phelps, Craig Williams certainly thought it important to know a site's degree-day classification. Beyond that, though, he paid little attention to *terroir* or grape growing, focusing instead on winemaking decisions. Insignia was a carefully selected blend. He thought that because the selection occurred in the winery, its character had to come from his and Walter Schug's science and art. But Williams slowly changed his mind. He gradually came to consider viticulture to be as important as vinification, and decisions made in the vineyard as significant as those made in the winery. From this new perspective, quality and style became reflections of wine growing rather than just winemaking.

Craig Williams was not the only person shifting his point of view. In the 1990s, a new wave of California vintners started to think about vineyards in terms of more than climate, in the process raising the level of achievement of American wine. Though they might not be able to identify exactly why grapes from two vineyards with comparable numbers of degree-days could yield significantly different wines, they acknowledged and indeed often worked to emphasize such differences. For they recognized that differences account for distinction, and that nuanced distinction forms the foundation of any great wine's identity.

Craig Williams and Joe Phelps had come to this realization almost a decade earlier, when they decided that in order for Insignia to become truly great, it needed to express a consistency of style rooted in place. This is not to say that they became as single-minded as some of their compatriots, the Francophile *terroiristes* who by the late 1990s were claiming that winemaking involves nothing more than being a caretaker for nature's gifts. Nonetheless, their recognition of the significance of place is what led them to alter the initial concept of Insignia, moving it from a generic *assemblage* of choice grapes to an *assemblage* of equally choice grapes always coming from specific sites.

"It's not that grapes from our vineyards are better than the ones we used to buy," Williams explains. "It's that they're ours every year. This means we have more control. The most important thing for any winemaker is identifying when the fruit is at the right level of ripeness for his wine. That's why it makes such a difference owning vineyards." Yet at first, having more control meant relinquishing control. Williams had to acknowledge that someone else's work was as important as his own. That someone else was Bulmaro Montes, the vineyard manager for the Phelps properties. These two men had to learn to work together, to listen to and acknowledge each other's expertise, and to make wine as a team. It took time. But gradually, as the vines matured, both men came to understand that they shared a commitment to a single principle. Whether in the vineyard or the winery, meticulous selection turned out to be the key to the *assemblage* of Insignia. The decision to lower yields, much like the decision to leave certain lots out of the final blend, had a direct effect on the wine. Even in a blend, exclusion ultimately proved more important than inclusion. So while in one sense the shift to estate fruit limited choices, in another sense it broadened them. Only now the choices were more specific, the issue no longer being which grapes to use but rather how best to grow them and then make wine from them.

The shift from purchased to estate grapes for Insignia did not happen all at once. Joe Phelps's acquisition of new vineyard land coincided with the Napa Valley phylloxera infestation of the 1980s, a blight that affected not only his own vineyards but also his outside sources. For a brief period in the second half of the decade, when the new properties had not yet fully come on line, overall quality declined. Beginning with the 1989 vintage, however, the first year in which the majority of the fruit came from estate vineyards, Insignia began to assume new form. That was a difficult because rain-soaked year, and the wine succeeded where many of its competitors failed, offering deep flavors with no trace of astringency. Then with the 1991 vintage it attained new heights, and was widely hailed by critics as the best yet. Richer, riper, and less aggressively tannic then before, this and subsequent releases displayed the sort of distinctive, identifiable character that earlier renditions had lacked. Full-bodied, these wines were richly perfumed, filled with dark fruit and concentrated but layered flavors. As important was their texture on the palate. For such powerful wines, they proved remarkably smooth, seductive, and satiny.

"This sounds odd," Williams says, "but I didn't really learn how to make wine until 1991. That wine was so good, I wanted to make something like it every year, not just occasionally." In order to do so, Williams needed a new model—not classified-growth Bordeaux, but Insignia itself. And Insignia could only serve as an effective model once he better understood the distinctions that came from the estate properties. "That was really a watershed year," he concludes. "From then on, we determined to exert more control over picking, and I focused more on the blending process within our vineyards."

The evolution of Insignia from multiple vineyard sources that changed frequently to a small set of sources that remains stable also means that the wine's varietal composition has become less variable. Cabernet Sauvignon, which is the grape planted most extensively on the estate vineyards, accounts today for the overwhelming majority of the blend. In fact, Insignia in most recent vintages technically could be identified on the label as Cabernet. Nonetheless, it remains very much an *assemblage.* What makes this wine exceptional, Joe Phelps and Craig Williams both insist, is the series of careful choices they make with it, first in the vineyard and then again in the winery, and they still do not want to be confined by anyone else's decisions.

In turn, those choices are responsible for the record of consistency that has characterized Insignia over the last decade. What is perhaps most impressive about that record is the wine's relatively high volume of production. A rigorously chosen *assemblage* is one thing when a winery is making 500 or 1,000 cases; but Joseph Phelps Vineyards produces 15,000 to 18,000 cases of Insignia each year. Craig Williams no longer is solely responsible for it, as he has nurtured the development of a top-notch winemaking team, and turned over many of the day-to-day chores to them. Nonetheless, he stays very much involved in selecting the lots for each year's Insignia blend. For the wine remains special to him, as it does to Joe Phelps, and as it should to anyone who cares about the emergence of great American wines over the past thirty years. During a period in which California winemaking as a whole attained a new level of excellence, Insignia has served as a benchmark for both overall quality and stylistic reliability. Year after year it outperforms all but a small and changeable number of wines, thus assuring itself a place in the pantheon of America's finest.

A NOTE ON VINTAGES:

Insignia has a great track record, being a wine that can be drunk with pleasure when young but that also ages beautifully. Wines from the 1970s and 1980s are still drinking well, and recent releases should evolve gracefully for a good two decades. Excellent older vintages include the groundbreaking 1974, 1984, 1986, and 1991; strong recent vintages include 1997, 1999, and 2001.

THE SUGGESTED PRICE FOR THE CURRENT 2002 INSIGNIA IS $135.

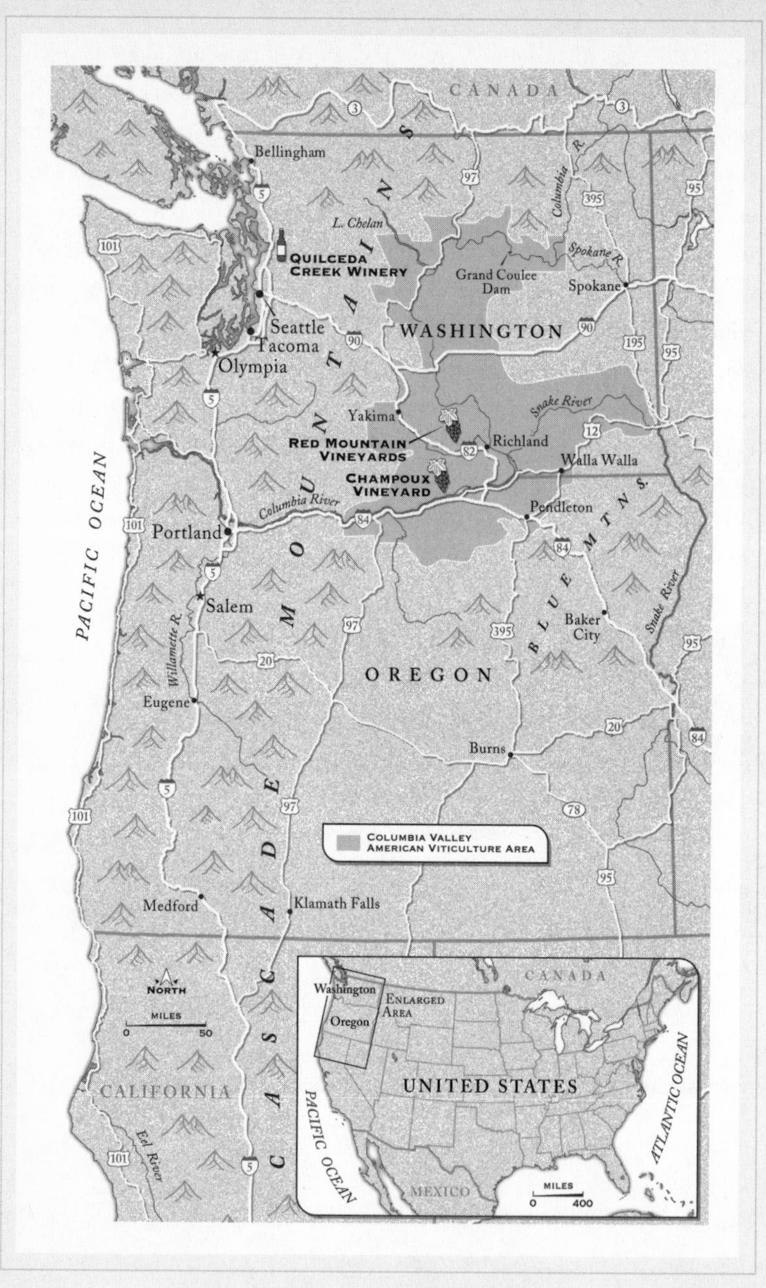

THE QUILCEDA CREEK WINERY
AND THE VINEYARDS FOR ITS CABERNET

CHAPTER 27

QUILCEDA CREEK VINTNERS CABERNET SAUVIGNON

Columbia Valley, Washington

...

The father and son team of Alex and Paul Golitzin share an audacious ambition. They aim to make nothing less than America's best wine, a Cabernet Sauvignon that, in their words, can be "tops worldwide." Though they worked for many years out of little more than a converted garage in Snohomish, Washington, some thirty miles north of Seattle, they may well be succeeding. The Golitzins' Quilceda Creek Cabernet, powerfully concentrated yet at the same time elegantly refined, is not as well known as some of the California wines profiled in this book, but it is every bit their equal if not their better. The Golden State, particularly the Napa Valley, produces more first-class wines than any other place in the country, but Washington's compelling contemporary Bordeaux-styled reds demonstrate that the Evergreen State is gaining ground fast. Of these, Quilceda Creek Cabernet, made since 2004 in a new, state-of-the-art winery just next door to their family home, is a clear leader.

Alex Golitzin

First produced commercially in 1979, when Washington wines were just beginning to attract attention beyond state lines, Quilceda Creek Cabernet started as a somewhat quirky experiment, and only evolved gradually into the standard-bearer it is today. Virtually everything about this wine, including grape sourcing, vinification, and most important, how the Golitzins conceive of it, has changed over the years. Alex Golitzin's initial aim, due, he recalls, "to the total lack of availability of fine wine in Washington at the time," was just to make something drinkable. Now, prodded in no small measure by his son, he wants much more. "Our quest," he says, "is the ultimate Cabernet."

That grail may be beyond their (or anyone's) reach, but Quilceda Creek's wines, especially those made over the past decade, compete favorably with the finest from both the New and the Old worlds. They combine the opulent fruit of California with the nuanced, earthy character of great claret, thus manifesting the sort of stylistic synthesis that vintners across the globe frequently proclaim as a goal but hardly ever actually achieve. Put simply, Quilceda Creek Cabernet Sauvignon is a New World wine that tastes more than new. Sampling it demonstrates both how much potential Washington's vineyards possess and how close the state's most ambitious vintners have come to realizing it.

Not that long ago, no one even imagined that Washington could produce top-flight wines. The absence of any significant pre-Prohibition history of wine growing, coupled with the presence of protectionist post-Prohibition laws, made the state an afterthought (if a thought at all) to American wine lovers. Things started to change in 1969, when the state legislature opened the market to competition, thus forcing local growers who wanted to stay in business to produce better wines. The first step involved shifting from labrusca and hybrid grapes to European vinifera varieties. In terms of large-scale production, American Wine Growers (now Ste. Michelle Wine Estates, owners of both the Chateau Ste. Michelle and the Columbia Crest wineries, among others) led the way, pioneering varietal wines, especially Chardonnay, Merlot, and Riesling, made in significant volume and sold at reasonable prices. As important, though, were a number of smaller operations, wineries such as Associated

Vintners, Kiona Vineyards, Leonneti Cellar, Preston, and of course Quilceda Creek. When these were bonded in the 1960s and 1970s, they represented something entirely new in Washington. Though they did not sell much wine, and though they often priced what they did sell quite high, their owners, committed to quality rather than quantity, made vinifera wines whose superiority inspired the state's large producers to follow suit.

Associated Vintners, for example, which was founded in 1962 by a group of University of Washington professors (and which later went on, under the Columbia Winery label, to become a large-volume producer itself), made a Gewurztraminer that the legendary Napa Valley vintner André Tchelistcheff declared in 1966 to be the best he had ever tasted from the United States. The managers over at American Wine Growers took note, and the next year they hired Tchelistcheff to work for them as a consultant. In turn, he helped them produce some of Chateau Ste. Michelle's first vinifera wines. But the story gets more complicated. Tchelistcheff's new job compelled him to travel to the Seattle area, where by chance he had family to visit—his nephew Alex Golitzin, then a wine drinker but by no means a winemaker. Golitzin, who had grown up in San Francisco and spent weekends as a child in Napa, used to complain frequently to his uncle about the quality of most Washington wine. Tchelistcheff could not disagree, but insisted that there was good reason to have faith in the future. He noted that independent vintners back home were helping improve the quality as well as the image of California wine. Perhaps the same thing could happen in Washington.

So it was at his uncle's urging that in 1974 Golitzin made an experimental barrel of Cabernet Sauvignon. The wine tasted good—so good in fact that after three more vintages and three more barrels, he and his wife, Jeannette, decided to go into business. They named their winery, only the twelfth commercial one in Washington, after the small stream that ran down from the mountains near their home, and they followed Tchelistcheff's instructions to the letter when making the first wines they offered for sale. In 1983, the year their initial Cabernet was put on the market, they won the Grand Prize from the Enological Society of the

Northwest for it. By then, more than a few people were beginning to believe that good, maybe even great wine could come from Washington.

Without André Tchelistcheff's vision, Quilceda Creek Vintners might not even exist. Certainly without his assistance, a wine of the quality of Quilceda Creek Cabernet would not exist. Yet a master is useless without a willing apprentice, and Alex Golitzin proved a quick study. "Uncle really helped," he acknowledges. "He taught me how to make technically sound wine. He was a little hard to keep up with, since he often was revising his advice, but he instilled in us the desire to continuously push the quality envelope."

Tchelistcheff saw in Washington the same sort of potential he had seen in Napa when he first came there after Prohibition. Continuous improvement was his mantra, repeated over and over again during his visits to the Golitzins' Snohomish home. Don't worry about vintage variation, he advised them. Do everything you can to make each year's wine better. Don't cut corners. If you really want to make good wine, concentrate on one varietal. And never forget that a wine will remember every little thing you do to it. These lessons took hold, first with Alex and then, perhaps even more deeply, with Paul, who can remember literally sitting, and learning, at his grand-uncle's knee.

Making wine was always Alex Golitzin's second job. A career chemical engineer, he worked full time for Scott Paper in Everett, Washington, for some twenty-seven years, retiring only in 1994. While grapes and wine came more and more to fill a special place in his heart, his day job supplied him with the income he needed to raise his family—two daughters, Lisa and Victoria, in addition to Jeannette and Paul. Egged on by his uncle, he had increasingly grand goals for Quilceda Creek, but for a long time he refused to let them overwhelm him. Excepting the first years when there was no wine to sell, he insisted that the business remain debt-free, resisting any temptation to purchase land or expand volume. The original winery, located right behind his house on a wooded lot overlooking the Cascade Mountains, stayed small, with production in the mere hundreds of cases. And the operation was always very much a family affair. Jeannette helped manage the books; Paul assisted in the winery; and though the girls never became all that involved with wine, their boyfriends and later husbands did. (One now works as an assistant winemaker, while the other is in charge of sales.)

Only after almost a decade in business did Golitzin cautiously allow his unsatisfied ambitions to begin to drive Quilceda Creek to a new level. In 1988, impressed by the quality of the vintage, he decided to designate a small percentage of that year's wine (50 out of 925 cases) as a "Reserve." He put Paul in charge. That wine proved so special that five years later he agreed to change the entire Quilceda Creek production to this "Reserve Style," one that now includes among other things a severe declassification to ensure quality and an aging program using 100 percent new French oak barrels. Not coincidentally, that same year saw him also agree that Paul should take over as the lead winemaker. The father had taken Quilceda Creek from a home winery to a state star. Now the son would raise the bar, fashioning wines that would bring national and even international acclaim.

Making the decision to hand over the winemaking reins proved surprisingly easy for Alex Golitzin, even though it came when he finally had the financial resources to devote himself full time to the business. Again, it was a matter of ambition, but ambition for the wine rather than for himself. He recognized that Paul was the member of the family who most clearly had inherited his uncle André's passion and talent. Paul, after all, was the one who pushed for the creation of reserve wines, who nurtured them like babies, and who when tasting through barrel lots could detect nuances and subtleties (sometimes assets, sometimes defects) that others missed. "Paul decided to follow me in winemaking," Alex says, "but really it would be more proper to say that I am following in his footsteps, as he is a far better winemaker. He has an outstanding palate and is extremely creative. Our wine is as good as it is today primarily due to Paul."

That may be a bit of an overstatement. The rise in quality at Quilceda Creek over the past decade has been due in large measure to responsibilities being so clearly defined. While the family tries to make most decisions by consensus, situations inevitably arise in which someone has to have the final say. "We taste together, using a hundred-point scale, when making the wine," Paul explains. "If a lot gets under ninety-five points, it's out." And what happens if they don't agree? "We usually do," he says with a smile; "but if we don't, it's my call." The opposite is true across the driveway in his father's office, where Alex has the final say in business decisions (involving, for example, what percentage of the profits to reinvest in the company). Father, son, and the two sons-in-law work together, in a clear but effective division of labor, all sharing but one goal: to make the very best.

When it comes to Cabernet Sauvignon, Paul Golitzin defines the best as a wine with ample but not heavy concentration, one that will taste appealing when young and then improve with time spent in the bottle. "We want to make a wine that will hit a plateau of maturity seven or eight years after the vintage," he says, "and then last for ten or twenty years more. That's what all the great Cabs do." He insists that he does not have a stylistic paradigm in mind, but at the same time concedes that he wants his wine to taste "like a real ripe version of first-growth Bordeaux." That in fact is a good description of the Quilceda Creek style—rich and opulent, but simultaneously refined and stylish. What most distinguishes this wine is its sumptuous but structured texture, not fleshy like so many New World Cabernets, but at the same time not tight and linear like much Bordeaux. "How the wine feels in your mouth is really important to us," says Paul. "Drinking it is all about pleasure."

Maintaining a consistent style can be a challenge at a Washington winery like Quilceda Creek because the facility is located some 200 miles away from the vineyards. All of Washington's important grape growing regions lie to the east of the Cascade Range. Since the Golitzins live and work west of the mountains, it takes a truck four to five hours to get grapes to them at harvest. As a result, father and son have to be fanatical about fruit quality. For most of its history, Quilceda Creek Cabernet was made exclusively with purchased grapes, as Alex Golitzin did not have the resources to invest in vineyard land. He initially bought fruit from Otis Harlan, whose vineyard in the Yakima Valley was one of the first in the state to be planted with red vinifera varieties. Then in the early 1980s he started purchasing grapes from the Kiona Vineyard, located on Red Mountain, just east of Benton City. A few years later, he began to experiment with grapes from Don Mercer's 150-acre vineyard on the north side of the Columbia River, near the town of Paterson. Of these, the Golitzins especially came to admire the Mercer Ranch. Its Cabernet vines yielded a consistently generous wine, with a full structure but without either the herbal edge that sometimes marked the Otis fruit or the aggressive tannins that characterized Kiona grapes.

In 1997, having made the decision to aim for the highest possible quality, the Golitzen family decided to purchase vineyard land. In partnership with a number of the state's other top wineries (including Andrew Will and Woodward Canyon), they bought Mercer, renaming it after the ranch's manager and now another partner, Paul Champoux. Then in 2001 they planted seventeen acres of Cabernet on Red Mountain in partnership with Jim Holmes of Ciel du Cheval Vineyard. Today, Quilceda Creek Cabernet is fashioned from Champoux fruit blended with grapes from Red Mountain. The former provides the expansive, voluptuous mouthfeel that Paul Golitzin so prizes, while the latter contributes deeper flavors and firmer tannins to ensure longevity.

As part of the effort to improve wine quality by exerting more control over the grape supply, the Golitzins increasingly have become hands-on viticulturalists. They no longer are willing to leave decisions to various vineyard managers, but instead supervise canopy control and green harvesting, monitor potential yields, and most important, make the long trek east many times each fall to sample grapes hanging on the vine in order to decide when exactly to commence harvesting. Always one of the last Washington wineries to pick grapes, Quilceda Creek insists on fully ripe fruit, and father and son trust their taste buds even more than scientific measurements. "Tasting," Paul Golitzin insists, "is the biggest part of research and development for winemaking."

This sort of self-reliance extends to the winery, where Alex Golitzin has designed a gentle semi-automatic punch-down device to extract concentration without excessive tannins. All the fermentations take place in temperature-controlled, mobile, 2- and 6-ton tanks, designed jointly by the winery and the manufacturer. Quilceda Creek now has almost fifty of these, enabling Paul Golitzin to keep each lot separate all the way from harvest through fermentation to barrel aging. One reason for this is his insistence on using only the best lots for his Cabernet. In 1997, he took what his palate told him were the weaker barrels and made a second wine, called simply "Quilceda Creek Red." Today, roughly 35 percent of the winery's production gets declassified in this way. Though selection is stricter than ever before, the acquisition of vineyard land has provided the Golitzins with a larger supply of fruit, and their production of Cabernet has increased from approximately one thousand cases in 1990 to over three thousand today.

Prior to 1995, Quilceda Creek's wines were virtually 100 percent Cabernet Sauvignon. Since then, inspired largely by Paul Golitzin's insistence that good blended wine can yield a greater whole, they have tended to include small percentages of Merlot and Cabernet Franc. (The winery also produces a varietally labeled Merlot, sourced from Champoux.) Nonetheless, their primary goal remains to produce a wine that displays a classic Cabernet flavor profile. "It's the grape my uncle was most excited about," Alex Golitzin remembers, "and it has been consistent for us all the way along." His son agrees. "The different vineyards provide grapes with different personalities, but taken together they show how good Washington Cabernet Sauvignon is. It's our best wine." Fans of Washington's finest Chardonnays, Merlots, Rieslings, and Syrahs might quibble, but few unbiased tasters can disagree.

Looking back on over a quarter century of winemaking at Quilceda Creek, Alex Golitzin marvels at how much has changed, as Washington has gone from a viticultural backwater to America's second most productive grape-growing state. In the process, overall quality has taken a huge leap forward. "We've played a part," he says modestly, "but other people's success has helped us, too. It used to be just about impossible to sell a bottle of Washington wine out of state. Now people from all over the world come knocking on our door." Quilceda Creek's wines currently are sold in over forty states and eleven countries, more than half of the production via a mailing list. The international wine press raves about them, and connoisseurs treasure them. Distribution has to be tightly allocated, as demand inevitably exceeds supply. The Golitzins' ambition has come very close to being realized. They, however, are not satisfied. Both father and son insist that this wine can get even better, for they are convinced that Washington has the potential to produce the world's finest Cabernet-based wines.

That is indeed an audacious claim, but the evidence in a tasting glass suggests that it just might be true. After all, if the next twenty-five years bring only a fraction of the improvement of the past twenty-five, Washington clearly will have arrived as one of the world's premier wine regions. Should that happen, there can be little doubt that Quilceda Creek Cabernet Sauvignon still will be on top.

A NOTE ON VINTAGES:

Firmly structured, Quilceda Creek Cabernet ages extremely well, over time augmenting its dark berry and black cherry fruit flavors with secondary notes reminiscent of spice, cedar, and tobacco—much like the finest red Bordeaux. Muscular in its youth, it becomes increasingly harmonious and elegant with age. Strong vintages include 1994, 1998, 1999, 2001, and 2002.

THE SUGGESTED PRICE FOR THE CURRENT 2002 RELEASE IS $90.

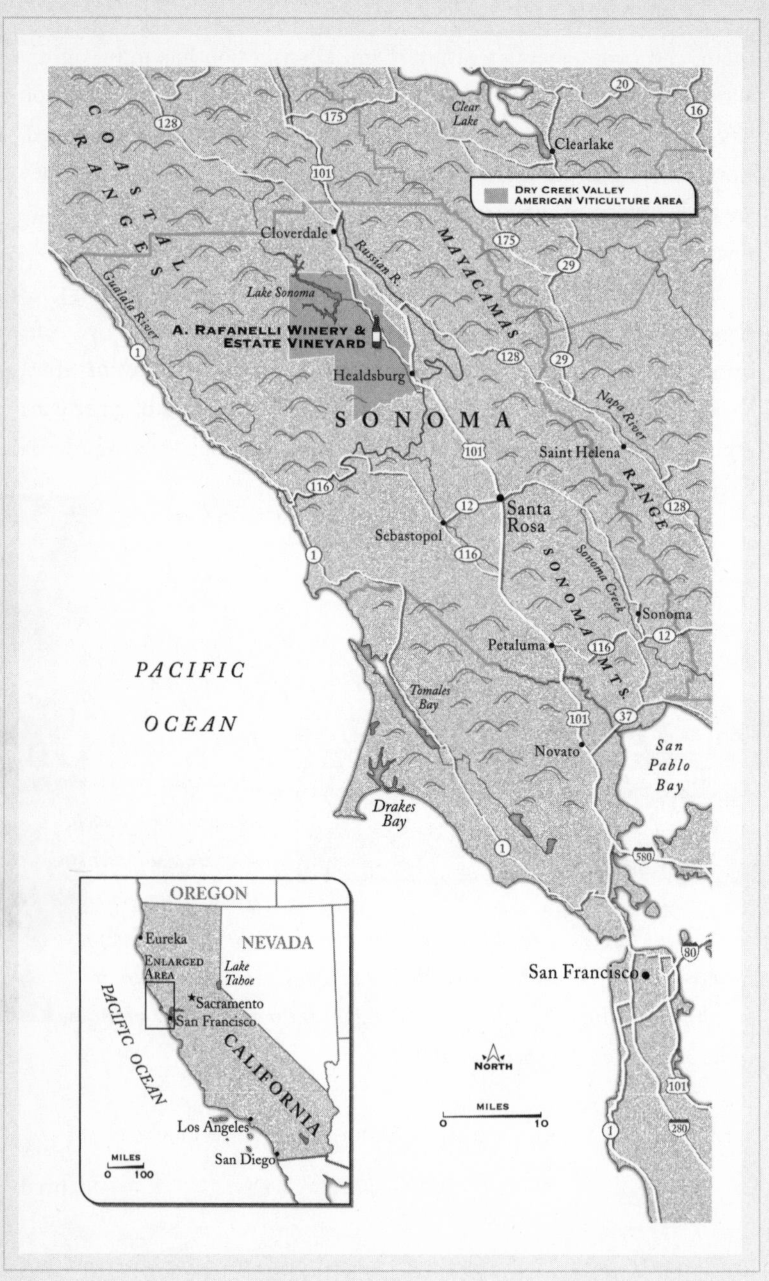

A. RAFANELLI AND THE DRY CREEK VALLEY AVA

CHAPTER 28

A. Rafanelli Winery Zinfandel

Dry Creek Valley, Sonoma County, California

...

For Dave Rafanelli, Zinfandel is a family affair. His grandfather, Alberto, an Italian immigrant from the island of Elba off the coast of Tuscany, first made wines from Sonoma County Zinfandel grapes in the not so "dry" 1920s, bootlegging them until he went into business legally after Repeal. Alberto later was joined by his son, Americo, who helped him sell both grapes and wine to some of California's leading producers. Only in 1974 did the Rafanellis start to bottle a small amount of wine under their own name. Although Alberto and Americo grew other grapes, Zinfandel always was their mainstay. "It was all they ever drank at home," recalls Dave Rafanelli, who today keeps the family legacy alive, and whose robust but refined Zins are some of the most nuanced made anywhere.

Dave Rafanelli

Zinfandel has been grown widely in California for some 150 years, but it has had a roller-coaster ride recently. First, late harvest, port-styled dessert wines were in vogue. Then, when sugary white Zin came along, sales of the red renditions, both sweet and dry, plummeted. Today, dry red Zinfandel has again become fashionable, but the trend is toward fleshy, extracted, alcoholic wines whose appeal is power rather than subtlety. Through all these changes, the Rafanellis steadily have made their wines in a "claret" style, meaning with the weight and body (though with markedly different flavors) of fine Bordeaux, wines principally designed to be drunk with food. "The old-timers drank lots of Zinfandel, but they only drank it with their meals," says Dave Rafanelli. "We're trying to make the same kind of thing now, only better." With the assistance of his daughter, Shelly (the winemaking heir apparent), he is succeeding. Ripe and spicy, but at the same time smooth and stylish, A. Rafanelli Zinfandel is an old-fashioned wine in a modern guise—both a reminder of why this grape has been popular in California for so long, and a testament to its contemporary status as a genuinely world-class varietal.

For much of its history in the Golden State, Zinfandel was the favorite grape of Italian immigrant families, and the Rafanelli story exemplifies the important place that those families occupy in the annals of American wine. Though few Italians grew grapes in California's early settlement days, by the end of the nineteenth century they were farming a considerable portion of the state's vineyards. They also were running some of the state's most successful wineries, including Italian Swiss Colony, a large agricultural cooperative in Sonoma County, and the Italian Vineyard Company, with a 5,000-acre vineyard in the Cucamonga district east of Los Angeles. Italians eventually came to dominate the wine business, beginning, paradoxically enough, during Prohibition. This was in part because their culture included wine in daily life, no matter what the law said, and in part because the Volstead Act, which made selling alcohol illegal, said nothing about grape growing.

All during the nearly fourteen "dry" years, Italian families continued to tend (and sometimes buy) vineyards, and to make wine. Some did so simply for home consumption. Others shipped their grapes east, where they sold them to like-minded city dwellers. Still others made and sold wine illicitly. By December 1933, when Repeal finally came, many of these families were set to go into business legitimately. Before long,

Italians owned the majority of the functioning wineries in the state, and for the next thirty years names such as Cribari, Gallo, Martini, Petri, Rossi, Sebastiani, and Vai directed the California wine trade. Some of the wine they made was cheap, fortified tipple sold primarily to skid row drunks, and in truth the public perception of American wine declined precipitously during the period. Yet much of their wine was dry table wine, usually red and rustic, the sort of stuff they drank themselves with lunch and supper. More often than not, the dominant grape variety turned out to be Zinfandel.

Since no one knew back then that Zinfandel is genetically the same as both Primitivo, an Italian grape that grows primarily in Apulia, the Italian boot's heel, and Crljenak Kastelanski from Croatia's Dalmatian coast, the predilection of immigrant families for this variety had nothing to do with Old World loyalty or tradition. Instead, their fondness for it came from its versatility. Zin's bold, brambly flavors made it a natural partner for the kinds of foods these families often ate, dishes flavored with garlic, olive oil, spicy peppers, and tomato-based sauces. In addition, it was relatively inexpensive to grow, producing large yields from untrellised vines, with the added advantage of a substantial second crop if hit by spring frost. The grape shipped well and proved forgiving during fermentation, so was widely planted in the 1920s, when home winemakers constituted the main market. And because it could serve different functions, it remained popular in the decades following Prohibition. Zin led itself readily to the production of heady fortified wines; and being dark in color and full in body, it made a superior blending grape for generic "burgundies" and "chiantis." So, no matter whether used in wines they drank or wines they sold, Zinfandel became the Italian American family's grape of choice. This was nowhere more true than in Sonoma County, particularly in and around the then sleepy town of Healdsburg, where a large number of such families lived, and where the Zinfandel grown in the nearby Dry Creek Valley tasted especially flavorful. Prominent names here included Pedroncelli, Seghesio, and Simi—and before too long, Rafanelli.

A sailor in the Italian Navy, Alberto Rafanelli had jumped ship in

Norfolk, Virginia, in 1903 and, like so many other immigrants, gone west. He first found a job as a carpenter in San Francisco, where he helped construct the Fairmont Hotel, eventually salvaging enough materials to build a house for himself and his new bride, Leticia Tognetti, herself an immigrant from Tuscany via Ellis Island. With the arrival of children, the couple moved north to Healdsburg, in search of a more peaceful, rural life. Alberto toiled there as a sharecropper, farming different fruits and vegetables, all the while slowly growing his small, homespun wine business. After nearly thirty years of careful saving, he finally had enough money to buy seventy-five acres in Dry Creek and become his own boss. His son helped him tend the vineyards and make the wines, and the Rafanelli name slowly acquired a cachet among those in the know. Wineries wanted their grapes, and consumers their wines. When Americo finally decided to bottle and sell some of those wines himself, he found a receptive local market. That was all he wanted. Unlike some of his more prominent neighbors, his ambitions never strayed far from home. "Dad was a farmer," recalls Dave Rafanelli. "He liked selling wine, but his heart was in the vineyard. He used to say, 'Pigs get fat but hogs get slaughtered.' He never wanted to grow the business too big."

Dave Rafanelli too is a farmer, as his callused hands and tanned visage plainly attest. In addition to everything his father taught him about growing grapes, he gleaned important lessons studying viticulture at UC Davis and then managing the vineyards at the nearby Lambert Bridge Winery. Specifically, he learned to focus only on what he could do best, and not to follow fads. When he took control at A. Rafanelli in 1986, he saw everyone around him making Chardonnay, but he steadfastly stuck to red wines. "Those were the best grapes we had," he says with a shrug. Another lesson came from watching the absentee owners at Lambert Bridge try to grow their business too quickly. "I learned to focus on quality, not quantity," he declares bluntly.

Today, A. Rafanelli produces about 11,000 cases of wine each year, two thirds of which are Zinfandel, the rest Cabernet Sauvignon. All of that wine is sold directly to consumers or restaurants, allowing the family to reap full profit and at the same time keep prices reasonable by bypassing wholesalers. Though Alberto and Americo are no longer alive, the operation remains very much a family affair. Patty Rafanelli, Dave's wife, runs the business side of things, taking orders, arranging deliveries, and managing the books, while father and daughter concentrate on the grapes and wine, much like father and son did a generation before, and a generation before that. True to his heritage, Dave Rafanelli insists that anything worth doing is worth doing oneself. "Keep things simple," he says, meaning keep them in the family, where everyone's interest will be personal even more than financial. He differs from his father and grandfather only in the scope of his ambitions. Though too modest to say so, everything he does at A. Rafanelli attests to his desire to reap more than regional renown. His Zinfandel now has a fervent global following, being sold in allocated amounts via a mailing list, as demand for it exceeds supply. "I guess if all those people want it," he says almost sheepishly, "we must be doing something right."

That something begins in the vineyard, where the Rafanellis long have prized hillside blocks over those on the valley floor. The leaner, well-drained soils on the slopes produce intensely flavored grapes at yields of roughly 3.5 tons per acre. By contrast, the rich, alluvial vineyards on the flatlands below can yield up to 8 tons. Dave Rafanelli still farms those, since they are part of the family property, but he sells the grapes to other wineries. "Even if you drop fruit from the vines there," he explains, "the wine won't be as good. Zinfandel likes the hills." Indeed, the presence of hillside vineyards, often filled with vines that are sixty or seventy years old, accounts in large measure for the Dry Creek Valley's well-deserved reputation as the home of superior Zin. Whether made by wineries located there or sold to producers elsewhere, old-vine Dry Creek Zinfandel has become a benchmark for the varietal. The best wines made from it display a degree of harmony and grace that those made from grapes grown elsewhere rarely achieve.

The finest Dry Creek Valley Zinfandels tend to come from the benchlands on both sides of this long but narrow AVA, which borders the warmer Alexander Valley region at one end and the cooler Russian

River one at the other. The Rafanelli property lies midway down the western side. Slightly brawnier wines tend to come from the east, where the largest landowner long has been Gallo, the producer of an excellent Zin from the Frei Ranch. Most growers in Dry Creek irrigate their vineyards these days, but previous generations dry-farmed the land, and some of the best fruit comes from their now gnarled, head-pruned vines. For a long time, most of the fruit from those vines went into bulk wine, including Gallo's "Hearty Burgundy," since Zinfandel rarely was used for stand-alone bottlings in the post-Prohibition era. Yields were larger then, the wines simpler and less distinctive. Over the past twenty-five years, as the vines have aged and Zin has come to be valued more for its own sake, growers increasingly have focused on improving quality. In the process they have discovered that this variety, though as easy to grow as ever, presents quite a challenge to anyone who wants to make truly fine wine from it.

"Zinfandel," Dave Rafanelli says, "can give a farmer gray hairs. You never know what you're going to get with it, so you have to care for it like you care for a baby." The extra level of attention that he has introduced has taken A. Rafanelli Zinfandel to new heights, making it not just one of many good Dry Creek Valley wines but an esteemed landmark. While the wine remains stylistically similar to the wines Alberto and Americo produced, Dave's meticulousness has made it more harmonious and less variable. Unlike his grandfather, he thins the crop in order to concentrate flavor. Unlike his father, he goes so far as to remove berries from individual bunches in order to encourage regular ripening. Zinfandel tends to mature unevenly within tight clusters, so the sugar levels can vary significantly. At A. Rafanelli, human hands touch each shoot on each vine at least three times during the growing season, cutting off loose "wings" of berries as well as small second-crop grapes. Then, at harvest, pickers pass through the vineyards multiple times in order to try to minimize differences in ripeness.

"We coddle each vine," Rafanelli says. "To make good wine here you have to start with good fruit. My dad taught me that." Americo, who witnessed the beginnings of the California wine boom, insisted that a winemaker is in essence a wine tender, someone who knows, and respects, the vines. His son agrees. "If you want to grow grapes and make wine," he says, "the first thing you need is patience. You have to let nature do its work at its own pace."

Care and patience characterize Dave Rafanelli's work in the winery as well. "I started out like my father," he acknowledges, "concentrating on farming. But as time went on, my interest in winemaking grew and grew." Though the basic process is much the same as the one Alberto and Americo employed (fermentation in small open-top tanks, followed by an extensive period of wood aging), small but significant changes have bettered the wine significantly. For one, Dave and Shelly now make sure to sort the grapes by hand before crushing them, removing not only odd bits of stem or leaf material but also any under- or overripe berries, again trying to minimize variations. For another, Dave has replaced his father's old wooden fermenters with stainless-steel ones, thus reducing the risk that off-flavors or aromas might be introduced into the wine. Like his dad, he punches down or submerges the cap of grape skins in the fermenting wine by hand, in order to extract maximum color and flavor; but he does it more often—on average, six times a day, every day, for about ten days.

The most significant change at A. Rafanelli involves the barrel program. Americo used only old, neutral American oak barrels. These affected the wine through oxidation, but imparted essentially no character of their own. His son today uses French barrels, discarding them after three or four years, when the supple vanilla flavor has been leeched out. Since these barrels run about $800 apiece, the cost of winemaking has gone up since he has taken charge. So too, though, has the overall quality of the wines. "If we are making better Zin nowadays," Rafanelli says, "it's only because we finesse it more."

A. Rafanelli Zinfandel is noteworthy not simply for its briary varietal character but also for its polish and refinement. Robust, as any red wine made from this grape should be, it nonetheless displays subtleties and nuances that enable it to stand out from all but a few others. With a perfume redolent of raspberries and black cherries, it offers deep fruit flavors augmented by secondary notes reminiscent at times of cedar and tobacco, with no hint of heat in the finish. Like all good Zinfandels, its primary appeal comes from vivid fruit, but unlike so many others, it tastes genuinely multifaceted and stylish. Perhaps most important, it is extremely food-friendly. Though not as showy as some others, particularly today's highly extracted Zins, it proves superior time and again when drunk with meals. And in this regard, A. Rafanelli Zinfandel has not changed at all over the years. Though the alcohol levels have crept up slightly, largely as a result of the efforts to cull out green fruit, it remains what it was when Alberto and Americo first made it: a wine whose proper place is at the supper table. "After all," Dave Rafanelli argues, "isn't that what any wine is for?"

This third-generation vintner, who grew up speaking Italian before he learned English, has taken a good but simple wine and, while retaining its basic character, made it ever more generous, graceful, and supple. In the process, he has helped bring new acclaim to a grape variety that, though long popular, only now is being recognized widely as having the potential to produce refined, world-class wines. He is not alone. Paul Draper does much the same thing with his Geyserville and Lytton Springs Zins from Ridge Vineyards, and fellow Dry Creek Valley vintners such as Doug Nalle, Fred Peterson, David Stare, and Grady Wann all share the conviction that Zinfandel can yield elegant as well as exuberant wines. Yet Dave Rafanelli's heritage, his lifetime of work in the valley, coupled with all the years in which his father and grandfather worked before him, sets his wine apart. Its prominence stems not only from the vines they planted, and not only from his own skill, but also from the vision that four generations share—a vision in which this grape and this wine are always very much in the family.

A NOTE ON VINTAGES:

Zinfandel is not a wine that ages very gracefully, as fresh, vibrant fruit flavors constitute its primary appeal. A. Rafanelli's Zin, though, fares better than most since it is deliberately fashioned in a refined rather than rambunctious style. Particularly strong years for this wine have included 1987, 1990, 1995, 1997, 2000, and 2001, with wines from the last four all drinking well now.

THE SUGGESTED PRICE FOR THE CURRENT 2003 RELEASE IS $35.

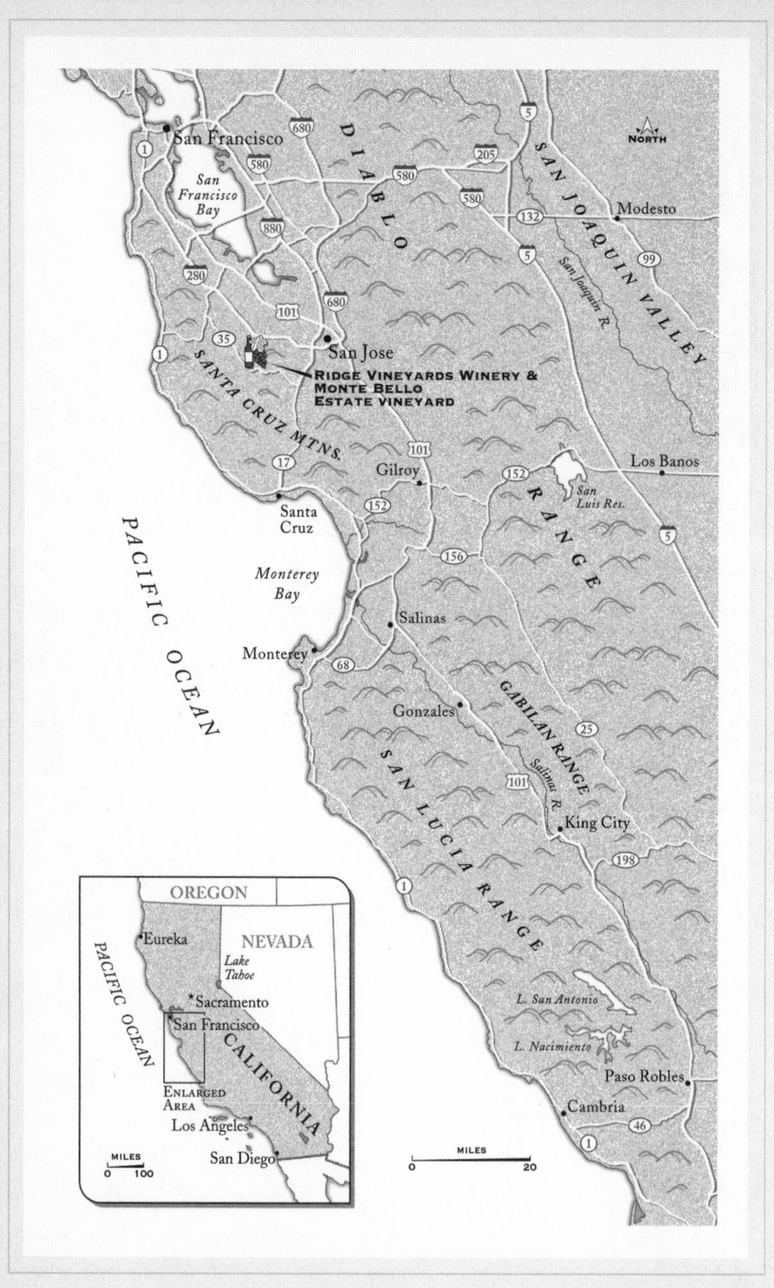

RIDGE VINEYARDS, ATOP MONTE BELLO IN THE SANTA CRUZ MOUNTAINS

CHAPTER 29

Ridge Vineyards Monte Bello

Santa Cruz Mountains, California

...

Go up. To reach the top of Monte Bello Ridge, you have to go up—2,600 feet above sea level, a trip of twenty minutes by car on a winding, sometimes vertigo-inducing mountain road, starting outside the Silicon Valley town of Saratoga. You climb above the clouds until you come to gnarled, scraggly vines, and then you climb even higher. The first vineyard you pass does not belong to Ridge. A second one does, and this is your first glimpse of Monte Bello, the "lower" vineyard at 1,300 feet. This now legendary block of land extends up the mountain, so you need to go all the way up. As the name suggests, the site is beautiful. The Pacific lies some fifteen miles over the mountains to the west, and on a clear day you can make out the sprawl of San Francisco's suburbs to the north. Below, way below, profit and gain are pursued frenetically in the high-tech corridor that stretches from Palo Alto to San Jose, but here nothing seems hurried or hectic. Birds sing peacefully; the breeze rustles the pines; and nature rather than commerce holds sway. It's hard to imagine a more idyllic place.

Paul Draper

No wonder that some forty-five years ago a group of friends from the nearby Stanford Research Institute bought this property as a weekend and holiday retreat. The estate included part of an old vineyard, and they enjoyed picking the grapes. Tranquility, however, does not explain what makes the wines from Monte Bello special. And for a long time, going back to the 1890s, they have been very special. The explanation comes from the place itself—from its thin and stony soils, long growing season, moderate temperatures, varied exposures, and non-irrigated vines, in a word, from its *terroir.* No American wine better exemplifies the effect of *terroir* than Monte Bello, and no American winery is more committed to expressing that effect in its wines than Ridge Vineyards.

"The Monte Bello character is stronger than any varietal character," notes Paul Draper, who has been making the wines at Ridge for over thirty-five years now. "That's because all the decisions, in the vineyard and in the winery, are made on the basis of taste." Predominantly Cabernet, but never fashioned by formula or recipe, the Monte Bello wine consistently tastes of its origin. No matter whether in the Old World or New, that is true of only a handful of wines made anywhere, anytime. And it explains why Monte Bello ranks near the top in the hierarchy of the world's great wines. Like the vineyard, it's way up there.

Terroir is a tricky because complex notion. A French word with no precise English translation, it frequently is used incompletely. That's because it means place, but in a multitude of senses. There's geology of course, and topography—the shape, structure, and situation of any specific site. And meteorology—not just regional weather, but meso- and microclimates, diurnal patterns, hours and intensity of sunlight, the influence of fog or frost, and more. These natural factors all interact to make any vineyard's ecosystem unique. But *terroir* involves more than environment. It also includes history, the history of the site, and this involves factors other than nature. Wine grapes are a cultivated crop, so without the work of human beings, a vineyard would never be a vineyard. That work, then, contributes to *terroir*. Much of what makes Monte Bello so special involves nature. Regardless of what might grow there, the place is extraordinary. But part also involves the human recognition of the site's potential for grapes and wine, and the subsequent realization of that potential. Put another way, *terroir* is the source of this wine's *typicité*—one more word with an imprecise translation. *Typicité* does not mean typical in the usual sense, as in representative of a category or group. Instead, it is self-referential, meaning representative of nothing so much as the object itself. And that characteristic can be recognized only through an awareness of history—in this case, the history of both the wine and the place.

The history of this place goes back some 67 million years, to when a ridge of limestone was formed on the floor of the Pacific Ocean near the equator. Over time, that ridge traveled north and east as the Pacific plate moved under the North American land mass. When the ridge reached the coast, it was sheared off and left behind. (Interestingly, observes Paul Draper, the geological term for land formed this way is "exotic terrain.") Since then, the Pacific plate has shifted course, moving north, parallel to the coast, creating the San Andreas Fault. That fissure sheers through the mountains at the western edge of Monte Bello, occasioning the spectacular but dizzying vistas.

In the vineyard, more important than the view is the resulting soil composition: Franciscan shale mixed with clay atop fractured limestone, soils that subsequent erosion has left thin and impoverished. Only people especially sensitive to the promise of *terroir* would go to the trouble to troop up Monte Bello and plant grapes. That was the next critical moment in this *terroir*'s history, and it first happened during the last decades of the nineteenth century. At the time, the eastern slopes of the Santa Cruz Mountains and broad Santa Clara Valley below were filled with orchards and vineyards. Much as now, ambitious vintners who cared more about quality than quantity prized the less vigorous mountain sites because they produced especially flavorful fruit. One of the first to climb up Monte Bello was Vincent Picchetti, who planted vines (mostly Zinfandel) near the top of the escarpment in 1877. Pierre Klein followed a few years later, with red Bordeaux varieties in a vineyard he planted even higher. Then, in 1886, Osea Perrone, a San Francisco physician, bought the land at the very top. Perrone planted grapes and bonded his business under the name of the Montebello Wine Company. He crushed grapes and made wine on the ridge, but bottled and sold it in San Francisco. Ridge Vineyards today uses Perrone's winery for the production and aging of its wines.

Wines from these different vineyards, though produced in small volume, soon reaped acclaim, and in the first decades of the new century the area developed a reputation for fine California claret. But the history of Monte Bello was soon interrupted by Prohibition and its bitter aftermath, and by the early 1940s most blocks in these vineyards were effectively abandoned, their *terroir* left unfulfilled. Later in that decade, a retired theologian, William Short, bought part of the Perrone estate. Aware of its past, he planted some vines—mostly Cabernet. This was the property that the Stanford researchers, four scientists and their families, purchased in 1959.

Their principal reason for coming up the mountain was relaxation. Picking grapes and making a little wine to sip at picnics was at best an afterthought. But one member of the group, David Bennion, intuitively sensed the possibilities latent in the Monte Bello *terroir*, and appropriated a small amount of the harvest for a more serious wine. It turned out to taste very good, so good that the group decided to reopen the winery and go into business, with Bennion in charge of production. Very much aware that they were reviving rather than inventing something, they wanted to call their enterprise "Monte Bello Ridge." But the New Jersey company that had purchased Osea Perrone's Montebello Wine Company facility in San Francisco would not allow it, so they settled on "Ridge." The first commercial release, seventy-seven cases of 100 percent Cabernet, came with the 1962 vintage.

Though the founding families initially thought of Ridge more as recreation than as business, they did not want to lose money, and it soon became clear that production had to expand. They replanted more of their own property; but since the young vines there needed time to bear quality fruit, they decided to purchase grapes in order to produce more wine and make ends meet. Old-vine, high-quality Cabernet was rare, so they had to find another varietal. They settled on Zinfandel, largely because some was growing lower on the ridge. A couple of acres on the old Picchetti property down the road still survived. In 1964, Dave Bennion pruned those eighty-year-old vines, and Ridge bought the whole crop, just about 2 tons. The wine turned out to be delicious—spicy, juicy, and unlike the more tannic Cabernet, ready to drink young. So over the next few years the Ridge partners went hunting for more sources of old-vine grapes. Some, like the Geyserville vineyard in Sonoma and the Dusi Ranch in Paso Robles, ended up being located far away, and before long, the winery's truck, loaded full with grapes, was laboring its way up the hairpin turns on Monte Bello Road.

By 1968, Ridge was producing some 2,300 cases of wine a year, 75 percent from grapes not grown at Monte Bello. By that point, the company had purchased the rest of the Perrone property, including the old winery. Bennion had quit his Stanford job; the original group had doubled; and the business had become viable. At much the same time, Bennion, whom the wine writer Jancis Robinson once described as "being so laid back he is almost horizontal," decided to hand over the day-to-day winemaking to someone younger and more vital, someone who could take Ridge to the next level. Enter Paul Draper, then thirty-three years old, thoughtful and analytical, a former student of philosophy at Stanford, so in touch with the academic world of the original partners, but at the same time more energetic and visionary, completely dedicated to one daring goal—as he put it to Robinson, "to make the finest wine not just in California but in the world."

In 1969, when he started working at Ridge, Draper did not talk about *terroir*, the word then being even more foreign than it is today. He did, though, talk a lot about vineyards—specifically, about the need to respect their individuality and to craft wines reflecting as much. Raised on a farm in Illinois, he came to winemaking interested less in conveying a personal or even a house style than in revealing particularities coming from the land. "That's what interested me about wine in the first place," he explains. "I wanted to take something from the earth, to carry it a step further through artisan ability, and make of it something sophisticated and complex." So he insisted on bottling the wine from each vineyard separately, showcasing the personality of the individual site. And for each wine's label, he penned an extended description of the site—not just the physical place but its effect on the grapes and the wine, the *terroir.*

Blending wines from different locations was never a serious option at Ridge, though blending different grape varieties was—so long as they grew alongside one another. Offering single-vineyard wines regardless of the particular grapes involved was a way of showcasing not just the vineyards but also the winery's ambitions, and Draper raised those very high. He made excellent Chardonnay and Petite Sirah, but the wines that brought the most renown were his Cabernets and Zinfandels. Ridge was one of the first wineries to treat Zinfandel seriously, keeping yields low and vinifying the wines much like fine Bordeaux, with extended aging in oak. During the 1970s and 1980s, the winery's claret-styled Zins and Zin blends became coveted collectibles, in the process bringing this then often maligned variety new respectability. The Geyserville rendition in particular emerged as one of Zinfandel's standard-bearers. All the while, though, Draper kept making wine from the estate vines at Monte Bello—originally only Cabernet, but with new planting, some Merlot, Cabernet Franc, and Petit Verdot as well. And while he regarded the various Zinfandels as princes in the realm of California wine, he always insisted that the wine from Monte Bello was a true king. After all, it alone evoked Ridge's own *terroir*.

Under David Bennion's watch, Monte Bello Cabernet almost made itself. "Dave was a real non-interventionist," recalls Draper, "and some of his wines were truly great." By contrast, "I'm a little more hands-on," meaning that he pays more attention to the details of winemaking—fermentation time and temperature, for example, or the size and shape of the fermentors (which he designed himself). At the beginning, Draper modeled the wine on top Bordeaux, particularly Château Latour and its legendary depth of flavor, but as time went by and he became more familiar with the *terroir*, both the vineyard and its expression in the wine, he began to take his cues from himself—or rather, from Monte

Bello itself. So as the wine acquired a history, it also developed a recognizable personality, one that has changed little over the years.

Back in the 1970s, when Monte Bello first came to the attention of connoisseurs, people often talked of it as a big or formidable wine. Today, when so many other California Cabernet-based wines have become substantially heavier and more alcoholic, it seems tame by contrast. But the field of comparison, not the wine itself, is what has shifted. Draper notes that alcohol levels still average around 13.5 percent, and that the tannins are as firm as ever. "Monte Bello always has been a wine designed for aging," he says. "In that, it's more like an old-fashioned Bordeaux than most Bordeaux or California wines being made today." But the Monte Bello Ridge is not the gravelly plain of the Médoc, and Draper's winemaking differs in significant respects from that practiced by his Bordelais compatriots. So, in truth, it resembles only one wine: Monte Bello itself.

When asked to detail what accounts for Monte Bello's individuality, Draper not surprisingly returns to the vineyard and the *terroir*. "Because we're so high up, nights here are cool," he explains. "But the growing season is long. That combination allows us to get full maturity with lower alcohols." It also keeps the acid levels high, making the fruit seem bright, especially when set against the initially stiff tannins. "The soils contribute, too," he continues. "Because they're thin and rocky, they keep the yield low. Selection and yield—that's what accounts for the intensity that's the trademark of this wine." Only about a third to a half of the grapes grown on the estate go into Monte Bello. The balance goes to another Cabernet made in a slightly softer style, called Santa Cruz Mountains, while the occasional lot deemed unworthy of the Ridge name gets sold in bulk. The vines atop the mountain range in age from ten to over fifty-five years old. More of the fruit from the older blocks tends to end up in Monte Bello, and the yields there are extremely low—only slightly more than a ton per acre. Also extremely important are the decisions made in the winery—Draper's insistence on natural instead of induced fermentations, his preference for malolactic fermentation in barrel not tank, his use of virtually all American rather than French oak barrels. These and a host of other choices clearly contribute to the wine's character—its simultaneously deep but delicate aromas, vivid black fruit flavors, classic structure, and exotic, evocative minerality, the series of secondary notes both in the bouquet and on the palate that elevate Monte Bello above all but a few other American red wines. And then, surely the result of natural as well as human influences, there is its ability to evolve and improve over the years. The 1974, for example, that I tasted in spring of 2004, was as complete and complex as anyone could ever want. It showed evident age but displayed nary a hint of brown color or fading flavors, and clearly had years if not decades of life left.

That wine was completely Cabernet. Today, Monte Bello contains up to 30 percent of the other Bordeaux varieties, mostly Merlot. And while all the grapes in 1974 came from one locale, Ridge today has three separate but adjacent sites, imaginatively named the "upper," "middle," and "lower" Monte Bello vineyards. As these have expanded, production has increased. The three sites, all containing the same soils, yield about 17,000 cases of wine, with about 5,000 selected as Monte Bello itself. Draper's goal in diversifying the varietal selection was to add nuance and subtlety to the wines, and so to better allow the *terroir* to express itself in them. "The blend for Monte Bello varies year to year," he says. "There's no formula. It all depends on what the particular year brings." That's because, again, Monte Bello is designed to taste like Monte Bello—nothing more and nothing less.

The Ridge partnership dissolved in 1986, when the investors, many nearing retirement age, sold the company to Akihiko Otsuka, the owner of a Japanese pharmaceutical firm. Draper, however, remained firmly in charge—of the winemaking and grape growing, and before long of the whole company, as he soon was promoted to the position of CEO. The new owner insisted that the winery sustain itself, but never became involved in its day-to-day operation. "He was attracted by the values that guide our company," says Draper. "He appreciates the work we do to make our wine, and he leaves us alone to do that work." Today, after more than thirty-five years on the job, Draper is assisted by a talented team, including vineyard manager David Gates, winemakers Eric Baugher and John Olney, operations officer Mark Vernon, and president and marketing director Donn Reisen. He happily credits them for much of Ridge's success, and notes that decisions regarding the final *assemblage* for Monte Bello are usually made by consensus. "We work as a team," he says simply. But there can be no doubt about who captains this team. Paul Draper, who makes his home atop Monte Bello Ridge, right beside the vineyard, remains inexorably linked to this *terroir*. His efforts are what have allowed it to realize its potential as one of the finest sites for one of the finest wines in the country. "Our goal up here," he says thoughtfully, "has always been to make something of real quality. That, not the bottom line, is still our bottom line."

A NOTE ON VINTAGES:

Ridge Monte Bello rewards patience. Tightly wound in its youth, it reveals myriad subtleties with bottle age, and so benefits from a good ten years of cellaring. Much like classic claret, it then remains delicious for a very long time—a good two or three decades in a strong vintage. There have been many such years atop Monte Bello, including 1970, 1974, 1984, 1991, and 1996.

THE SUGGESTED PRICE FOR THE CURRENT 2002 RELEASE IS $120.

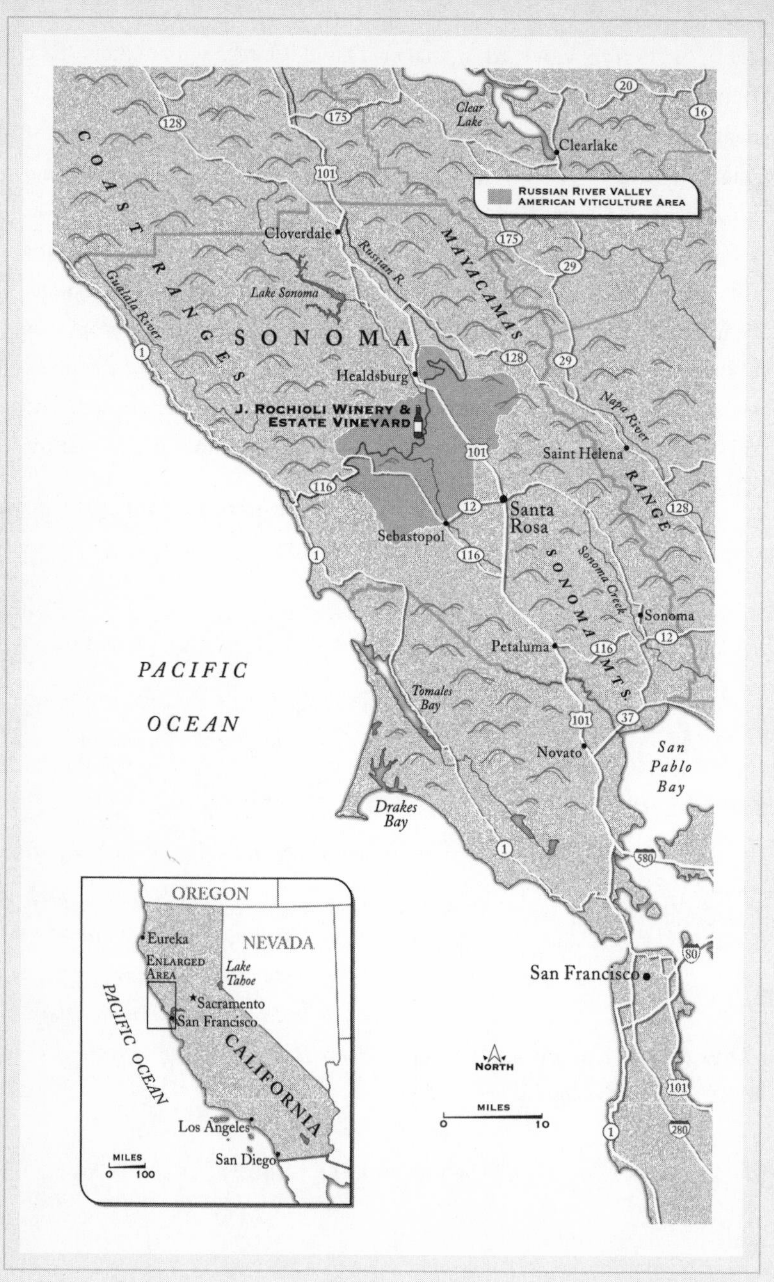

J. ROCHIOLI VINEYARDS AND THE RUSSIAN RIVER VALLEY AVA

CHAPTER 30

J. Rochioli Vineyards Pinot Noir, West Block

Russian River Valley, California

. . .

"I started off by losing my shirt," Joe Rochioli, Jr., chuckles when he recalls first attempting to grow wine grapes on his family's farm, some 160 acres bordering the Russian River in western Sonoma County. This was in 1958. A few years earlier, his father, who had leased the property since the late 1930s, finally saved up enough money to buy it. Beans, hops, and prunes were his main crops, but young Joe wanted to try wine grapes. So he interplanted French Colombard, a popular white variety at the time, with the beans—a row of vines, then a row of beans—and at harvest he sold the fruit to E & J Gallo and Martini & Prati, two big companies that were buying grapes from growers all over California. "But being here, we just couldn't compete," he remembers. "Back then, grapes were grapes. No one differentiated. We'd get eight tons per acre while growers in the Central Valley got twenty. So I started off by losing my shirt."

Tom and Joe Rochioli

Still, Joe Rochioli was nothing if not stubborn. He was convinced that the future in the Russian River Valley belonged to wine. After all, low yields were a problem with other crops as well, and the qualitative difference with grapes seemed far greater than with beans. Though few people at the time cared all that much about specific varieties, Joe intuitively sensed that particular grapes would do particularly well in the Russian River Valley. It helped that his father, who had come to California from Tuscany in Italy as a young boy, liked to make wine at home. It helped too that the grapes Joe started growing yielded good wine—ripe and fruity but also balanced. Gradually, he began to experiment with different, more noble varieties—first Sauvignon Blanc, then Cabernet, Zinfandel, and more. Ahead of his time in growing grapes, he was equally pioneering in his search for just the right grapes for just the right place.

Joe Rochioli planted an initial four-acre block of Pinot Noir in 1968, and the next year purchased cuttings for a second one from Carl Wente, whose vineyard in the Livermore Valley, north of San Jose, was widely considered to be the best source of both Pinot and Chardonnay in California. Then, when some of the wines that other people made with his grapes started winning plaudits, he began thinking about making wine himself. In 1976, he formed a partnership with two outside investors. That operation sputtered, so when his son, Tom, expressed an interest in winemaking, the two agreed to join forces and bond J. Rochioli Vineyards as a commercial, family-owned enterprise. Their first wines were released, to considerable acclaim, in 1985. Four years later, Tom Rochioli crafted a Reserve Pinot Noir from what he and his father agreed was one of the best sites in the vineyard: the West Block, planted to the now mature Wente selection vines. Today, the Rochioli Vineyard Pinot Noirs, including four other block designates, sell from $40 to $90 a bottle, and rank among the country's most esteemed expressions of this most capricious grape variety. Clearly, no one is losing his shirt anymore.

The Rochiolis use only about a third of the fruit they grow for their own wines, selling the remainder to other producers, including Davis Bynum, Gary Farrell, and Williams-Selyem, all of whom identify the family vineyard on their labels. Joe Rochioli is pleased that people want his grapes as well as his wines, but admits being surprised by the prices they are willing to pay. "I grew up simple," he says, "so money doesn't mean much to me. What I do does. I'm proud of my wife, of my kids, of my old cars. And I'm very proud of my grapes."

For a long time, though, no one else thought those grapes were anything out of the ordinary. That's because the Rochiolis sold them to large companies who blended them into generic jug wines. For nearly fifteen years, wine growing on the farm was an avocation rather than a viable business, and so brought the family neither profit nor renown. When asked why he kept at it all that time, Joe Rochioli says: "Because I knew these grapes could make good wines. I had the foresight to believe in varietal grapes for varietal wines." And when pressed as to why he planted Pinot Noir, a variety that, until the 1970s, few producers in California took seriously, he notes that he tried a great many different varieties—"all in order to find out what worked, what I liked. And I liked Pinot. I just really liked Russian River Pinot Noir."

Pinot Noir is the ultimate real estate varietal, its value wholly dependent upon location. But determining why one location is better than another can prove perplexing. Though Pinot likes good drainage and dislikes excessive heat, the grape does equally well in a diversity of soils and with a variety of temperatures. The Rochioli vineyard is relatively cool, being in the middle of the Russian River Valley Viticultural Area, a few miles from where the river makes its final turn toward the ocean, and so benefits from morning fog and afternoon sea breezes. Still, the site is warm enough for Cabernet, thus belying the notion that Burgundy and Bordeaux varieties should not be planted in the same place. And while the soil contains quite a bit of gravel, due to the river's proximity, so too do nearby vineyards that yield poor Pinot but good Zinfandel and Petite Sirah. "I don't know," Tom Rochioli admits, "why we do well with Pinot and they don't three farms down the road." Whatever the confluence of factors, this *terroir*, particularly in the vineyard blocks near the river, yields majestic wines—simultaneously deep and delicate, marked by both force and finesse.

Though the Russian River Valley is widely acknowledged today as one of America's three or four best sources of Pinot Noir, proven sites still come few and far between. Of these, the two most illustrious are the Rochioli and Allen vineyards, both off Westside Road. The second, named for its absentee owner, also has gravelly, well-drained soils, enjoys a maritime-influenced climate, and contains some Wente selection vines. But perhaps the most important commonality is the fact that Joe Rochioli planted it and still farms it, much as he does with his own property across the way.

Howard Allen, a San Francisco real estate entrepreneur, first hired Joe to plant and manage his vineyard in 1972. No one in the region had a better track record. Much as at his family estate, Joe has been able to coax something from the Russian River *terroir* that most other growers cannot—ripe, supple fruit that yields rich, elegant wines. Though he modestly contends that "anyone can grow grapes here," the fact of the matter is that many others try and fail, at least with Pinot Noir. Joe Rochioli was the one who first divided these vineyards into small blocks, based on soil properties and elevation, and then farmed each one slightly differently. He was the one who decided to pull leaves off the vines so as to expose the maturing fruit to the sun, "because it made sense, no matter what the folks from Davis told me." And he is the one who still goes row by row and vine by vine, removing first shoots and then later green bunches so as to ensure even ripening. In short, Joe Rochioli cares for his vines as a mother cares for her babies.

That care, coupled with the Russian River Valley's natural but for a long time untapped potential, is what yields superior fruit and then superlative wines. Today, other vintners in the valley, including Tom Dehlinger, Merry Edwards, Gary Farell, and Steve Kistler, make excellent Pinot Noirs with grapes grown in other sites. Still, the Allen and Rochioli vineyards remain the region's *grand crus*. While Mother Nature has a great deal to do with what makes them special, so too does "Papa Joe," whose master's touch first revealed their promise.

Of the multiple vineyard blocks that Joe Rochioli farms, his favorites tend to be those on the east side of the road, near but not right next to the river, where he first planted grapes almost half a century ago. And of the seventeen blocks of Pinot Noir in the Rochioli vineyard, he has found that the most consistent fruit quality comes from the one he planted back in 1969, the West Block. That explains why, as he has reconfigured and expanded the vineyard over the years, he has used cuttings from it in other places. Both father and son think it important to have a diversity of plant material, so they grow six separate clones or selections of Pinot Noir in the one vineyard. Still, they devote more acres to selections from the West Block than the other five combined. Descended from vines originally brought to California from France, these plants are naturally low-yielding, and produce fruit with intense, deep flavors.

Though originally obtained from one source, the Wente estate in Livermore, these vines do not represent a single clone of Pinot Noir. That is because their ancestry is somewhat obscure. The Livermore vines can be traced to (at least) two sources: Charles Wetmore's initial introduction of cuttings from Burgundy in the 1880s, and Ernest Wente's importation of vines from the nursery at the University of Montpellier in southern France right before World War I. During the decades following Repeal, the Wentes provided budwood to those few California vintners interested in Chardonnay and Pinot Noir. Wente selections then went on to form the backbone of many of California's best wines when interest in those varieties took off in the 1970s. But in the meantime, the Wente family had planted a new vineyard in Monterey County, using budwood from UC at Davis, and much of the Pinot they sold to growers in the late 1960s consisted of those selections. Moreover, since natural changes and mutations in grapevine cells can result in shoots that are genetically different from the rest of the vine, even the original Livermore vines were not all of a piece. So when the Rochiolis talk about their Pinot Noir, they refer to their own "West Block Selection," the similar but not identical cuttings that they have propagated elsewhere on the farm. Other growers in California prefer more recent imports, French clones from the research center in Dijon that are identified with numbers like 115 and 777. Joe Rochioli has planted these too, but he and Tom especially prize their heirloom California grapes. That is why they vinify the wines from their original Pinot vines separately—the East and West Blocks.

A trip to Burgundy in 1990 is what convinced Tom Rochioli to keep these wines separate in the winery, and then to bottle them as vineyard designates. He had made some reserve wines previously, but starting in 1992 he introduced the two J. Rochioli Vineyard block wines. (He since has added five other block-designates, two of Chardonnay and three more of Pinot Noir.) Traveling and tasting in France showed him the importance of distinguishing between adjacent vineyard sites. As a farmer, his father knew that the different blocks on the family farm produced subtly different fruit. Now the son became determined to let those differences express themselves in the finished wines. Even today, blending the best blocks into a reserve might make better business sense, as he would be able to sell nearly fifteen hundred cases of one well-recognized Pinot instead of much smaller lots of five fairly obscure ones. But he insists that the combination of separate vineyard sites and a diversity of plant material yields wines that display distinctly different personalities, and that blending would invariably result in a less distinctive wine. "What I learned on that trip," he says, "was to respect those kinds of differences." It's very much a traditional Burgundian principle, realized in an overtly Californian wine.

Succulent, ripe fruit flavors that echo black cherries and raspberries, backed by plenty of heft and muscle, clearly mark Rochioli West Block Pinot Noir as a sun-drenched California wine. At the same time, its spicy aromas, sumptuous texture, and layered complexity combine to set it apart from all but a handful of other Golden State Pinots. Especially with a few years of bottle age, it becomes silky smooth and extremely luxurious. Tom Rochioli is a self-taught winemaker. He also is somewhat self-effacing. "Look," he says, "if you grow good grapes, you can make good wine. And my dad grows very good grapes." Still, the success of the J. Rochioli wines owes a great deal to Tom's skill in the winery. Because he prefers to let his wines speak for themselves, he may not be as well known as some more publicity-conscious vintners. Few others, though, craft as enthralling wines.

Perhaps precisely because he did not take university classes in enology, Tom Rochioli learned early on that the best winemaking is non-interventionist. When he started in the business, he turned to friends and neighbors in the Russian River Valley for advice. Burt Williams from Williams-Selyem and Steve Kistler from Kistler Vineyards were especially supportive, and both advised him when to leave well enough alone. In addition, his father and grandfather made home wine, without the bells and whistles of commercial production. "I just let a wine go through all the fermentation it can, and then let it be," he says, when asked to explain his winemaking philosophy, "so as not to muck it up." He is being too modest. Keeping hands off requires plenty of skill, because with a minimum of human intervention, each decision becomes critical. Knowing exactly when—and when not—to ferment, rack, and bottle requires a sensitive touch. That Rochioli has such becomes evident as soon as one considers both the quality and the range of the wines he makes. In addition to the different Chardonnays and Pinot Noirs, the J. Rochioli label has adorned many bottles of Cabernet, Zinfandel, and one of the few consistently top-notch American Sauvignon Blancs. All have been beautifully crafted, made with such precision and sensitivity that the vintner's hand seems almost invisible—which of course is exactly what any first-rate winemaker wants.

Though aged for fifteen months in 100 percent new French oak barrels, the fruit in J. Rochioli West Block Pinot Noir tastes so pure and expressive that the wood plays only a minor, supporting role, even when the wine is drunk young. Tom Rochioli cold-soaks the destemmed grapes for up to five days, gently extracting initial color and flavor without tannin or alcohol, and then, following fermentation, moves the young wine to barrel without letting it settle completely, thus keeping as much of the spent yeast and sediment in it as possible. He only racks, or clarifies, it once, and he bottles the wine unfiltered, so as to retain all of its natural character. Production averages just four hundred cases, and save for allocation to a few restaurants, it is sold exclusively through a mailing list.

While the East Block can produce a more powerful, long-lived Pinot Noir in some vintages, Tom and Joe Rochioli both think that the West Block is more dependable. "It's really the wine that made our name,"

Tom says. "Back in 1985, when Williams-Selyem first designated a Rochioli Vineyard Pinot, all the fruit came from the West Block. And when I made our first reserves, they were all West Block." The yield averages 2 tons, but Tom insists that tons per acre is "an irrelevant figure." What's more important, he argues, is total ripening, no matter the crop size, because "even a small number of green, unripe berries will affect the wine." This emphasis on fruit ripeness means that the wine has a relatively high alcohol level, usually somewhere around 14 percent. But it never tastes hot or seems heavy. Instead, while full-throttled, it retains remarkable elegance and purity. That combination of ripe power and nuanced gentility is what makes it one of the finest expressions of New World Pinot Noir.

The western Russian River Valley has not changed all that much over the nearly half century in which Joe Rochioli, Jr., has grown wine grapes there. Still verdant and bucolic, it remains largely farmland or forest, with small, winding roads that, save during the touristy late summer months, see little traffic. But where once hops, beans, and prunes were the main moneymakers, now grapes are cultivated in abundance. For devotees of the two Burgundy varietals, Chardonnay and Pinot Noir, this part of Sonoma County has become a land of promise and possibility. Many natural factors make it so—the gravelly soils, the cool ocean influence, the fog-shrouded *terroirs*. But evidence of human accomplishment and success is just as important. And no one in the area has accomplished more than the two Rochiolis, father and son, who in their proud but unassuming way go on growing grapes, making wines, and proving to the world that great Pinot Noir indeed can come in an American form.

A NOTE ON VINTAGES:

West Block Pinot Noir tastes of vivacious cherry fruit and smoky oak when young. With a few years of bottle age, however, it becomes ever so much more refined—an alluring, enticing wine that seduces with a smooth, seamless, and yes, sexy texture. In a good vintage, it should drink well for a decade. Strong years include 1992, 1994, 1999, 2002, and 2003.

THE SUGGESTED PRICE FOR THE CURRENT 2003 RELEASE IS $75.

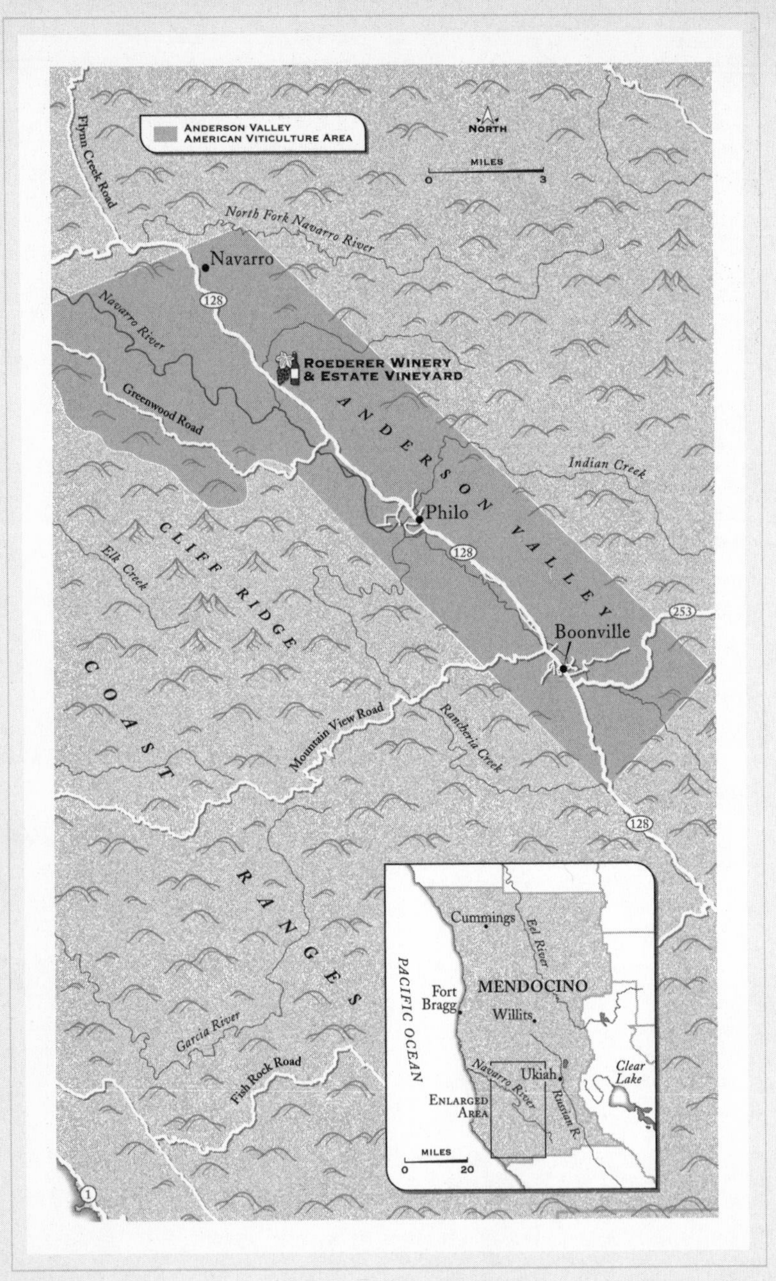

ROEDERER ESTATE, IN MENDOCINO COUNTY'S ANDERSON VALLEY

CHAPTER 31

ROEDERER ESTATE BRUT SPARKLING WINE

Anderson Valley, California

...

Jean-Claude Rouzaud was not first. As president of the highly respected, family-owned Champagne house of Louis Roederer in Reims, he started building a California sparkling wine estate in 1981, a full eight years after Möet & Chandon had made the initial French entry into American bubbly. And Möet had invested in California only after Jack and Jamie Davies of Schramsberg had proved that quality sparkling wine could be made there. So, in the modern history of *méthode champenoise* California wine, the Davies came first, Domaine Chandon soon after, and Rouzaud was but one of many who followed. Yet he has separated himself from the proverbial pack by overseeing the production of the one California sparkling wine that consistently displays the depth of flavor and textual finesse of first-class Champagne. Roederer Estate's Anderson Valley Brut tastes beautifully rich but finely balanced, with toasty, brioche-scented complexity and a long, evolving finish. Other wines approach it, but none enjoys its record of unswerving excellence.

Michel Salgues and Arnaud Weyrich

Vineyard location and meticulous winemaking account for this wine's superiority, and both are part of a larger vision—Jean-Claude Rouzaud's effort to craft a prestige American *cuvée* not only via the Champagne method but also in a specific Champagne style. That style, exemplified in France by his family's multivintage Brut Premier, is marked simultaneously by power and grace. No other American sparkler exhibits those qualities in such fine balance. That is because other producers, particularly the Franco-American ones, often have been befuddled by the growing conditions in California as opposed to Champagne. But Rouzaud, along with his winemakers, Michel Salgues and now Arnaud Weyrich, has mastered them. So, while Roederer Estate was not first, it has ended up on top, as California's and indeed America's best.

By all accounts, the vineyards of Champagne in northeastern France produce the world's finest sparklers. In one sense, these are *terroir* wines. Champagne's combination of chalky, limestone soil and a razor-edge climate, with a mean annual temperature of only 50°F (10°C), is unique in the wine-growing world. The region lies at the northernmost limit of viticulture. As a result, its vineyards receive a good deal of sunshine in summer, but its grapes always retain a very high level of acidity at harvest. Young wines from those grapes, so tart as to be almost undrinkable as table wine, prove ideal as base material for bubbly. Thus, as the Champenois are fond of telling visitors, their wines taste so good because they express an inimitable place. But virtually all Champagnes, even prestige cuvées, are blends of separate vineyard lots from separate villages, often located far apart from one another. The reason is plain enough. Though each vineyard produces grapes with distinct flavors, their fruit is barely ripe, so those flavors inevitably remain incomplete and undeveloped. Consequently, the blend or *assemblage* is what yields depth and complexity. Using multiple lots of different wines made with different grapes and often from different vintages, the winemaker works to express not a particular site but rather a recognizable "house" style, one that customers will recognize bottle after bottle and year after year. Hence in another sense, Champagnes are very much vintner's wines.

In California, where grapes rarely struggle to ripen, the aim of the *assemblage* has to be different—less depth than elegance and restraint. To make a good wine in a Champagne style, the basic method thus needs to be adapted to the peculiarities and particularities of a different place. Even more than with still wines, such adaptation is the crucial factor in the success or failure of New World sparklers to taste nuanced and refined—much like good Champagne. That many instead are simple and cumbersome reflects less the inadequacy of locale than the difficulties involved in modifying techniques that have been refined over centuries in a very different *terroir*. As Jean-Claude Rouzaud puts it: "We cannot reproduce what we do in Champagne. But in the right place, we can produce good sparkling wine."

But what is the right place? The Champenois have been growing grapes for sparkling wine for over three hundred years, during which time they have identified the very best vineyard sites. (Those sites pop up all over the region, as a glance at a map of Champagne, with its Rorschach-like splotches of *grand* and *premier crus*, indicates.) By contrast, quality sparkling wine in any significant volume has been made in California for only about a generation. The answer, then, is still very much up in the air. Many producers, including both the Davies and the directors at Möet, chose to locate in Napa and to source their grapes primarily from Carneros. Others set up shop in Sonoma County. Still others went south, to Arroyo Grande and Santa Maria.

Rouzaud looked at all these places (as well as the Willamette Valley in Oregon), but after a two-year study, he ultimately opted to buy land in the Anderson Valley in northern Mendocino County. His rationale was not that it carbon-copied Champagne. (No place in California does.) Rather, he thought that its *terroir*, though constituted differently, with nary a trace of chalk and significantly higher daytime temperatures, could cause similar viticultural effects and so, perhaps, yield the material for a wine with both depth and grace, like Louis Roederer's Brut Premier in France. Though grapes get riper in the Anderson Valley than in Champagne, sugar levels rise gradually and the ripening tends to be even—precisely the effects that Rouzaud wanted.

Slow ripening is crucial for California sparkling wine because the grapes have to be picked earlier than those destined for still wines. Whereas the fruit in Champagne simply does not get ripe enough for good table wine, grapes mature fully in all wine-growing regions of California. This means that even if a vintner harvests at the same sugar level as in Champagne, the wines will taste different. (The grapes in Champagne, being at their optimal stage of maturity, will have converted abrasive malic acid into softer, more appealing tartaric acid, while those in California, being physiologically immature, will taste harsher.) Californians thus often face a set of unpleasant choices: Leave things alone, resulting in green, excessively tart wines; induce total malolactic fermentation, yielding potentially cumbersome wines; or harvest later, resulting in excessively alcoholic, heavy ones. The only way to minimize those difficulties is to ripen the fruit as slowly as possible. And the only way to do that is to use grapes from vineyards that enjoy an extended growing season.

Jean-Claude Rouzaud's crucial insight was that the length of the season was ultimately more important than either soil or temperature. At Roederer Estate, budbreak comes in February and the grapes are not picked until early September. The period between fruit set and harvest averages one hundred days, much as in the Roederer vineyards in Champagne. Of all the facts and figures in the study Rouzaud commissioned, that was the one that impressed him the most. This place, he thought, has the potential to produce fruit for his family's "house" style.

A sliver slicing through the coastal mountains, starting only ten miles from the Pacific, the Anderson Valley enjoys such a long growing season because of the pronounced ocean influence. Late evening and morning fogs regularly blanket the vineyards, and cool winds flow inland almost every summer afternoon. Roederer owns four separate parcels of land, two north of the town of Philo in the coolest part of the AVA, and two smaller ones slightly farther inland, near Boonville. The estate totals 580 acres, some 420 of which are under vine, and only grapes from these vineyards are used for the wines. Roederer Estate is by far the largest wine-growing concern in the area. When Rouzaud bought the properties, some wine already was being crafted in the valley. But virtually all production (at wineries like Edmeades, Husch, Lazy Creek, and Navarro) was small and artisanal, and no one was trying to make serious sparkling wine. By force of visionary coincidence, John Scharffenberger started producing bubbly, initially all from purchased grapes, at about the same time. His facility, since purchased by Maisons Marques & Domaines USA, the marketing arm of Louis Roederer, produces good wines today under the Scharffenberger Cellars label. Yet despite the region's now obvious aptness for bubbly, they are the only other *méthode champenoise* wines made there. That's because the Anderson Valley remains, literally as well as figuratively, well off the beaten track, far removed from the glitz and glamour of more touristy "wine country."

Though only a couple of hours from Napa, these two California wine valleys seem worlds apart. A refuge for ex-hippies, the Anderson Valley tends to attract people looking for a relaxed, alternative lifestyle, not glamour. Marijuana long has been the leading cash crop, and many locals drive flower-decaled Volkswagens or old, dented Volvos. The Anderson Valley thus is also unlike Reims, the cultured northern French city in whose cathedral the kings of France were crowned and under whose streets many of the world's greatest Champagnes are aged. Michel Salgues trained at Louis Roederer in Reims before Jean-Claude Rouzaud tapped him to head the company's California outpost, and surely he experienced a considerable amount of culture shock when he moved. "Yes, it was different," he says with a grin, hastening to add, "different, but not bad." Salgues in fact settled in quite comfortably, adapting easily to the tranquil pace of life, and making many friends in the wine community as well as the neighborhood at large. He and his wife, Sylvie, raised two daughters, and for eighteen years they called the Anderson Valley home. Sylvie, however, was never really happy there, and in 2003, when Michel retired, the couple moved back to France. Arnaud Weyrich, also trained in Reims, then took over. His instructions from Jean-Claude Rouzaud were clear: "Keep doing what Michel has done."

That, however, was a tall order. For what Michel Salgues did during his tenure at Roederer Estate was create the wine that the British author

Tom Stevenson, the world's leading authority on bubbly, dubbed "the greatest non-Champagne sparkling wine." Soft-spoken but instinctively curious and energetic, Salgues was an ideal choice for the job. He brought to the Anderson Valley not only experience in the vineyards and cellars of Champagne but also extensive technical knowledge of viticulture and enology in different locales, having been a professor at the University of Montpellier and a researcher at the Institut de la Recherche Agronomique in Paris, where he studied virtually all aspects of winemaking. So, while he had intimate knowledge of Champagne production, he was open to new possibilities and, as important, aware of techniques that might prove beneficial.

In the vineyard, Salgues oversaw the initial planting of Chardonnay and Pinot Noir (but not Pinot Meunier, Champagne's insurance grape, because, he says, "we don't need insurance here"). Little more than a decade later, he supervised replanting, as phylloxera appeared on the property in 1993. That infestation constituted a financial blow but, much as elsewhere in California, a benefit in terms of wine quality. Much of the initial Pinot Noir turned out to have been in fact Gamay (the less noble red grape of Beaujolais), and too many acres of Chardonnay had been planted with one clone. "It's important to have diversity, especially in terms of ripeness," he explains, as he details the selection of plant material he used when replanting. In Champagne, a multiplicity of vineyard sites provides that diversity; at Roederer Estate, with only four ranches, the different clonal material does it. Still, much as in Reims, the goal is to harvest grapes with a variety of different flavors for the *assemblage*.

"Yes," says Salgues, "it's different here. We never have to fight to get fruit or intensity. Instead, we fight to get elegance." No matter the locale, making superior sparkling wine involves a myriad of decisions. Three loomed especially large when Salgues first attempted to craft an Anderson Valley wine in an authoritative but nuanced Roederer style. The first involved pressing; the second malolactic fermentation; and the third reserve wines. With so much potentially ripe fruit at his disposal, Salgues could afford to be persnickety, and so he used only the first, gentle *cuvée* pressing (not the potentially harsher second or third *taille,* as many wineries do). And he was perfectly willing to sell any of the pressed wine that did not fit the flavor profile he wanted, on average 30 percent of the total each year. He at first decided not to induce malolactic fermentation, thinking that the wines would need sharp acids in order to taste graceful, but he subsequently decided that the malic acid was a bit too sharp, so began to experiment with between 10 to 20 percent malolactic for the blend. In Reims, the Louis Roederer winemakers fashion the Brut Premier blend from at least four vintages, using oak-aged reserve wines to augment each year's base wine and hence attain the "house" style. Salgues followed suit in California. The large, aged casks do not contribute wood flavor, but help provide body in the wine.

Of course, at the start Salgues did not have many reserve vintages at his disposal. That may explain why the first Roederer Estate Brut, made from the base 1986 vintage and released two years later, while certainly good by California standards, was the weakest wine he made. But since the subsequent release the very next year turned so many heads (including Tom Stevenson's), perhaps Salgues simply needed to have one commercial vintage under his belt. No matter, since 1989 Roederer Estate Brut has ranked at the head of its class. If anything, it has gotten better, since Salgues and now Weyrich have a superior stock of aged reserves with which to work the magic of the *assemblage.*

That magic is communal. Each year a team of winemakers comes to Mendocino from Reims to help craft, first the base wine, and then the final blend, incorporating on average 15 percent reserve wines. The bottled wine then spends a minimum of two years on the yeast, attaining effervescence, until disgorgement, dosage, and finally release. Proof that the magic works can be found in the wine both when young—full and somewhat austere—and when aged. "When I came to California," Salgues admits, "I expected the wines to go downhill very fast. But I have been surprised at how well they develop—as well if not better," he adds with a sly smile, "than those in Reims." A tasting in March 2003 with base wines from 1988 onward bore him out, as the older offerings seemed remarkably refined. Without having lost their fruit, they had added layered toasty, nutty aromas and flavors, revealing a level of complexity that even many Champagnes (let alone other California sparklers) never attain. Most impressive, they all stayed true to type, that is, the Roederer style: rich and full but at the same time very, very stylish.

Since 1993, Roederer Estate also has offered a prestige, vintage-dated sparkler. Named "L'Ermitage," it spends a full five years on the yeast, so tastes toastier than the Anderson Valley Brut. Since only the finest lots of grapes are used, the taste of fruit is more overt, and the wine ultimately seems quite Californian. As such, it is part of a set of expensive, prestige Golden State sparklers—including "Le Rêve" from Domaine Carneros, "Etoile" from Domaine Chandon, "DVX" from Mumm Napa, and "J Schram" from Schramsberg—that over the past decade have raised expectations in California. At times exceptional but also sometimes excessive, they tend to taste both yeasty and fruity, bespeaking their Golden State origins. Perhaps in the future these wines will help establish a distinctive California mode of sparkling wine, much as has happened with Cabernet Sauvignon and to a lesser extent Chardonnay. Perhaps, too, one wine-growing region someday will become identified exclusively with exceptional bubbly. For now, though, first-class California sparkling wine is still a work in progress.

The best California bubblies, coming from different regions, display finesse and focus as well as fruit, but many other wines err by going to extremes. They either taste too fruit-driven or too austere and angular. To date, the finest remain those that are consciously crafted to echo Champagne, and the finest of those is Roederer Estate's non-vintage Brut. Like its French model, it expresses both nature and art, God-given *terroir* and a human vision. It did not come first and, given the overall improved quality of California sparkling wine, no longer is the obvious best every year. But for reliability at a very high level, it has no real rival.

A NOTE ON VINTAGES:

Like the finest Champagnes, Roederer Estate's non-vintage Brut improves with bottle age, becoming more refined as it becomes less rambunctious. I've enjoyed delicious wines from bottles over ten years old. Just be sure to store them well—in a cool place, away from bright light.

THE SUGGESTED PRICE FOR THE CURRENT RELEASE IS $22.

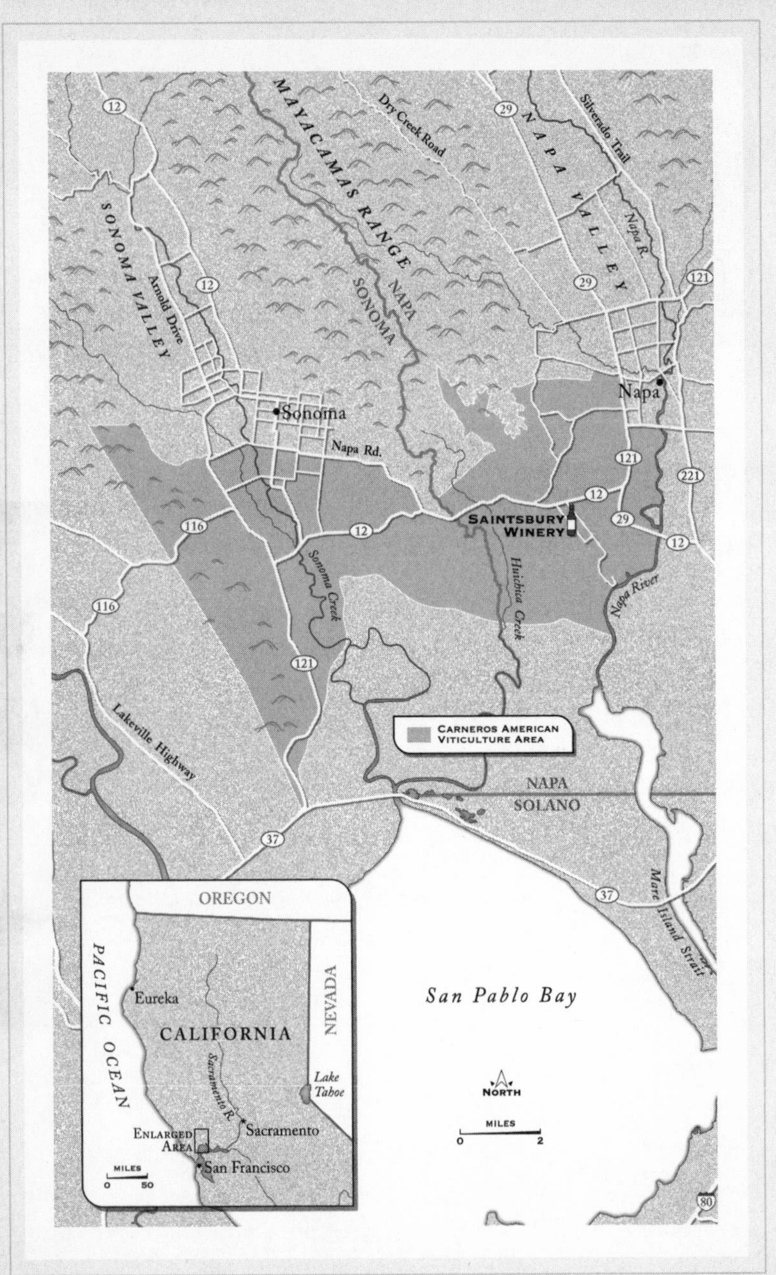

SAINTSBURY AND THE CARNEROS AVA

CHAPTER 32

SAINTSBURY PINOT NOIR

Carneros, California

...

The low hills of Carneros roll gently through southern Napa and Sonoma counties, ending in the salt marshes and tidal flats that mark the upper reaches of the San Pablo Bay. Though grapes have been cultivated there for a long time, Carneros was better known until recently for dairy farms and sheep ranches. Markedly cooler than sites some five or ten miles to the north, it can be a difficult place to grow grapes, as yields and even berries are small. Still, visionary vintners, ranging from John Stanly and George Husmann in the nineteenth century to André Tchelistcheff in the twentieth, long have recognized the region's potential as a source of fine wines. Today, that potential has been realized—particularly with the two cool-climate, Burgundy varietals, Chardonnay and Pinot Noir. With both, Carneros wines display graceful,

David Graves and Dick Ward

almost sweet flavors, purity of expression being their great appeal. No matter the producer, the finest Carneros wines invariably seem elegant.

Because delicacy is the primary virtue of Carneros wines, they easily can be overwhelmed by a vintner's heavy hand, and restraint becomes crucial to successful Carneros winemaking. The finest renditions taste clearly of fruit, with wood playing only a minor role, and alcohol levels held in check. Of these, the wines from Saintsbury set a clear standard, both stylistically and qualitatively. Though not the first to win renown for Carneros, they more than most define what the region is capable of delivering. Saintsbury's Pinot Noir in particular demonstrates that wines from Carneros, while obviously different from the French originals, can share much the same virtues: elegant, expressive flavors and silky, seductive textures. "Of course Burgundy is our model," says Richard Ward, who along with his friend and partner, David Graves, founded the winery in 1981. "How could it not be?" That does not mean, he hastens to add, that the two vintners have tried to replicate France in California. "We want to make the best wine we can using the raw material we have. If that leads us down the same path as winemakers in Burgundy, that's fine. But we're not going to say, a priori, 'This is the way to do it.' We have to adapt what we do to our own circumstances here."

Those circumstances are unique to Carneros—its natural *terroir* as well as its human history. Graves and Ward were conscious of both when they first decided to make wine there, since Carneros was the only place in the United States at the time with anything resembling a record of achievement with Pinot Noir. In the nearly quarter century since then, other regions—the Russian River and Sonoma Coast, Santa Barbara and Monterey counties, Oregon's Willamette Valley—have come into their own. But Carneros too has evolved, and its top wines, exemplified by those from Saintsbury, remain among the country's finest.

The San Pablo Bay forms the upper third of an inland sea, the remainder being the waters of the San Francisco Bay. Both bays flow from one source—the Golden Gate, the only break in the long California coastline through which the cold Pacific surges. The water's presence accounts for virtually every aspect of *terroir* in Carneros. Soils here are a thin layer of silty topsoil above deep clay, the latter left behind some 5 million years ago when an even larger body of glacial water receded to form the current shoreline. The bay brings fog many summer mornings, and then stiff breezes in the afternoons. Those sometimes severe winds distinguish Carneros from other cool-growing California regions, as they reduce crop levels by literally breaking off young shoots or flowers, and then cause the vines to shut down in order to prevent dehydration. At the same time, the maritime influence keeps temperatures relatively constant, promoting early budbreak and allowing for a late harvest.

Thus, while Carneros has a comparable number of degree-days to Beaune in Burgundy, its growing season is significantly longer, with more intense sunshine. The grapes have similar acid levels but are riper, and the wines taste more of fresh fruit. With Chardonnay, citrus and apple flavors predominate. With Pinot Noir, red berries and sweet cherries come to the fore. Rarely is there anything wild—the animal scent of the Côte d'Or—about these wines. Instead, they seem gentle. Their allure is an almost virginal grace.

Wine grapes have been cultivated in Carneros since before the Civil War, and the region enjoyed a boom of sorts at the turn of the last century. Thanks largely to the efforts of the transplanted Missouri viticulturalist George Husmann, growers there planted on phylloxera-resistant rootstock before most of their California compatriots. The best-known property was the Riverdale or Stanly Ranch, named for its original owner, and located just south of the current Saintsbury winery. (Beringer Vineyards owns a significant portion of the Stanly Ranch today, and produces a vineyard-designated Pinot Noir under that name.) John Stanly grew all sorts of grapes, including at least some Pinot Noir. In fact, a bottle of 1910 Pinot, made with grapes from that property, was what convinced André Tchelistcheff that Carneros could be "California's Burgundy."

Tchelistcheff first tasted that wine in 1937, but by then grapes had largely disappeared from the region, Prohibition having claimed yet another victim. They returned only gradually. After World War II, Louis

Martini purchased part of the Stanly Ranch (which he renamed for Stanly's old winery, La Loma). Martini planted Pinot Noir there and made wine with it during the 1950s. Then in 1960, René di Rosa bought a 400-acre Carneros ranch. He found the remains of an old winery on it (the Talcoa property, once managed by Husmann), a discovery that led him to experiment with grape growing at a place he dubbed "Winery Lake." At about the same time, Tchelistcheff convinced Hélène de Pins, the owner of Beaulieu Vineyards, to purchase a Carneros property—the now famous BV 5 Vineyard. Later that decade, the Sangiacomo family began converting their Carneros pear and apple orchards into vineyard land, and a few years after that Francis Mahoney built the first new Carneros winery in some thirty years, Carneros Creek. Still, in 1972 there were only about 200 acres under vine in the whole region. Within twenty years, that number had ballooned to more than six thousand, and Carneros had developed a reputation as a source of high-quality grapes and wines.

Although others, notably Mahoney at Carneros Creek and Larry Brooks at Acacia, made wines that contributed to that reputation, no one did more to raise awareness of Carneros as a quality wine-growing region than Graves and Ward at Saintsbury. They had met in 1977 as UC Davis graduate students—in, of all things, a brewing class. ("Go figure," quips Graves.) But wine was their shared passion, and a few years later they were working at different Napa facilities when they began to talk about going into business together. "There were so many other people starting wineries at that point that we worried we might be too late," Graves recalls with a laugh. "We had some different ideas, though. We wanted to do Pinot, not Cabernet. And neither of us cared for either the high-alcohol, high-oak style, or the lean, mean 'food wine' style. We wanted to make wines like the ones we liked to drink." They both liked to drink Burgundy—red and white, but especially red—and they named their new venture after another Burgundy lover, George Saintsbury, the nineteenth-century British author whose idiosyncratic reflections on wine, *Notes on a Cellarbook*, they admired.

Starting on something of a shoestring, Graves and Ward had no money with which to buy vineyards or build a winery, so they leased production space and purchased grapes—from vineyards in Carneros as well as from growers in western Sonoma County. But from the beginning, they focused only on the two Burgundy varietals, Chardonnay and Pinot Noir. "Beaune in the U.S.A.," read the joke on their T-shirts. After their second vintage, they had sold enough wine to afford a down payment, and began building a facility of their own. That was when they decided to use exclusively Carneros grapes, and to label their wines as Carneros rather than Napa or Sonoma. "It just made sense to become identified with one place," Graves remembers. "And for the wines we wanted to make, there was no better place."

That same year, 1983, was when the federal authorities approved the Carneros Viticultural Area, a bit of fortuitous timing for the two young vintners, since the government's approbation encouraged people to think of Carneros as a distinct place, home to distinct, different wines. Unlike many American Viticultural Areas (AVAs), where the boundaries are largely political, Carneros makes sense as an appellation. That's because the borders are largely natural. To the south, they begin where the marshland turns into solid ground. To the north, they end where the elevation reaches roughly 400 feet. The Napa River defines the AVA's eastern edge; the crest of the Sonoma Mountains its western one. Carneros is one of the few AVAs to cross a significant political line, in this case the boundary separating Napa and Sonoma counties. It is fairly large, some 37,000 acres, 15,000 or so of which have been deemed plantable. Merlot and even Cabernet grow in the warmer western and northern portions, but a full 80 percent of the Carneros vineyards are planted to Chardonnay and Pinot Noir. Those two varieties, whether used for still or sparkling wines (and Carneros fruit goes into many Champagne-styled sparklers), define what the region is all about.

Production at Saintsbury increased steadily during Graves and Ward's first decade—from 3,000 cases the first year, to 12,000 in 1985, then 35,000 in 1991. "We grew bigger," Ward explains, "by getting new sources of fruit." Those sources came to include their own vineyards, 12.5 acres at the winery as well as another 10 that they planted nearby;

but at that point the Saintsbury wines always were based primarily on purchased grapes. As more Carneros pastureland became converted to vineyards, the quality of the fruit available to them and other vintners increased, and the resulting wines got better.

After ten vintages, during which Chardonnay constituted some two thirds of their production, Graves and Ward made the decision to concentrate more directly on Pinot Noir, the wine that Ward calls their "first love." They did not cut back on Chardonnay, but instead increased production of Pinot as more and better fruit became available. These days, Saintsbury produces roughly 60,000 cases of wine, 45,000 of which are Pinot Noir. There are four separate bottlings. At one end of the range comes a light, quaffable rendition called Garnet, at the other end, a Reserve and a vineyard designate. In the middle, with nearly 25,000 cases each year, is the wine they consider their flagship: Saintsbury Carneros Pinot Noir.

Graves and Ward's commitment to Pinot Noir, and specifically to this wine, led to changes in both the winery and the vineyards from which they acquired their grapes. Today, they have over a dozen different vineyard sources, and they insist that this diversity has led to markedly better wines. "Some of it is site, some new clones being grown now, some better viticulture," Graves argues, "but there's no doubt that Carneros Pinot Noir is better today than it was ten years ago." Much of the improvement comes from Saintsbury now owning a significant amount of vineyard land, and estate fruit being a significant part of the blend. Graves and Ward planted their first vineyard, twelve and a half acres adjacent to the winery, back in 1986. Six years later they added thirty-four more acres and acquired the Brown Ranch, a warm (for Carneros) site that they planted in a dense spacing format, using Dijon clones. Pinot Noir from Brown Ranch tends to display black fruit flavors, while grapes from the other sites tend more toward red berry and cherry ones. As a result, today's Carneros wine seems more complex and multifaceted, while retaining the region's trademark purity of fruit expression.

So too, techniques in the Saintsbury winery have changed over the years. Through 1997, fermentations took place in large pump-over tanks. Today, only small open-top tanks are used, the goal being gentle handling for gentle fruit. For a time, Graves and Ward refused to filter their wines. Now, they use a high-tech, cross-flow filter because, as Graves puts it, "We couldn't taste the difference." The resulting wine is cleaner and brighter. And whereas they used to age every lot of wine separately and blend right before bottling, they now select lots for an initial blend right after fermentation. That way the various components have more time to integrate with one another, especially as the wine ages in barrel—all French oak, and all from coopers known for using long-aged so less astringent wood.

"Just as the growers in Carneros have learned to grow better Pinot Noir," says Ward, "the winemakers here have learned how to make better wines." Tasting a vertical series of Saintsbury Carneros Pinots bears him out. Though elegant and graceful, the wines made before the mid-1990s seem simpler than those that follow, the later vintages being the ones in which the characteristically sweet Carneros fruit is accompanied by firmer tannins and more complex secondary flavors and aromas. Still, Ward insists, "I'm not sure we've ever gotten to the point where we've made the wine we want to make." Or, as Graves puts it, "We've reinvented our project a few times, and we probably will again."

The evolution of Saintsbury Carneros Pinot Noir mirrors the evolution of Carneros as a whole. What Graves calls "the old Carneros," winemaking during the 1970s and 1980s, yielded wines that were light-bodied and relatively simple. They impressed people at the time because, unlike virtually all other American renditions, they tasted legitimately of the varietal; but compared with today's wines, they can seem uninspired. Starting in the 1990s, improved viticulture—meaning better irrigation practices, canopy management, and clonal selection—produced deeper, darker, more complex Pinots, wines with riper tannins, fewer harsh vegetal notes, and more nuanced flavors. Some people still think of Carneros Pinot as inherently light and simple, but contemporary versions can hold their own with the best from other regions. Both Graves and Ward insist, though, that they don't want their wine to become too deep or rich. A level of concentration and extract that will seem appropriate in, say Cabernet, will obscure Pinot Noir's varietal integrity, making the wine seem clumsy instead of classy, and lumbering rather than lithe. "Moderation in all things is our motto," says Graves, adding with a grin, "or at least in most things."

Graves and Ward oversee the process, but they employ a winemaker to take care of the day-to-day operation at Saintsbury. Bill Knuttel was the first. Byron Kosuge and Mark West followed. Each brought something new to the winery, but each also understood his job to be maintaining rather than creating a stylistic identity for the Saintsbury wines. "At the end of the day," says Ward, "you want to be able to pull the cork out of the bottle and pour a glass of wine that tastes good. You don't care who made it or what's on the label. From the beginning, that's all we wanted—to make wines that taste really good." Graves amplifies: "The first sip of a lot of wines today is great, but they're so big and extracted that the second glass is no fun to drink. We want our whole bottle to taste good." Ward then chimes in. "Even a second bottle," he says with a laugh.

More than other grape varieties, Pinot Noir distinguishes itself in distinct ways in distinct places. When Graves and Ward started Saintsbury, Carneros was essentially *the* place—Pinot's one proven locale in the United States. Today, other regions have come to the fore, and as a result American Pinot has begun to come of age, much as American Cabernet did a generation before. In the process, Carneros wines sometimes get overlooked. "We don't get the hype anymore," notes Ward, "but that's because we've been doing it so long." And in their particular case, doing it so well.

Saintsbury Carneros Pinot Noir is not America's richest rendition. Nor is it the flashiest. But for sustained merit, it ranks at the very top. "Carneros is still a damned good place to grow grapes and make wine," Graves declares. Tasting a vertical set of vintages demonstrates that he's right. This wine's virtues—forthright fruit flavor coupled with delicacy and grace—express nothing so much as the character of the region, a character worth cultivating. George Husmann and André Tchelistcheff recognized as much way back when. Graves and Ward do so now. Unlike earlier visionaries, however, they have been able to do more than make a wine that promises potential. Their track record, particularly with Pinot Noir, is one of remarkably unfailing accomplishment—Carneros's potential realized and excellence achieved.

A NOTE ON VINTAGES:

This wine is light and lithe, an elegantly graceful expression of both a region and a varietal. It benefits from a few years of aging but is not necessarily a candidate for extended cellaring. It won't crack up or fall apart with time in bottle, but it also won't improve noticeably. Drink it, then, within five to ten years of the vintage. Strong recent years have included 1995, 1996, 1999, 2001, and 2002.

THE SUGGESTED PRICE FOR THE CURRENT 2003 RELEASE IS $30.

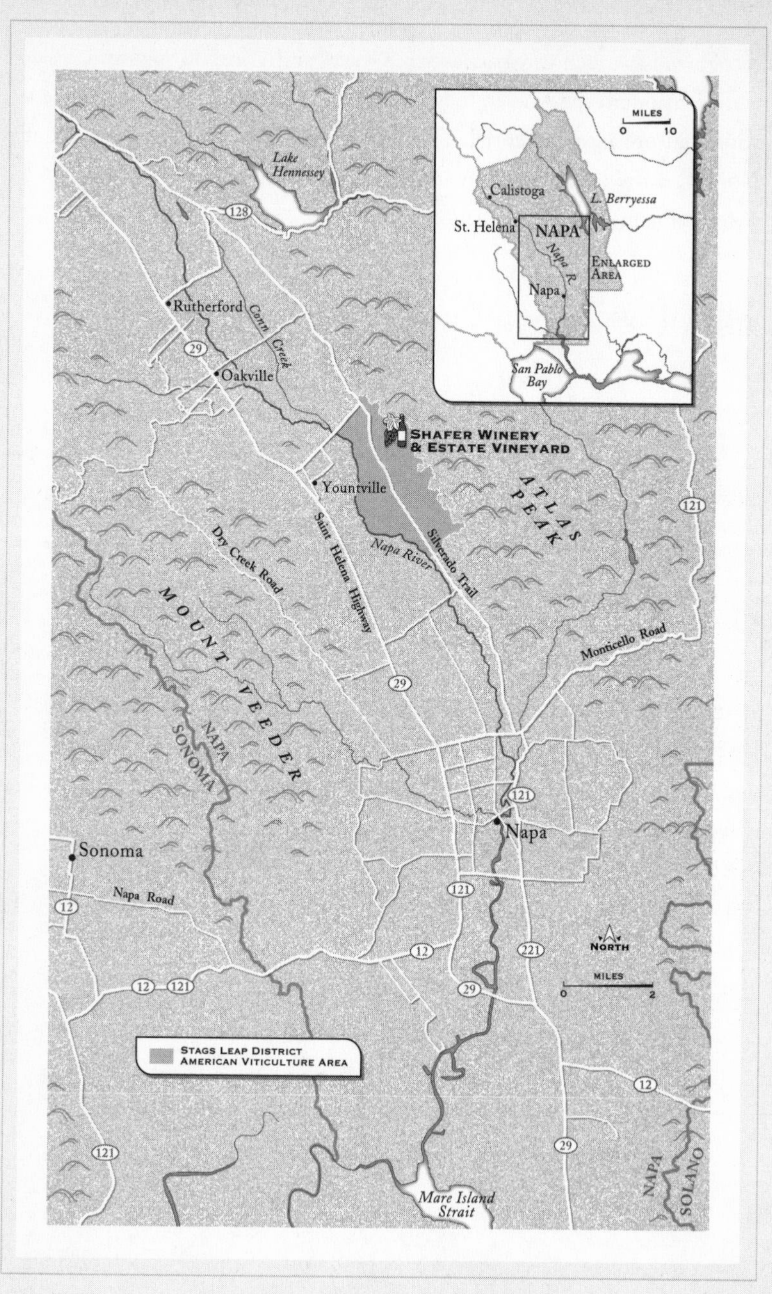

SHAFER VINEYARDS AND THE STAGS LEAP DISTRICT AVA

CHAPTER 33

SHAFER VINEYARDS CABERNET SAUVIGNON, HILLSIDE SELECT

Stags Leap District, Napa Valley, California

...

They had grand ambitions. The two young men—Doug Shafer, the winery owner's son, full of brash bravado, and Elias Fernandez, more reserved but equally confident—were sure that they could make a wine to challenge Napa's elite. After all, they had the right training, enology degrees from UC Davis, and the right vineyard, a block of prime hillside land at the northern edge of the Stags Leap Viticultural Area. The wine they wanted would be big and powerful, like the wines they admired from Randy Dunn up on Howell Mountain or Al Brounstein at Diamond Creek. It would also have high acids and a firm structure, like those from the top Bordeaux châteaux. And as their professors preached, it would be clean, with nothing obscuring the flavor of the fruit. Shafer, who had graduated from Davis a few years earlier, was making wines for his dad, and the winery had a reputation for better than average Merlot. Now with Fernan-

John Shafer, Doug Shafer, and Elias Fernandez

dez's help, he was going to raise the bar with Cabernet, the varietal that everyone agreed was Napa's best.

The two self-styled "amigos" made their first wine together in 1984. It tasted fine—not as good as they wanted, but fine. Much the same thing happened the next year. And the year after. Then came 1987, a vintage that seemed ideal, the fruit perfectly ripe according to their measurements. This was their moment. So they picked the grapes, fermented the juice, and waited for the magic. It never came. "We did everything by the book," Shafer recalls, "and then the wine didn't taste right. That's when we started to realize that we weren't all that smart after all." Perhaps paradoxically, that was also the moment when their fortunes began to change. "We recognized that we had to alter our approach," he explains. "We had to start over, and literally learn from the ground up." Before long Shafer Hillside Select began what became a rapid rise to its current status as one of Napa's very best Cabernet-based wines. That rise involved returning to the initial vision of the estate's owner, as well as better understanding the vineyard's distinct *terroir*. Today, Fernandez and Shafer take great pride in their achievement with Hillside Select Cabernet, their initial ambitions having been realized. Their pride, though, has its roots in humility. "We remember," says Fernandez. "We remember all the mistakes we made."

Those mistakes involved paying too much attention to things other than their own grapes—to academic lessons and scientific numbers, as well as models from afar. "We had to learn to listen to the vineyard," says Fernandez. "And," adds Shafer, we had to learn "how to taste." He explains: "We needed to stop trying to make a wine that was like something else. We needed to learn how to be ourselves." Their success over the past fifteen years with this particular wine suggests that they learned those lessons well, for no Napa Cabernet today is held in higher critical esteem. Powerfully expansive, yet at the same time seductively supple, it embodies the qualities that make Cabernet Sauvignon California's (and by extension America's) finest red varietal. As such, Shafer Hillside Select occupies a somewhat peculiar position in the pantheon of top American wines. With an initial release back in 1978, it clearly has a track record, but at the same time it is a relatively recently risen star. Its story, then, is one of maturity—the developing maturity of both a vineyard and a winemaking team. In turn, it exemplifies how Napa Valley Cabernet as a category has evolved—both stylistically and in terms of renown. From a wine whose greatest recognition came when it was mistaken for something else (first-growth Bordeaux), Napa Cabernet now has an identity all its own. And no wine better embodies that identity—dense and concentrated, with vibrant fruit yet pliant tannins—than Shafer Hillside Select.

John Shafer came to the Napa Valley from Chicago in 1972, leaving behind a successful, twenty-three-year career in textbook publishing in order to pursue a new one in wine. He was not alone. The decade of the 1970s saw a host of entrepreneurs and refugees from corporate life enter the California wine industry. Many were attracted by the appeal of something chic, the emerging "wine country" lifestyle. Others felt the lure of working on the land rather than in a boardroom. Still others were betting on the future—on wine becoming a bigger part of mainstream American life. All these were part of Shafer's rationale. Because he focused from the start on premium production, he went hunting for a hillside vineyard, having read that such a locale likely would produce the best grapes. Hillside soils are thin, so yields tend to be low, with small berries and intense flavors; in theory, the fruit from them should prove superior. Shafer found what he wanted off the Silverado Trail, a few miles east of the town of Yountville, in what is now the Stags Leap District. The area is widely recognized today as the source of many of the finest Napa Valley wines, but back then hardly anyone thought of it as unusual. Nathan Fay was growing Cabernet down the road, and both Warren Winiarski and Bernard Portet had recently planted vineyards; but not until the close of the decade, after wines from Winiarski's Stag's Leap Wine Cellars and Portet's Clos du Val had reaped considerable acclaim, did people begin to conceive of Stags Leap as a distinct place. "No one really knew its potential," Shafer told an interviewer years later, admitting that his buying land there was in large measure just "dumb luck."

But luck, as the old adage suggests, can result from design, and while Shafer surely was fortunate in buying this particular property, he always had clear ideas about what to do with it. He wanted to grow grapes that would go into top wines and, as important, fetch top dollar. To do so, he first replanted and then expanded the property's small, neglected vineyard, terracing the hillsides and hauling away literally tons of rock. He concentrated on Cabernet, and he did much of the work himself. "I'll never forget," recalls his son, who was seventeen when the family moved west, "coming home from school in the afternoons and seeing my dad riding a tractor wearing a big grin. It was quite a change from the Chicago days in three-piece suits." When the new vines bore fruit, Shafer sold his crop to the local co-op. The only problem was that he had lots of company. All the investment and planting in Napa during the 1970s led to an oversupply of grapes, and fruit from hillsides did not fetch a significantly higher price than fruit grown on the valley floor. So in 1978, he decided to use some of his grapes to make his own wine. The first Shafer Vineyards bottling was a Cabernet, fashioned entirely from fruit grown on the hill he had cleared five years earlier. By the time it was released onto the market three years later, Shafer had modified his original design and committed himself completely to the new label. No more sales to the co-op. From then on, all the grapes would go into his own wines.

That initial Shafer wine turned a few heads, as it took first place in an annual tasting run by the San Francisco Vintners Club. But there were only a thousand cases, and the big-city connoisseurs had seen plenty of new Napa wines shine brightly for a vintage or two, only to dim under the force of market pressure and the strain of growth. That's precisely what seemed to happen to Shafer Cabernet. Subsequent vintages were sound and safe but not really special. Doug Shafer assumed the winemaking duties in 1983, and he immediately started making a Merlot, presciently perceiving that this second Bordeaux varietal was about to skyrocket in popularity. When it did, the Shafers rode the wave, and Merlot more than Cabernet first brought them to people's attention. But Shafer Merlot was made primarily with purchased fruit, and father and son (along with Elias Fernandez, who was working by then as the assistant winemaker) chafed at not making as good a wine as they wanted with their own hillside grapes. More to the point, they were haunted by the memory of that first Cabernet. Why had it been better than what they were making now?

The answer lay in what John Shafer had not understood when he had harvested that initial vintage—namely, that he was supposed to pick the grapes at 23 degrees of sugar, and then make a squeaky clean wine from them. At least that was what he was supposed to do according to the accepted wisdom of the day, the same wisdom that the UC Davis professors had imparted to Doug Shafer and Elias Fernandez. "Dad used to say that he'd been too busy to pick the grapes on time that year," his son remembers. "But after we missed with our 1987 Cabernet, it occurred to Elias and me that maybe he was wrong. Maybe he'd picked them just right, and we'd come in with our university degrees and screwed things up." A similar lesson dawned upon them in the winery. "Dad had pretty much let that first wine make itself," Shafer explains, "so we figured maybe we should go back to that." Helping them reach those conclusions was Tony Soter, the highly respected Napa winemaking consultant who worked with them for two critical years. "Tony always told us to listen to the vineyard," recalls Fernandez, "to ask what the wine wants. He helped turn our mind-set." In sum, the key to the change at Shafer came in a change of attitude. Instead of growing grapes and making wine according to a textbook model, they began to trust themselves—their own palates and their own experiences. That trust involved listening and tasting: in short, reacting rather than instructing or imposing. And while self-trust often suggests confidence, here it was self-effacing. As Fernandez puts it, "We had to stop doing what we wanted, and start doing what the grapes wanted."

"One of our mistakes back then," admits Shafer, "was paying too much attention to Bordeaux as a model. That meant trying to hold back—in the vineyard and in the winery. We've since learned that we have to maximize what we have. The best thing this place does is give lush, rich fruit. So now that's what we want in our wine." And today, that's exactly what they get. Shafer Hillside Select is an intense wine, full of both red and black fruit flavors, broodingly dark, with a long, deep finish. At the same time, it feels supple on the palate, its tannins silky rather than abrasive. Though designed for cellaring, it proves exceptionally seductive when young, as the combination of power and elasticity render it deliciously accessible. "That's this vineyard," argues Fernandez. "All we do is optimize what it gives us." But before doing that, Fernandez and Shafer first had to recognize as much—meaning recognize what exactly it is this particular place provides, and what exactly they needed to do in response. Such recognition marked their maturity as vintners, and it accounts in large measure for their achievement with the wine.

That maturity is emblematic of California Cabernet at large, or more precisely, of the state's top vintners' approaches to it. At the start of the contemporary California wine boom, in the late 1960s and 1970s, success with this varietal invariably entailed making a wine that would resemble top-growth Bordeaux. Despite the track record of domestic Cabernets from wineries such as Beaulieu and Inglenook, the foreign model was what most people wanted to emulate. Whether in Paris, New York, or San Francisco, the ultimate accolade a California Cab could get came when supposedly expert palates were unable to distinguish it from a French wine. That happened frequently enough, not only at publicized events such as Steven Spurrier's Paris tasting in 1976 but also in scores of sales calls and marketing meetings, as American wine, led by California Cabernet, made its way into tony restaurants, connoisseurs' cellars, and most important, the consciousness of a growing number of consumers. The problem, of course, came in the fact that California is not Bordeaux. With a different climate, topography, and geology, its vineyards naturally produce grapes with different flavors and textures—as a general rule, lower acids, richer fruit flavors, less of an earthy or vegetative character, and so on. And within California, even within a relatively small region like the Napa Valley, different locales do this to different degrees. Cabernet grown up-valley, in Calistoga or St. Helena, for example, generally has slightly thicker skin and hence more tannin than Cabernet grown down-valley, so the resulting wines will taste subtly but significantly distinct. The recognition of those differences—differences both within and between regions, let alone countries—marked the second stage in American wine's ascent to international prominence. And it indeed was a mark of maturity—the maturity of a vintner having both the confidence and the humility to trust his or her grapes and his or her experience with them.

What distinguishes Shafer Hillside Select Cabernet is both the vineyard, John Shafer's "dumb luck" of thirty years ago, and the winemaking team's continuing commitment to realizing its potential. Within the fifty acres of Cabernet on the property, separate blocks, each carrying separate names, yield fruit with individualistic character. Because the soil compositions vary subtly, the exposures range over the points of the compass, and because the different blocks are planted to different clones, the one vineyard yields a patchwork quilt of Cabernet flavors—some resembling blackberries, others dark plums, still others with a minty leafiness and intense tannins. If human hands do not interfere, that variety of plant material will produce complexity in the resulting wine. At Shafer, the hillside grapes are picked into small bins, so that they are not crushed by their own weight. In the winery, maceration and fermentation are extended so as to allow the fruit to express itself fully. And the aging, in tight-grain new French oak, takes nearly three years, so that the wine and wood can integrate at their own pace. In both vineyard and winery, Fernandez and Shafer pay meticulous attention to this wine, micromanaging it by not interrupting its development. The result is a Napa Valley Cabernet with a classic (because elusive) New World combination of muscle and grace.

The commitment to Hillside Select Cabernet at Shafer Vineyards is in part financial and in part philosophical. Doug Shafer runs the business side of things these days, his father having semi-retired under the title of company chairman, and he spares no expense in either the management of the vineyard or the production of the wine. "What Elias needs," he says, "Elias gets." As that statement suggests, Fernandez is now in charge of the actual winemaking. One of the few Mexican Americans to have risen to a position of such authority in the California wine business, he takes charge of all phases of the process—from sampling the grapes in the field through deciding when to harvest, all the way to blending and bottling. An extremely talented but at the same time modest craftsman, his dedication to quality has been a prime factor in this wine's emergence as one of Napa's best.

"I saw during my very first harvest here that the Cabernet off the hillsides was special," Fernandez says. "The juice developed an intensity of flavor and deepness of color within hours of crushing that might take other grapes days to get. It just took us a while to figure out how to capture all that in the wine." That process of discovery is the story of this wine. It took years, all the years in which the wine did not live up to Fernandez and Shafer's expectations because, as they came to learn, it did not fully express its origins. Today, the two men are no longer all that young, but with age has come wisdom—the wisdom to recognize what they should and should not do. And with Shafer Hillside Select, not doing is just as important as doing. In the vineyard, they practice sustainable agriculture, using native cover crops to control erosion and reduce the need for chemicals. In the winery, their meticulous attention to detail allows them to practice hands-off winemaking, the concentrated grape juice naturally but slowly evolving into something deep and delicious. They are both very proud of the wine they make, but they both also insist that they are not really responsible for it. "It's the vineyard, stupid," says Shafer with a grin. "That's what all the years have taught us." And that's why this wine, which at other wineries might be labeled "Reserve" or called by a fabricated proprietary name, is labeled simply as what it is—the best selection from Shafer's Stags Leap hillside.

A NOTE ON VINTAGES:

This concentrated, intense Cabernet has all the requisite components for successful long-term aging. In my experience, however, it does not so much improve with cellaring as maintain its vibrant character. In most vintages, it certainly needs a few years of bottle age to soften and settle, but from that point on, it's delicious—an intense but beautifully integrated Napa Valley wine. Top vintages include 1991, 1992, 1994, 1997, and 1999.

THE SUGGESTED PRICE FOR THE CURRENT 2001 RELEASE IS $175.

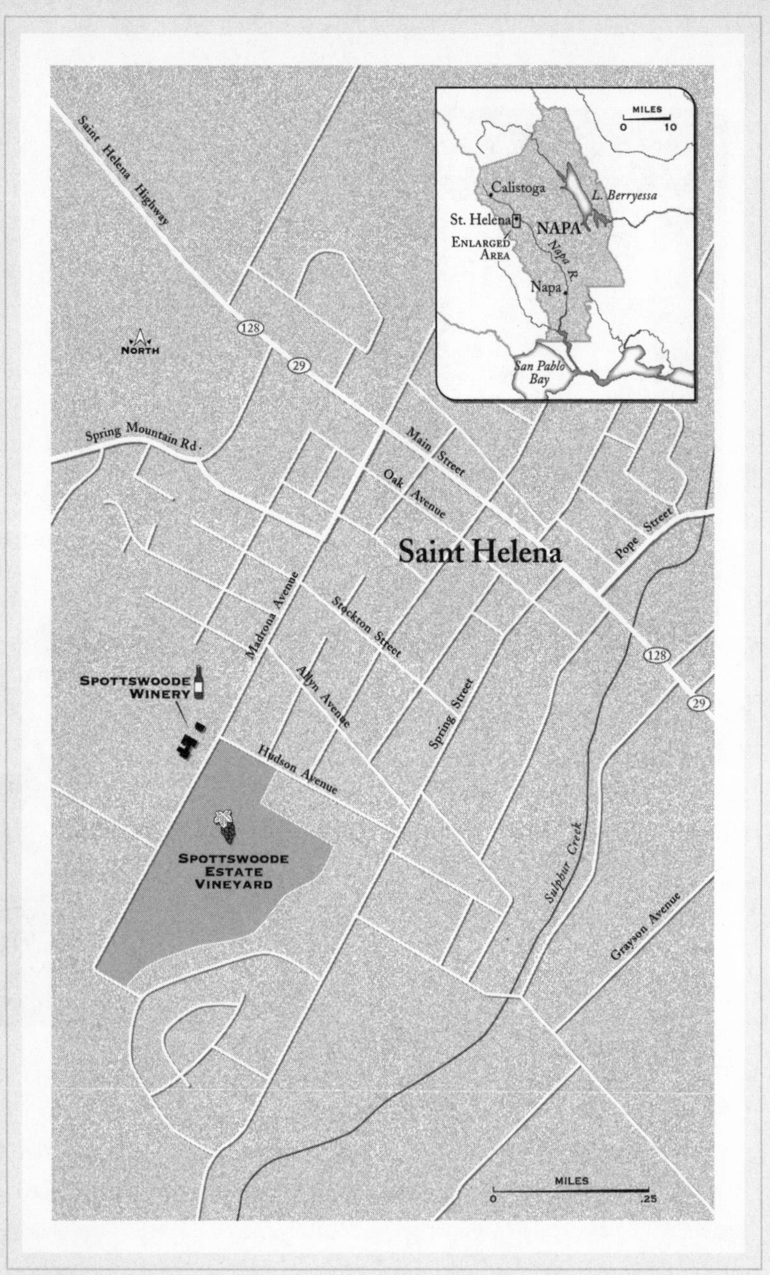

THE SPOTTSWOODE WINERY AND VINEYARD IN ST. HELENA

CHAPTER 34

SPOTTSWOODE CABERNET SAUVIGNON

Napa Valley, California

...

The women of Spottswoode produce an unfailingly elegant Cabernet Sauvignon—the Grace Kelly of Napa Valley wines, conveying an almost aristocratic impression of refinement and class. The estate's owner, Mary Novak, her daughter Beth, who directs the business, and her other daughter Lindy, who manages sales, are committed to a style of wine that might well be called feminine. So too are the current winemaker, Rosemary Cakebread, and her assistant, Jennifer Williams. Is their gender the reason? "I really don't think so," says Cakebread. "I know how to make big, brawny wines; I just don't want to do so here." She's right, of course. As demonstrated by the work of Heidi Barrett and Helen Turley (to cite two prominent examples), a female hand in a California cellar need not result in a particularly tender wine. Yet wines often do reflect the character of the people behind them, and the focused gentility that distinguishes Spottswoode Cabernet most definitely is echoed by the soft-spoken determination of the women responsible for it.

Mary Novak

"Lots of men work with us and have worked with us over the years," notes Beth Novak Milliken, "so I can't say that our wine tastes as it does because women are in charge. But gender may make a difference in our philosophy." That philosophy emphasizes above all else care and constancy, staying the proverbial course. Since the initial release in 1982, Spottswoode Cabernet has set itself apart—first from tight, austere "food wines," and later from more extracted, alcoholic ones. Though the thirty-eight-acre estate vineyard had to be completely replanted in the 1990s, neither the wine's stylistic profile nor its qualitative edge ever shifted or slipped. It remains today what it was at the start: a remarkably graceful example of Napa Cabernet that seduces rather than overwhelms. Even Robert Parker, who tends to prefer much more muscular wines, sings its praises, calling it "the Château Margaux of the Napa Valley." Like that French exemplar, Spottswoode is more lithe and supple than most of its peers. It too is distinguished by an evocative perfume and extraordinary length, only here the aromas and flavors are Californian—echoing not violets and cassis but black and blue berries, baking spices and cookie dough. "That's what this fabulous place gives us," Mary Novak remarks softly. "We try to stay true to that gift."

The Spottswoode story begins well over a century ago, when George Schoenewald, the manager of the Hotel Del Monte in Monterey, and one of the first true connoisseurs of California wine, built a home and winery a few blocks off Main Street in St. Helena. Schoenewald's Esmeralda wines enjoyed a fine reputation, but the winery changed hands and then fell into disrepair following Prohibition. Meanwhile, the house and vineyard too were sold—to a family named Spotts, who named it after themselves. Many years later, in 1972, when Jack and Mary Novak purchased the property, they kept the name but not the winery, as the Town Council refused to issue them a permit to make wine in what had become a residential neighborhood. At that point, they were more interested in grape growing than winemaking anyway. They had moved, along with their five children, from a suburb of San Diego, where Jack worked as a family physician, because they had fallen in love with the Napa Valley—not today's glitzy, boutique-filled tourist mecca, but the sleepy and bucolic farming community of times past. "Jack just wanted to grow things," remembers Mary. "Everyone back home thought we were crazy to come up here, but he just wanted to be on a tractor."

In St. Helena, Jack worked part time in the emergency room at the local hospital in order to make ends meet. But he spent most of his time up on that tractor—clearing the overgrown Spottswoode vineyard in order to replant it, and later tending the young vines. Rick Forman, then the winemaker at Sterling, lived across the street, and advised planting Bordeaux grapes. So did Jack's friend Justin Meyer, late of Christian Brothers and recently embarked on a new project, Silver Oak Cellars. Jack did just that, and when his vines produced a decent crop, he sold the grapes to some of the valley's top wineries, including Duckhorn, Heitz, St. Clement, Shafer, and Spring Mountain.

Meanwhile, Mary kept busy raising the family and remodeling the house. She turned George Schoenewald's old Victorian manse into an inviting home, filled with the laughter of children and the warmth of familial fellowship. Living there, with her kids settled comfortably into the gentle rhythm of small-town life, all seemed right with the world. Then, five years into their new life, with no hint of warning, Jack died, the victim of a heart attack. Mary, forty-five years old, her children ranging from eleven to twenty, was on her own. "I had to think hard about what to do," she remembers. Should she uproot her family once again, or should she stay put? "I opted to stay, and try to keep the business going," she says, "because I didn't really have anything else to do."

Before long, she decided to expand into winemaking instead of just grape growing. "I didn't really know much about wine," she recalls, "but the people we were selling grapes to kept telling me that ours were special." The Spottswoode Cabernet grapes simply were too good to be relegated to the role of a blending component in wines from other producers. So, even though she had no winery, Mary took the plunge, hiring a young man to handle the winemaking duties in rented space down the highway. His name was Tony Soter, and it proved to be an inspired choice.

A former student of philosophy at Pomona College, Soter would go on to become one of the most successful consulting winemakers in the country, working in Northern and Southern California as well as Oregon. His clients came to include a roll call of elite wineries, names such as Araujo, Dalle Valle, Niebaum-Coppola, Shafer, and Viader, as well as his own labels, Etude and Soter. Perhaps because he had no formal university training, Soter made the initial Spottswoode wines without preconception. More than anyone else, he defined the estate Cabernet's style. As he told Mary Novak, elegance was what the vineyard dictated.

Unlike many consulting vintners, who try to realize a predetermined mode or form of wine, Soter pays meticulous attention to the peculiarities of each vineyard, so the wines he makes (or helps make) can be quite different from one another. That focus on place, so common today as to be clichéd, was relatively rare back in the early 1980s, and it was what inspired Soter to craft a wine at Spottswoode that was understated and subtly seductive rather than bold or brash. "Tony is scholarly and thoughtful," notes Beth Novak Milliken, "and those qualities are reflected in our wine. He sensed something special in our vineyard, but it took a special person to be able to do that." Her mother puts things more simply. "I had faith in the vineyard, and I had faith in Tony."

Tony Soter too had faith—in this vineyard and this family. "He didn't just work for us," says Beth Novak Milliken. "He quickly became our very good friend. And even though he doesn't help with our wines anymore, he still is." Spottswoode Cabernet established Tony Soter's reputation as a preeminent California vintner. In turn, Soter established a wine style that has remained constant despite personnel changes in the cellar. In 1992, he handed the winemaking reins to Pam Starr, staying on to tender advice and assistance when needed. Starr left four years later, and one of Soter's last assignments for Spottswoode was to help find a new winemaker. (With his wife expecting their first child, he soon quit the consulting business altogether to devote more time to his family.) Soter suggested Rosemary Cakebread to Mary Novak and Beth Novak Milliken, insisting that though much of her background was in sparkling wine, she had a similar sensibility when it came to Cabernet.

Indeed she does. "I love balance and finesse in any type of wine," she says, when asked what attracted her to the job. "Being part of a Napa family [she is married to Bruce Cakebread, of Cakebread Cellars], I was very familiar with Napa Valley Cabernet. It's the tour de force here. It's what makes this place tick. So of course I knew Spottswoode. And I knew that, stylistically, it's a wine that speaks to my heart. For myself, I'm more interested in elegance than anything else. How to achieve that in Napa, with our hot summers—that's the challenge. Tony showed it could be done here."

It's done in the winery, where Cakebread, like Starr and Soter before her, insists on gentle handling, slow fermentations, minimal intervention, and extended aging in French oak, some 60 percent of the barrels being new each year. Most important, it's done in the vineyard, where the roughly thirty-five acres of red grapes (primarily Cabernet Sauvignon, with four acres of Cabernet Franc, and a half acre or so of Petit Verdot), produce roughly twenty-five separate lots of wine, each managed, harvested, and then vinified separately. That attention to individual plots and parcels contributes crucially to the Spottswoode style, for it provides Cakebread with ripe fruit that is not marred by excessive alcohol or heat.

The vineyard, abutting the Novak home and gardens, sits flat on the valley floor, just to the east of the point at which the Mayacamas Range meets Spring Mountain. The small gap between those two provides a cooling maritime influence, tempering the hot summer sun, and allowing for an even development of the grapes. David Abreu, one of Napa's preeminent vineyard managers, oversaw the viticulture for many years; but in 2004, Matt Novak, Mary's youngest son, and Jennifer Williams, took control. "We recognized," says Beth Novak Milliken, "that we are better positioned to keep a close eye on our estate." Jose Luis Lopez, who has worked at Spottswoode since 1982, manages the day-to-day operation. The goal with this particular vineyard is slow ripening, so as to attain full maturity in the grapes, resulting in fruit with supple tannins and rich, potentially complex wine flavors, but without excess sugar or potential alcohol. The vineyard crew cuts off unwanted green grapes so as to keep yields low, usually under 3 tons per acre, enabling Rosemary Cakebread to produce an average of four thousand cases of wine. Though demand inevitably exceeds supply, no one at Spottswoode evidences any desire to increase production. "This fabulous piece of land is what we focus on," insists Mary Novak. "We want to improve as we go along, but our intention is not to grow."

Part of that improvement came in 1990, with the purchase of the old Frank Kraft winery just across the road, to the north of the vineyard. The authorities in St. Helena permitted it to be modernized and used for production; and though the work took longer than hoped, this ghost facility (built in 1884 but long since abandoned) now has been brought back to life. The first step involved restoring an old stone cellar for barrel storage, since the wine previously had been aged in Mary Novak's basement. Then an adjacent farmhouse was converted into an office, and finally a new winery was constructed beside the pre-Prohibition one. Designed specifically to handle only the grapes grown across the way, the new facility enables Cakebread to micromanage production, overseeing each lot individually. "It also allows us to become a true estate winery," she notes. "Everything now is done here."

All this renovation and construction took the better part of a decade, because the purchase of the property coincided with the discovery of phylloxera in the vineyard, which led to an inevitably costly replanting program. Bit by bit, parcel by parcel, the vulnerable AXR1 rootstock vines that Jack Novak had put in back in the 1970s were ripped out and new ones planted—on four different rootstocks this time, so as to hedge all bets. "The plan was to have sufficient old-vine fruit so as not to alter the quality, or style, of the wine," explains Beth Novak Milliken. "That's why we went so slowly. It was a business of patience." The last plots were replanted in 2002, and the entire vineyard (including 2.5 acres of Sauvignon Blanc, the only other wine that carries the Spottswoode label) should be on line by 2008. To further ensure constancy, some 80 percent of the new vines were planted with budwood taken from the vineyard. "We replanted because of disease," notes Milliken, "not because we wanted to change the wine."

Meanwhile, in a further illustration of the Novak family's desire to improve but not substantially alter what they do, their vineyard became certified as an organic farm property, meaning one in which natural rather than synthetic products keep the ecosystem in balance and the crop healthy. The Spottswoode vineyard team plants selected flowering shrubs to control unwanted insects, and cover crops of clover, peas, oats, and vetch to fertilize the soils. They remove weeds manually rather than with chemical sprays, and have installed owl boxes and bird feeders to further check the insect and rodent population. "Sure, organic farming takes more work," says Milliken. "But for us, it's philosophical. We just believe it's the right thing to do. And you know, it's also better farming. You have to think more deeply. You have to make a long-term commitment."

That sort of commitment is what Spottswoode Cabernet Sauvignon is all about. As Mary Novak puts it, "We don't want to ride the fads. We want to stay true to ourselves." In terms of the wine, that means an unswerving commitment to a single style, one that comes from the estate vineyard but that needs to be recognized and realized by the people responsible for it. Especially in the northern portion of the Napa Valley, where the heat tends to produce ripe, heavy wines, that style is indeed a "feminine" one. The tannins in this wine are refined rather than aggressive, the fruit succulent but not jammy or stewed, and the body almost willowy, length of layered flavor being one of its principal charms. The significant roles played by, first Jack Novak, then Tony Soter, David Abreu, Jose Luis Lopez, and now Matt Novak, prove that this style does not come from women being exclusively in charge. Still, the commitment of the women responsible for it contributes significantly to Spottswoode Cabernet being what it is today—an American first growth.

"The goal back when we started," says Beth Novak Milliken, "was to pursue a classic Bordeaux model. But we don't really think in those terms anymore. Now, after more than twenty years, we want to hold true to what we do best *here*." That focus on the estate itself—the vineyard, its unique character, and the wine, its distinct style—sets the women of Spottswoode apart from many of their colleagues and compatriots, in Napa and beyond. Few American wineries have a track record that enables a vintner to work without a model, no matter whether foreign or domestic. Spottswoode does. Cakebread, Milliken, and Novak all recognize that riper, headier—yes, more "masculine"—wines tend to get the headlines these days, and that many well-known wineries have shifted stylistically, sometimes subtly, sometimes blatantly, in pursuit of this press. At the same time, they insist that they in no sense feel left behind.

"Our consistency is appreciated by our customers," notes Milliken. "People buy our wine because they understand what it is." Her mother amplifies: "Because we're family-owned, we can take a long-term view, and not have to answer to anyone else." That sense of quiet confidence characterizes the Spottswoode operation. "We're smart enough here to know what we're capable of and to do it," says Rosemary Cakebread. "We don't have to mirror either Bordeaux or a California cult wine. We just have to do what we do best, and stay true to ourselves."

For these women, and all the people, male and female, who work with them, the confessed goal now is to be recognized as one of the world's very best wine estates—meaning a privileged place that produces a wine that stands apart, with unswerving quality in a recognizable style, a place that remains true to its own identity. Getting there will take time, "a long time," acknowledges Milliken. But tasting through the vintages of Spottswoode Cabernet, and noting the wine's class and refinement as well as its stability, suggests that they are well on their way. Napa's most consistently stylish Cabernet, it is a genuine American star.

A NOTE ON VINTAGES:

Spottswoode Cabernet ages gracefully, but being more refined than most Napa Cabernets from the start, neither needs many years to display subtleties nor changes significantly in middle age. Older vintages seem interestingly delicate, but to experience the wines at their best you probably should consume them within ten to fifteen years of harvest. Top vintages at Spottswoode include 1987, 1991, 1994, 1999, and 2001.

THE SUGGESTED PRICE FOR THE CURRENT 2002 RELEASE IS $90.

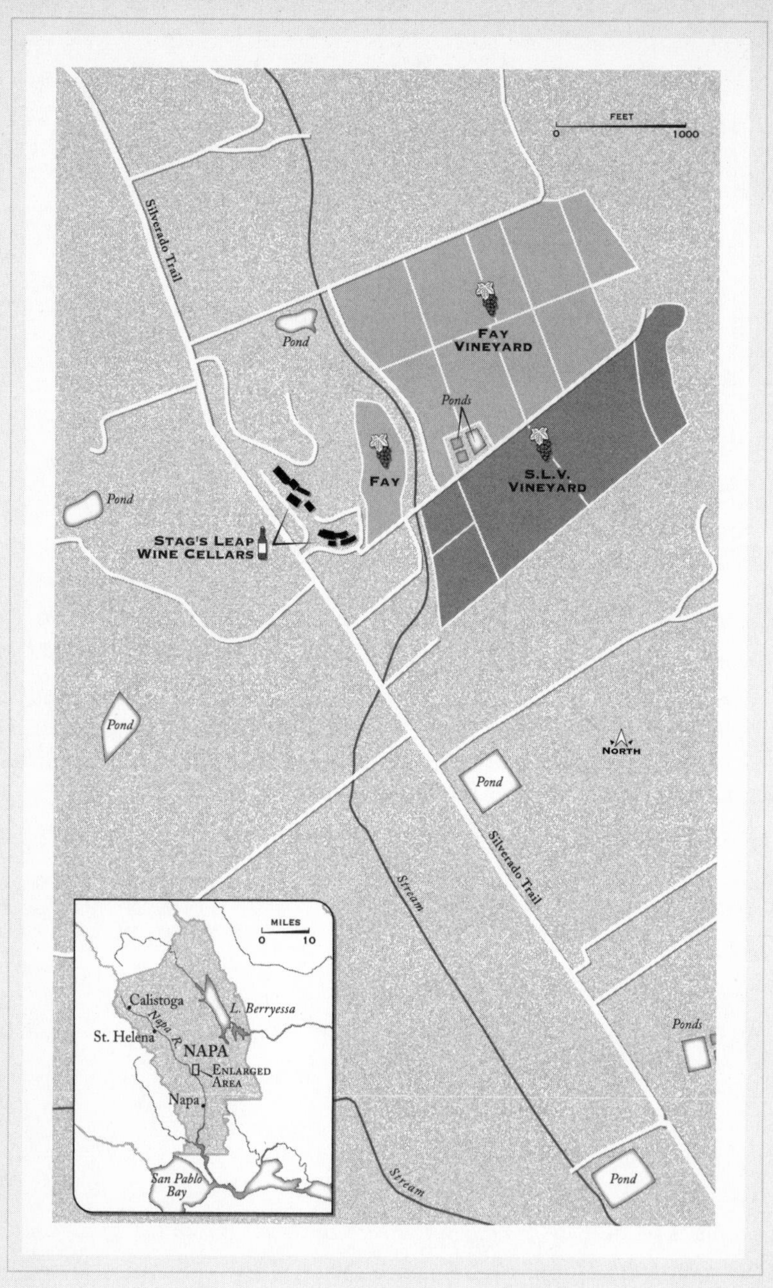

THE S.L.V. AND FAY VINEYARDS

CHAPTER 35

STAG'S LEAP WINE CELLARS CABERNET SAUVIGNON, S.L.V.

Napa Valley, California

...

Cabernet Sauvignon from the Napa Valley is the one American wine that enjoys truly international renown. Its fame has penetrated even the most hidebound Old World cellars, so much so that for many people it serves as a symbol of American wine at large—the country's vinous achievements but also its excesses. Over the years, many individual labels—from groundbreakers like Beaulieu Vineyard Georges de Latour and Inglenook Cask, through heavyweights like Heitz Wine Cellars Martha's Vineyard and Dunn Vineyards Howell Mountain—have contributed to its fame. But one particular wine, and one seminal moment, stands out. In 1976, a three-year-old Cabernet from Stag's Leap Wine Cellars, made with grapes from equally young vines, triumphed at Steven Spurrier's now legendary Paris tasting, besting a set of first- and second-growth Bordeaux. From that point on, Napa, and by extension all American wine, began to emerge from a cocoon of provincial isolation. As important, the Paris tasting initiated a process in which critics, consumers, and vintners all began to rethink what

Warren Winiarski in the mid-1970s

constitutes merit or greatness in wine. For generations, people had associated wine quality with history, a history of storied vintages. Since only a handful of European wines enjoyed such a legacy, only those wines could be considered great. But the Paris tasting suggested that quality involves something else. The fact that a new wine from a new winery and a new vineyard could be judged superior to top Bordeaux meant that merit could no longer simply be equated with pedigree. Add to this the fact that the wine came from a country that only a generation earlier had deemed all wine contraband, and it became clear that excellence in wine, no matter the wine's origin, had to be defined in terms of present composition rather than lineage.

This shift in understanding had wide-ranging ramifications. For vintners, it inspired rededication and reinvention, while for critics and consumers, it led to a new sort of wine appreciation, exemplified by blind tastings and numerical scores. Most important, it enabled not only the United States but also Australia, South America, and the rest of the New World to emerge as legitimate sources of increasingly superior wines. And within the New World, no category of wine became more acclaimed than Napa Valley Cabernet Sauvignon. As Warren Winiarski, the man responsible for the Cabernet that prevailed in Paris, acknowledges: "We were struck by lightning."

That particular wine, from Winiarski's very first commercial vintage at Stag's Leap Wine Cellars, tasted rich and ripe, but at the same time restrained—its components all in balance. A tasting of it and a series of subsequent vintages in early January 2004 demonstrated that S.L.V. (this vineyard designation was first employed in 1985) consistently displays those qualities—what Winiarski likes to call "the three Rs." The 1973 showed its age that day, but it still exhibited refinement and finesse, while later releases, including an outstanding 1985 and a breathtaking 1997, tasted remarkably harmonious, their flavors deep but never heavy. According to Winiarski, that was his goal from the start. "I made this wine," he says, "in a deliberate effort to counterbalance some California wines of the time. Yes, we were struck by lightning. However, we did climb to the top of the tree, or the top of the hill, to be exposed to the possibility of being struck by lightning."

Of course, Stag's Leap Cabernet was not the only winner at the 1976 Paris tasting. Chateau Montelena Chardonnay bested a set of Côte d'Or white Burgundies that same day, the two Napa wines enjoying a bicentennial triumph that gave American vintners what Winiarski describes as the "confidence that we only sort of wished we had before." Today, nearly thirty years later, that confidence is more apparent with Napa Cabernet than with Napa Chardonnay, if only because of the greater affinity the red grape has for most of the valley. Yet despite the category's renown, few Napa Cabernets display the sort of subtle, complex flavors that characterize Stag's Leap S.L.V., just as few have such a fine-grained texture, the tannins in this wine, even a young rendition, being firm but seductively pliant.

S.L.V.'s distinctive character comes in part from the vineyard; but even more important is the human vision behind it, *terroir* always expressing itself through choice and action. Warren Winiarski's philosophy of wine and winemaking has evolved over the years, becoming less instinctive and more reasoned with the passage of time—something that is not surprising considering his background as a student of the Great Books at St. John's College in Annapolis, Maryland, and then a lecturer in the liberal arts at the University of Chicago. As a vintner, he strives not simply to make a wine that tastes good, but to comprehend why it tastes good and, even more to the point, what in this context constitutes "goodness"—the unchanging, ideal form to be emulated in the transitory reality of the grape's passage from vine to glass. Winiarski believes that a great wine is one that transcends both regionality and varietal assertion, so as to express a Platonic essence, what he calls "the lure of the classic," considerations such as "harmony, balance, proportion, [and] scale." His S.L.V. Cabernet does just that.

Winiarski purchased this property "on the basis of taste"—not the taste of a wine made from grapes grown there, but the taste of a wine made from grapes grown next door, a homemade wine fashioned by

Nathan Fay, that vineyard's owner. Fay had bought his property, then a fruit orchard, in 1953, and eight years later had become the first person to plant post-Prohibition Cabernet in the southern portion of the Napa Valley, defying the experts of the day who declared the region too cold. By 1969, when Winiarski first tasted Fay's wine, it had become clear that the area was in fact well suited to Cabernet, as some of Napa's most prominent wineries, including Heitz Wine Cellars and Charles Krug, regularly purchased his crop. But since they used the grapes in their Napa blends, only Fay's homemade wine presented this *terroir* in undiluted form.

When Winiarski tasted Nathan Fay's wine, he experienced an epiphany. "I said to myself, 'Eureka! That's it. This wine satisfied what I hoped was possible in the Napa Valley. It had not only regional character but also elements of classic or universal character." What exactly did it taste like? "It had a perfume of violets," he recalls thoughtfully, "and a complex structure that combined softness and strength. There was also a note of freshness, a red fruit character embedded in black that persisted from beginning to middle to end. No other Napa Valley Cabernet tasted like it." So the next year, using his own savings, along with a gift from his mother as well as money gathered from a group of investors, Winiarski purchased the property immediately to the south, assuming that it would produce grapes and wine with a similar taste. "My hope," he explains, "was that this would be a place that would express most fully the character of the wine I wanted to make."

As he cleared the land, then planted mostly to prunes, cherries, and walnuts, but containing a small, Prohibition-era vineyard (a field blend of primarily Alicante Bouchet and Petite Sirah), Winiarski thought frequently about what those characteristics might be. Only later did he find the right words. Speaking in London, at the 1987 International Wine and Spirits Competition, he argued that the difference between Old World and New World wines is not as important as the distinction between regional and classic ones—the former representing the character of a grape in a place, the latter moderating or even negating such character in order to express more universal qualities such as harmony, balance, complexity, and completeness. "In every place where vines are grown," he contended, "they will express the regional character of soil, the climate and other natural circumstances. They will also betray the work of the winemaker: his intent and his methods. [But] in some places, favored because of the special character of the soil, climate, and those other natural circumstances, the wines seem to possess another possibility. . . . [They] seem to lend themselves to the possibility of transcending the merely regional and reach what might be called the classic dimension."

The idea of that dimension, its *ideal*, is what Winiarski wanted to express through his wine when he bought what would become S.L.V. He did not want to make a wine that shouted, "Cabernet!" or screamed, "Napa!" or even whispered, "I taste like Bordeaux." Instead, he wanted to make a wine that could approximate what he called "wine perfection itself." He had tasted one that hinted at that when he sipped Nathan Fay's homemade wine, and as he planted his vineyard, he was gambling that this neighboring site could bring to fulfillment what seemed to him incomplete because of the merely regional and varietal character of so many other Napa Valley Cabernets.

Winiarski admits freely that he did not know then what about this location might prove special. But he thinks he knows now. In part, it's the climate—cooler than more northern sites in Napa, with warm afternoons that give way to chilly, often breezy evenings. And in part it's the soil, or soils—volcanic rock in the blocks that stretch up onto the steep hillsides, combined with alluvial deposits in the lower ones. "It's fire and water," he maintains; "soil made by fire and soil transported by water, a combination of unity and opposition."

In the wine, the volcanic "fire" contributes concentration and structure, while the alluvial "water" yields softness and perfume. The balance so critical to Winiarski's ideal, restraint alongside richness and ripeness, thus originates in the site. Yet following this logic, all the Cabernet-based wines from vineyards on the eastern edge of the Stags Leap District Viticultural Area should exhibit this sort of harmony, and they clearly do not. Shafer Hillside Select, for example, tastes significantly deeper and more powerful than S.L.V.—not because the *terroir* is all that different, but because Elias Fernandez and John and Doug Shafer pursue a different ideal, one in which concentration and intensity are valued more highly than restraint. Both are exceptional wines, as is neighboring Stags' Leap Winery's Petite Syrah, and less consistently, the top wines from Chimney Rock, Clos du Val, and Steltzner Vineyards, all of which display berry fruit checked by persistent, fine-grained tannins. (When all is said and done, those tannins may well be the district's mark of distinction.) The region yields related but markedly different wines because, as Winiarski acknowledges, *terroir* by itself is a powerful but mute force. "*Terroir* can find its true voice," he argues, "only through the deliberate, painstaking, fastidious, and correct process of human choices—through trial and error. Or, more accurately, through trial and trial again."

The trials at Stag's Leap Wine Cellars involve managing the vineyard so as to regulate its annual cycle, trying to compell each vine to devote maximum resources to the production of berries rather than leaves or wood. The vineyard workers, overseen by Winiarski's daughter, Julia, and led by Charlie Hossom, prune and thin the vines so as to restrain natural vigor. They regulate yields, often working cluster by cluster, and at harvest they make multiple passes through each block, with up to two weeks passing from when the first until the last grapes in this thirty-six-acre vineyard are picked. The trials continue in the winery, where each lot is fermented slowly and separately, and the wine is aged in French oak barrels that are stored in caves and chambers tunneled in a low-lying hill. Winiarski made the initial 1972 vintage of S.L.V. in rented space in Oakville, and then aged it in the basement of his home. He started building a production facility on the estate in 1973 (completing the first part in time to make that vintage's Cabernet), and has added onto it over the years as production of Stag's Leap Wine Cellars and Hawk's Crest (his other label) wines grew. Today, the vast majority of the wine made there comes from other vineyards in Napa. But for Winiarski, the pride and joy remains the Cabernet Sauvignon that brought him here in the first place.

Along with his wife, Barbara, he lives in a home overlooking the estate vineyards. It's a place, he says, in which "every day is Christmas."

There are now two estate Cabernet vineyards at Stag's Leap Wine Cellars, Winiarski having purchased Nathan Fay's historic property in 1986. (The winery owns two other vineyards, both closer to the city of Napa, one devoted to Chardonnay, the other to Chardonnay and Sauvignon Blanc.) Fay and S.L.V. were replanted gradually in the later 1980s and 1990s, not due to phylloxera since the vines were not on vulnerable AXR1 rootstock, but simply because of age. In both, the effect of trial and experimentation is evident. The spacing is tighter now, with vertical trellising and cordon rather than cane pruning, and Winiarski thinks the fruit is even more expressive than before. In strong vintages, a selection of the top lots goes into a separate bottling: Cask 23, the winery's most exclusive offering. Originally sourced only from S.L.V., but now using fruit from Fay as well, it too tastes graceful and elegant, as it is crafted with much the same stylistic ideal in mind.

That ideal, precisely because it is an ideal, has not changed over time. Winiarski may not have been able to convey it all that clearly when he first moved to Napa back in 1964, but even then the form of his desire was fixed in his mind. "I've always wanted a wine that can *dwell*," he says; "a wine with a euphonic relationship between the parts—the smooth, sensuous parts and the harder tannic parts—a wine with no predominance, no excessively forceful elements, with a certain complexity, a depth, a length, a persistence of flavors, no shortness and no interruptions, a wine with continuity and completeness." Those "classic" or "universal" or "transcendent" qualities are what he has aimed to express from the start. In order to do so with the early vintages of S.L.V., he deliberately tried not to focus on varietal character, for he wanted his wine to do more than announce itself as an expression of the grape. In an era of sometimes excessively hard and tannic Napa Valley Cabernets, richness was an appropriate goal. With more recent vintages, of Cask 23 and Fay as well as S.L.V., Winiarski and his winemaking team (currently led by Nicolette Pruss) consciously counterbalance the contemporary California craze for highly extracted, superripe wines. "People have gone too far," Winiarski argues. "In recent years, there has been a paradigm shift away from classically styled wines. I think that's unfortunate." And he adds emphatically, "It's not a direction we're ever going to go here."

Winiarski's insistence on all three Rs—*R*estraint as well as *R*ipeness and *R*ichness—has led many of the influential critics, who today can be blinded by their infatuation with extract and power, to undervalue his wines. James Laube of *The Wine Spectator*, who once dubbed Stag's Leap Wine Cellars Cabernet a Napa "First Growth," now tends to score it in the high 80-point or occasionally low 90-point range; and Robert Parker, who called the 1985 Cask 23 "perhaps perfect," now wonders publicly, "What's going on?" To be fair, Parker in the same review admits that "wine tasting is very subjective." His personal preferences, more than the wines in question, may well be what have changed. My own tasting of S.L.V., with a set of vintages from 1973 through 2000, suggests that the wine is remarkably consistent. Production dropped in the late 1990s because of the vineyard replanting program, but the wine retains its distinct character—with a stylish bouquet, full fruit, evocative secondary flavors, and great length. (Indeed, the 1997 S.L.V. , which was made under the direction of Julia Winiarski, sticks in my memory as one of the very finest of the hundreds of excellent wines I tasted while doing research for this book.) Stag's Leap Wine Cellars' Cabernets are definitely not as powerful as many of today's blockbuster Napa wines, but they undoubtedly are more nuanced and tasteful than most.

"We've never had trouble getting ripe fruit," notes Winiarski. "Our challenge is getting ripeness at a lower degree of sugar so as not to sacrifice restraint." He met that challenge successfully in 1973, crafting a wine that brought unprecedented notice to Napa Valley Cabernet Sauvignon. In the years since, he has continued to do so, vintage after vintage and wine after wine, aspiring after the always elusive Platonic ideal. If critical attention now sometimes goes elsewhere, well—"so be it," he says softly, adding, "our wines are what they are." They continue to have legions of admirers, and to my mind remain exemplars of why Napa Cabernet clearly deserves to be America's most renowned wine.

A NOTE ON VINTAGES:

Stag's Leap Wine Cellars S.L.V. is delicious in its youth but perhaps even more delectable with seven to fifteen years of age, when its affinity to classic red Bordeaux comes to the fore. Of the many excellent vintages over the years, 1973, 1985, 1991, 1997, and 1999 stand out.

THE SUGGESTED PRICE FOR THE CURRENT 2001 RELEASE IS $100.

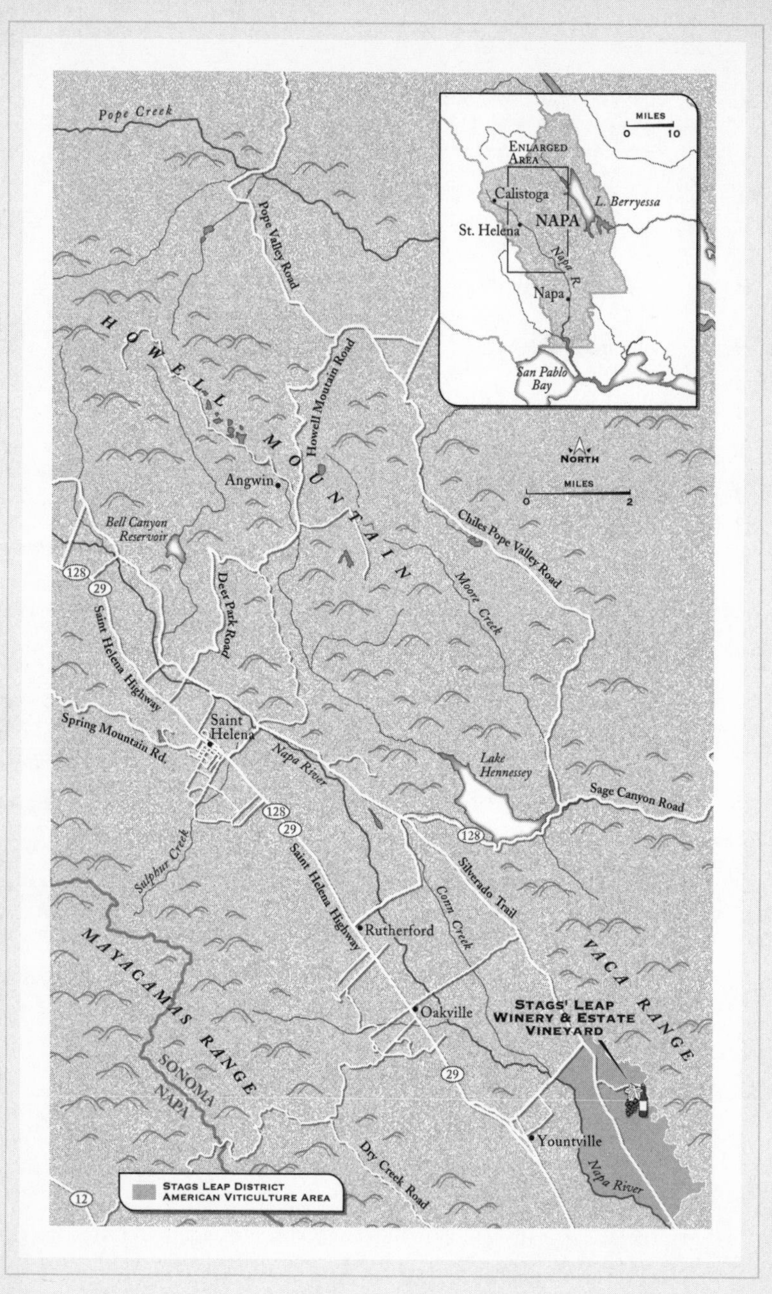

THE STAGS' LEAP WINERY, IN NAPA VALLEY'S STAGS LEAP DISTRICT AVA

CHAPTER 36

Stags' Leap Winery Petite Syrah

Napa Valley, California

...

Robert Brittan

Petite Sirah—both the wine and the vine—can be perplexing. For one, the grape is related to but very different from true Syrah, the classic *cépage* from the Rhône Valley in France. For another, vines called "Petite" do not always comprise a single variety, and the usually powerful wines made from them taste anything but small or dainty. Even the spelling can prove puzzling, since some people use an "i" and others a "y," as in "Syrah." Petite—or "Petty," as old-time grape growers like to call it—was once a mainstay in California, but it is largely ignored or forgotten today. Trendier varieties fetch higher prices, so this one rarely gets planted anymore. Most winemakers, particularly those in the Central Valley, use it as a blending agent, but some vintners, especially those up north who have access to old-vine fruit, do bottle varietal versions. At bucolic Stags' Leap Winery in the Napa Valley, Robert Brittan has produced many stunning examples, wines that illustrate how class and quality can transcend visceral fashion. Beginning with the 2005 vintage, Kevin Morrisey will take over the winemaking reins. "That wine," he says when asked about Stags' Leap Petite, "just makes you dream."

An extremely long-lived wine, Stags' Leap Petite Syrah (this label spells the name with a "y") exhibits beauty as well as brawn, its muscular structure softening with age to reveal subtle but distinguishing nuances of aroma and flavor—echoes of such things as tobacco and molasses, brown sugar and citrus peel, all of which become especially enticing five to ten years after the vintage. The winemakers at Stags' Leap treat Petite Sirah with the sort of respect neighboring Napa vintners reserve for Cabernet Sauvignon. In this, they follow Robert Brittan's lead. A decade ago, Brittan and geneticist Carole Meredith from UC Davis used DNA mapping to identify the different vines in the estate vineyard, and then propagated new plants in order to keep the original selections alive—vine by vine and row by row. His analytic effort to preserve a piece of Napa's viticultural past was motivated by his sense of how special what comes from this historic property can be. Petite Sirah, when tended attentively in an appropriate locale, clearly can yield noble results, and Brittan describes his restoration efforts as "labors of love"—love for a remarkable place and an equally remarkable wine.

The place has a rich history. Founded in 1893 by socially prominent San Franciscans Horace and Minnie Mizner Chase, the estate initially included a working winery as an adjunct to a gracious country residence. Chase grew grapes as a gentleman farmer, and he constructed a grand manorhouse overlooking the vineyards for himself and his wife, replete with the first in-ground swimming pool in Northern California. That house still stands, as do the guest cottages that the property's second owner, the Grange family, rented to guests when they turned it into a resort frequented by the elite of San Francisco society. Legends abound of Jazz Age flappers attending summer soirées on the manorhouse porch, or sneaking off for late night trysts in the cottages. The property later served as a billet for military wives during World War II, and then gradually fell into disrepair, finally closing its doors in the early 1950s. All the while, grapes grew there; but for a long time no one thought of this relatively isolated part of the Napa Valley as prime wine territory. Instead, Stag's Leap became a piece of Napa lore, a relic of fabled days gone by, dilapidated and deserted, save for the occasional ghost.

Winemaking returned to the area in the 1960s and 1970s, beginning when Nathan Fay planted a few acres of Cabernet among the fruit trees on his nearby property, and reaching a climax of sorts when Warren Winiarski's Stag's Leap Wine Cellars Cabernet triumphed in the famous 1976 Paris tasting. That wine did not come from Horace Chase's original property, but rather from an adjacent vineyard to the south. Winiarski had adopted the name, which refers to an Indian legend of a deer that escapes hunters by leaping across the craggy palisades to the east, in homage to the past. But at about the same time, Carl Doumani, an entrepreneur from Los Angeles, purchased the old Chase estate, with the hope of turning it into a hotel. When Doumani decided to go into the wine business instead, he started selling bottles labeled with the name of his property. A protracted legal squabble ensued, with different judges ruling different ways, until Winiarski and Doumani finally agreed on separate though similar monikers: Stag's Leap Wine Cellars for one and Stags' Leap Winery for the other. The press joked about pugilistic punctuation marks, but by then a number of other vintners had begun using the name to identify the region at large. Finally, in 1989, after ongoing boundary disputes, it became officially recognized as the designation not of one or two properties but of an entire Viticultural Area, the Stags Leap District. The government refrained from using an apostrophe.

Over the years, the Stags Leap District has developed an enviable reputation for Cabernet Sauvignon, being widely regarded as one of the best places in Napa to grow this most prestigious and profitable grape variety. Cooler than most other parts of the valley, with gravelly, eroded rhyolite rock soils washed down from the Vaca Mountains (home of the legendary Leap), it tends to produce supple, stylish Cabs marked by an initial fruity softness, fine-grained tannins, and subtle secondary nuances—the proverbial iron fist in a velvet glove. The best examples rank among the finest anywhere (Shafer Hillside Select and Stag's Leap Wine Cellars S.L.V. are profiled in this book), and not surprisingly they sell for prices reserved for very rarified company. By contrast, Petite Sirah today usually is cultivated in hotter, less prestigious regions of California. It often is used to add color to blends, and even most varietal bottlings taste rustic rather than refined. Neither the grapes nor the wines tend to fetch top dollar. Why, then, is the restored Stags' Leap Winery still producing its Petite Syrah?

Robert Brittan has two answers to this question. Sitting on the porch of the manorhouse, overlooking the vineyard, he talks first about the history of the property, and speaks reverently about the gnarled Petite vines that he has nurtured so attentively each season. But then sheer pleasure takes over. Reaching for a glass of wine, he declares, "Just open your taste buds, dummy!" And he's right. For whatever reasons—climate, soil, human care and attention—this wine tastes like no other. Neither rough and excessively tannic nor syrupy and clumsy, it displays an elegance and sophistication that may seem to belie its varietal foundation but that clearly affirms its geographical and historical origin. Put simply, it doesn't just taste like Petite Sirah. It also tastes of Stags Leap.

Brittan came to Stags' Leap Winery in 1988, right when the new district appellation was being approved. He did not focus initially on Petite. Carl Doumani's winery at that point produced big, brawny wines, and operated very much in the shadow of the other, more renowned Stag's Leap, where Cabernet was king and the wines cultured and gracious. Brittan's understanding was that his job included upgrading quality and shifting styles. So one of the first things he recommended was that Doumani rip out a motley block of old head-trained Petite Sirah vines and replant with Cabernet. The boss resisted, and in an attempt to try to prove his point, Brittan vinified the fruit from that block separately.

He fully expected the result of this exercise to taste crude and coarse, but to his surprise found instead the potential for much more. Yes, this undeveloped wine was inky black and chock-full of astringent tannins, but beneath all that ran a rich vein of complex flavors. The vines that had produced it clearly were special. "I went back one day and literally stood in front of them, scratching my head, trying to understand them," he recalls. That effort would consume his attention for much of the next decade. In part, it involved adjusting his winemaking techniques so as to render the wines more palatable when young. Even more important, though, it involved working in the vineyard and caring for the vines, many of which were infected with leaf roll virus and other diseases, and so getting to know them on an almost individual basis. In the process, he became even more confused. Vines that looked alike, with nearly identical leaves and clusters, made wines that tasted different from each other. What, he wondered, is really going on in this vineyard? What exactly is Petite Sirah?

Grapevines can mutate unpredictably. A cross of two varieties will create a new one, and even an offshoot of a single variety is likely to yield a noticeably different plant from its parent. (The propensity of vinifera vines to mutate explains why all commercial vine propagation is done with cuttings, not seedlings.) According to research conducted some thirty years ago by the renowned French ampelographer, or vine scientist, Pierre Galet, Petite Sirah is the French grape Durif going under an American alias. Durif was first cultivated in southern France in the late nineteenth century, and apparently imported soon afterwards to California, where records indicate that a nursery sold cuttings of something advertised as "petite sirah," a variation of a name used by *vignerons* in the Rhône to identify their better (because smaller and more concentrated) grapes. Pre-Prohibition California vintners loved it. Their most admired wines back then were "burgundy" or "claret" blends, not single varietals, and Petite's dark color, deep flavors, and aggressive tannins gave otherwise thin, pale wines power and verve. Rather than create such blends in the winery, many vintners preferred to grow them in the vineyard. That is, they interplanted Petite Sirah with other varieties, including Carignane, Mourvèdre, and Zinfandel. In short, an old Petite Sirah vineyard like the one at Stags' Leap might well include different clones of one variety—the original Durif—as well as specimens of other varieties altogether.

That other grapes were growing in this old, pre-Prohibition vineyard seemed clear to Brittan. Some plants simply looked different, with dissimilar leaves, shoots, and clusters, and he found it fairly easy to identify many of them. By the time he got in touch with Carole Meredith at UC Davis, he was able to tell her that Carignane, Grenache, and Mourvèdre were mixed in with the more prevalent Petite. What he still did not understand, and what he needed her help for, was the fact that some of the Petite vines looked alike yet yielded diverse wines.

Meredith had been researching this variety for some time. Her work had confirmed that Petite is genetically identical to Durif, but she did not know that variety's exact parentage. Using DNA fingerprinting on samples from vineyards throughout Northern California, she ultimately determined that it is a cross of Syrah from the Rhône and an obscure French variety called Peloursin from the Midi. Testing samples from Stags' Leap, Meredith found that the vineyard there contained both Syrah and Peloursin. The Peloursin vines looked almost exactly like the Durif ones growing beside them, but analysis proved them to be genetically separate. So too did Robert Brittan's palate, for these were the plants that yielded the wines that tasted so different.

Brittan's next challenge was to map the precise composition of the Stags' Leap vineyard. He purchased DNA testing equipment, hired a young technician with a degree in genetics, and began identifying the plant material. Younger blocks consisted of offspring from the original block, so the task proved extensive. Many vines needed to be replaced, some due to age, others to phylloxera, but Brittan refused to change anything until he knew exactly what each vine was, and so exactly what he should plant in its stead. Whenever possible, he tried to use cuttings from healthy vines in the vineyard, his goal being not just to maintain the multiplicity within the vineyard but actually to improve it.

Varietal composition only partially accounted for the diversity of plant material at Stags' Leap. Over the years of post-Prohibition neglect, many of the old vines had spawned new selections. Brittan wanted to know which of these produced the most consistently distinctive fruit. With only one harvest each year, finding this out took a long time, but once he identified specific vines as especially desirable, he used cuttings from them in his replanting program. After nearly fifteen years of work, Brittan finally can say what makes Stags' Leap Winery's Petite Syrah so special. "It's diversity and constancy together," a rich diversity of selections and varieties, combined with a constancy of place.

Many of the same traits found in the best Stags Leap District Cabernets characterize this Petite Sirah. It too marries power with finesse, and while its flavor profile and tannic structure are clearly different, it exhibits a similar interplay of primary and secondary attributes. These parallels evidently result from the locale. The Stags Leap District's morning fog, midday heat, and cool nights, coupled with its well-drained soils, work to extend the ripening process. As a result, the growing season tends to be longer than in other areas of the Napa Valley, with budbreak coming early and harvest relatively late, thus ensuring physiological maturity as well as sugar ripeness in the grapes. Vineyards on the eastern side of the district, particularly those abutting the craggy palisades that loom overhead, benefit most from these factors. Not surprisingly, the most arresting Stags Leap wines, all Cabernet-based save for this extraordinary exception, come from there. The Stags' Leap Winery produces Cabernet and Merlot as well as Petite from grapes grown on its historic estate. Those wines, while certainly good, have many worthy rivals. The Petite, however, stands alone.

Making this wine is something of a challenge. "Petite can be a more delicate wine than most people think," says Brittan, noting that managing tannins is the key to producing a graceful rendition. "If you don't remove the grapeskins at just the right time, you can easily create a monster." At harvest, the fruit is handpicked and transported to the winery in small bins, so as not to break the skins and prematurely release tannin. The winemakers then carefully control the fermentation, monitoring the temperature, using irrigators to keep the cap of grapeskins wet and supple, and slowing the process as much as possible so as to extract color and flavor without excessive astringency. The wine is aged in a combination of French and American oak barrels for about eighteen months. Upon release, it tends to display bold blue and black berry flavors and a firm structure, but with time spent in bottle develops a host of intriguing secondary notes. As it matures, it displays all the classic attributes of a truly noble red wine, no matter the varietal—depth, length, balance, and complexity. So, while it probably will never be as exalted (or expensive) as the best Stags Leap District Cabernets, it is very much their equal in terms of inherent quality.

All of this work, the research, replanting, attentive viticulture, and meticulous winemaking, costs money. In this regard, Stags' Leap has benefited enormously from Carl Doumani's decision to sell it in 1997 to Beringer Wine Estates, a company with deep pockets as well as a deep commitment to quality. Beringer immediately started a program of both restoration and expansion. Since then, the manorhouse and guest cottages have been refurbished, the gardens revived and replanted, and a series of caves for barrel aging tunneled into the hillsides. In addition, the winemakers have been given all the financial resources they need to make the best wines they can.

"The winery and vineyard were in bad shape when I came here," Robert Brittan recalls. "Carl and I worked hard to make things better, but with Beringer's help, everything is much, much better." In early 2005, after seventeen years at Stags' Leap, Brittan decided that he wanted to be his own boss. That's when he handed over the winemaking to Kevin Morrisey, his former assistant who had spent the previous two harvests working with Tony Soter at Etude, another prestigious winery in the Beringer stable. Morrisey considers stewardship of the estate and the wines that come from it his primary responsibility. Like Brittan, he will bottle a Stags' Leap proprietary blend—"Ne Cede Malis," sourced primarily from the oldest Petite Sirah vines, with small amounts of other grapes (including Grenache, Mourvedre, and Viognier) added to the cuvée. The name, which comes from a motto that Horace Chase inscribed in a stained-glass window in the manor house, means "do not give in to misfortune." It aptly describes both this once-neglected estate and this often-ignored grape.

As a varietal, Petite Sirah does have its admirers, a small but loyal group of fans who like their wines powerful and pungent, and so are happy to sacrifice subtlety for muscle. Most all the other top California renditions fit that profile. Whether coming from such producers as Concannon in Livermore, Foppiano in Sonoma, or Turley Cellars in

Napa, they tend to be extremely concentrated, sheer weight being what offsets the often fierce tannins. Such wines will always attract adherents, but they rarely can be considered world class, as they usually lack the necessary grace and complexity. In this respect, Stags' Leap Winery's Petite Syrah stands out. While there is nothing shy about it, there also is nothing simple or heavy, and no one can doubt that it acquires genuine finesse as it ages.

Petite probably never will be as chic as Cabernet or other international varieties, but of course tastes change and fashions come and go all the time. This wine demonstrates that, in the right hands and the right site, it can rank with the very best. Stags' Leap Winery's consistent track record, particularly in vintages over the last decade, suggests that Petite Sirah, so often confusing to consumers and disdained by vintners, can yield truly noble wines. As Robert Brittan and Kevin Morrisey know well, real class in the glass never perplexes.

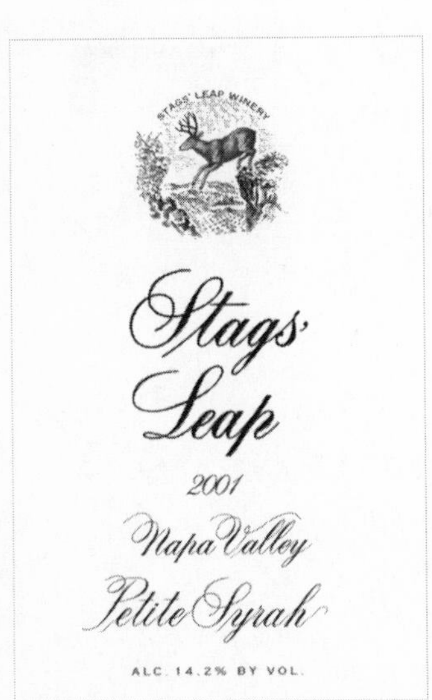

A NOTE ON VINTAGES:

More elegant than most Petites, Stags' Leap Winery's Petite Syrah benefits from about five years of cellaring—time in which the tannins soften and the secondary, non-fruit flavors emerge. It ages well, becoming quite leathery after fifteen years or so, and is probably at its best roughly a decade after the vintage. It can last, though, considerably longer still. Strong years include 1982, 1988, 1993, 1997, and 1999.

THE SUGGESTED PRICE FOR THE CURRENT 2002 RELEASE IS $35.

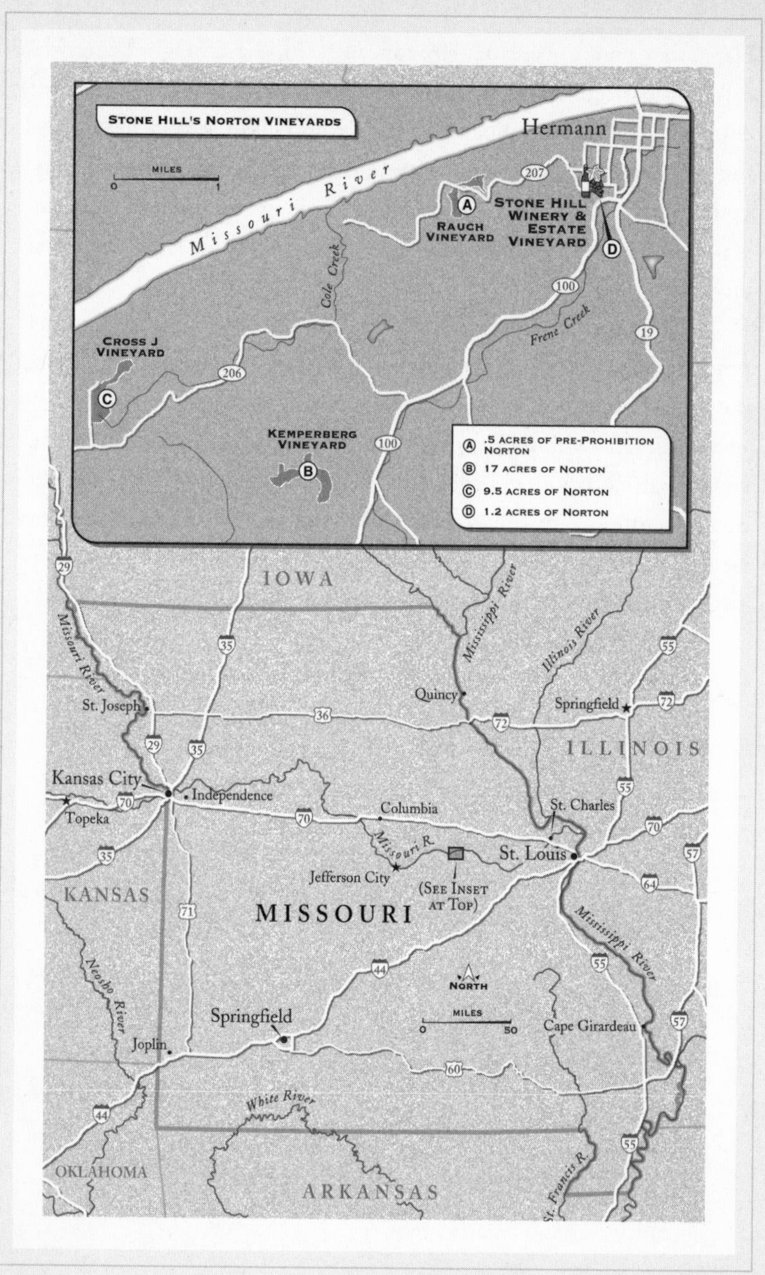

STONE HILL'S NORTON VINEYARDS

CHAPTER 37

Stone Hill Winery
Norton

Hermann, Missouri

...

Grapes grow wild in much of North America, the continent that Norse explorers once dubbed "Vineland." But compared with European vinifera grapes, native American ones yield usually undistinguished and often downright ghastly wines. Early settlers dubbed them "fox grapes" (because of their "rank Taste when ripe, resembling the Smell of a Fox," according to Robert Beverley's 1705 *History and Present State of Virginia*), and wines made from them can smell and taste something akin to nail polish or hairspray. Happily, cross-breeding can reduce the offputting foxiness in many varieties. Some primarily native crosses, like Catawba, were accidental. Others, like Delaware, were intentional. Still others were designed to temper native character with 50 percent vinifera parentage. Grapes such as Seyval and Vidal Blanc, Chambourcin and Vignoles are French-American hybrids, cultivated crosses between domestic and imported vines. And then there's Norton. Though a completely native variety, it produces the continent's finest dry non-vinifera wines—fruit-filled, robust reds that at

The Held family: (left to right) Tom, Betty, Jon, Jim, and Patty

their best display remarkably rich, nuanced flavors. These wines do not taste at all like they belong in a beauty parlor. "That's because Norton isn't a labrusca variety," explains Dave Johnson, the long-time winemaker at Stone Hill Winery in Hermann, Missouri. "When people say that Norton doesn't taste native, they mean it doesn't taste like other labrusca varietals—Concord, for example. But it's an aestivalis, not a labrusca grape. So I can't really say it doesn't taste native. It just tastes like Norton."

And that's all to the good. Fine examples of Norton are truly distinctive. Like top-flight vinifera reds, they offer seductive because subtle aromas, with fruit flavors that do not need to be sweet to be appealing. At the same time, unlike vinifera wines, those flavors do not so much resemble other fruits as taste of the grape itself. Norton is an American original, the one completely native variety capable of yielding wines that can hold their own with the world's best. And year after year, the finest Norton wines come from Stone Hill—where Dave Johnson and the Held family, the winery's owners, rediscovered it and then committed themselves to it. Together, they have championed this native's return to glory.

A little history is in order. Norton was widely grown east of the Rockies before Prohibition, and wines made from it were commonly considered to be among America's finest. In 1873, a Norton made just south of St. Louis was declared the "best red of all nations" at a prestigious international competition in Vienna; and soon afterward the celebrated British journalist and connoisseur Henry Vizetelly declared Norton the virtual equal of "first-rate Burgundy." The reason it performed so well, and merited comparison to top French vinifera bottlings, was that unlike most wines made from indigenous American grapes, Norton tasted, well, like *wine*. That is, when vinified dry, it displayed a genuinely vinous character—in Vizetelly's words, "full-bodied, deep-colored, aromatic, and somewhat astringent." And the reason it did that is that it belongs to a wholly different species from most of the other indigenous American grapes fermented into wine.

All grapevines belong to the genus *Vitis*, but that broad category includes around sixty separate species. And within each species, there can be numerous varieties—more, many more, varieties within a species that has been domesticated as opposed to one that grows wild. *Vitis vinifera*, the European wine grape, once grew wild. The fact that it has been cultivated for many millennia is what accounts for the remarkable number of varieties within it today—well over five thousand separate ones. In the early nineteenth century, when North American grapes first began to be cultivated in significant number, multiple varieties began to appear in nurseries. Most of these, however, were labrusca crosses or hybrids, labrusca being a common species in the eastern United States and one that is simple to propagate from cuttings. These were the grapes that smelled and tasted so foxy. By contrast, grapes of the aestivalis species, while equally native, do not root easily from cuttings and so were cultivated less frequently. Some people called them "summer grapes" or "pigeon grapes." Small and flavorful, they were rarely grown in vineyards but made for good eating out in the woods.

Sometime around 1820 a physician in Richmond, Virginia, discovered that this grape also made pretty good home "claret." It's unclear whether he first hybridized it from existing varieties or grew it from seed (the latter seems more likely, since it later would be sold as "Virginia Seedling"), but in order to propagate it, he needed to go to considerable effort and "layer" canes from each vine underground so as to force new roots to grow. By 1830 he had enough young vines to offer some for sale through William Prince's nursery in New York. Prince's catalogue listed it by name: Norton, named after Dr. D. N. Norton, the amateur Virginia vintner who first domesticated it.

Norton would go on to be cultivated widely in the Old Dominion in the decades after the Civil War. But it was grown with even greater success in Missouri, where German immigrants first planted it in the 1850s near the town of Hermann. Show-Me-State viticulture boomed in the second half of the nineteenth century. Missouri soon became the largest wine producer in the Union, its output surpassed by California only around 1900. Missourians grew other grapes and made other wines as well, but Norton was their pride and joy. "No red wine has ever been produced in America equal to that made by the Germans of Missouri," declared the humanitarian Charles Loring Brace. Ulysses S. Grant served it in the White House, and it regularly won medals in national and international competitions.

As grape growing and winemaking on the bluffs of the Missouri River, some ninety miles west of St. Louis, became big business, one Hermann winery became particularly prominent. The Stone Hill Wine Company grew to be the second largest in the country in the first decades of the new century, its production of table wine surpassed only by Italian Swiss Colony in California. And Norton, while not its largest volume wine, was certainly its most prestigious. Then, in 1919, with the passage of the Volstead Act and the advent of National Prohibition, everything screeched to a sudden halt—a cessation that would last for nearly five decades. That's because after Repeal, during all the years in which the country preferred spirits to wine, there simply was no market for a varietal like Norton. The few Americans who drank non-fortified wines bought either European ones or domestic wines that aped Old World models—American "burgundy," "chablis," and the like. Before long, hardly anyone knew what Norton was.

Jim and Betty Held certainly didn't when they started growing grapes. Family corn and hog farmers, they planted their first small vineyard—all Catawba—as an experimental, alternative crop in 1961. Fully ripe Catawba was then in high demand at New York wineries, and once their vines bore fruit, the Helds shipped the grapes east. The profits proved good, so they were receptive when the owner of the old Stone Hill Winery proposed that they try to make wine there. By then, the impressive redbrick facility overlooking Hermann had fallen into disrepair. The vaulted cellars were being used to grow mushrooms, not age wine, but the Helds were intrigued by the possibility of restoring it. They leased the property in 1965, and then a few years later purchased it. In the meantime, they acquired more vineyard land and produced the first legal, commercial Missouri wine since Prohibition.

Marketing Missouri wine was difficult at first. A few of the old bootleggers in the area told Jim Held to get gallon jugs, since no one would buy anything in little wine bottles. Before long, though, the Helds ran out of little bottles. The local market grew slowly but steadily, impelled in large measure by the family's hard work—not only in the winery but also in Hermann, where they played a leading role in turning this sleepy Germanic town into a tourist center. They promoted Hermann's Octoberfest in the fall and Maifest in the spring, started a restaurant where they held wine and food dinners (including a "beast feast," featuring local game), and opened the winery year-round for tours—often led by one of the Held children. By the mid-1970s, Stone Hill was producing some 25,000 cases of wine annually. Soon, the oldest son, Jon, went west to study oenology at Cal State Fresno. He would be followed by his sister, Patty, and his brother, Tom—and even today Stone Hill, with production over 90,000 cases, remains very much a family affair.

Jim Held taught himself the rudiments of winemaking when he came to Stone Hill. From the start he was intrigued by Norton, largely due to its reputation among local home winemakers. One of his first wines was "Held's Virginia Seedling," a dry red in a Germanic green bottle. He changed the name on the label to Norton after one too many customers asked him why he was selling Virginia wine in Missouri; but the wine proved popular no matter its moniker. Initially it was aged in used whiskey barrels, then later in old, 1,000-gallon casks. Though lighter and less compelling than today's rendition, it always sold out. Jon Held remembers that his parents only opened it on special occasions at home, and then recounts how he turned more than a few heads with bottles of Stone Hill Norton during his student days in California. No one there knew anything about this grape, but they sure liked the wine.

By 1976, Jim Held's business had grown too large for one man to keep doing everything all at once. Because he was more a farmer than a cellarmaster at heart, he decided to hire a full-time winemaker. Joe Norman, a UC Davis graduate, was Stone Hill's first non-family vintner; but after two years, in which Norman found he couldn't take the harsh midwestern winters, Dave Johnson, fresh from the wine and grape program at Michigan State, came aboard. Johnson also knew little about Norton. "But I started reading about it," he remembers, "in the old, pre-Prohibition books, where all the authors spoke so highly about it.

Everyone called it the best American red grape for making fine red wines." At that point, the few other wineries with Norton tended either to use it in blends or to produce a pale, sweet wine by diluting the juice with water and adding sugar to the must. "No one was making Norton the way the literature described it," recalls Johnson. He wanted to try. So, in 1979, he and Jim Held decided to make a more serious red wine from old-vine Norton.

Johnson handled the grapes for this wine much as he knew vintners in Bordeaux handle Cabernet or Merlot, with a lengthy fermentation on the skins and an extended period of aging in small oak barrels. The results were outstanding. "Folks loved it," he says. Before long, people who had never even thought to drink Missouri wine were clamoring for Norton. The market was still local, as production remained very small, but in St. Louis and to a lesser degree Kansas City and Chicago, knowledgeable wine consumers and connoisseurs came to recognize Stone Hill Norton as something special. So too did other ambitious vintners—in Missouri, Arkansas, and in the variety's birthplace, Virginia, all sources today of fine dry red Norton. Looking back, Johnson can note with satisfaction: "We were the ones who got the ball rolling. That's not to say it wouldn't have happened without us. But we were the ones who got Norton started again as a serious wine varietal."

Norton is a relatively easy grape to grow in Missouri, a state in which many other varieties struggle to survive. The combination of harsh winters and hot, humid summers can wreck havoc in vineyards, especially since temperatures often fluctuate wildly within a short period of time. "A warm spell followed by a deep freeze can be really hard on vines," says Johnson. "But Norton, being native, does okay with it." Part of the variety's appeal also comes from its being extremely resistant to fungus—a constant headache with other grapes in Missouri. In the winery, however, Norton can prove difficult. That's because its combination of high acid and high ph is something of a rarity, and the winemaker always runs the risk of spoilage. "You have to watch it very carefully," notes Johnson, "and you need to know the chemistry of what's happening at any given time." But if handled with care and attention, Norton can yield beguiling wines.

When young, Stone Hill Nortons taste intensely fruity—grapey to be sure, but also redolent with an aroma resembling ripe blueberries. With time, the fruit calms down, and the wines develop earthy, even meaty secondary flavors, in this regard something like wines from the southern Rhône Valley in France. At a vertical tasting held in December 2004, the most impressive because most complete and complex wine was from 1994, and both Johnson and Jon Held agree that in a good vintage, Stone Hill Norton needs five to ten years to reveal all its charms.

"Yes, it's an easy grape to grow," argues Johnson, "but I'm not sure that Norton's easy to grow if you want to make the best wine." Because the variety's revival is still nascent, no one yet has conducted much research on it. "It's still very much a seat-of-the-pants effort," he continues. "We have to base many of our decisions on research that's been conducted on other grapes from other species!"

Much of that effort is being conducted at Stone Hill. Jon Held is now the general manager, and he is even more committed to Norton than his father was before him. Upon his return to Hermann from Fresno, he pushed for more planting, and new blocks of Norton were added in 1984, 1987, 1995, 1997, and 2002, with still more planned for 2006. The family now owns seven estate vineyards, four of which contain Norton. In addition to the estate vineyard beside the winery, they farm a small, half-acre plot of old, pre-Prohibition vines at the Rauch Vineyard, and two larger vineyards west of town, Cross and Kemperberg. "We've learned a lot over the years," Held notes. For one, Norton grows best in light-colored, fine-grained loess soils that were once windblown from what is now the Missouri River bottom. For another, because the variety can be quite vigorous, he thins the shoots early in the growing season, aiming to effect a balance between fruit and vegetative growth and increase both ventilation and sun exposure. Stone Hill's current fertility regime—organic compost combined with the total avoidance of synthetic fertilizers and herbicides—further lowers vigor and improves fruit quality.

Similar adjustments have taken place in the winery. Norton can be quite aggressive, so Dave Johnson tries to treat it gently during fermentation—racking some tanks and then returning the juice instead of simply pumping the fermenting wine over the cap of skins and seeds, thus extracting a minimal amount of harsh tannins. Rather than move the young wine to cask immediately after fermentation, he keeps it in tank through the winter, thus allowing some of the tartaric compounds to settle out. He then puts it in barrel—a mix of French and American oak, roughly a third new each year. "It's a grape that can stand up to oak," he says. Tasting young wines from cask bears him out. When grown and vinified well, Norton displays a rich fruitiness that isn't at all overwhelmed by wood.

Stone Hill today only makes some five thousand cases of Norton each year. Jon Held would like to increase production, as his stated goal is to see the winery "repositioned to the grand stature it held in the years prior to Prohibition." To realize as much, he knows that he needs to get more people to sample the wine—not just locals but knowledgeable wine drinkers far afield. At present, two thirds of Stone Hill's total output is sold through the company's three Missouri retail outlets (in Hermann, Branson, and St. Florence), and the company's wines are available through wholesalers in only five states—Missouri, Arkansas, California, Illinois, and Kansas. "We need to grow that side of the business if we're going to be taken as seriously as we want to be," Held acknowledges.

Proof of his and his family's seriousness can be found in the impressive array of medals Stone Hill wins in wine competitions: over 250 in 2004 alone. Many of those awards are given to wines other than Norton; Stone Hill's luscious late harvest Vignoles, for example, its impressive *méthode champenoise* Vidal-based sparkler, and its full-flavored Port (which is made with Norton grapes). But much as has been true in Hermann, Missouri, for some 150 years, dry red Norton retains pride of place.

Because this wine has been so good for so long, vintners elsewhere have been inspired to follow its lead. Augusta and Hermanhoff in Missouri, as well as Chrysallis and Horton in Virginia, make some excellent wines from Norton these days, as does Cowie from time to time in Arkansas (where confusingly enough, the grape often is called

Cynthiana). Production at all these wineries is small, so many American wine lovers still don't know Norton. But as more good wines from conscientious producers come onto the market, more and more of them surely will. For unlike any European vinifera varietal, this is America's own grape and own wine. Some fifty years ago, it was nearly lost. But thanks to the pioneering work of the Held family and Dave Johnson, the native has returned—as delicious as ever.

A NOTE ON VINTAGES:

Norton needs time. When young, it tastes almost too fruity, something like blueberry jam. But with seven to ten years of bottle age, spicy, peppery aromas emerge, and the wine becomes leaner, longer, and more refined. Stone Hill's Nortons from strong vintages like 1989, 1992, 1994, 1999, 2000, and 2001 need that bottle age to show their best.

THE SUGGESTED PRICE FOR THE CURRENT 2003 VINTAGE IS $18.

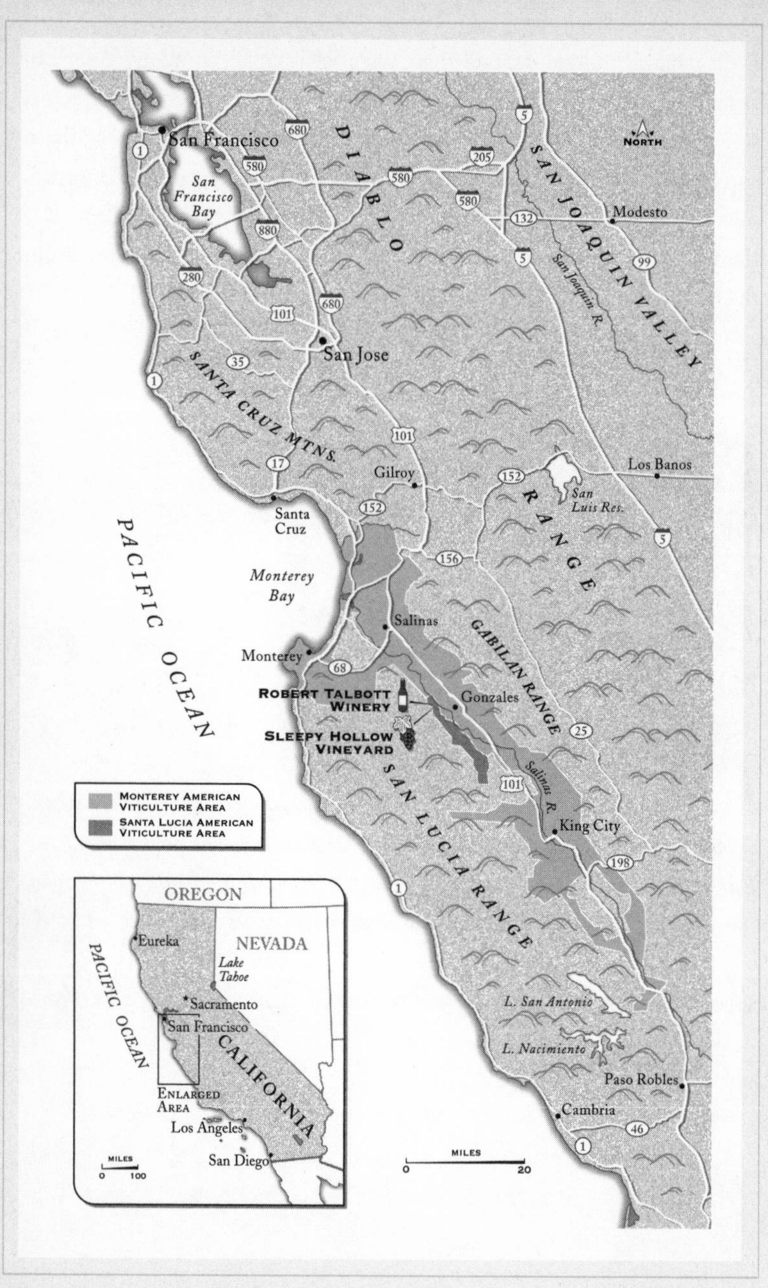

TALBOTT VINEYARDS AND THE MONTEREY COUNTY AVAs

CHAPTER 38

TALBOTT VINEYARDS CHARDONNAY, SLEEPY HOLLOW VINEYARD

Monterey County, California

...

"We still have to work hard to sell Monterey wine," says Robb Talbott. "Bad news lingers a long time." Talbott is the founder and president of Talbott Vineyards in the Santa Lucia Highlands, a low-lying bench on the western edge of the Salinas Valley. Most of Monterey County's 45,000 vineyard acres lie on the valley floor, where grapes grow alongside lettuce and broccoli in what has been called America's salad bowl. Vast, flat tracts of fertile land yield massive amounts of correct but often characterless wine, the majority of which is used by California producers in inexpensive, big-volume blends. Back in the 1970s, when large-scale viticulture first came to Monterey, many of those vineyards were planted to red grapes, and the resulting green, weedy wines came to be known as "Monterey veggies." Things improved when more white varieties were planted, but like the warmer Central Valley, the Salinas Valley still serves largely as a fruitful source of good but rarely outstanding grapes for wineries situated elsewhere. Robb Talbott has lived almost all his life in Monterey, and he

Robb Talbott

believes passionately in the region's potential for high-quality grapes and wine. He knows, though, that only a handful of growers share his vision, success in Salinas, as in San Joaquin, often being measured simply in terms of volume. "We have to work hard to get people to understand," he says, "but certain places in Monterey can yield something special, something truly unique."

At Talbott's Sleepy Hollow Vineyard, Chardonnay is what proves special. This vineyard-designated, estate wine displays the sort of ripe tropical fruit flavors typically associated with top New World Chardonnays, as well as mineral ones more often characteristic of white Burgundies, and so manages to taste both richly concentrated and subtly nuanced. Made from grapes grown in selected, naturally low-yielding vineyard blocks, it has been prized by those in the know for nearly twenty years now. Its unquestioned quality bespeaks both accomplishment and ambition—what already has been achieved in Monterey, and what more may be in the future.

In Monterey, as in so many vineyard regions, the most distinctive wines come from grapes grown on the hillsides, where the soils are rocky and sparse, and vines have to struggle to bear fruit. On the eastern side of the Salinas Valley, the limestone-rich Chalone Vineyard has a long history of producing such wines, while on the northwestern flank, the most individualistic wines come from vineyards in the Santa Lucia Highlands Viticultural Area. This AVA is a nearly twenty-mile sliver of land, separated from the valley floor by a visible fault. Its east-facing vineyards are a series of alluvial fans containing well-drained loam and gravel soils. Notable producers include Mer Soleil and Morgan in addition to Talbott, and while Santa Lucia Pinot Noir shows considerable potential, Chardonnay is the region's proven star. This variety does so well because the soils compel each vine's roots to extend deep below ground in a search for nutrients, with the result that subsoil minerals contribute complexity to the wines. In addition, the Monterey Bay, its cold waters less than twenty miles away, profoundly affects the vines. Morning fog blankets these sloping, northeast-facing vineyards, and strong marine breezes sweep through every afternoon, keeping temperatures low and allowing the grapes to retain high levels of acidity. In turn, that acidity is what gives the wines their beguiling combination of richness and refinement.

In the case of Talbott's Sleepy Hollow Chardonnay, even after complete malolactic fermentation and extended *sur lie* barrel aging, the wine tastes beautifully balanced, with plenty of acidity and structure to support the almost opulent fruit flavors. Though big and bold, it impresses most of all with its harmony, and never seems heavy or coarse. As Robb Talbott says, the place—in Monterey County, but on the Santa Lucia bench so up away from the salad bowl—is special.

The 400-acre Sleepy Hollow Vineyard was first planted in the early 1970s, one of the initial viticultural ventures in the Monterey hills. "It was a happy accident," says Sam Balderas, who has managed the Talbott vineyards and has made the Talbott wines for nearly all of the company's history. Growers didn't plant on the Santa Lucia bench because they knew the resulting wines would be good. "They planted on the hillsides," he explains, "because it was just grazing land. And grazing land was cheaper than the more fertile agricultural land on the valley floor. No one knew at the time that the wines would be better."

Sleepy Hollow at that point was owned by a group of businessmen from near San Francisco who were looking to profit from the emerging American wine boom. A well-publicized Bank of America economic forecast had promoted grape growing as an investment, and people from far and near were sheltering income in California vineyard land. In Monterey, Sleepy Hollow was small fry when compared with the much bigger vineyards going in to the south and east. The largest was San Bernabe, nearly 8,000 acres of vines in the gently rolling swales that extend down from the hills to the flat Salinas Valley floor. Planted between 1972 and 1974, and financed initially by Prudential Insurance in New Jersey, San Bernabe is today owned by Delicato Vineyards, and produces fine but largely unexceptional fruit.

That's not the case at Sleepy Hollow. Though the absentee owners were interested in profit more than prestige, they soon came to realize that their vineyard was capable of growing unusually good grapes. For nearly twenty years, they sold those grapes to a myriad of companies, including large producers like Gallo and Fetzer, and small ones like Talbott. The label did not yet say so, but Talbott's Chardonnay was sourced exclusively from Sleepy Hollow beginning with the winery's third vintage, in 1985. That wine received critical plaudits; Robert Parker called it "full-bodied, creamy and weighty," and *The Connoisseur's Guide* dubbed it one of the potentially best in California—quite a claim for a wine from Monterey. The vineyard owners took note, and when they decided to sell the property and collect their profit, they offered Robb Talbott first refusal.

"I'll never forget getting that phone call," Talbott says. "The fellow's name was Tom Wolfe. He was one of the owners, the spokesman for the group. He called me out of the blue and said, 'Well, Robb, I like what you do with our vineyard, so I'll give you the first shot.' But then he told me that I only had two days to decide, because there was a big wine company all ready to buy, waiting right behind me." This was in the summer of 1994. The non-negotiable price was $4 million, and while the name of the big company was never officially revealed, Talbott knew that whoever it was (he guessed Kendall-Jackson) would want to keep all the grapes. He asked Sam Balderas whether they could continue to make as good a wine, in the same style, without grapes from this vineyard. The answer came back simple and short—no. "So I swallowed hard and we bought it. It scared me to have to go to the bank for so much money, but we just needed this vineyard." Beginning with the 1993 vintage, the first released with the land under Talbott ownership, their Chardonnay has carried the Sleepy Hollow name on the label.

"We had to do a lot of work when we got this vineyard," remembers Balderas. Wolfe and the other absentee owners had used various farming companies to manage Sleepy Hollow over the years, with different blocks cared for differently, depending on who had contracted for the fruit at what price. As a result, much of the property was in shambles, with greasewood trees sprouting up between the rows, and many of the vines in chaotic sprawl. Balderas and his team cleaned away the unwanted undergrowth, pruned severely, and replaced much of the trellising. In addition, they began to replant some blocks in a denser pattern, and to graft some of the less successful varietals, such as Gewurztraminer, to Chardonnay, Pinot Noir, and later Syrah.

Sleepy Hollow is really two separate parcels, designated unromantically as "SH A" and "SH B." They share much the same soil composition and exposure, but Balderas usually only picks grapes from two blocks of "SH B" for Talbott Chardonnay, one at the highest point in the vineyard, the other at the lowest. He uses Chardonnay from "SH A" for one of the winery's other labels, Logan, and the resulting wine is rich but youthful, a less riveting rendition of both the varietal and the site. Balderas also makes Pinot Noir from Sleepy Hollow grapes, but he uses less than 20 percent of all the fruit that grows there for all the Talbott and Logan wines. The rest continues to be sold to other producers, some of whom now use the vineyard designation with their own wines. "We want to build the Sleepy Hollow name as well as our own family name," explains Robb Talbott. That's why he has trademarked it, so that wineries need to receive his permission to print it on their labels. "We're happy when other good wines announce that they come from Sleepy Hollow," says Balderas. "We just want to be sure they're really good."

Sam Balderas came to Talbott Vineyards in 1985. An immigrant from Mexico, he already had worked with vines and wines for nearly a quarter century, beginning when he first hoed weeds as a summer job for Martin Ray in Santa Cruz, and continuing when he went on to make wine for Mirassou and then Stony Ridge. Those last two were big companies, and while Balderas enjoyed the challenge of a large production operation, he wanted to try something new. In fact, he was ready to change careers completely and move to Southern California, where he had an offer to manage a water filtration company, when Robb Talbott offered him a job. "I saw his commitment to quality," Balderas says, "and I liked it a lot. So I decided to stay." That commitment echoed his experience at Martin Ray. He had worked in various capacities for the celebrated but idiosyncratic vintner for some thirteen years, and while he shakes his head and smiles wryly at the memory of Ray's quirks, he also credits his time there with teaching him how to make wine in a hands-on, artistic manner. Today, Balderas manages a relatively large property, some 600 acres, including Talbott's two other vineyards, but a relatively small winery, some 28,000 cases of total production, roughly 9,500 of which contain bottles of Sleepy Hollow Chardonnay.

Much like Martin Ray, Balderas's approach to Chardonnay is decidedly Burgundian. He ferments it in small French oak barrels, only a third of which are new. He encourages the advent of malolactic fermentation very early in the process, so that both the primary alcoholic fermentation and this second bacterial one can finish together. He then leaves the wine to age for a full year, stirring the spent yeast cells, or lees, regularly, and topping each barrel every three weeks or so. He samples it frequently, and finds that the young wine invariably develops slowly. "There's no real change in flavor over the first six months," he says, "but lots happens toward the end. That's when the different parts start coming together." At that point, Balderas makes a preliminary blend, almost always declassifying a small percentage, and transfers the selected lots, lees and all, into a holding tank, where they rest for a month or so before being bottled. Though the wine could then be sent out for sale, Balderas holds it back, so that there always are at least two years between harvest and market. "It needs time to harmonize," he explains.

Harmony, in fact, is a hallmark of Talbott Sleepy Hollow Chardonnay. Clearly Californian in its forward fruit, the wine also displays a distinct minerality, evident in its simultaneously flinty and floral aromas as well as its intriguing layers of secondary flavors. Its appeal, though, comes not just from a multiplicity of sensory components but from their seamless integration, something that becomes especially evident as time passes. Once its initial exuberance settles into a refined middle age, five or six years after the vintage, it tastes remarkably subtle and sophisticated. The 1997, for example, that I sampled at the winery in early 2004, proved stunning, each element of aroma, flavor, and structure in near-perfect symmetry. And the 1990, tasted blind in October 1997 as part of a *Wine Spectator* California versus Burgundy "Chardonnay challenge," was given a perfect score of 100 points by Per-Henrik Mansson, the magazine's Burgundy expert. He mistook it for a *grand cru* from the Côte de Beaune, and reported that the wine "took my palate and emotions by storm."

The 1990 vintage was the first fashioned at the current winery, located on River Road, just beneath the "SH A" vineyard. Before then, the Talbott wines had been made in a facility in the Carmel Valley, on the other side of the Santa Lucia Highlands, near Robb Talbott's home. Originally a cabin he built himself, that now spacious house sits below another vineyard, "Diamond T," which is the source of yet another critically acclaimed Talbott wine. Diamond T Estate Chardonnay is even more blatantly Burgundy-inspired, as Robb planted the rocky, almost topsoil-free property with a Corton-Charlemagne clone back in 1982. That was the year in which his parents, who ran a successful fashion business, decided to diversify into grapes and wine. They gave him free rein to run the new venture. "I had an itch," he recalls. "I wanted to do something creative. I wanted to make something from scratch." He was thirty-four years old, and although he had enjoyed success in various ventures, everything from teaching to beekeeping to restoring antique cars and trucks, he had not yet found a calling. Wine, specifically Monterey wine, turned out to be it. "I found my passion," he says. "It got under my skin. That itch just never went away."

From the very beginning, Talbott's goal was to prove that Monterey could grow wines of extremely high quality. As he puts it, "I wanted to try to combine this locale with time-proven methods, and see if we could produce something unique." That focus on the singular and distinctive is what led him over the Santa Lucia Highlands to Sleepy Hollow. In turn, the promise of the grapes he purchased there compelled him to buy land and then build a winery, and when the opportunity arose, to purchase Sleepy Hollow itself. "We found out," he says with evident pride, "that this place really is special. Quality drove us here." A great many Monterey wines, including plenty made with hillside grapes, taste pleasant enough but evoke no real sense of place, and so seem generic rather than individualistic. "*Terroir* disappears under bad winemaking," says Talbott. "Some wines are representative of their mini-climates. Others are not." Sam

Balderas is even more blunt. When asked what it will take for Monterey to become better known as a source of truly fine wine, he responds simply: "Grow fewer grapes per acre, and make better wines."

Talbott Vineyards is not the only producer making first-rate wines from grapes grown in Monterey. Using Santa Lucia fruit, sometimes from Sleepy Hollow, small producers like Arcadian, Barnett, and Testarossa are crafting some delicious wines, primarily Chardonnays and Pinot Noirs. Dan Lee at the Morgan Winery, located in the town of Salinas, has long bought grapes from growers up and down the Santa Lucia bench. He now owns vineyard land himself, and the wines from Morgan can be superb. And Chuck Wagner has set up shop at the northern edge of the Santa Lucia AVA, right next to Talbott. A Cabernet specialist at Caymus Vineyards in the Napa Valley, Wagner grows Chardonnay in Monterey, and his Mer Soleil offerings, rich, ripe, and intensely flavored, offer further proof that these hillsides can yield superlative grapes and wines.

Still, as Robb Talbott notes wryly, few consumers think of Monterey or Santa Lucia as being in the same league as Napa or Sonoma. "I know our wines would be scored higher if we were located up there, even if we still sourced the grapes from here," he maintains. "There's such prestige in Napa. We're five miles from Gonzales. Who's ever heard of Gonzales?" But then he pauses, and acknowledges an advantage in seclusion. With prestige comes pressure—the pressure to conform to expectations, to follow trends, to try to make wines in the latest style or mode. "Not us," he says. "We don't copy. You never achieve real success by copying." Talbott's may be a minority voice in Monterey, but the wine that results from his and Sam Balderas's shared commitment is a proven winner—one of the entire country's, not just this one California county's, best.

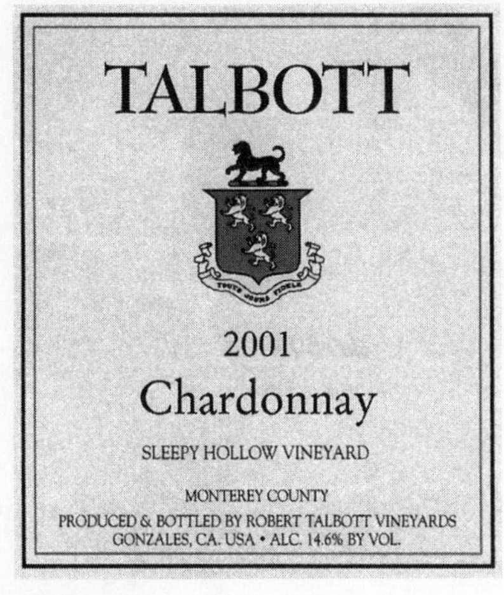

A NOTE ON VINTAGES:

Talbott Sleepy Hollow Chardonnay ages surprisingly well, gaining mineral-tinged complexity with time in bottle. Still, holding on to it for more than ten years is something of a gamble, as the wine probably tastes best about five to eight years after the vintage. Particularly strong years for this Chardonnay include 1990, 1994, 1996, 1997, and 2001.

THE SUGGESTED PRICE FOR THE CURRENT 2002 RELEASE IS $42.

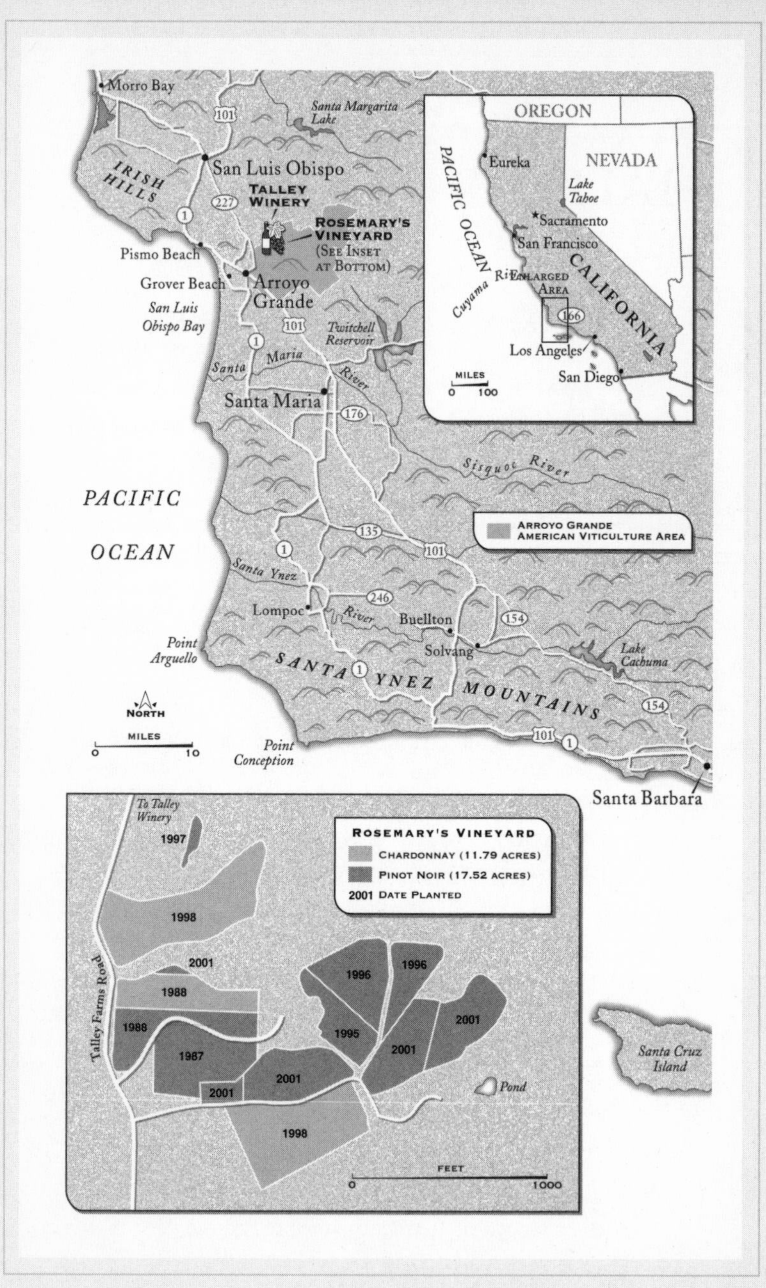

ROSEMARY'S VINEYARD, IN THE ARROYO GRANDE AVA

CHAPTER 39

Talley Vineyards Chardonnay, Rosemary's Vineyard

Arroyo Grande Valley, California

...

"We're farmers," says Brian Talley with a shrug of his shoulders. "Maybe that explains why we aren't as flamboyant as some others in the wine business." The Talley family has been growing fruit and vegetables in California's Arroyo Grande Valley for nearly sixty years. Bell peppers are their biggest crop, and Talley Farms is one of the state's prime pepper producers, shipping up to seven thousand boxes each day during the harvest. The Talleys have been growing grapes only since 1982, and wine makes up a small percentage of their family business. Still, they are extremely proud of it. Though not prone to self-promotion, their goal is to produce estate-grown Chardonnay and Pinot Noir at the highest level. They let their wines do the proverbial talking, and their single-vineyard bottlings from the Rincon and Rosemary's vineyards frequently declare themselves the qualitative equal of the country's very best.

Steve Rasmussen

The Talley Pinots taste quite rich, with forward fruit flavors, a spicy undertone, and a silky texture, while the Chardonnays seem even more nuanced, simultaneously ripe and refined. The Rosemary's Vineyard Chardonnay in particular stands out because it combines exuberant fruit with elegance and finesse. Fairly full-bodied, it exhibits superb balance and ages effortlessly, making it one of the very finest renditions of America's most popular (and widely planted) white varietal. "It's the vineyard," Brian Talley says simply, when asked to account for the wine's exceptional character. "That's what this vineyard gives." But no vineyard simply bequeaths wine of this quality, and the rich complexity of Rosemary's Vineyard Chardonnay has as much to do with how the Talleys treat it as with the site itself. The third-generation son to make his career on the farm, Brian acknowledges as much when he notes the learning curve that he and his family underwent with wine. When they planted their first vineyards, they treated the grapes like any other crop—like avocados, or lemons, or peppers. Not anymore. "We've learned," he explains, "that we have to think of what we do as wine growing, not grape growing. It's a different approach, a whole different mentality."

The difference is in part a matter of yield—only slightly more than 2 tons per acre at Rosemary's Vineyard. Unlike other fruits, an abundant crop of wine grapes often produces an inferior result. That's because low-vigor vines tend to produce more concentrated, flavorful grapes, and concentration in the fruit translates into both intensity and complexity in the wine. But while high quality requires low yields, a small crop is by itself no guarantee of merit. Without proper vineyard management, a low-yielding site can still produce monolithic wines, the grapes being either under- or overripe. The issue of yield, then, is really an issue of balance—of having the right amount of grapes per vine (as well as per acre) so that the vineyard experiences neither undue stress nor excessive growth. And that involves getting just the right amount of light on the leaves and grapes, without so much shade as to result in green flavors, or so much sunshine as to produce raisined ones. Each growing season brings with it new weather conditions, so none of this can be accomplished by following a formula. Instead, a conscientious grower needs to pay attention to detail, and to keep looking ahead, foresight being perhaps the most essential part of vineyard management.

The guiding principle at Talley is sustainable viticulture, minimizing the use of pesticides, utilizing compost and cover crops, and coaxing rather than compelling nature to yield superior fruit and then superior wine. With this sort of farming, as Brian Talley notes, it's essential to remember always that grapes are not the ultimate crop. Wine is.

The Talley family enjoys one big advantage when it comes to farming their estate vineyards: a trained, experienced labor force. Unlike other comparably sized wineries (total production is about 15,000 cases), the Talleys do not have to rely on seasonal or migrant workers. Instead, because the vegetable operation requires year-round attention, full-time employees do all the actual hands-on work in the vineyards. They know the vines intimately, and under the watchful eyes of vineyard manager Rodolfo Romero and winemaker Steve Rasmussen, they work throughout the year with a sole goal—ever-improved quality. From planting cover crops in fall, pruning during the dormant winter months, then removing shoots, leaves, and unripe clusters during the summer, and finally harvesting the grapes, their objective is simply to nurse the vineyards so as to produce optimally mature fruit, and then optimally expressive wines.

Commercial viticulture in what is now the Arroyo Grande Viticultural Area has a long if somewhat spotty history, beginning in the 1880s in the warm, eastern edge of the valley, a source then as now of some impressive Zinfandels. Planting in the cooler western side of Arroyo Grande, much as in the neighboring Edna Valley, is a more recent phenomenon, dating only from the 1970s, when Chardonnay as a varietal first began its remarkable surge in popularity. Though Talley is not the region's only small-volume, high-quality producer, most grape growing takes place on a considerably larger scale. Both of these AVAs are located in the southern half of San Luis Obispo County, a largely agricultural region with over 3,000 acres under vine. Wine grapes are San Luis Obispo' s leading crop, with Chardonnay accounting for the majority of the planting. Though much of the fruit tastes rich and ripe, few if any of the wines approach the quality of the Chardonnay from Rosemary's Vineyard.

San Luis Obispo County is the heart of California's prodigious Central Coast, the source of much of the juice that went into big-production "fighting varietal" Chardonnays in the 1980s and 1990s, and much that today goes into "coastal" wines from big producers, many sporting Napa or Sonoma addresses. These Chardonnays tend to taste fun and fruity, with more than a hint of sweetness. Bright and bouncy, they're "good but simple," notes Steve Rasmussen. He should know. Having worked four harvests in Napa, he first came to the Central Coast in 1985 as the winemaker at Corbett Canyon Vineyards, one of the era's more successful "fighting varietal" producers. "The grape grows pretty easily here," he notes, "and most of the wines are easy to enjoy. They have the kind of tropical fruit flavors that lots of people want when they order a glass of Chardonnay. Here and there, though, there are some special spots, places where you can push the envelope. Wines from those places offer much more, and Rosemary's Vineyard is one of them."

Rosemary's is located on a hillside surrounding Brian Talley's childhood home. His parents, Don and Rosemary, were the ones who first planted grapes on the property, their original idea being to sell the fruit much as they sold the peppers and other produce they grew. But their timing proved bad, as the mid-1980s saw a glut of grapes come on the market, so they decided to use some of the crop to make their own wine. "I think Dad secretly had that idea from the start," Brian says with a smile. "He just didn't tell anyone." Rosemary's was their second site, and they planted it with the benefit of lessons learned at Rincon, the original Talley vineyard located beside the current winery. Those lessons included a number of varietal and clonal trials. By 1987, when the first vines went in the ground at Rosemary's, they had become convinced that Chardonnay and Pinot Noir (not Riesling or Sauvignon Blanc, Semillon, Melon, or Cabernet Franc, small blocks of which all still grow in Rincon) were the best varieties to plant. As Brian explains, "Dad's principle is that a farmer should stick with what grows best in his place. By the time we planted Rosemary's, we knew that Chardonnay and Pinot made the best wines here."

Rosemary's is a slightly cooler vineyard than Rincon because it's located a mile or so closer to the ocean. Its soils are rocky, with a layer of fragmented sandstone beneath the surface that evidently contributes mineral-tinged aromas and flavors to wines made from grapes grown there. For the initial block of Chardonnay, two acres directly in front of the family house, the Talleys used clone 4 nursery stock, a UC Davis selection sometimes said not to be especially good for premium wine because of its tendency to be vigorous in warm locales. This site, however, is cool. The Talleys knew from decades of farming experience that Arroyo Grande's climate would hold the yields in check, and so judged clone 4 to be the appropriate choice. Ten years later, when they planted nine more acres of Chardonnay at Rosemary's, they did use a number of other clones and selections. The original block, though, still produces superior fruit and consistently makes up most of the vineyard-designated wine. Chardonnay, though, only accounts for about a third of the vineyard, the majority being Pinot Noir.

"I have to tell you," confesses Steve Rasmussen, "I didn't like Rosemary's Chardonnay in the beginning." The grapes from this vineyard have abundant acidity and quite low levels of nitrogen. As a result, yeasts find it hard to get going, and fermentations have a tendency to stick or stop altogether—a winemaking nightmare. "I didn't think it was worth it," Rasmussen admits. "My advice back then was to graft the whole vineyard over to Pinot." Thankfully, the Talleys didn't take that advice. Brian was running the wine side of the business by then, and he had faith in the vineyard's potential for both grape varieties. By 1994, the fourth viable crop, it had become clear that his faith was justified, as the Chardonnay from Rosemary's Vineyard was proving very special. Unlike the vast majority of Central Coast renditions, it did not taste especially tropical. Nor was it particularly round or lush. Instead, it had a tight structure, and the flavors more closely resembled lemons and apples—more akin to a top Burgundy than to other Californians.

"We all learned that we had to think about this wine differently," Rasmussen recalls. "Tasting it was all about tasting potential. It wasn't like most wines from around here. But you just knew it was going to get better and better." It did. At a retrospective tasting of all of the Rosemary's Vineyard Chardonnays held in May 2004, this initial release impressed me with its clean aromas, firm backbone, and fresh flavors.

Though not as complex as the 1996 or 1998, both of which approached perfection that day, it was still going strong. Very few ten-year-old American Chardonnays can make that claim.

According to Rasmussen, "our goal isn't really to make a wine to age. It's to make the best wine we can from the vineyard. It just so happens that with this vineyard and this grape, the wine needs time." The reason surely is the high acid level, but the reason for that is harder to discern. Part of the explanation has to do with the soil at Rosemary's—white, rocky sandstone and loam. Part involves the steep slope, which provides excellent drainage. Then there is the relatively unsheltered location, less than eight miles from the Pacific, so open to cool, sometimes stiff ocean breezes every afternoon. Add the long, extended growing season, with budbreak coming as early as mid-February but harvest not arriving until early October. The grapes at Rosemary's mature slowly, gaining sugar incrementally. Unlike Chardonnay grown in a warmer site, the acid level does not decrease due to heat spikes. All of these factors (and more) combine to produce a crop that, when managed properly in both vineyard and winery, results in a wine that impresses with both richness and refinement. "Rosemary's at its best gives you an impression of austerity, even leanness," says Rasmussen, now fully converted to its charm, "but when you put it in your mouth, it feels rich and luxurious." That combination is what makes it so special.

Because fermentation can be difficult, sometimes taking a full year to complete, Rasmussen uses cultured rather than wild yeasts when making this wine. All of his other vinification techniques, however, are old-fashioned. The grapes are whole-cluster-pressed and fermented in French oak, roughly a third of the barrels being new each year. The lees are stirred frequently, both to help impart a layer of creaminess to the wine and to encourage the alcoholic fermentation. "It's tricky," he explains. "Because I refuse to filter it before bottling, I have to make sure it's completely dry. But it often doesn't want to get there. I've learned to be very, very patient with it." The wine then undergoes complete malolactic fermentation, further softening the texture and harmonizing the flavors. It stays in barrel for a fairly long time, about sixteen months, and receives only a gentle fining to remove solids before being bottled. The whole idea is to retain subtlety and nuance by not interfering with what the vineyard has provided.

"As a winemaker, I started off with a varietal focus," Rasmussen says. "But I've moved more and more to a vineyard emphasis. I think Rosemary's special character is what's pushed me in that direction." Production of the wine varies by vintage, as not all the grapes from the vineyard ends up in the vineyard-designated wine. Rasmussen selects only the most balanced fruit and the best barrels, using the rest as part of the blend in Talley's Arroyo Grande Estate Chardonnay. Even in an abundant year like 2002, Talley Rosemary's Vineyard Chardonnay is extremely limited—450 cases at most.

This wine sets a benchmark for Central Coast Chardonnay. With the possible exception of the estate wines from Calera and Chalone high in the mountains, no other Chardonnay produced from grapes grown south of the Santa Lucia Highlands and north of the Santa Maria Valley is in its league. At the same time, it clearly is atypical for the region, the rich, lush Chardonnays from Edna Valley Vineyards just up the road being much more representative. Those coconut-scented and pineapple-flavored wines taste delicious. But they are superior versions of something that has become so common as to be ubiquitous, so are not especially distinctive. That is, they taste first and foremost of the grape variety, no matter where it's grown. Chardonnay has become so successful internationally precisely because such varietal character proves pleasant. But an exceptional wine needs to taste of more than the grape, and Rosemary's Vineyard Chardonnay is one of only a handful from the Central Coast that succeeds in doing so.

Most Central Coast Chardonnays feel fleshy and forward. Full of honeyed, buttery aromas atop tropical fruit flavors, they flirt with excess, and are invariably fragile, losing allure quickly. By contrast, Rosemary's Vineyard Chardonnay is initially tight, gains appeal with time, and without sacrificing flavor, offers an extra level of flair, a patina of refinement and class that distinguishes the very best wines, no matter the varietal or region. If many California Chardonnays taste so big and blowsy that they seem almost to be trying too hard, this wine does just the opposite. Its charm is gently seductive. It entices with balance, depth, and length, offering concentration and complexity rather than power.

"This is a wine on the edge," offers Steve Rasmussen. "It's a struggle from a winemaking perspective. But maybe, in order to have a really great wine, you have to struggle. Maybe you need to be on the edge." A confluence of natural factors enables this particular vineyard to provide fruit of extraordinary potential, so how that potential is realized in both the vineyard and the winery becomes crucially important in the creation of the wine. Before he and the Talleys understood that, they grew grapes and then made wine from them. Now they try to make those two endeavors one.

"Just as it's a different kind of farming," says Brian Talley, "it's a different way of thinking about winemaking. With both, you have to pay attention to so many details." He and his parents have been growing grapes on this particular plot of ground for less than twenty years; Rasmussen has been crafting this particular wine for slightly more than ten. They all readily acknowledge that they still have much to learn. But the wine itself, particularly if tasted a number of years after the vintage, when it's had a chance to soften and integrate, demonstrates that they already have earned high marks. Since they too are not very forward or showy, their wine may not be as well known as some others. But in terms of inherent quality, it already is on a par with the very best.

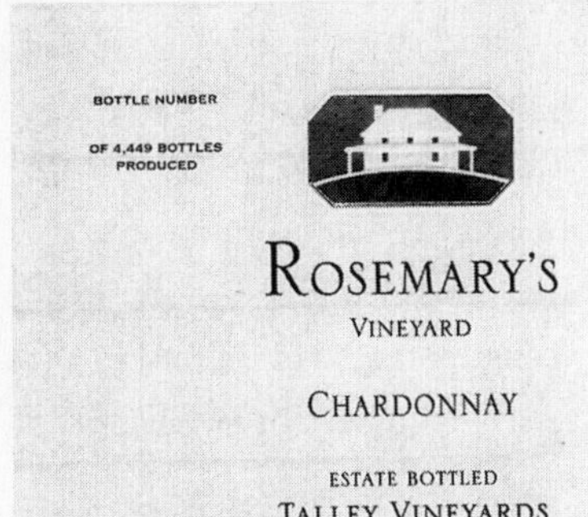

A NOTE ON VINTAGES:

Unlike the vast majority of American Chardonnays, Talley's Rosemary's Vineyard Chardonnay virtually begs for a few years of bottle age to show its best. At four to seven years after the vintage, though, it has few equals. Particularly strong years for this wine include 1996, 1998, 1999, 2000, and 2002.

THE SUGGESTED PRICE FOR THE CURRENT 2003 RELEASE IS $44.

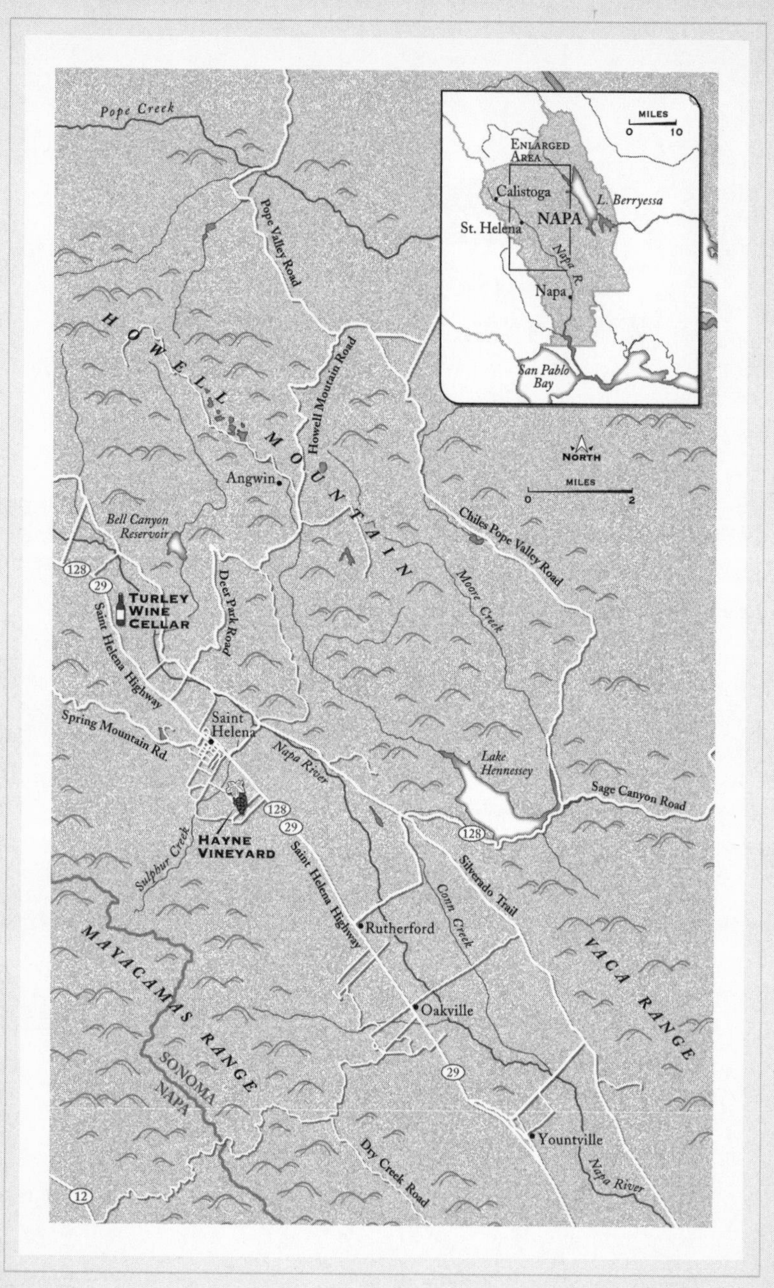

THE TURLEY WINE CELLARS WINERY AND THE HAYNE VINEYARD

CHAPTER 40

TURLEY WINE CELLARS ZINFANDEL, HAYNE VINEYARD

Napa Valley, California

...

San Francisco's Fort Mason, a former military base on the waterfront between Fisherman's Wharf and the Golden Gate, is today a cultural and educational center, hosting over 15,000 meetings, conferences, and performances each year. Of these, none proves more popular than the annual "ZAP" wine tasting held in late January. At this event, more than ten thousand people pay $50 or more in order to sip, swirl, and spit out wines from nearly three hundred producers. Though well over five hundred different wines are poured, only one varietal is offered. ZAP stands for Zinfandel Advocates and Producers, and it is the largest varietal-specific wine group in the world. No one would dare bring any other wine to a ZAP event, Zin fanatics being just that when it comes to their favorite grape. These days, they tend to be especially passionate about new-styled, high-alcohol Zinfandels, wines

Ehren Jordan and Larry Turley

whose powerhouse personalities have fueled this varietal's renaissance, and whose commercial and critical success has gone hand-in-hand with the organization's growth. Enthusiasm for these wines is what makes the ZAP tasting such a hot ticket; and not surprisingly, crowds tend to congregate where particularly coveted wines are poured.

Elbow room is always in short supply at the Turley Wine Cellars table. A Napa-based winery, Turley produces fifteen or more different Zins, most in small lots from single vineyards all over coastal California. All are highly regarded, but the most esteemed one comes from a scant six acres of pre-Prohibition vines in the Hayne Vineyard in St. Helena. It serves as a standard-bearer for the intense Zins that so many ZAP members crave, and so is the hottest ticket of all at Fort Mason—the one wine you just have to try.

Yet what is most remarkable about this wine is that it is *not* hot. Though it typically contains between 16 and 17 percent alcohol, Turley's Hayne Vineyard Zinfandel does not seem at all abrasive or harsh, but instead displays a seductive, opulent charm. Unlike an earlier generation of high-alcohol Zins, it feels heady rather than heavy, and so tastes deliciously harmonious. As such, it has helped change perceptions of this varietal, turning Zinfandel, long misunderstood and even maligned as a minor player, into a major star.

ZAP began in 1991 as a marketing effort by a group of vintners to promote Zinfandel as a wine worthy of serious attention. The grape had a long history as a California workhorse, but at the time it seemed in danger of being overshadowed by other, supposedly more elite varietals. There were plenty of vineyards planted to it, but the great majority of the fruit was used to make off-dry, blush wines, and many consumers thought of Zin primarily, if not exclusively, as something pink. Even those who knew it as a red table wine rarely considered it to be in the same league as varietals like Cabernet, Chardonnay, and Pinot Noir, wines made with grapes that went into great European cuvées. Instead, it was something quirky and homespun, pleasant enough but not sufficiently pedigreed to be ranked with the world's noblest grapes. To be sure, some people did love it. But as David Darlington admitted in his *Angel's Visits*, published that same year, they too thought of it as something out of the vinous mainstream, and hence of themselves as a breed apart, "almost . . . a cult."

When ZAP started, the cult was quite small. Though some vintners treated red Zinfandel as seriously as Cabernet, others paid it scant attention. In fact, a number of prominent producers, including Robert Mondavi, had dropped it from their portfolios. At the first ZAP tasting, in 1992, only twenty-two wineries showed their wines. And only about a hundred people showed up. The event began to become popular a few years later (and then really took off at the end of the decade), when the organization expanded to include consumers as members, and when a new breed of wines, including those from Turley Wine Cellars, began appearing in the market. The top Zins of the 1980s (from producers like A. Rafanelli, Ravenswood, and Ridge) had been claret-styled, meaning restrained rather than rowdy, with alcohol levels usually hovering between 13 and 14 percent. The new wines of the 1990s were much bigger, with higher alcohols, more forceful flavors, greater concentration, and in general, more vivacious personalities. By the turn of the new century, people were flocking to ZAP tastings to try them, ordering them from mailing lists, and paying previously unimaginable prices for them. The cult had become a movement, and a wine that for generations had been considered pedestrian was suddenly chic.

Price is a good barometer of Zinfandel's newfound prestige. In 1987, when Robert Parker first began reviewing the varietal in *The Wine Advocate*, his two top-rated wines, 1985 Ravenswood Dickerson and 1985 Ridge Lytton Springs, sold for $10 and $12, respectively. Fifteen years later, when Turley's Hayne Vineyard received his highest score, its suggested retail price was $75—higher than many Napa Valley Cabernets and classified-growth Bordeaux. Even more revealing, though, is the language Parker used to describe these different wines. He had written that the Ridge wine exhibited "superb balance . . . character and complexity," while the Ravenswood's bouquet seemed so "classic" that he confessed confusing it with an older bottle of Mouton-Rothschild. By contrast, he characterized the 2000 Turley as "immense" and "enormous," with tremendous "intensity" and "palate-staining extract"—language that to the uninitiated might well sound offputting. Clearly something had changed (including, perhaps, the critic's own preferences). Zinfandel became more expensive as it became both more popular and more critically esteemed. But that only happened when styles shifted, and more vintners began making big, vigorous wines without either a European or an old California model. They aimed to fashion something compelling because concentrated rather than "classic."

High levels of alcohol come from superripe grapes, and this stylistic shift toward ever fuller ripeness was not confined to Zinfandel. Nor was it an exclusively American phenomenon. Beginning in the early 1990s, alcohol levels started to creep up in all sorts of red wines, including many from Bordeaux, as vintners all across the globe tried to encourage fruit development rather than vegetative growth in their vineyards. Advances in viticulture, principally involving canopy management and trellising, allowed them to harvest more mature grapes, with richer, more developed flavors and, inevitably, higher sugars. As with all shifts in fashion, some people took it too far, and a fair number of wines ended up tasting hot and heavy—as indeed had many high-alcohol Zinfandels a generation before, when ripeness was defined solely in terms of sugar.

Zin, though an uneven ripener, produces berries with unparalleled sweetness. The trick is to pick them at just the right point, before they become so sweet that they shrivel up like raisins, but after they lose any vegetal characteristics. Virtually all the top Zin producers make richer, riper wines today. Some, like Dave Rafanelli at A. Rafanelli and Paul Draper at Ridge, continue to think of claret-like restraint as a virtue. Not Larry Turley. "I like big wines," he says bluntly, "and I want to make what I like." But he then quickly adds: "I also like balanced wines. So what I really want is a wine that's big and at the same time balanced." That's what he gets in the Zinfandel he sources from the Hayne Vineyard. "Year in, year out," he notes, "it's one of the biggest alcoholically, but also one of the most elegant wines we make."

Although it is admittedly difficult to conceive of a wine with such intense alcohol and extract as elegant, tasting a series of Hayne Vineyard Zins proves Turley right. The wine is every bit as prodigious as Robert

Parker claims, but it also displays genuine gentility and a wonderfully nuanced complexity. The 1994 that I tasted in early 2004, proved surprisingly fresh, with aromas reminiscent of sweet tobacco as well as red and black berries, and deep, expansive flavors that culminate in a chocolate-tinged finish. At over 17 percent alcohol, it certainly felt big on the palate, but there was nothing at all brooding or brutish about it. So too with more recent vintages, the fruit in them tasting even fresher. Most impressive of all, none of the wines seemed hot, and none tasted raisined. Instead, all were sweet and succulent, their structural elements in near-perfect proportion. That sort of symmetry is what sets this wine apart from other high-alcohol, powerhouse Zins, and makes Larry Turley, along with winemaker Ehren Jordan, the most important architects of Zinfandel's new style.

Turley, a former emergency-room physician, got into the Napa wine business when he co-founded the Frog's Leap Winery back in 1981. Always interested in small, hands-on winemaking, he left twelve years later, when production there grew to some 50,000 cases, in order to start a new winery behind his house, this time under his own name. From the start, he focused primarily on Zinfandel, and powerful Zinfandel at that. "In the 1970s and 1980s, Zin was all over the board," he remembers. "And the big wines were hot. I just thought you could have a big wine without heat or raisin-ness."

Turley's thinking was influenced by his sister, Helen, then as now one of California's most admired vintners. Helen has made wine for many of the state's top producers, including Bryant Family, Colgin, Pahlmeyer, and Peter Michael. Today, while she continues to consult, she concentrates on her own Marcassin wines on the Sonoma coast. But back in 1993, she worked alongside her brother at Turley Wine Cellars, where their shared philosophy was deceptively simple: Find great vineyards, farm them precisely, be sure the grapes ripen fully, and then make the wines as naturally as possible, with minimal intervention. Though she only made two vintages at Turley, leaving when the demands at Marcassin grew too strong, she left her mark. That's because her assistant, Ehren Jordan, stayed behind. Extremely talented himself, Jordan took over full-time winemaking and viticultural duties in 1996, and he deserves considerable credit for the Turley style. In turn, he credits Larry and Helen for showing him how to practice what he calls "ostrich winemaking"—get things right in the vineyard, "and then leave the stuff alone!"

Jordan came to wine circuitously, starting as a college student in Washington, D.C., when he got a part-time job as a stockboy in a wineshop. After graduation, he moved to Colorado, and sold and served wine in an Aspen restaurant in order to finance time on the ski slopes. Then he started spending summers in Napa, working variously as a tour guide, cellar helper, and sales manager. Soon enough, having been seduced by the grape's magic, Jordan decided he wanted to try his hand at winemaking. But he had no desire to go back to school. So he asked himself, "Where do people with no degree go to make wine?" He packed his bags and headed off to France—where he threw himself into all aspects of traditional winemaking and what he calls "endurance-sport viticulture," working for Jean-Luc Colombo in the Rhône Valley. Colombo, an influential consulting enologist who owns his own estate in Cornas (much like Helen Turley in California), taught him that the best wines are those left alone. "I learned that a wine has a memory," Jordan explains. "You can't manipulate it and have it come out resembling something that was once alive." Upon his return home, that lesson led him to Helen and Larry Turley. As he puts it, "We were all thinking the same way."

That way runs counter to an academic emphasis on numerical analysis. Jordan and Turley are both openly disdainful of what they call "textbook" viticulture and winemaking. Conventional wisdom may say to pick Zinfandel at 25 degrees of sugar, "but if you do that in the Hayne Vineyard," Turley insists, "you end up with green fruit." Jordan expands on the point: "Look. Plenty of winemakers think in terms of pH and sugar level and potential alcohol. They calculate all the numbers. But we think it's better to go outside the box, and taste the fruit. Your mouth tells you when it's ripe." A similar approach governs their winemaking. Turley Hayne Vineyard Zin ferments only with natural, indigenous yeasts, and is bottled without any fining or filtering. "We let it make itself," says Jordan. "From a winemaker's perspective, it's humbling. You realize that what you do doesn't have all that much to do with what you get."

That's a bit misleading. What the two men choose *not* to do in the winery surely proves important, as does everything they end up doing (and not doing) in the vineyards. Larry Turley produces wine from grapes grown in eighteen different California vineyards, only four of which he owns; but he and Jordan, along with a crew of eight full-time vineyard workers, control the farming in all of them. If they try not to intervene as winemakers, they do just the opposite as viticulturalists, since they micromanage each property. As Turley explains, "every vine requires some human judgment. That's why it's important to have the same people work on them every year."

Turley and Jordan prefer to farm organically, using no herbicides, and irrigating only newly planted vines. To optimize their chances of harvesting fully concentrated grapes, they pay a great deal of attention to the vine's canopy, thinning leaves so that the fruit clusters are exposed to the morning sun. Then, at verasion, when the grapes change color, they discard any that remain green or only turn pink, in some vineyards leaving fully half of the crop on the ground. Their goal is even ripening, and full, physiological fruit maturity. "We can get there," says Turley, "if we prune and thin properly."

The Hayne Vineyard, planted soon after the turn of the last century, ripens remarkably evenly. Family-owned, it sits on an alluvial fan that extends down from the Mayacamas Range, and consists of fifty-two gravelly acres planted to Cabernet, Petite Sirah, and Zinfandel. Turley Wine Cellars contracts for some of the Zin and all of the Petite, while the Cabernet is sold primarily to Cathy Corison and Joseph Phelps. In years past, the owners sold grapes to many different wineries, but they now are quite selective. Otty Hayne, a retired diplomat, runs the business, and he credits the Turley crew for raising his own expectations concerning the quality of these grapes. "I was impressed with Turley from the start," he says, "with how they cared for the vines, and then with the wines they made." Yields from the old, dry-farmed Zin vines average about 2 tons per acre, which means that Jordan and Turley make only about 650 cases of the wine each year. They have used budwood from Hayne in other vineyards (and they are the only growers Otty Hayne allows to do so), but they know that this vineyard has its own personality and that the wine they make from it cannot be replicated. "People must have thought it was special way back," speculates Jordan. "Any vineyard kept going through Prohibition had to have been special."

What, then, accounts for the remarkable combination of power and grace in Turley Hayne Zinfandel? "It's there in the vineyard," says Jordan. "If you can achieve balance in the vineyard, you'll be able to translate that into the wine." The age of these vines helps, as older Zinfandel grapes tend to retain acidity. But the harmony that makes this wine so special is no accident of age. Jordan and Turley know exactly what they want, and they work tirelessly to try to get it—in the winery, certainly, but first and foremost in the vineyard, where they care for these wines, as Otty Hayne says, "from beginning to end." In the process, they produce an intense, forceful wine that simultaneously tastes evocatively supple. "There's no other Zin consistently like it," acknowledges Larry Turley. Ehren Jordan makes the point slightly differently. "Why worry about the alcohol?" he asks rhetorically. "That's just a number. Instead, ask yourself if you like the wine."

Plenty of people clearly do like this wine, for no Zinfandel is in greater demand at the big ZAP tasting, as well as at select shops and restaurants all year long. It represents a new style for this varietal, one that, while not intrinsically superior to the older claret style, has provided Zin with a new audience and given it new appeal. Just go to Fort Mason and see for yourself.

A NOTE ON VINTAGES:

This wine is packed with flavor—ripe, jammy fruit certainly, but also secondary notes reminiscent of dried herbs, pepper, and leather. What is most impressive about it, though, is what's not in it—namely, alcoholic heat. It holds up well for a decade or so, but since it does not become particularly nuanced with time in bottle, why defer gratification? After all, this style of Zin is a hedonist's delight. Strong vintages that are drinking especially well now include 1997, 1999, 2002, and 2003.

THE SUGGESTED PRICE FOR THE CURRENT 2003 RELEASE IS $75.

ART CREDITS

...

Maps with each chapter were designed by The M Factory, Inc.

All labels are reproduced courtesy of the respective vineyards.

PHOTOGRAPH CREDITS ARE AS FOLLOWS:

Chapter 1: Photograph by Marguerite Thomas

Chapter 2: Photograph by Kirk Irwin

Chapter 3: Photograph by Marguerite Thomas

Chapter 4: Photograph courtesy of Beringer Vineyards

Chapter 5: Photograph courtesy of Calera Wine Company

Chapter 6: Photograph by Marguerite Thomas

Chapter 7: Photograph by Marguerite Thomas

Chapter 8: Photograph courtesy of Ste. Michelle Wine Estates

Chapter 9: Photograph courtesy of Cristom

Chapter 10: Photograph courtesy of Far Niente Winery

Chapter 11: Photograph courtesy of Domaine Drouhin Oregon

Chapter 12: Photograph courtesy of Dr. Frank's Vinifera Wine Cellars

Chapter 13: Photograph courtesy of Dry Creek Vineyard

Chapter 14: Photograph by Marguerite Thomas

Chapter 15: Photograph by Marguerite Thomas

Chapter 16: Photograph by Marguerite Thomas

Chapter 17: Photograph by Marguerite Thomas

Chapter 18: Photograph by Marguerite Thomas

Chapter 19: Photograph courtesy of Horton Vineyards

Chapter 20: Photograph by Marguerite Thomas

Chapter 21: Photograph by Marguerite Thomas

Chapter 22: Photograph by Marguerite Thomas

Chapter 23: Photograph courtesy of Robert Mondavi Winery

Chapter 24: Photograph by Marguerite Thomas

Chapter 25: Photograph by Marguerite Thomas

Chapter 26: Photograph courtesy of Joseph Phelps Vineyards

Chapter 27: Photograph courtesy of Quilceda Creek Vintners

Chapter 28: Photograph by Marguerite Thomas

Chapter 29: Photograph courtesy of Ridge Vineyards

Chapter 30: Photograph by Marguerite Thomas

Chapter 31: Photograph by Marguerite Thomas

Chapter 32: Photograph courtesy of Saintsbury

Chapter 33: Photograph courtesy of Shafer Vineyards

Chapter 34: Photograph courtesy of Spottswood Vineyard and Winery

Chapter 35: Photograph courtesy of Stag's Leap Wine Cellars

Chapter 36: Photograph courtesy of Stags' Leap Winery

Chapter 37: Photograph courtesy of Stone Hill Vineyard

Chapter 38: Photograph courtesy of Talbott Vineyards

Chapter 39: Photograph by Marguerite Thomas

Chapter 40: Photograph courtesy of Turley Wine Cellars

INDEX

Page numbers in *italics* refer to illustrations.

A Note About the Author

...

PAUL LUKACS is the chair of the English Department at Loyola College in Maryland, where he teaches American literature. He also is the wine columnist for *The Washington Times* and *Washingtonian* magazine. In that capacity, he tastes and evaluates thousands of different wines each year. The author of *American Vintage: The Rise of American Wine* (winner of the James Beard, IACP, and Clicquot book of the year awards in 2001), he teaches wine appreciation classes and consults on wine for restaurants in the Washington, D.C., area. He lives in Federal Hill in Baltimore, with his wife, Marguerite Thomas, and his daughter, Helen.